THE IMPLICATIONS
OF EMBODIMENT

*This collection copyright © Wolfgang Tschacher & Claudia Bergomi, 2011.
Individual chapters copyright © their authors, 2011.*

The moral rights of the authors have been asserted.
No part of this publication may be reproduced in any form without permission, except for the quotation of brief passages in criticism and discussion.

Published in the UK by
Imprint Academic, PO Box 200, Exeter EX5 5YX, UK

Published in the USA by
Imprint Academic, Philosophy Documentation Center
PO Box 7147, Charlottesville, VA 22906-7147, USA

ISBN 978184540 240 2

A CIP catalogue record for this book is available from the
British Library and US Library of Congress

THE IMPLICATIONS OF EMBODIMENT

Cognition and Communication

edited by
Wolfgang Tschacher
and
Claudia Bergomi

imprint-academic.com

Contents

Wolfgang Tschacher and Claudia Bergomi
   Introduction   vii

Scientific Roots of Embodiment

Jiri Wackermann
   In Quest of Human Nature: Rediscovery of the Body   3

Matej Hoffmann and Rolf Pfeifer
   The Implications of Embodiment for Behavior and Cognition:
   Animal and Robotic Case Studies   31

Shaun Gallagher
   Interpretations of Embodied Cognition   59

Embodiment: Formal Approaches

Hermann Haken and Wolfgang Tschacher
   The Transfer of Principles of Non-Equilibrium Physics
   to Embodied Cognition   75

Karl Friston
   Embodied Inference: or "I think therefore I am,
   if I am what I think"   89

Social Embodiment

Sanneke de Haan, Hanne De Jaegher, Thomas Fuchs, and Andreas Mayer
  Expanding Perspectives: The Interactive Development
  of Perspective-Taking in Early Childhood   129

Sabine Koch
  Basic Body Rhythms:
  From Individual to Interpersonal Movement Feedback   151

Karl Grammer, Elisabeth Oberzaucher, Iris Holzleitner, and Silke Atmaca
  Dance: the Human Body as a Dynamic Motion System   173

Fabian Ramseyer
  Nonverbal Synchrony in Psychotherapy:
  Embodiment at the Level of the Dyad   193

Wilma Bucci
  The Role of Embodied Communication
  in Therapeutic Change: A Multiple Code Perspective   209

Embodiment and Ecological Psychology

Naoya Hirose
  Affordances, Effectivities, and Extension of the Body   231

Wolfgang Tschacher and Martin Tröndle
  Embodiment and the Arts   253

Name Index   264
Subject Index   271
List of Contributors   277

Introduction

Wolfgang Tschacher and Claudia Bergomi
University Hospital of Psychiatry, University of Bern, Switzerland
{tschacher, bergomi}@spk.unibe.ch

This book is about the implications of embodiment, but how is embodiment defined? Is it a theory, a paradigm, a perspective, a methodology, or a scientific field? Seen from the different angles of the chapters in this volume, it may well mean all of the above.

Embodiment goes beyond a neurobiological interpretation of cognition. It rests in the much broader idea that the body— including behaviors and properties such as facial expression, movement, prosody, gesture, and posture — influence, and at the same time are influenced, by the mind. Therefore, embodiment research is not restricted to neurobiological methods but includes behavior observation, subjective assessments and engineering approaches as well. Embodiment research involves the complete range of measurements and methods in psychology and biology.

The most general way to think of the implications of the embodiment perspective is to call for the acknowledgement of a simple fact: that there is no easy way of circumnavigating the mind-body problem. While the word 'embodiment' seems to emphasize the body as the means of every cognitive act, it also points to that which is embodied: The mind. In contrast to the currently prevalent tendency towards the reduction of mental processes to their neural correlates, the embodiment perspective emphasizes the mutual influence and interconnectedness of body and mind. To conceive of the mind as embodied means that the mind must be viewed in its context. Three different contexts *come to mind* here: the context of the body and body movement (embodied cognition), the context of the physical environment (situated cognition) and the social context (embodied communication). Functional mental processes need the interplay of both mind and context, of both perception and action, of both cognition and social resonance. Mind and context are different, yet both form a necessary unity.

Such embodiment positions have been proposed repeatedly in the last two decades, during which different fields have converged in their views on mental process: Dynamical systems theory (Haken & Stadler, 1990; Port & van Gelder, 1995; Tschacher & Dauwalder, 1999, 2003), philosophy of mind (Clark 1997; Lakoff & Johnson 1999), biology (Varela et al., 1991; Núñez & Freeman, 2000) and psychology (Neisser 1994; Niedenthal et al., 2005). What are the commonalities in this broad movement of embodiment? In addition to the defining characteristics of embodiment — the mind is understood fully only as embedded in its context — one may notice that an emphasis on the *social* embedding of the mind has come to the fore. This may well be the aspect of embodiment that will have to be considered in more detail in the future: That social interaction generally occurs through embodied communication. Therefore, we have dedicated the most detailed section of this volume to 'Social Embodiment'.

The book starts with a section on the 'Scientific Roots of Embodiment'. These roots are explored in three fields, philosophy, computer science and cognitive science. *Jiří Wackermann* gives a detailed account of the history of philosophical inquiry of the body in relation to the psyche. Starting with the Presocratics, he finds with "some historical irony" how the present emphasis on embodiment may actually be a rediscovery of many precursors, e.g. in phenomenology and theoretical biology (*Gestaltkreis*) of the last century. *Matej Hoffmann and Rolf Pfeifer* illuminate embodiment from a completely different field, that of robotics and Artificial Intelligence. They show how information processing and movement, i.e. an agent's functioning in the real world, depend heavily on the morphology and material properties of the 'body' of the (robotic) agent. Thus, cognition is seen as emerging on top of what they call morphological computation, a basic sensory-motor dynamics. *Shaun Gallagher* gives an overview of the assumptions held by proponents of embodied cognition, distinguishing minimal embodiment from more radical notions. Notably, there are differing positions with respect to representation and computation. According to Gallagher, embodied cognition must be informed by a variety of scientific fields including brain science, and must deal with brain-body-environment couplings.

The section 'Embodiment: Formal Approaches' details two proposals of how embodiment can be given a formal mathematical foundation in circular causality. *Hermann Haken and Wolfgang Tschacher* derive their theory of embodiment from the field of synergetics, a transdisciplinary field hat applies dynamics and statistical physics to complex systems, which are embedded in non-equilibrium environments. This treatment entails a naturalization approach of intentionality ('self-organizing systems are *about* their environments'). *Karl Friston* puts the free-energy principle at the center of his elaboration of embodiment. Free energy is a quantity that biological agents, as self-organizing adaptive systems, must minimize in order to remain within the bounds of the attractor of survival. Thereby agents avoid 'surprise', the complement of value. This principle can be applied to the brain, leading to a Bayesian hypothesis of how the brain manages to arrive at optimal models (representations) of what has caused its sensory input.

The third section 'Social Embodiment' exhibits that embodied cognition is especially significant for communicating agents. *Sanneke de Haan, Hanne De Jaegher, Thomas Fuchs and Andreas Mayer* address childhood development: They approach second-person understanding, the process underlying social perspective-taking and empathy, from the point of view of embodiment rather than following the prevalent account given in Theory of Mind theory. Using infants' games such as hide-and-seek and peek-a-boo as materials, they identify social interaction as the core mechanism by which social capacities are learned, instead of assuming that social capacities are pre-wired as hidden cognitive modules. *Sabine Koch*'s chapter is on basic rhythms of the body, focusing on movement qualities that affect emotion, attitudes and cognition. Building on social-psychological research on static body feedback she advances to empirical studies of these dynamic qualities and to bidirectional kinaesthetic resonance, showing that embodiment research should also consider these intercorporal aspects. *Karl Grammer, Elisabeth Oberzaucher, Iris Holzleitner and Silke Atmaca* study dance and movement based on the Darwinistic assumption that movement serves a signal function for sexual selection. Quantifying dance movement by motion energy, they find correlations of factors of motion dynamics with the 'big five' personality traits and with sexual-hormone markers. *Fabian Ramseyer* makes use of a similar measure, motion energy analysis (MEA), for the investigation of the psychotherapy dyad consisting of patient and therapist. He finds that the nonverbal synchrony of this dyad is a characteristic of the relationship quality in therapy process and the patient's interactional abilities, and predicts the overall positive outcome of psychotherapeutic treatment. *Wilma Bucci* addresses psychotherapy from a psychoanalytic starting point. She connects embodied communication with her multiple code theory, especially the subsymbolic processes necessary to change emotion schemata. The common coding of perception and action, also supported by the findings on the mirror neuron system, allows addressing the referential process that is the basis of dyadic interchange.

The final section widens the scope to 'Embodiment and Ecological Psychology'. *Naoya Hirose* builds on ecological psychology to discuss the concept of affordance, which addresses the relation between an animal and its environment. Affordance is understood as a property of the environment that encourages a specific action. Such an action possesses a certain effectivity: This concept complements, on the side of the animal, the affordance concept. Special cases are body attachments such as tools, which effectively extend the boundary of the body. *Wolfgang Tschacher and Martin Tröndle* finally apply the embodiment perspective to aesthetic perception. They present a research project in which locomotion and physiology of visitors of an art museum were closely monitored and imaged. Discussing single mappings of the 'psychogeography' of art perception, the attracting forces that artworks exert on visitors' physiology and locomotion are visualized.

The 'Herbstakademie' conference we organized in Bern, Switzerland, in October 2009 provided the inspiration for this thematic volume. We cordially thank the participants of this conference for their intellectual and emotional involvement, and for laying the foundations of this book. To complement those authors who had presented at the conference, we invited several further scholars. In sum, we are confident that all chapters together paint a coherent and full picture of what today is the scientific essence of embodiment and its implications.

We would like to express our gratitude to all those who contributed to the success of the meeting, notably Jean-Pierre Dauwalder, who co-organized the meeting, as well as Marlise Matti, Marcel Meyer, Fabian Ramseyer, Stefanie Feuz, Georg Rees and the team of the City Hall facilities of Bern, the splendid venue of this Herbstakademie. The financial and administrative support given by the Universität Bern, the Kantonale Gesundheits- und Fürsorgedirektion and the Swiss graduate program 'troisième cycle romand' is gratefully acknowledged. We also thank Hannah Schmidt and Marianne Hänni for their help during the final stages of the editing process, and Andrea Lüthi, who created the cover art of this book. The cooperation with Anthony Freeman of Imprint Academic was a pleasant and satisfying process.

Bern, January 2011   Wolfgang Tschacher
                                                  Claudia Bergomi

References

Clark A. (1997). *Being there: Putting brain, body, and world together again.* Cambridge: MIT Press.
Haken H. & Stadler M. (eds.) (1990). *Synergetics of cognition.* Berlin: Springer.
Lakoff G. & Johnson M. (1999). *Philosophy in the flesh: The embodied mind and its challenge to western thought.* New York: Basic Books.
Neisser U. (ed.) (1994). *The perceived self: Ecological and interpersonal sources of self knowledge.* Cambridge: Cambridge University Press.
Niedenthal P. M., Barsalou L. W., Winkielman P., Krauth-Gruber S., & Ric F. (2005). Embodiment in attitudes, social perception, and emotion. *Personality and Social Psychology Review, 9,* 184-211.
Núñez R. & Freeman W. J. (eds.) (2000). *Reclaiming cognition. The primacy of action, intention and emotion.* Exeter: Imprint Academic.
Port R. & van Gelder T. J. (eds.) (1995). *Mind as motion: Explorations in the dynamics of cognition.* Cambridge: MIT Press.
Tschacher W. & Dauwalder J.-P. (eds.) (1999). *Dynamics, synergetics, autonomous agents – nonlinear systems approaches to cognitive psychology and cognitive science.* Singapore: World Scientific.
Tschacher W. & Dauwalder J.-P. (eds.) (2003). *The dynamical systems approach to cognition.* Singapore: World Scientific.
Varela F., Thompson E. & Rosch E. (1991). *The embodied mind.* Cambridge: MIT Press.

Section 1

Scientific Roots of Embodiment

In Quest of Human Nature: Rediscovery of the Body

Jiří Wackermann

Institute for Frontier Areas of Psychology and Mental Health,
Freiburg i. Br., Germany
jw@igpp.de

Introduction

Living in the world, experiencing the world, means understanding. Articulated and communicable understanding is knowledge; rational, organized, systematic knowledge is science. It is commonly believed that science enables us to understand the world. This belief becomes problematic when it comes to understanding ourselves. There is an amazing contrast between the knowledge of nature, of all the things that are around us but not us — stones and rocks, tides and storms, planets and stars — on the one hand, and of human being, of our place among things of nature, and ultimately of our own nature, on the other hand.

The particular ethos of human sciences consists in asking questions and, in turn, questioning not only the answers, but the questions themselves — in the quest for the proper form of the question. The history of natural sciences is a record of progress and success, of cumulative findings and discoveries, while the history of human sciences is an erratic process of conquests and abandonments, of gains and losses, discoveries and rediscoveries.[1]

One of these rediscoveries is the topic of this chapter: namely, the rediscovery of the body as a natural ground of our existence. The method of our essay is not historical in the proper sense of the word; rather it is a series of short excursions, strolls through the history of human thought about human nature.

Tomb of the soul

The fact of our being incorporated in the world — seemingly the most trivial fact of life — raises a problem at the very basis of our existential condition. The usual phrasing, the duality between 'being a body' and

---

[1] The picture sketched here is certainly schematic; a closer look at the history of natural science reveals numerous gaps and disruptions. Yet, there is a large-scale coherence in this knowledge, which cannot be claimed by the science of human being. There is more continuity between the cosmologies of early Greek philosophers and modern physical theories than, for example, between different directions of psychological thought in the last century.

'having a body', is only one aspect of the problem. All the contrasts, tensions and dualities between 'being with me' and 'being for others', between 'being here' and acting in space, between 'being now' and existing in time, etc., find a meeting point in the facticity of human 'embodiment' in the physical and social world.

It is not by chance that the problem of the body comes back, with all its disquieting moments, to *psychology*. A psychological approach to human existence is grounded in one particular tradition of thought, identifying the principle of one's individual life with a substantial carrier of this life, its 'soul', or *psychē*, and aiming at the knowledge of the nature of *psychē*. Although the rise of psychology coincides with the beginnings of philosophical inquiry of nature — with the celebrated transition from *mythos* to *logos* — a critical reconstruction reveals its connections to ancient mysterianism present in early Pythagorean philosophy. It is not only to the name of the universe a well-ordered whole, *kosmos*, and the intuition of the number, *arithmos*, as a principle underlying this cosmic order, that we owe to this tradition. The same tradition preserved and cultivated the ancient Orphic notion of the body (*sōma*) as a tomb (*sēma*) of the soul: resulting in a view of *psychē* as an individual entity, independent and separable from the body, carrying on its proper life on its own.

It is the quality of the soul that determines the form of an individual life: the body is merely a temporary *habitat*, while the soul's proper *habitus* is formed throughout numerous cycles of bodily lives. In some way, psychology amounts to *morphology of human lives*; indeed, we are told that Pythagoras used to compare life to a festival where "some people came... to contend for the prizes, and others for the purposes of traffic, and the best as spectators; so also in life, the men of slavish dispositions are born hunters after glory and covetousness, but philosophers are seekers after truth." (Diogenes Laërtius,1853, book VIII, section 6). This observation of the variety of the aims and goals of human lives finds a direct counterpart in Aristotle's distinction of life-forms in his *Nicomachean Ethics*. Even more importantly, we will see a projection of this ethical trichotomy into Plato's mythopoietic portrait of the psyche.

Let us note in passing that the mysterianist tradition was not the only possible path for the new-born psychology. Heraclitus was aware — as well as Pythagoras was — of the varieties of human inclinations and the psychological relativity of their motivations.[2] Yet, he had a possibly clearer and broader view of *psychē* as the instance connecting, at least potentially, human being with the order of the universe (Kahn, 1979, frgs.

---

[2] There is an almost symbolic counter-position between eloquent Pythagoras, an authoritative teacher of self-styled image, and Heraclitus, an aloof-standing, word-terse thinker of aristocratic manners who rudely criticized Pythagoras for "much learning and artful knavery"; see fragment XXV in Kahn (1979).

XXXVI and XXXVII), and as immense as the universe: "You will not find out the limits of the soul, even if you travel over every way, so deep is its logos." (Kahn, 1979, frg. XXXV). This view does not exclude a physical grounding of the soul; *psychē* may be dry, pyrophorous, participating in the world's proper element, fire, and thus the "wisest and best"; or moist and heavy, such as the soul of a drunk man (cf. Kahn, 1979, frgs. CVI and CIX). In Heraclitus' seemingly naïve — in fact deeply symbolic — psycho-physiology there was no schism between the nature of *psychē* and the material nature.

Freedom of psyche

> *– We shall try our best to do as you say, said Crito.*
> *But how shall we bury you?*
> *– Any way you like, replied Socrates, that is, if you can catch*
> *me and I don't slip through your fingers.*
> *— Plato, Phaedo*[3]

It is the ethos of taking freedom from earthly things, and from the needs and desires of the body, that permeates ancient Greek philosophy and philosophical psychology — from Pythagoras to Plato, and further on. This ethos finds its memorable expression in Plato's *Phaedo*. There we find the Orphic–Pythagorean theme, *sōma – sēma*, in a new context: the body as an obstacle to true knowledge, and philosophy as a way of liberating the soul from this hindrance:

> We are in fact convinced that if we are ever to have pure knowledge of anything, we must get rid of the body and contemplate things by themselves with the soul by itself. (*Phaedo* 66d)

> Every seeker after wisdom knows that up to the time when philosophy takes it over his soul is a helpless prisoner, chained hand and foot in the body, compelled to view reality not directly but only through its prison bars, and wallowing in utter ignorance. [...] Philosophy takes over the soul in this condition and by gentle persuasion tries to set it free. (*Phaedo* 82e–83a)

Socrates' conversations with friends take place in an extreme situation, in the prison where he is expecting his execution; and it is Socrates who brings consolation to his friends, explaining that it is not *he* who will be buried, but only his body; that nothing harmful happens to *him* by his enforced death; since he is not identical with his body. The argument is well-known: it is soul that brings life by taking possession of a body; hence it is a vital principle essentially different from the body; therefore indestructible with the body; therefore immortal. But then the soul "demands our care not only for that part of time which we call life, but for all time. And indeed it would seem now that it will be extremely dan-

---

[3] This and other Plato's works are quoted from the edition by Hamilton & Cairns (1961).

gerous to neglect it." (*Phaedo* 107c)

Hence the existential relevance of the theme discussed above: philosophy is not merely a way of spending time in amusing discussions; its proper task is "taking care (*epimeleia*) of the soul". And those who "have purified themselves sufficiently by philosophy live thereafter altogether without bodies"; this was the promise and the "great hope." (*Phaedo* 114c)

Threefold structure of psyche

The psychological eschatology of *Phaedo* is complemented by the myth of the souls' lifecycles, told in Plato's *Phaedrus*. There the living being is defined as a temporary composition of soul and body; but also the soul is conceived in its inner structure, as a threefold entity:

> Let it be likened to the union of powers in a team of winged steeds and their winged charioteer. ... [O]ne of them is noble and good, and of good stock, while the other has the opposite character, and his stock is opposite. Hence the task of our charioteer is difficult and troublesome. (*Phaedrus* 246b)

This picture serves to illustrate the inner tension involved in the choice of a life-form; the conflict between the search for the ideal, true reality, represented by the rational instance of the soul (the charioteer), and the earthly desires and bodily drives represented by the instinctive component (the horses). The reward for those in whom the higher, rational instance prevails, is the contemplation of the divine truth and beauty; and there Plato again emphasizes the liberation from the bonds of the body:

> ... pure was the light that shone around us, and pure were we, without taint of that prison house which now we are encompassed withal, and call a body, fast bound therein as an oyster in its shell. (*Phaedrus* 250c)

The intra-psychic structure is discussed in the 4th book of Plato's *Republic*, where the question arises "whether there are three things [in the soul] and we do one thing with one and one with another... or whether it is with the entire soul that we function in each case." (*Republic* 436a) Then, by analogy to three societal classes, "the money-makers, the helpers, the counselors," three constituents of the soul are identified (*Republic* 441a *et seq*): the appetitive (*epithymētikon*), the 'high spirit' (*thymoeides*), and the spirited and rational (*logistikon*). A one-to-one correspondence to the threefold structure depicted in the *Phaedrus* is obvious. In the mythopoietic picture of the soul, it was the charioteer's task to control the irrational, dynamic powers of the soul. Also here, the rational part of the soul has to govern the whole, supported in its task by the 'high spirit':

> These two ... will preside over the appetitive part which is the mass of the soul in each of us and the most insatiate by nature of wealth ... filled and infected with the so-called pleasures associated with the body. (*Republic* 442a)

The parallel between social and psychical constituents establishes the method of 'psycho-political correlation' used later in the dialogue in a critical examination of different forms of constitutions of a *polis*.

In sum, in Plato's theory the *psychē* appears as a compound of three constituents; the superior instance of these three is in touch with the eternal, ideal being; while the inferior instance is being enchained by contact with the body, driven by the pleasure principle. Manifestations of the three instances can be observed in the variety of political forms of as well as in individual life-forms (*Republic*, 580c *et seq.*)

In the same vein, Aristotle[4] distinguished in *Nicomachean Ethics* (1095b) "three prominent types of life," namely, "the life of enjoyment," which most people, and particularly people of the most vulgar type, lead; the political life, seeking honor; and the contemplative life, *bios theōrētikos*, seeking wisdom, the noblest of all three types. The trichotomy closely matches the three life-forms enumerated in Pythagoras' festival-parable. But Aristotle's theory avoids all transcendentalism or mysticism; instead, it aims at a life-immanent "happiness [which] is something complete and self-sufficient... the end of action." (*Nic. Eth.*, 1097b) While Plato's dissection of psyche into three instances parallelizes his idealist ontology, Aristotle's realist ethics is based on a division of "goods ... into three classes ... external, others relating to soul or to body; and we call those that relate to soul most properly and truly goods." (*Nic. Eth.*, 1098b)[5] However, the ordering principle of the goods is roughly the same as the ordering principle of Plato's psychic instances: that is, the distance from body; the dismissal of body, abstention from its 'slavish' urges,[6] and the preference for the contemplative life-form as the one of highest dignity.

---

[4] Aristotle's works are quoted from Barnes' (1984) two-volumes edition.

[5] In spite of the obvious parallelism between Pythagoras', Plato's and Aristotle's typologies of life-forms, there are profound differences between Plato's and Aristotle's psychologies, which should not be left without mention. Against the Pythagorean–Platonic view of the soul as an immortal, only temporarily embodied entity, separable from the body, Aristotle puts a much more realist concept of the soul as "the cause or source of the living body" (*De anima*, 415b). The facticity of the body is a key for a correct understanding of Aristotle's definition of *psychē*, based upon his polar concept of matter/potentiality and form/actuality: "the soul is an actuality (*entelecheia*) ... of a natural body having life potentially in it" (*De anima*, 412a); a living animal is thus a unity of the soul and the body. For Pythagoras or Plato, the body was only accidentally related to the soul; for Aristotle, the body of this individual animated being is *its* unique body. Therefore "the soul is inseparable from its body" (*De anima*, 413a), and if some parts of the soul may be separable, then it is because they are "not actualities of any body at all" (*ibid.*) – Aristotle's doctrine of *psychē* as *entelecheia*, a purpose-oriented life principle in an *animated and embodied* being, contains virtually many elements which we later meet in modern, biologically informed and anthropologically motivated streams of thought of the 20th century.

[6] Interestingly, the attribute "slavish" is used concordantly by philosophers of such different temperaments as Pythagoras and Aristotle: "the mass of mankind are evidently quite slavish in their tastes, preferring a life suitable to beasts."

This intellectual prejudice helped to keep the problem of the body out of the scope of philosophical inquiry for a long time.

Contingency of the body

In the Orphic-Pythagorean view, the body is merely a temporary housing for the soul; the relation between the body and the inhabiting soul is as contingent as that of a tomb to a buried corpse. In Plato's psychology, the body–soul link is a more intimate one, as tightly binding as the bond between an oyster and its shell; however, its role is only negative, it is just a hindrance for the spiritual life of the individual, which is realized in *psychē*.

In the *Phaedo* the relation between the body and the soul is discussed again, from a different angle. In the well-known passage where Socrates contrasts his philosophical method with that of natural philosophy of his times, he criticizes Anaxagoras (and others) who "... made no use of mind and assigned to it no causality for the order of the world but adduced causes like air and æther and water and many other absurdities." (*Phaedo* 98b) To illustrate the inaptitude of physicalist 'explanations', Socrates adds ironically, this is

> as if someone were to say, The cause of everything that Socrates does is mind — and then, trying to account for my several actions, said first that the reason why I am lying here now is that my body is composed of bones and sinews, and that the bones are rigid and separated at the joints, but the sinews are capable of contraction and relaxation ... and since the bones move freely in their joints the sinews by relaxing and contracting enable me somehow to bend my limbs, and that is the cause of my sitting here in a bent position. (*Phaedo*, 98cd)

The true reason for Socrates' acts is his "conviction of what is best", that is, *knowledge of the good*, which of course is a function of his mind — the physical circumstances, including bodily functions, are merely contingent. Now, Socrates points out a category error inherent to such physiological accounts:

> If it were said that without such bones and sinews and all the rest of them I should not be able to do what I think is right, it would be true. But to say that it is because of them that I do what I am doing, and not through choice of what is best — although my actions are controlled by mind — would be a very lax and inaccurate form of expression. Fancy being unable to distinguish between the cause of a thing and the condition without which it could not be a cause! (*Phaedo* 99ab)

According to Plato the true causes of human actions are meanings and values; in his idealist interpretation, value is a form of knowledge, realized in the *psychē*. Plato correctly dismisses naturalist explanations by physical/physiological mechanisms;[7] but, unfortunately, with this clear cut he also cuts away all the causes (motives, reasons) originating from the irrational parts of the soul and their bonds to the body.

Descartes' ultimate doubt

It is common-place to make Descartes responsible for psycho-physical dualism, for the split between mind and body. This is certainly exaggerated; Descartes did not invent the soul as an instance independent from the body; he merely inherited it, with all the complexity of tradition ranging from ancient via medieval authors down to him. What Descartes really did was cast the psyche–body duality in the form of *substance dualism*, in an extreme opposition of *res cogitans* and *res extensa*. The sharpness with which he separated the attributes of the *res* had its price: if the ancient philosophers were facing a problem how to release the bonds between soul and body, Descartes and his followers had to face a problem how the two 'things' could have anything in common — how could there be anything binding them together.

There was, no doubt, an extra penalty paid with the price. All the richness of mental life was reduced to pure *cogitationes*; all the diversity of the material world was reduced to pure extension, and had to be reconstructed from scratch, in Descartes' corpuscularist view of the nature's mechanism. This applies to the body — that is to say, the "mind's own body" — as well. One's body is just a *corpus* among many, in principle not different from all other physical bodies, except for inner innervation, the working of which was always a weak point of Descartes' construction. That he was aware of this weakness is witnessed by the passage in the *Sixth meditation* (Descartes, 1641) concerning the rôle of interoceptive sensations such as hunger and thirst:

> Nature teaches me by these sensations ... that I am not merely present in my body as a sailor is present in a ship, but that I am very closely joined, and as it were, intermingled with it, so that I and the body form a unit. If this were not so I ... would not feel pain when the body was hurt, but would perceive the damage purely by the intellect, just as a sailor perceives by sight if anything in his ship is broken.

This observation suggests certain reservations to the utterly cognitivist conception of the soul as an instance monitoring the bodily states, and

---

[7] We may wish that this passage from the *Phaedo* be an obligatory reading for psychologists and neuroscientists. Indeed, replacing the 'bones and sinews' in Plato's text by neural cells and fibers, and transposing the 'freedom' of the bones' motions in the joints to the 'degrees of freedom' of the neural mechanism — do not we obtain a naturalist picture of human being, including a theory of 'freedom' of human action? Such a hermeneutic exercise might be more helpful to students of human sciences than reading hundreds of pages of modern philosophical writings.

acting *'puro intellectu'*.

It is thus not a doubt about a 'ghost in the machine' that makes Cartesian anthropology questionable; it is rather a 'twitch in the machine', providing a subtle but sensible evidence that "there is an important sense in which these faculties cannot be properly accommodated within Descartes' official dualistic schema." (Cottingham, 1986, p. 127) However, nothing more than a hint of doubt is admitted in Descartes' metaphysical writings. A more realistic account of the human condition as a psycho-physical unity is to be found in his anthropological-ethical work, *Passions de l'âme*, where "Descartes brings us closest to a conception of man as an embodied being, a creature of flesh and blood." (Cottingham, 1986, p. 153)

The fourfold unity

In Descartes' separation of *res cogitans* and *res extensa* the psycho-physical dualism reached its extreme point. We can only cursorily mention alternative conceptions, avoiding the difficulties inherent to Cartesian dualism, such as Leibniz's monadology, amounting to panpsychism, and Spinoza's theory of the identity of the spiritual reality and the material nature. They have, however, no direct bearing on the course of our report.

On the other hand, we should note a renewed interest in biopsychological questions and speculations in the 'romantic period' of philosophy at the end of the 18th century. That period is characterized by a peculiar amalgamation of advances of physical sciences (electricity, magnetism, chemistry), medical sciences and physiology (including newly discovered phenomena of 'animal magnetism', hypnotic trance, etc.) and philosophical speculation (*Naturphilosophie*). This intellectual situation was favorable for rethinking questions and problems concerning the human nature *sub specie* of its unity, of spiritual dimension and physical condition.

Worth mentioning in this context are the anthropological writings of a Swiss philosopher of early 19th century, Ignaz Troxler.[8] Troxler's conception, presented in his first philosophical work, *Insights into Human Nature* (1812) is based on two polar oppositions: that between the *spirit* (*Geist*) and the *corporeal body* (*Körper*) on the one hand, and that between the *soul* (*Seele*) and the *vital body* (*Leib*) on the other hand.[9]

> I conceive of the spirit, the soul, the vital and the corporeal body as being different one from the other, yet by no means as entia sui generis; rather, I maintain that a human being in its entirety is spirit and corporeal body, soul

---

[8] Ignaz Paul Vital Troxler (1780–1866), Swiss philosopher, physician and politician. Important works: *Blicke in das Wesen des Menschen*, 1812; *Naturlehre des menschlichen Erkennens oder Metaphysik*, 1828. Biography: Lauer & Widmer (1980).

[9] Our translations, 'corporeal' and 'vital' body, respectively, attempt to reproduce the connotations of the German words *Körper* and *Leib*, which we will meet repeatedly in the subsequent sections.

and vital body, that in these the human being is uniquely and completely reproduced. (Troxler, 1989, p. 36)

Human nature is, essentially, a *twofold duality*. The unifying principle of those four constituents is named *Gemüt* — a term which cannot be adequately translated to English. Human being *qua* individual person is not a composite entity but rather a fourfold unity:

> It is in *Gemüt* where the two relations [*viz. Geist-Körper* and *Seele-Leib*] come in touch, where the spiritual and material, the ideal and the real world meet and penetrate one another. *Gemüt* is the true individuality of man, through which he is properly himself; the focus of his selfhood, the vital center of his existence. (Troxler, 1989, p. 36f)[10]

The task of anthropology, according to Troxler, is then to interpret the manifold of human phenomena — ranging from physiological and psychological functions to language and creativity — out of this fourfold unity, or 'Tetraktys' (Troxler, 1985, p. 46).[11] We cannot follow in detail Troxler's development of his anthropological insights into a metaphysical system. What makes his thoughts interesting specifically for our purpose, is his questioning of all substance-based conceptions — idealism, materialism, or psycho-physical dualism — his emphasis on the primordial unity of human being, and his expressly relational view of the four different instances of that unity.

Most of these characteristics apply equally well to another original author of the 19th century, Gustav Th. Fechner.

Psychophysical unity

Fechner is known, first of all, for his 'dual aspect' theory of the material and the mental reality, based on his metaphysical hypothesis of psychophysical unity. In fact, Fechner himself was a 'dual aspect' character on the intellectual stage of his time:[12] an experimental physicist, devoted to rigorous laboratory routine and quantitative data analysis; and a speculative thinker, expressing himself in flowing streams of poetico-philosophical reflections.

In a short treatise *On the problem of the soul* Fechner (1907) identifies the four key terms to be examined, and related one to another: *Körper, Leib, Seele, Geist*. Fechner distinguishes, as already Troxler did, between

---

[10] Elsewhere Troxler uses an artificial term *wesentliches Teilganze* = 'constitutive whole-part' for the four aspects of the unity.

[11] This expression is an allusion to the 'fourness' principle (*tetraktys*) of the Pythagorean philosophico-mystical teachings.

[12] Gustav Theodor Fechner (1801–1887), German physicist and philosopher, founder of psychophysics and experimental æsthetics. Important works: *Zend-Avesta*, 1851; *Elemente der Psychophysik*, 1860; *Über die Seelenfrage*, 1861; *Vorschule der Aesthetik*, 1876; *Die Tagesansicht gegenüber der Nachtansicht*, 1879. Biography: Arendt (1999). Monographic study of Fechner's scientific work and philosophy: Heidelberger (2004).

Körper and *Leib*: *Körper*, the corporeal body, being a "material system graspable only in its external appearance," while *Leib* is the *one* body in a relation to *one* soul (*Seele*): in a relation known to everyone of us as the relation between *my* body and *my* soul. Fechner thus also assigns a special rôle to the 'subject's own body', which only from an external point of view appears as one among many physical bodies. Nature (*Natur*) is then conceived as the totality of physical things; as for the Spirit (*Geist*), Fechner shows a confusing multiplicity of the use of this term as correlated with, or opposed to the notion of the (individual) soul.

By contrast to Troxler, Fechner does not seem to differentiate so sharply between the two polar dimensions, *Leib–Seele* and *Natur–Geist*. This is not necessarily a failure of distinction; rather it is because, for Fechner, the problem of the soul amounts to the question of animation of individual bodies in a hierarchical scheme up to the world as a whole. The ultimate horizon of Fechner's study of the problem of soul is a sort of panpsychism.

Fechner's conception of psycho-physical unity is briefly sketched in the introductory remarks of his foundational work, *Elements of Psychophysics*. Fechner explicates the difference between the physical and the mental phenomena from a difference of 'standpoints', as two mutually exclusive appearances of one reality in the outer or the inner view. This conception sets the framework for the definition of a new scientific discipline, psychophysics, as an "exact study of functional relations of mutual dependence between the body (*Körper*) and the soul (*Seele*) or, in more general terms, between the corporeal and the spiritual world." (Fechner, 1860, p. 8) Ever and again, Fechner emphasizes that psychophysics is concerned with physical and mental *phenomena*, as given in immediate experience, not with metaphysical questions. However, his diction leaves no doubts that he considers his monist conception as superior to the traditional substance dualism. Fechner further distinguishes between external and internal psychophysics, exploring the relations between the mental (*Geistiges*) and the external or internal corporeal world (*körperliche Aussenwelt, körperliche Innenwelt*), respectively (Fechner, 1860, p. 10).[13]

---

[13] There is, however, a hidden difficulty: Fechner seems to identify the "corporeal inner world" with the nervous system as an alleged substrate (*Träger*) of mental processes. But phenomenologically, the neural substrate is there only for an external observer – a neurophysiologist, for example – not for the subject of the mental processes himself: "Es ist ein Unterschied, ob man mit dem Gehirne denkt, oder in das Gehirn des Denkenden hineinsieht." (*op.cit.*, p. 4). Therefore, a study of quantitative relation between e.g. the impulse frequency in a neural fibre and the intensity of corresponding sensation still belongs to external psychophysics – that the physical correlate is located in the nervous tissue and not in the outer space, does *not* make an *essential* difference. Strictly speaking, an internal psychophysics proper would be a psychophysics of the subject's own body as *Leib*. Fechner's proposal of two branches of psychophysics obscures rather than reveals this distinction.

Beyond the psycho-physical problem

There is obviously an intimate link between the psycho-physical problem and the problem of the body, as indicated by Troxler's and Fechner's metaphysical speculations. This link becomes even more pertinent in Ernst Mach's[14] attack on the psycho-physical problem; or more precisely, in his attempt to dispose of the problem by rephrasing it in non-metaphysical terms.

In Mach's view, there is only one phenomenal reality, consisting of qualitative elements or 'sensations' (*Empfindungen*): "Thing, body, matter, are nothing apart from the combinations of the elements — the colors, sounds, and so forth — nothing apart from their so-called attributes." (Mach, 1922, Chapter I, §3)[15] Mach rejects the idea of material bodies as external 'causes' of sensations as a metaphysical assumption. The relation is exactly the opposite: 'bodies', 'things' are relatively stable complexes or aggregates of the sensations. Therefore

> the world does not consist of mysterious entities, which by their interaction with another, equally mysterious entity, the ego, produce sensations, which alone are accessible. For us, colors, sounds, spaces, times ... are provisionally the ultimate elements, whose given connexion it is our business to investigate. It is precisely in this that the exploration of reality consists. (Mach, 1922, I, §13)

The apparent duality of the 'physical' and the 'psychical' arises from two large systems of connections: the *same* element, *e.g.* a sensation of green, can be considered as 'physical' or as 'psychical' — depending whether it is determined by its position in the numerical system of wavelengths or by its place in the manifold of perceived colors — yet it is still the same element.[16] In this radically phenomenalist account, questions about primacy of the material over the mental, or *vice versa*, disappear as void metaphysical phantasies. However, Fechner's hypothesis of a unitary reality underlying the appearances is rejected as a metaphysical residue, too.[17] For Mach, there is *nothing behind* the phenomena, nothing 'in the background'; the unitary and psychophysically neutral reality is 'in the

---

[14] Ernst Mach (1838–1916), Austrian physicist and philosopher of great impact in the early 20th century (e.g. Vienna Circle, unitary science). Important works: *Die Mechanik in ihrer Entwickelung historisch-kritisch dargestellt*, 1883; *Die Analyse der Empfindungen*, 1886; *Erkenntnis und Irrtum*, 1905. About Mach: Cohen & Seeger (1970); Haller & Stadler (1988); Banks (2003).

[15] This and the following English quotes are taken from the translation by C.M. Williams, *The Analysis of Sensations*, New York: Dover, 1959.

[16] Unfortunately, Mach often uses the word 'sensations' as synonymous with the 'elements', thus confounding the psychological construct with the psycho-physically neutral phenomenon; cf. Wackermann (2010).

[17] The young Mach was greatly inspired by Fechner's psychophysics, and much in his later intellectual development can be understood as revisions of fundamental problems of psychophysical science; cf. Heidelberger (2004), pp. 172ff, and Heidelberger (2010).

foreground', that is, in the sensations themselves.

The problem of one's own body shows up in the very beginnings of Mach's *Analysis*:

> That complex of memories, moods, and feelings, joined to a particular body (the human body), which is called the 'I' or 'ego', manifests itself as relatively permanent. (Mach, 1922, I, §2)[18]

Then there is a particular complex of elements,

> known as our own body [*unser Leib*], which is a part of the former complexes distinguished by certain peculiarities ... Precisely viewed, it appears that the group $A \ B \ C$ ... [*viz.* elements composing external things] is always codetermined by $K \ L \ M$ ... [*viz.* elements composing one's own body]. (Mach, 1922, I, §5.)

This distinguished *Leib*-complex is also of only *relative* stability — exactly as ego is — and cannot be delimited sharply and definitely. All concepts of ego or of material bodies as permanent 'substances' have to be abandoned:

> the supposed unities 'body' and 'ego' are only makeshifts ... The antithesis between ego and world, between sensation (appearance) and thing, then vanishes, and we have simply to deal with the connexion of the elements ... (Mach, 1922, I, §7)

We could say, in a sloppy abbreviation, that Mach's solution of the psycho-physical problem equals to its dissolution; with this turn, the traditional notion of 'substance' is dissolved in a mass of qualitative elements. Problems inherent to this conception are manifest and cannot be easily ignored. Nonetheless, abandoning rigid psycho-physical dualism, a new, psychophysically neutral ground has been gained[19] and prepared for a novel, more radical approach to the problem of the body.

Life-based categories

Deconstruction of the substance duality — the inanimate material body versus the immaterial animating principle — enforces new attention to the *phenomenon of life* itself. Philosophy has to recognize life as a problem of its own standing; biology has to become aware of philosophical problems in its very foundations. An ultimate challenge for this intellec-

---

[18] In German original: "Als relativ beständig zeigt sich ferner der an einen besonderen Körper (den Leib) gebundene Komplex von Erinnerungen, Stimmungen, Gefühlen, welcher als Ich bezeichnet wird. ... Allerdings ist auch das Ich nur von relativer Beständigkeit." – Note the use of the term *Leib* for the body belonging to the subject.

[19] For further examination and interpretation of Mach's theory see Banks (2003). Here we cannot follow multiple relations between Mach's concepts and the sympathetic lines of thought (Continental: Avenarius; Anglo-American: Clifford, James, Russell); see Stubenberg (2005) and Banks (2010).

tual motion is then understanding of human life in its entirety, in its biological, social and cultural aspect. Hence the alliance between philosophically oriented anthropology and theoretical biology, which in the early 20th century produced a number of new and original approaches to the human condition.

Facing new problems, philosophy may need a novel conceptual framework, a changed set of thought habits. Wilhelm Dilthey had lucidly seen the possibility and necessity of rethinking traditional categories — such as 'subject' and 'object' — out of the facticity of life:

> ... the life-unity [*Lebenseinheit*], or subject, and the thing, or object, are not only correlated, not separable one from another, and inexistent without the other — they are also analogous. Although the life-unity and the object occur to us in totally different ways, their structure is to some extent similar, nay, intimately related. (Dilthey, 1984, p. 169)

A primary characteristic of every one, of a human being qua person, is being him- or her-*self*. The 'selfness' (*Selbigkeit*) is a category of life itself, while 'identity' is merely a formal category. Saying that a thing θ is identical with itself, $\theta = \theta$, is nothing but tautology; pointing out the unique being of a living thing out there refers to its selfness. Dilthey suggests that the notion of a thing, of any thing, is grounded in the category of selfness:

> By transferring [the selfness] onto the object, the object also contains an interior, an inner central point, a kernel of reality, since it is there for the life only as a life, for the will as a resistance to the will. Every idea of a thing ... is thus, for a natural attitude, endowed with such an interiority, which, ultimately, is understandable as [a form of] life. (Dilthey, 1984, p. 175)

This idea implies a complete reversal of the usual ways of thinking: one's own body is no more just one among many bodies, many things of physical nature, only accidentally exhibiting some special features. One's own body is the primary reality, upon which the concept of a body, *any* body — including cosmic bodies as well as corpuscles of physical theories — is constituted.

Positionality of the body

The correlation between philosophical anthropology and theoretical biology was thoroughly elaborated in Helmut Plessner's[20] work *Stages of organic life and the human being* (Plessner, 1975).

Its foundational thesis is, "The only human way of living is to con-

---

[20] Helmuth Plessner (1892–1985), German philosopher and sociologist, one of the proponents of 'philosophical anthropology' (along with A. Gehlen and M. Scheler). Important works: *Die Einheit der Sinne*, 1923; *Die Stufen des Organischen und der Mensch*, 1928; *Anthropologie der Sinne*, 1970.

duct a life." (p. 310)[21] In other words, human life is not merely biological functioning; its outstanding sign is 'self-relatedness' resulting in the consciousness of and the responsibility for him-self [*rückbezügliches Selbst*]. However, Plessner wants to explicate this specific character from its biological foundation, out of the continuity of human being with the organic life: "to understand the human being as a spiritually-moral and natural existence, on the ground of *unitary* experience." (p. 14) In this undertaking, not only the psycho-physical dualism but all related dualist notions, conceptually splitting up human being, are to be abandoned: object *vs.* subject, nature *vs.* culture, etc. The core of philosophical anthropology should be a "study of essential laws of psychophysically neutral human person." (p. 28)

Submitting the psycho-physical dualism to a closer scrutiny, Plessner criticizes identification of 'corporeality' [*Körperlichkeit*] with 'spatial extension' [*Ausdehnung*] in Cartesian *res extensa*, and exclusion of all qualitative phenomena to the realm of 'interiority' [*Innerlichkeit*] as *res cogitans* (p. 42–44).[22] There he also briefly touches "the attempt to overcome the dualism of worlds in terms of its own perspective", resulting in the notion of 'sensation' as a psychophysically neutral 'boundary phenomenon' (p. 59).[23]

These critical remarks delimit the starting point of Plessner's own examination: it is the 'dual-aspectivity' [*Doppelaspektivität*] as a characteristic of all life: "the dual-aspectivity must be objectively, property-like, present at a thing if we are to name the thing a living being."[24] Plessner's method is a *phenomenology of the living*, or, in his terms, of the organic reality; his goal as a theory of 'organic modals' — the essential and irreducible features of the living — making up an 'axiomatic theory of the organic'.[25] What all living beings have in common? They are bodies, as other physical things; what makes the difference between a living and non-living body is a special character of the boundary:

> In order to distinguish in a formed entity [*Gebilde*] the inward from the outward direction, there must be something given, relative to which this directional difference is neutral. ... Since this directionally neutral zone cannot occupy any spatial area, anything really between the exterior and the

---

[21] German original: "Der Mensch lebt nur, indem er ein Leben führt."

[22] Let us note in passing that 'interiority' [*Innerlichkeit*] is the key notion in the phenomenological biology of the Swiss biologist and anthropologist Adolf Portmann (1897–1982).

[23] Plessner does not name Mach here, although he unquestionably refers to Mach's theory of neutral elements.

[24] Duality in terms of the 'outer' and 'inner' aspect is, of course, a truly Fechnerian theme; but Plessner mentions Fechner only cursorily in the opening of his examination (Plessner, 1975, Chapter 3, p. 81).

[25] Before turning to philosophy, Plessner studied medicine and biology, and was influenced by Hans Driesch; cf. the use of the substantive 'the organic' in Driesch's *Philosophie des Organischen* (1909).

interior, it is a *frontier*. (p. 100)

Importantly, the frontier is not just a contour-like boundary of the body, such as the surface delimiting a geometrical body: "living bodies have a frontier of visible appearance"; and more, "the frontier belongs really to the body, which *realizes* its delimitation." (pp. 100, 103) Therefore, a living body is not merely a passive spatial extension within a given boundary. An organic body *positions* itself in space; it *sets* actively its frontier, and by this setting relates itself to the surrounding space and thus 'transcends' the frontier:

> In its being-living, the organic body differs from an anorganic body by its *positional character*, briefly, by its *positionality*. (p. 129)
>
> A living organism appears as confronting its environment. (p. 131)[26]

Now, the organic body is an articulated, functionally structured, 'organized' body. The place of an organ within the functional whole is determined by its purpose; the purpose of the entire body is then *life itself*.[27] Two organization forms, distinguished by the body's articulation and its positioning in the environment, are the *open* organization, typical for plants, and the *closed* organization, typical for animals. Characteristic for the 'closed organization' are (1) *frontality* — the animal faces and confronts objects and bodies in its environment — and (2) *centrality* — the ability to 'take distance' from the body's frontier.

The ability of 'double distancing' is the ground for the potential duality between the spatial body [*Körper*] and the vital body [*Leib*], for the spontaneity of acting, and by this virtue a condition for *subjectivity*. It is also on this ground that the nervous system — that is, the organ mediating between the frontier and the inner, vital kernel — is created. The existence of neural centers and subjectivity admits the 'dual-aspectivity' in terms of the inner and outer aspect; but, as Plessner reiterates, the domain of 'positionality' as such is *psychophysically neutral*.

This brief report should sufficiently illustrate Plessner's original method, deriving the basic structural/functional principles of living beings from the primordial fact of the body and its positionality. Proceeding to specifically human life-forms, Plessner puts forward the notion of 'excentric positionality': the ability to take distance *from its own center*, and thus the condition of reflective consciousness: [Human being is] "Not only living and experiencing, but also experiencing his own experience." (p. 292)[28] Plessner further seeks interpretation of various cultural pheno-

---

[26] German original: "Ein Lebewesen erscheint gegen seine Umgebung gestellt."

[27] Greek *organon* = instrument, tool, etymologically related to *ergon* = work. Plessner (1975, p. 191) writes, "der organisierte Körper im Ganzen, wie er leibt und lebt", inventing a verb *leiben* for the function of the vital body, *Leib*. A straightforward translation to English is impossible.

[28] German original: "Er lebt und erlebt nicht nur, sondern er erlebt sein Erleben."

mena out of the fact of human 'excentric positionality', a path that we will not follow here.

Action and perception: Gestaltkreis[29]

An organism not only 'is in' an environment but transcends itself in a relation to its environment as its 'world' (*Umwelt*). The organism 'positions' itself (speaking with Plessner) and thus *enters* the relation: it acts toward the environment and is being acted upon. The living body is the locus where the two functional bundles linking the organism and its world — that is, perception and motor action — meet, intersect and interact. If physiology in the Cartesian tradition was concerned with the analysis of afferent and efferent paths within the body's (physical) mechanism, the new view of biological reality requires a new approach to perception and action, understanding these functions from a unitary perspective. Such an approach was taken by Viktor von Weizsäcker[30] in his *Gestaltkreis* theory (von Weizsäcker, 1997a).

The point of departure was von Weizsäcker's study of disturbed function in neurological patients. Whereas the traditional neurophysiology sought to explain neurological symptoms in terms of 'processing errors' on neuronal stimulus–reaction pathways, thorough clinical observations revealed a 'functional transformation' [*Funktionswandel*] of the structure of sensorimotor acts. On this ground von Weizsäcker contrasted the 'conduct principle' against the 'conduction principle',[31] suggesting to abandon the simple reflex-path doctrine and to study sensorimotor acts in their entirety. Phenomenological analyses of acts such as eye-tracking, pointing, grasping etc. reveal the 'coherence' between the subject's acts and the perceived objects. More than just co-ordination, it is a kind of 'entanglement' [*Verschränkung*] of the perceiver and the perceived, making the perception of an object and the action toward the object a unitary biological act. Therefore, "perception must not be conceived as a fabricated image, but rather as a dynamical activity ... it is not a final product for the subject, but rather a process of encounter between the 'I' and the environment." (p. 219) — Von Weizsäcker introduced for this principle a new term, *Gestaltkreis*, to emphasize the holistic character and

---

[29] This section is partly based on our earlier essay (Wackermann, 2009).

[30] Viktor von Weizsäcker (1886–1957), German neurologist, founder of 'medical anthropology' and one of pioneers of psychosomatic medicine in Germany. Important works: *Der Gestaltkreis*, 1940; *Natur und Geist*, 1944; *Begegnungen und Entscheidungen*, 1945; *Psychosomatische Medizin*, 1949; *Pathosophie*, 1956. Biographical sketch: C.F. von Weizsäcker (1992).

[31] Our translation attempts to mimic the word-play in German original: *Leistungsprinzip vs. Leitungsprinzip*. The 'conduct principle' aims at achievement of the same result on different pathways (teleology), while the 'conduction principle' states the conduction of neural impulses along the same path (causality).

the circular form of the subject–object entanglement.

Importantly, Gestaltkreis is not merely a theory of interaction or co-ordination between two pre-existent neural subsystems. Von Weizsäcker elaborates the concept into a general theory, "introducing the subject into biology" (p. 83) and vindicating the *unity of subject and object* in a biological act. It is a dynamic, unstable unity, permanently disturbed, endangered, and continuously re-established in the ongoing action. For the traditional neurophysiology, 'stimulus' is just an event in the physical environment eliciting a sensory experience *or* an immediate motor response; while in von Weizsäcker's theory, 'stimulus' is a disturbance of the Gestaltkreis unity, which is restored in an adaptive response involving both sensory *and* motor components. In this way, the artificial separation between the afferent and the efferent subsystem, between perception and motor action, is removed. Moreover, the psycho-physical dualism implied in the subject-versus-object split is abandoned as well:

> A biological act understood as *Gestaltkreis* should serve as an example of a genuine, intimate unity. … We replace the superficial dualism of substances, of psyche and physis, by a polarly bound unity of the subject and the object. (pp. 310–311)

Biological functions are understandable only as 'formations' [*Gestaltungen*] of this unity; whereby the subject's body and its articulations are of crucial importance. Von Weizsäcker critically commented on the physiologists' tendency to "forget that there are not only centripetal and centrifugal nerves, but also hands and fingers" (von Weizsäcker, 1933, p. 640) parts of the body usually involved in both 'half-circles' of a unitary sensorimotor act. He also pointed out the relativity of the frontier between the subject and the world, observed on the living body:

> The question where my environment ends and my corporeal and mental ownership[32] begin cannot be read out from phenomenal data but must be judged by the dynamics of the Gestaltkreis processes. … The relocatability of the frontier is an expression of the functional manifold of the organism. (p. 655)

But the variety of 'formations' includes much more:

> There are turns toward the objects of the environment, and there are turns away from them; there are transpositions of the 'I' into the environment, there are releases, crises, total interruptions of the coherence between 'I' and the environment. And all these [phenomena] reveal the importance of the functional transformation; they are of constitutive necessity for the reality of perceived things, of our own body, of events that happen. (von Weizsäcker 1997a, p. 285–286)

The above-mentioned 'crises' allude to another important component of

---

[32] In German original: "leiblicher und seelischer Besitz"; von Weizsäcker here refers to works of Plessner and Buytendijk.

von Weizsäcker's thought, building a bridge between his Gestaltkreis theory and the medical anthropology: it is the category of 'the pathic' [*Pathisches*].[33] This term refers to the reverse side of the life's activity; the subject is passive with respect to contingencies of the surrounding world, of its own vital impulses and urges: "Not only that it sets itself, and so it is active; it also happens to be, and in this sense it is passive." (von Weizsäcker, 1997a, p. 313)[34] — In the domain of the pathic, the depths of the life continuity are revealed in *existential* situations.

The body-image

In the preceding sections we have seen the importance of the 'frontier', the zone of the body–world differentiation. The subject is bound to the body — not a deliberately moving and purely cognizing instance, like Descartes' sailor in the ship — but *relatively* free with respect to the boundary.[35] But there is more: our body itself is a variable sensuous field, with its own gradients of pleasure and displeasure, re-structuring itself autonomously, without conscious effort. Neuropathology exhibits a broad variety of alterations of the subjective topology of the body; a domain of study from where the important notion of 'body scheme' arose.

The term *body scheme* was coined by the neurologist Paul Schilder.[36] Schilder's work is highly original as well as amazingly eclectic, integrating approaches from neuro- and psychopathology, Gestalt psychology, psychoanalysis, and phenomenology. Schilder began his researches with a study on self-consciousness and its alterations in the 'depersonalization' syndromes, and continued with a monographic study, *Körperschema* (Schilder, 1923), later re-worked and expanded in his monumental *Image and Appearance of the Human Body* (Schilder, 1935). There, Schilder points out the absence of the body in traditional psychology; that is, body conceived not merely as a source of proprio- and interoceptive sensations,

---

[33] Derived from Greek verb *paschō* = suffer, stem *path-*; cf. 'pathos', 'sympathy', 'empathy', 'pathology', and (mediated by Latin) 'passive' or 'passion'.

[34] In German original: "Nicht nur setzt es sich selbst und ist so aktiv; es geschieht ihm und so ist es passiv." – As examples of situations belonging to the category of the pathic von Weizsäcker names 'intention', 'expectation', 'surprise', 'danger', 'threat', 'security', 'liberty' and 'freedom', 'decision' and 'constraint'.

[35] This internal positionality is well-known from everyone's experience: we are able to re-distribute our 'sensible presence' *within* the body, for example, distancing ourselves from a pain occurring in a distal extremity, or retracting temporarily from our body during a painful dentist surgery.

[36] Paul F. Schilder (1886–1940), Austrian neurologist and psychiatrist, from 1930 living and working in USA. Important works: *Selbstbewußtsein* and *Persönlichkeitsbewußtsein*, 1914; *Körperschema*, 1923; *The Image and Appearance of the Human Body*, 1935.

but "body as an entity and as a unit," "the inner body," *Leib*:[37]

> the body in this sense ... is not the product of sensations, but is co-ordinated with the sensations which get their final meaning only from the unit which is one of the fundamental units of our experience. (Schilder 1935, p. 283)

It is this body of subjective experience that is in the focus of Schilder's interest:

> the picture of our own body which we form in our mind ... the way in which the body appears to ourselves. ... Beyond [sensations] there is the immediate experience that there is a unity of the body. This unity is perceived, yet it is more than a perception. We call it a schema of our body or ... postural model of the body. ... We may call it 'body-image'. (p. 11)

The totality and unity of the experienced body, which is not merely a collection, a 'sum' of singular sensations, suggests the approach of the Gestalt psychology; and Schilder straightforwardly names the body-image "the human Gestalt" (p. 14). Experimental data on subjective perception of one's own body, clinical observations of variations and disturbances of the body-image caused by brain lesions, alterations of consciousness, etc., and their intepretations fill the first part of Schilder's book.

But the subjective body is not only a scheme of spatio-temporal coordinates; it is a sensing and sensuous entity, an experiential field of *Lust* and *Unlust* and, correspondingly, of libidinous cathexis, *Besetzung* in Freud's sense. These aspects are studied in the second part of the book within the conceptual framework of psychoanalysis.[38] In particular, Schilder discusses the rôle of sensations of pain and pleasure during the early phases of mental development for the emergence of the body–world distinction, and then for building up the body-image. "Body and world are experiences which are correlated with each other. One is not possible without the other."(p. 123) The mobility of the frontier between the two, and the existence of the 'indifference zone' between the body and the world are explained by the developmental interplay between ego-controlled sensations and motility, and the body's proper libidinous tendencies.

As seen from what has been said above, Schilder's work definitely dismisses the concept of body as a purely physiological vehicle of mental functions, a psychologically indifferent carrier. Moreover, Schilder does not stop at the analyses of the meaning and importance of the body-image for an individual subject. The subject's body is the place of communi-

---

[37] In his use of the German word *Leib*, Schilder refers especially to Max Scheler's phenomenological studies.

[38] Schilder did not accept psychoanalytical concepts uncritically; in fact, he rejected most of the Freud's theory contained in the *Beyond the Pleasure Principle*, and exhibited views which make him closer to ego-analysis than to the classical Freudian psychoanalysis.

cation with other subjects, present as visible and tangible body-images. A disturbance of the subject's own body-image implies an alteration of the others' body-images:

> Experiences in pathology show clearly that when our orientation concerning left and right is lost in regard to our own body, there is also a loss of orientation in regard to the bodies of other persons. The postural model of our own body is connected with the postural model of the bodies of others. There are connections between the postural models of fellow human beings. (p. 16)

Consequently, the third part of Schilder's book, 'The sociology of the body-image', is devoted to these aspects of human embodied existence: social interaction, personal identity and identification, sexuality, beauty, æsthetics and, ultimately, ethics:

> Just as the integrity of our own body and its preservation is a moral value, the preservation of the bodies of others is a moral value, too. ... There is a moral law not only to preserve the form of the body of another as we perceive it with our senses, but also to preserve or to restore his libidinous structure, the regulated function of which is the only basis for a full and harmonized postural model of the fellow human being. ... The study of the psychology of the body-image may lead to a system of ethics and a system of morals. (pp. 281–282)

Interim summary

The history of human body is a counter-part of the history of psyche. From the early Greek thinkers on, accounts of the human nature were mostly *psychologizing* accounts: it was 'something in us' what makes us what we are; yet not entirely identical with our presence in this world. The Platonic outlook at the ideal — conceived as the only true reality — conserved and confirmed the link between psyche and the transcendental, releasing the bonds between the soul and the body, and leaving the body with earthly matters. A shadow image of this separation can be seen in Cartesian substance dualism.

From the pole, all ways go to the equator; from an extreme intellectual position, all ways lead to its revision and reassessment. The history of embodiment is a history of continuous corrections of the metaphysically motivated disembodiment. A decisive move on this path was the anti-metaphysical turn of the late 19th century, followed by the phenomenological turn in the early 20th century: 'back to things themselves'. Indeed, all authors referred to in the three preceding sections were significantly influenced by Husserl's phenomenology, and their researches parallelized investigations in phenomenological philosophy and psychology.[39] And there are, of course, many more precursors and shared influences than could be treated in the limited space; let us mention J. von Uexküll's theoretical biology,[40] Gestalt psychology, K. Goldstein's holistic approach in neurology, and psychosomatic medicine. Because of those numerous affinities and parallel influences, a brief overview may help to reveal a common structure:

1. Anti-Cartesianist attitude

The dualism of psyche and physis — in modern parlance, of mind and matter — was recognized as unproductive, conflicting with our own experience of ourselves and of the world, and plainly untenable. Instead of speculative 'alternative' metaphysics (Troxler, Fechner), the later authors shifted the focus to the phenomenon of life as a natural psychophysical unity, and attempted to demonstrate the differentiation of the two seemingly separate realms out of one common, psycho-physically neutral background:

> Theory of organism could and should be incorporated in a psychological doctrine which sees life and personality as a unit. ... There is no gap between the organic and the functional. Mind and personality are efficient entities as well as the organism. Psychic processes have common roots with other processes going on in the organism. (Schilder, 1935, p. 7)

The rejection of *dualism* was accompanied by a more or less explicit rejection of *mechanism* as an explanatory principle.[41] The dominance of causally-mechanistic explanation was relativized by Fechner's emphasis on functional relations, and this program was further radicalized in Mach's concept of phenomenological science (cf. Heidelberger, 2010). The mechanistic paradigm in psychology, represented particularly by Pavlov's 'reflexology', was criticized by Buytendijk & Plessner (1935).[42] Von Weizsäcker's refutation of the 'conduction principle' as inadequate to the observed phenomena has been already mentioned; his aversion to the mechanistic manner of thought can be summarized in one quote: "Nature does not build machines." (von Weizsäcker, 1997b, p. 406)

---

[39] If we do not penetrate deeper into the field of phenomenological psychology, and phenomenology proper, it is not because of a thematic blindness, but rather due to a vast extension of the field. Among authors sympathetic to the above discussed approaches, at least E.W. Straus and F.J.J. Buytendijk should be named.

[40] J. von Uexküll (1926) introduced the circular scheme of the organism's embedding in its environment [*Umwelt*], which was understood as a unity of the 'world-of-signs' [*Merkwelt*] and 'world-of-action' [*Wirkwelt*]. Von Weizsäcker's *Gestaltkreis* appears as a variation of the circular scheme, applied to the subject–object situation.

[41] Another part of Cartesian legacy, still present in physiology up to the present day, is the insistence on mechanism as the preferred, or the only explanatory model.

[42] Cf. simultaneous criticism of Pavlov's physiological psychology by Goldstein (1934), Straus (1935), and Merleau-Ponty (1942).

2. Focus on phenomenal life-world

Mach's phenomenalism, dissolving natural structures of perception into a mass of 'elements', was perhaps too radical — and, ironically, 'atomistic' — but it removed the artificial cleft between 'being' and 'appearance' and prepared the terrain for a discovery of immediate, 'pure' experience, which continued in the phenomenological movement[43]. Phenomenology, originally conceived as a study of pure facts of consciousness, abandoned the idealist perspective and acknowledged the 'life-world' [*Lebenswelt*] as the primary reality. This move not only legitimated the natural, pre-scientific attitude to the life-world, but also opened totally new field of problems to study: "we find ourselves in the presence of a field of lived perception which is prior to number, measure, space and causality." (Merleau-Ponty, 1963, p. 219) The task for phenomenological study is to reveal the paths along which cognitive constructs and scientific concepts — such as those of time and space — are constituted. Interestingly and significantly, it occurs that their constitution is intimately related with experience of and at one's own body.

The revisionist approach to space and time begins with Mach (1906; see also Mach, 1922, Chapters VI and XII), who held spatial data and temporal durations for 'sensations' not essentially different from qualitative sensations of, say, sound or color; and he emphasized the precedence of experienced (in his somewhat unfortunate nomenclature: 'physiological') space and time before the abstract spatial and temporal continua of mathematical physics. The notions of space and time received even more problematic status with the shift of focus to biology, as it was felt that the physicalist concepts were not adequate for the understanding of space and time *in which the life process itself takes place.*[44] Plessner considered the 'positionality' of a living organism as *the* condition necessary for its being in time: "A thing of a positional character can be only in becoming; the way of its being is being a process," (Plessner, 1975, p. 132)[45] and specified a living body as a "positional unity of space and time." Von Weizsäcker, focusing more on the experience of worldly things in the I–body–environment entanglement, remarked that "the world and its things are not in space and time, but space and time are in the world, at the things." (von Weizsäcker, 1997a, p. 234) Schilder pointed out the anisotropy and diversity of qualitative characters of experienced space, "the space in and around the postural model is not the space of physics. The body-image

---

[43] Concerning relations between Mach's phenomenalism and Husserl's phenomenology, see Fisette (in press)

[44] It is not by chance that the first two chapters of von Uexküll's *Theoretical Biology* (1926) are dedicated to problems of space and time.

[45] German original: "Ein Ding positionalen Charakters kann nur sein, indem es wird; der Prozeß ist die Weise seines Seins."

incorporates objects or spreads itself into space." (Schilder, 1935, p. 213) Cf. also Erwin Straus' (1930, 1952) analyses of the rôle of human body in the constitution of subjective space.

3. Existential dimension

The studies referred above do not stop at an explication or clarification of human sensorimotor or cognitive functioning; they all have higher ambitions; they all attempt, in their individual way, an outlook at the human being as *existence* — not a thing, be it a material or a mental (cognizing) thing, or a 'psycho-physically indifferent' thing. Correlatively, human body is discovered as being not-just-a-thing, but rather as a prerequisite — that is, a model and a condition at the same time — for the experience of any-thing. In von Weizsäcker's analysis, the body is the ground of pathic crises, revealing the existential depths of human being; in Schilder's view, the body's integrity is not reduced to its mechanistic functioning, but is understood as integrity of the embodied subject — not only in terms of its efficiency, but also of its *dignity*.

Human being and bodily acting in the world cannot be conceived as an interaction among $n+1$ physical bodies, one arbitrarily chosen and some n objects being 'just around', contingently. The interaction has rather a character of *encounter* (*Begegnung*) between the subject and the world. Von Weizsäcker permanently emphasized the encounter-like of the subject–object entanglement.[46] Also Plessner referred to this essentially 'dialogic' structure, writing

> It is in agreement with the nature of human being to say 'thou' to his environment, and to search what he is himself, in the reflected image of the world. (Plessner, 1975, p. 71)[47]

Speaking about a 'discovery' of the body, we make use of an imprecise and somehow confusing metaphor. It is not a single entity that has been found, but rather an overwhelming multitude of phenomena:

> There is the body as mass of chemical components in interaction, the body as dialectic of living being and its biological milieu, and the body as dialectic of social subject and his group; even all our habits are in impalpable body for the ego at each moment. (Merleau-Ponty, 1963, p. 210)

In sum, the discovery of the body is not like a discovery of a new planet, or of a yet unknown chemical element. It is rather like a discovery of gravitation, or of an ordering principle of the known elements. With the

---

[46] von Weizsäcker, *Gestaltkreis*, pp. 235ff and elsewhere; cf. p. 335 (Glossary): "The term 'encounter' should express the opposition between 'I' and the environment, by contrast to the constructively-mechanical synthesis, e.g. of a stimulus and a motor reaction."

[47] German original: "Denn es entspricht dem Menschen, zu seiner Umgebung Du zu sagen und, was er selbst ist, im Widerschein der Welt zu suchen." – Cf. also E.W. Straus (1952) and J. H. van den Berg (1952).

discovery of the lived body, human existence is fully embedded into the natural order; but at the same time the existential dimension of human nature is revealed.

New embodiment?

It may seem that, during the last two centuries, the spell over the body has been broken, and the reality of embodiment as a biologically, psychologically and existentially important fact has been recognized.[48] 'Embodiment', 'enacted cognition', 'situated perception' have gained currency in the philosophy of mind as well as in cognitive science and related disciplines.[49] The parole of the day is to "put brain, body and world together," not to keep them apart. Themes and theses mentioned above — unity of perception and action, importance of the body-image in the inter-subjective communication, etc. — are no new discoveries, rather commonplace topics. And yet, we may and should ask, What is the meaning and true motivation of the present 'embodiment' turn?

Firstly, there seems to be a kind of historical short-sight with regard to the anthropologically and phenomenologically motivated approaches of the early 20th century. It is not that the foundational ideas of early authors were forgotten; but it appears that the attention is rather selectively focused. For example, the works of Merleau-Ponty are almost obligatorily cited, while works of some other, arguably no less relevant authors are rarely mentioned;[50] or, in some cases, they never overcame the language barrier between continental Europe and Anglo-American literature. Moreover, lists of references suggest that the 'working memory' of the present-day science has quite a short span.

There is a striking latency of about 50–60 years between the ground-making[51] works and the present wave of 'embodiment' enthusiasm. What

---

[48] The post-modern thematization of human body, merging the phenomenological perspective in various contexts such as cultural anthropology, medical anthropology, sociology of illness/disability, gender studies, the move toward 'new sensuality', etc., is beyond the scope of this chapter.

[49] See, for example, Part III of Gallagher & Schmicking (2010); or the special issue 'Subjectivity and the Body' (Legrand, 2007).

[50] This comment is not meant to question the importance of Merleau-Ponty's work which I highly value. What makes him unique among philosophers of his time is his paying thorough attention to results of empirical sciences, studying and scrutinizing them; thus we should be aware not only of his own contribution, but also of his sources. A brief look at references in his major works, *Structure of Behavior* and *Phenomenology of Perception*, reveals how much Merleau-Ponty owes to our authors.

[51] *Sic!* – this is not a typing error. The ambitions of modern authors are 'ground-breaking' findings or ideas; but a broken ground is not the proper place to build upon. Here I agree with Plessner (1975, p. 76): "Lösungen von Problemen sind wertlos, solange nicht das Fundament der Phänomene, auf denen sich die Probleme erheben, gesichert ist"; therefore, ground-making approaches are required.

was the cause of this delay? The answer is simple but unequivocal: Exactly those characteristics of the early 'embodiment' movement (though never named this way) listed above — anti-mechanistic, phenomenologically trained and existentially oriented approach — made its thought-style obsolete, if not plainly incomprehensible to the *Zeitgeist* of the post-WW2 period, marked by the apparent success of mechanistic, 'information-processing' and computational paradigms.

Yet, it is well possible that the comparison of the strength and 'explanatory power' is ill-placed. One example for many: von Weizsäcker's Gestaltkreis theory may in some aspects appear as a precursor of the 'reafference principle' (von Holst & Mittelstaedt, 1950); or, more strongly, it could be argued that von Holst's theory solves the problems which were only named and described by von Weizsäcker in his theory (see C.F. v. Weizsäcker, 1982). However, such interpretation would ignore the broader context of von Weizsäcker's work, and cut away the links from his Gestaltkreis theory to fundamental problems of natural science (*e.g.* the rôle of subjectivity in biology) or of philosophical and medical anthropology (*e.g.* the 'pathic' dimension of human existence). Briefly, Gestaltkreis was *not* just a precocious branch of biological cybernetics, but a theory of its own standing and reach;[52] and the reafference principle was not the last word in the perception–action coordination, anyway (cf. Feldman, 2009).[53]

So it is not without some historical irony if the discovery of the body is nowadays celebrated as an advance in the cognitive science. There is an intrinsic tension that cannot be easily disputed away: If 'embodiment' does not mean anything more than that the alleged symbolic operations of the mind are implemented in the neural 'wet-ware', then it is nothing but a fashionable label. If the facticity of the body is taken seriously, the traditional cognitivist picture of human being as a biological computer is untenable. The present situation is quite confusing: the emphasis on 'embodiment' may be interpreted as a move toward a 'new cognitive science' — or as an attack of 'new anti-cognitivism' (Richeimer, 2006). Still, disregarding such ideological labels, the question remains open: Are we witnessing a truly new discovery? or a late fruitful phase of an early rediscovery? or still waiting for a re-rediscovery?

---

[52] Cf. a critical reassessment of the theoretical approaches of Gestaltkreis and of cybernetics by Buytendijk & Christian (1963).

[53] On the other hand, reading general statements such as "Perception is not itself a bodily activity, but it does underpin such activity – it makes possible fluid, interested interaction with the world." (Roberts, 2010, p. 110), we may wonder if there has been any substantial progress since von Weizsäcker's Gestaltkreis theory?

J. Wackermann

Epilogue

*"Alle Naturwissenschaft ist nur ein Versuch,
den Menschen, das Anthropologische zu verstehen:
noch richtiger, auf den ungeheuersten Umwegen immer
zum Menschen zurückzukommen."*
— F. Nietzsche (1872)

We are not only minds, we are also bodies; this may seem trivial. The less trivial part of the lesson: we are not only minds, and not only cognizing organisms; we are embodied lives.

The rediscovery of our embodied nature is a step toward a rational, scientific, yet non-reductionist theory of human being; but not the last step to a final theory in a form of 'revised cognitivism'. Rather, it should be a new beginning, an initial step on a path leading away from cognitivist and cybernetic paradigms to an understanding of multiple aspects of human existence: cognitive, existential and ethical.

All these aspects meet in the facticity of the body. Paraphrasing Pascal, we could say that the body has its own reasons; listening to them means accepting the wisdom and the foolishness of the body; and so accepting our being down to its pathic depths.

References

Arendt H.-J. (1999). *Gustav Theodor Fechner*. Frankfurt: Lang.
Banks E. C. (2003). *Ernst Mach's World Elements: A Study in Natural Philosophy*. Dordrecht: Kluwer.
Banks E. C. (2010). Neutral monism reconsidered. *Philosophical Psychology, 23*, 173–87.
Barnes J. (1984). *The Complete Works of Aristotle*. (2 vols.) Princeton: Princeton University Press.
van den Berg J. H. (1952). The human body and the significance of human movement. *Philosophy and Phenomenological Research, 13*, 159–83.
Buytendijk F. J. J. & Plessner H. (1935). Die physiologische Erklärung des Verhaltens. *Acta Biotheoretica, Series A, 1*, 151–71.
Buytendijk F. J. J. & Christian P. (1963). Kybernetik und Gestaltkreis als Erklärungsprinzipien des Verhaltens. *Nervenarzt, 31*, 97–104.
Cohen R. S. & Seeger R. J. (eds.) (1970). *Ernst Mach – Physicist and Philosopher*. (Boston Studies in the Philosophy of Science, vol. VI.) Dordrecht: Reidel.
Cottingham J. (1986). *Descartes*. Oxford: Blackwell.
Descartes R. (1641/1904). *Meditationes de prima philosophia*. In C. Adam & P. Tannery (eds.), *Œuvres de Descartes, Vol. VII* (pp. 1–90). Paris: Cerf.
Dilthey W. (1912/1984). Leben und Erkennen. In W. Dilthey (ed.), *Das Wesen der Philosophie* (pp. 169–212). Stuttgart: Reclam. [Original work written 1912]
Diogenes Laërtius (1853). *The Lives and Opinions of Eminent Philosophers* (C. D. Yonge, transl.). London: Bohn.
Fechner G. Th. (1860). *Elemente der Psychophysik*. (2 vols.) Leipzig: Breitkopf & Härtel.
Fechner G. Th. (1907). *Über die Seelenfrage*. (2nd ed.) Hamburg/Leipzig: Voß.
Feldman A. G. (2009). New insights into action–perception coupling. *Experimental Brain Research, 194*, 39–58.

Fisette D. (in press). Phenomenology and phenomenalism: Ernst Mach and the genesis of Husserl's Phenomenology. *Axiomathes*.
Gallagher S. & Schmicking D. (2010). *Handbook of Phenomenology and Cognitive Science*, Dordrecht: Springer.
Goldstein K. (1934). *Der Aufbau des Organismus*. The Hague: Nijhoff.
Haller R. & Stadler F. (eds.) (1988). *Ernst Mach – Werk und Wirkung*. Wien: Hölder-Pichler-Tempsky.
Hamilton E. & Cairns H. (eds.) (1961). *The Collected Dialogues of Plato, Including the Letters*. Princeton: Princeton University Press.
Heidelberger M. (2004). *Nature from Within: Gustav Theodor Fechner and His Psychophysical Worldview*. Pittsburgh: University of Pittsburgh Press.
Heidelberger M. (2010). Functional relations and causality in Fechner and Mach. *Philosophical Psychology*, 23, 163–72.
von Holst E. & Mittelstaedt H. (1950). Das Reafferenzprinzip. Wechselwirkungen zwischen Zentralnervensystem und Peripherie. *Naturwissenschaften*, 37, 464–76.
Kahn C. H. (1979). *The Art and Thought of Heraclitus*. Cambridge: Cambridge University Press.
Lauer H. E. & Widmer M. (1980). *Ignaz Paul Vital Troxler*. Oberwil: Kugler.
Legrand D. (ed.) (2007). Subjectivity and the Body. *Consciousness and Cognition*, 16, whole issue 3.
Mach E. (1906/1988). *Space and Geometry in the Light of Physiological, Psychological, and Physical Inquiry* (Th. J. McCormack, transl.). La Salle: Open Court. [Reprint 1988]
Mach E. (1922). *Die Analyse der Empfindungen und das Verhältnis des Physischen zum Psychischen*. (9th ed.) Jena: Fischer.
Merleau-Ponty M. (1942). *La Structure du comportment*. Paris: Presses Universitaires de France.
Merleau-Ponty M. (1962). *Phenomenology of Perception* (C. Smith, transl.). London: Routledge.
Merleau-Ponty M. (1963). *The Structure of Behavior* (A. L. Fisher, transl.). Boston: Beacon Press.
Nietzsche F. (1872). *Posthumous fragments*, series 19
　<http://www.nietzschesource.org/texts/eKGWB/NF-1872,19>.
Plessner H. (1975). *Die Stufen des Organischen und der Mensch*. (3rd ed.) Berlin: de Gruyter.
Richeimer J. (2006). Familiarity and the inferential theory of perception. *Theory and Psychology*, 16, 505–25.
Roberts T. (2010). Understanding 'sensorimotor understanding'. *Phenomenology and Cognitive Science*, 9, 101–11.
Schilder P. (1923). *Das Körperschema*. Berlin: Springer.
Schilder P. (1935). *The Image and Appearance of the Human Body*. New York: International Universities Press.
Straus E. (1930). Die Formen des Räumlichen. Ihre Bedeutung für die Motorik und die Wahrnehmung. *Nervenarzt*, 3, 633–56. [Reprinted as Chapter 1 in (Straus, 1966).]
Straus E. (1935). *Vom Sinn der Sinne. Ein Beitrag zur Grundlegung der Psychologie*. Berlin: Springer. [2nd ed. 1956]
Straus E. W. (1952). The upright posture. *Psychiatric Quarterly*, 26, 529–561. [Reprinted as Chapter 7 in (Straus, 1966).]
Straus E. W. (1966). *Phenomenological Psychology*. London: Tavistock.
Stubenberg L. (2005). Neutral monism. In *Stanford Encyclopedia of Philosophy*
　<http://plato.stanford.edu/entries/neutral-monism/>
Troxler I. P. V. (1989). *Blicke in das Wesen des Menschen*. Oberwil: Kugler. [Original work published 1812]

Troxler I. P. V. (1985). *Naturlehre des menschlichen Erkennens oder Metaphysik.* Hamburg: Meiner. [Original work published 1828]
von Uexküll J. (1926). *Theoretical Biology.* New York: Harcourt.
Wackermann J. (2009). Anthropological turn: a missed chance for psychophysics? In M. A. Elliott & S. Antonijević (eds.), *Fechner Day 2009* (pp. 143-8). Galway: International Society for Psychophysics.
Wackermann J. (2010). Psychophysics as a science of primary experience. *Philosophical Psychology, 23*, 189-206.
von Weizsäcker C. F. (1982). Die Einheit von Wahrnehmen und Bewegen. In C. F. von Weizsäcker (ed.), *Der Garten des Menschlichen* (pp. 206-224). München/Wien: Hanser.
von Weizsäcker C. F. (1992). Viktor v. Weizsäcker zwischen Physik und Philosophie. In C. F. von Weizsäcker, *Zeit und Wissen* (pp. 922-46). München/Wien: Hanser.
von Weizsäcker V. (1933). Der Gestaltkreis, dargestellt als psychophysische Analyse des optischen Drehversuchs. *Pflügers Archiv gesamter Physiologie, 231,* 630-61.
von Weizsäcker V. (1997a) Der Gestaltkreis. Theorie der Einheit von Wahrnehmen und Bewegen. In P. Achilles, D. Janz, M. Schrenk, & C. F. von Weizsäcker (eds.), *Viktor von Weizsäcker. Gesammelte Schriften, Vol. 4* (pp. 77-337). Frankfurt: Suhrkamp. [Original work published 1940, 4th ed. 1950]
von Weizsäcker V. (1997b) Über das Nervensystem. In P. Achilles, D. Janz, M. Schrenk, & C. F. von Weizsäcker (eds.), *Viktor von Weizsäcker. Gesammelte Schriften, Vol. 4* (pp. 405-19) Frankfurt: Suhrkamp. [Original work published 1943]

The Implications of Embodiment for Behavior and Cognition: Animal and Robotic Case Studies

Matej Hoffmann and Rolf Pfeifer

Artificial Intelligence Laboratory, Department of Informatics
University of Zurich, Switzerland
{hoffmann, pfeifer}@ifi.uzh.ch

Abstract. In this paper[1], we will argue that if we want to understand the function of the brain (or the control in the case of robots), we must understand how the brain is embedded into the physical system, and how the organism interacts with the real world. While embodiment has often been used in its trivial meaning, i.e. 'intelligence requires a body', the concept has deeper and more important implications, concerned with the relation between physical and information (neural, control) processes. A number of case studies are presented to illustrate the concept. These involve animals and robots and are concentrated around locomotion, grasping, and visual perception. A theoretical scheme that can be used to embed the diverse case studies will be presented. Finally, we will establish a link between the low-level sensory-motor processes and cognition. We will present an embodied view on categorization, and propose the concepts of 'body schema' and 'forward models' as a natural extension of the embodied approach toward first representations.

Introduction

Intelligent behavior has always fascinated researchers. Traditionally, intelligence was attributed solely to the control or the neural system. In 'classical' (also Good Old-Fashioned — GOFAI) Artificial Intelligence and cognitive science, the focus was on problem-solving through computation on internal symbolic representations of the world (e.g., Pylyshyn, 1987). In computational neuroscience, the focus is essentially on the simulation of certain brain regions. For example, in the 'Blue Brain' project (Markram, 2006), the focus is, for the better part, on the simulation of cortical columns — the organism into which the brain is embedded does not play a major role in these considerations. However, recently there has been an increasing interest in the notion of embodiment in all disciplines dealing with intelligent behavior, including psychology, philosophy, artificial intelligence, linguistics, and neuroscience. In this paper, we explore the far-reaching and often surprising implications of embodiment for

---

[1] Parts of the ideas presented in this paper have appeared in previous publications; they will be referenced throughout the text.

behavior and for cognition.

While embodiment has often been used in its trivial meaning, i.e. 'intelligence requires a body', there are deeper and more important consequences, concerned with connecting brain, body, and environment. The behavior of any system is not merely the outcome of an internal control structure (such as the central nervous system); it is also affected by the ecological niche in which the system is physically embedded, by its morphology (the shape of its body and limbs, as well as the type and placement of sensors and effectors), and by the material properties of the elements composing the morphology. This embedding impacts the physical as well as the information (neural, control) processes that all together manifest themselves in a particular behavior (Pfeifer & Bongard, 2007).

Physical constraints shape the dynamics of the interaction of the embodied system with its environment (for example, because of the way it is attached to the body at the hip joint, during walking a leg behaves to some extent like a pendulum) and can be exploited to achieve stability and energy efficiency. We will speak about 'intelligence by mechanics' or 'morphological computation' when morphology and materials take over some of the functions normally attributed to the brain (or the control). A direct link also exists between embodiment and information: coupled sensory-motor activity and body morphology induce statistical regularities in sensory input and within the control architecture and therefore enhance internal information processing (e.g., Lungarella & Sporns, 2006).

The above-mentioned points apply to any agent interacting with its environment, animal or robot. We will present some case studies from biology, however, our selection will be biased toward case studies on robots. The advantage of using robots is that embodiment can be investigated quantitatively: robots are much simpler to manipulate and monitor. That is, first, we can change the control structure without much effort, and we can even manipulate the morphology relatively easily. Second, all sensory stimulations, motor signals, and internal states can be recorded as time series for further analysis. Having discovered some principles or put forth some hypotheses, we can turn back into the biological realm and verify the ideas. Such a method corresponds to the synthetic modeling approach, or 'understanding by building' (Pfeifer & Scheier, 1999; Webb, 2001). At the same time, these principles will enable us to design and build intelligent systems (computer programs, robots, other artifacts) for research and application purposes.

We will demonstrate that embodiment not only plays a crucial part in low-level sensory-motor activities (such as locomotion), but also in capabilities that would be considered cognitive. To illustrate that, we present an embodied view on categorization. Still, we stop short of the so-called higher-level cognitive capabilities such as planning, abstract reasoning, or language. In an effort to bridge this gap, we will sketch how the bottom-up, embodied, approach can be naturally extended to form representations, providing a way to higher-level cognition. The way is through the concepts of 'body schema' and 'forward models'.

We will proceed as follows. First, we will present a number of case studies to illustrate the physical and information theoretic implications of embodiment. The case studies have been chosen from different domains — locomotion, grasping, and visual perception — to demonstrate the broad import of the concept of embodiment. Then we will deal with the extension of the concepts toward cognition. Finally, we will attempt to integrate the diverse case studies into a general overarching scheme that captures the essence of embodiment and morphological computation, and conclude.

Locomotion Case Studies

The fact that moving from one place to another, or locomotion, requires a body, comes as no surprise. However, it has been treated predominantly as a control problem by many; the body playing the part of a mere tool that has to be commanded appropriately. In this section, we will try to illustrate the contrary: shaping the body morphology and thereby the dynamics that result from the interaction with the environment can lead to stable and efficient locomotion, requiring very little control. We will illustrate these physical implications of being embodied on several machines and animals that walk or run. After that, a case study on leg coordination in insect walking will elucidate the impact of embodiment on information or control processes.

Physical Implications of Embodiment in Locomotion

In this section, we want to demonstrate that the body and its dynamics in the interaction with the environment, not control, are the key determinants of locomotion behavior. First, the passive dynamic walkers — brain-less machines — will serve as a powerful illustration of this concept. Second, we will present case studies that extend this idea to powered and controlled machines. However, the goal of the brain (or controller) is not to override, but to exploit the underlying body-environment dynamics and only tune it or channel it in desired directions. We will demonstrate how such an approach leads to greater stability and energy efficiency.

Passive dynamic walking. The passive dynamic walker, which goes back to McGeer (1990), is capable of walking down an incline without any actuation and without control. In other words, there are no motors, no sensors, and there is no microprocessor on the robot; it is brainless, so to speak. Its locomotion is an outcome of the slope of the incline (gravity is the only power source), and the mechanical parameters of the walker (mainly leg segment lengths, mass distribution, and foot shape). The original walker had four legs to provide stability in the lateral direction; Collins et al. (2001) have constructed a two-legged version which balances by using a counter-swing of the arms that are attached rigidly to their opposing legs (see Fig. 1, A).

As the passive dynamic walkers demonstrate, locomotion can be realized through pure, but carefully tuned mechanics only. However, the 'ecological niche' (i.e. the environment in which the robot is capable of operating) is extremely narrow: it only consists of inclines of certain angles. Therefore, the next objective is to extend this concept to machines with some practical capability — that can actively walk on level ground (or even uphill) and that can cope with rough terrain.

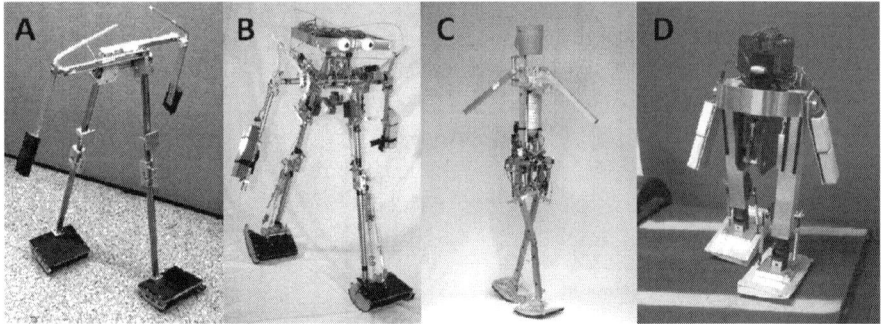

Fig. 1. Passive dynamic and passive dynamic based walkers. (A) The Cornell passive dynamic walker. It walks completely passively down an incline (Collins et al., 2005). (B)-(D) Passive dynamic based walkers are an extension of passive dynamic walkers. Actuation is added, such that they can walk on flat ground, but the energy-efficiency thanks to the exploitation of passive dynamics is preserved (Collins et al., 2005). (B) is an actuated extension of the passive walker (A).

Passive dynamic based walkers. These machines (Collins et al., 2005; Fig. 1, B-D) are a direct extension of the passive dynamic walking concept. Gravity (in the form of the incline) is substituted by small power sources. The robots can thus walk on level ground. However, they strive to preserve the advantages present in the entirely passive solution: minimal control and superior energy efficiency. The former goal can be illustrated on the Delft and Cornell bipeds that walk with simple control algorithms. Their only sensors detect ground contact, and their only motor commands are on/off signals issued once per step. The latter goal — superior energy efficiency — was also accomplished, as the cost of transport estimates testify[2].

What is the reason for the unprecedented energy efficiency of the passive dynamic based walkers? It is a consequence of the careful design of the body and of the minimalistic control scheme that only 'piggybacks' onto the underlying body dynamics. As is well known in physics, energy transfer is maximum at resonant modes of a system. The passive dynamic walkers and their active descendants contain a number of elements with pendulum-like dynamics: (1) a simple pendulum corresponds to the passive swing of the leg forward; (2) an inverted pendulum describes the motion of the hip mass over the stance leg; (3) another inverted pendulum characterizes the lateral rocking motion of the walker. The step frequency, stride length, and speed of the robots that can be observed are a direct consequence of the natural dynamics (the pendulums operating at their eigenfrequencies) that are exploited by the controller.[3]

The passive dynamic based walkers not only pave the way for energy-efficient robots of the future, but they also serve as models of human walking. The Cornell and Delft bipeds use anthropomorphic geometry and mass distributions in their legs and demonstrate ankle push-off and powered leg swinging, both present in human walking. They walk with human-like motion and human-like efficiency (Collins et al., 2005). The ease of altering different parameters and observing their effects helps us to better understand human walking.

Self-stabilization. Passive dynamic walkers have shown that locomotion can be realized through pure, but carefully tuned mechanics. However, how stable or adaptive is such a solution? In other words, how does a brainless machine cope with different slopes or with disturbances? The theory of nonlinear dynamical systems is often employed to analyze the phenomena involved in the mechanical (and also neural) aspects of locomotion. The walker is an example of a nonlinear dynamical system and walking patterns (which are periodic motions) correspond to limit cycles. Limit cycles in a nonlinear system can display attractive behavior, i.e. nearby trajectories are 'pulled' toward the limit cycle.

Mechanical self-stability, i.e. robustness to disturbances through local attractivity of the mechanical system, has been shown in a physical (McGeer, 1990) and mathematical (Coleman et al., 1997) walking model. In hopping or running, the dynamics is even more prolific. Fig. 2 illus-

---

[2] The dimensionless mechanical specific cost of transport, c_{mt} = (positive mechanical work of actuators)/(weight * distance travelled), was 0.055 for the Cornell biped, 0.08 for its Delft colleague, which is similar to the value estimated for humans (0.05), but vastly outperforms the estimated value for the state-of-the-art Honda humanoid Asimo (1.6) (Collins et al., 2005).

[3] The problem of a controller, in this case a central pattern generator, adapting to the resonant frequencies of a walking machine has been addressed by Buchli & Ijspeert, 2008 and Verdaasdonk et al., 2006.

trates this phenomenon schematically. A monopod hopper driven by an open-loop controller compensates for disturbances without any explicit feedback mechanism, that is, without measuring the disturbances or altering the system. Self-stabilization has been investigated in a monopod (Ringrose, 1997), or quadruped (Poulakakis et al., 2006; Ringrose, 1997), for instance. Kubow & Full (1999) designed a dynamic model of a hexapedal runner and observed the recovery from rotational, lateral, and fore-aft velocity perturbations. Perturbations altered the translation and/or rotation of the body that consequently provided mechanical feedback by altering leg moment arms. Koditschek et al. (2004) provide an excellent review of the mechanical aspects of legged locomotion, analyzing cockroaches in particular and showing how this inspired the construction of the RHex robot — a robot with unprecedented mobility (Saranli et al., 2001). These studies show that running on rough terrain can be accomplished with simple feed-forward control in concert with a mechanical system that stabilizes passively. In the biological realm, the intrinsic properties of muscles further aid self-stability (Blickhan et al., 2007) and further assist in making the neural contribution to locomotion control simpler.

Body dynamics vs. control. This confrontation is already expressed in McGeer's original paper (McGeer, 1990). The passive dynamic walker has nothing but (passive body) dynamics. On the other end of the spectrum are traditional robots with strong emphasis on control. The Honda humanoid Asimo often serves as a representative of state-of-the-art of this approach to robot locomotion. We identify the following characteristics: (1) joint trajectories are planned and enforced rather than negotiated in interaction with the environment; (2) stabilization is achieved actively (through the famous zero-moment point control scheme: Vukobratovic & Vorovac, 2004) rather than passively; (3) stiff, high-power, and high-frequency actuation is used. As a consequence of these characteristics, both computational and energetic requirements are high. On the other hand, the robot is very versatile — it can move its limbs into every possible position, it can walk uphill, downhill, even up and down the stairs.

By contrast, all the passive dynamic walker can do is walk, and it can only walk down an incline. Nevertheless, the descendants of the passive dynamics exploitation approach, the passive dynamic based walkers (Collins et al., 2005) or RHex (Saranli et al., 2001), demonstrate that the narrow ecological niche can be gradually expanded, while preserving the merits of this approach.

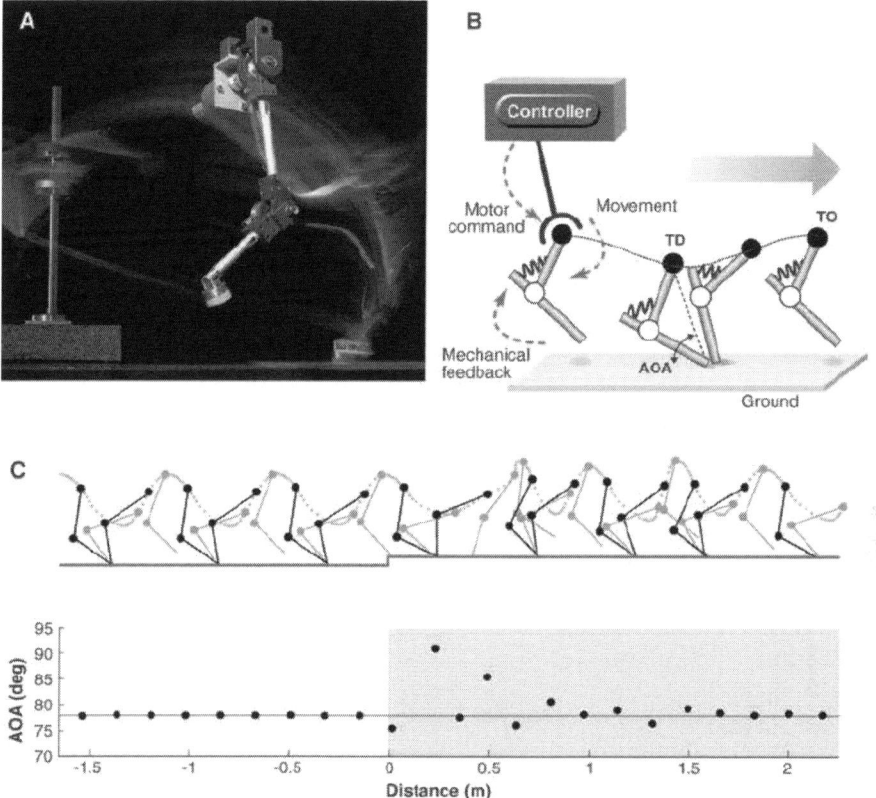

Fig. 2. Self-stabilization. Adaptivity is part of the mechanical structure itself. (A) Picture of a two-dimensional underactuated monoped hopping robot attached to a central rod with a rotational joint (courtesy of A. Seyfarth and A. Karguth). (B) A schematic representation of the hopping robot in the different phases of locomotion: flight, touchdown (TD) [with angle of attack (AOA)], and takeoff (TO). Only the joint depicted by the black circle (hip joint) is actuated, the knee (white circle) is passive, and the lower limb is attached to the upper limb with a simple spring. (C) Output of a simulation of the robot. The upper part of the panel shows the trajectory of the model over time as a sequence of stick figures; in the lower part, the angle of attack (the angle at which the leg hits the ground) is plotted. The model exhibits a stable hopping gait with a periodic hip motor oscillation, as indicated by the constant AOA at every step in the left side of the panel. At distance d = 0 m, there is a step in the ground that disturbs the robot's movement but to which the robot adapts without the need for any changes in the control. This purely mechanical phenomenon is called self-stabilization (Figure from Pfeifer et al., 2007; there adapted from Blickhan et al., 2007).

Information Theoretic Implications of Embodiment in Locomotion

The view presented in the previous section overly polarizes the situation. Body and brain should not be viewed as competitors, but rather collaborators. The tasks can be distributed and accomplished by the substrate that is more appropriate. What we have demonstrated so far is that in many locomotion-related tasks, the body itself is the candidate of choice. Nevertheless, for versatile locomotion, control is indispensable. Traditionally, control algorithms need to be fed with information about the state of the system, as obtained from sensors. Based on that, a decision, regarding the leg coordination for instance, is taken centrally. However, there are alternatives to the centralized control paradigm, which take embodiment into account. What we want to elucidate in this section is that embodiment is as important for the physical processes as it is for the informational processes. The inputs to a control scheme necessarily come through the body dynamics (see Iida & Pfeifer, 2006, for an account on sensing through body dynamics in a dynamic quadruped robot). The following case study illustrates how the body and interaction with the environment can replace a central communication between legs in insect walking.

Leg Coordination in Insect Walking[4]. Leg movements in insects are controlled by largely independent local neural circuits that are connected to their neighbors. There is no central controller that coordinates the legs during walking. The leg coordination comes about by the exploitation of the interaction with the environment (Cruse, 1990; Cruse et al., 2002). If the insect stands on the ground and moves forward by pushing backwards with one of its legs, as an unavoidable implication of being embodied, all the joint angles of the legs standing on the ground will instantaneously change. The insect's body is pushed forward, and consequently the other legs are also pulled forward and the joints will be bent or stretched. This fact can be exploited to the animal's advantage. All that is needed is angle sensors in the joints — and they do exist — for measuring the change, and there is global communication between the legs! But the communication is through the interaction of the agent with the environment, not through neural processing.

Inspired by the fact that the local neural leg controllers need only exploit this global communication, a neural network architecture called WalkNet has been developed which is capable of controlling a six-legged robot (Dur et al., 2003). This instance of morphological computation takes over part of the task that would have to be done by the brain — the communication between the legs and the calculation of the angles on all the joints — is performed by the interaction between the insect and the world.

---

[4] This case study has previously appeared in Pfeifer & Gomez, 2009.

Grasping Case Studies

At first sight, grasping and locomotion do not seem to have much in common. However, as we will show in this section, the implications of embodiment illustrated thus far in locomotion can be equally well demonstrated in case studies that involve grasping. In essence, the rich and dynamic interactions of walking or running bodies with the ground will be replaced by equally complex interactions of hand morphologies and objects being grasped.

Physical Implications of Embodiment in Grasping

In this section, we discuss how morphology and materials contribute to grasping behavior. Hand joint structure, muscle mechanics, and the distribution and density of bone to joint movements and muscle recruitment during manipulative behavior are all important variables, as investigated by Marzke & Marzke (2000). It has also been reported that ridged structure of human skin offers better grip due to increased friction (Cartmill, 1979). However, we will use two robotic case studies for our illustration of 'cheap grasping', i.e. grasping that is stable and reliable, yet requires little control. First, we will demonstrate a robotic hand, in which the attention paid to the mechanical construction leads to self-adaptation of the grasp to different objects. Second, we will present a recent universal robotic gripper, where the morphological approach was taken to its extreme.

Cheap Grasping with a Robotic Hand[5]. The 18 degrees-of-freedom (DOF) tendon driven 'Yokoi hand' (Yokoi et al., 2004; Fig. 3) which can be used as a robotic and a prosthetic hand, is partly built from elastic, flexible, and deformable materials (this hand comes in many versions with different materials, morphologies, sensors, etc.; here we only describe one of them). The tendons are elastic, the fingertips are deformable and between the fingers there is also deformable material.

Fig. 3: 'Cheap' grasping with a robotic hand: exploiting system-environment interaction. (A) The Yokoi hand exploits deformable and flexible materials to achieve self-adaptation through the interaction between environment and materials. (B)-(C) Final grasp of different objects. The control is the same, but the behavior is very different.

---

[5] This case study has previously appeared in Pfeifer & Gomez, 2009.

When the hand is closed, the fingers will, because of the anthropomorphic morphology, automatically come together. For grasping an object, a simple control scheme, a 'close' is applied. Because of the morphology of the hand, the elastic tendons, and the deformable fingertips, the hand will automatically self-adapt to the object it is grasping.

Cheap grasping with a universal gripper. As our everyday experience confirms, a multifingered hand is an extremely dexterous manipulator. However, from a robotic perspective, this approach is highly complex from a hardware as well as software point of view. Brown et al. (2010) have therefore devised a gripper that utilizes a completely different strategy. Individual fingers are replaced by a single mass of granular material (e.g., ground coffee). The principle of operation is illustrated in Fig. 4, D. The 'bag' containing granular material is pressed onto an object, flows around it, and conforms to its shape. Then, a vacuum pump is used to evacuate air from the gripper, which makes the granular material jam and stabilize the grasp. The gripper conforms to arbitrary shapes passively, that is without any sensory feedback, thanks to its morphological properties only. Brown et al. identify three mechanism that contribute to the gripping: (i) geometric constraints from interlocking between gripper and object surfaces; (ii) static friction from normal stresses at contact; and (iii) an additional suction effect, if the gripper membrane can seal off a portion of the object's surface. The properties of the gripper can be changed by using a different granular material. Objects of various shapes (see Fig. 4, E) as well as hardness (from steel springs to raw eggs) can be gripped. An additional advantage is that the orientation of objects that are picked up and placed again does not change.

In the two case studies presented, there is no need for the agent to 'know' beforehand what the shape of the to-be-grasped object will be (which is normally the case in robotics, where the contact points are calculated before the grasping action: Molina-Vilaplana et al., 2007). In the first study, the shape adaptation is taken over by the morphology of the hand, the elasticity of the tendons, and the deformability of the fingertips, as the hand interacts with the shape of the object. In the second study, the physical properties of the granular material and how they change when air is evacuated play a key part. In both cases, control of grasping is very simple, or, in other words, very little 'brain power' is required. Clearly, these designs have their limitations; for fine manipulation more sophisticated sensing, actuation, and control may be required (Borst et al., 2002). However, a powerful fundament on which the next layers can rest has been provided.

For prosthetics, there is an interesting implication. EMG signals can be used to interface the robot hand non-invasively to a patient: even though the hand has been amputated, he or she can still intentionally produce muscle innervations which can be picked up on the surface of the skin by EMG electrodes. If EMG signals, which are known to be very noisy, are used to steer the movement of the hand, control cannot be very precise and sophisticated. But by exploiting the self-regulatory properties of the hand, there is no need for very precise control, at least for some kinds of grasping: the relatively poor EMG signals are sufficient for the basic movements (Hernandez Arieta et al., 2006; Yu et al., 2006).

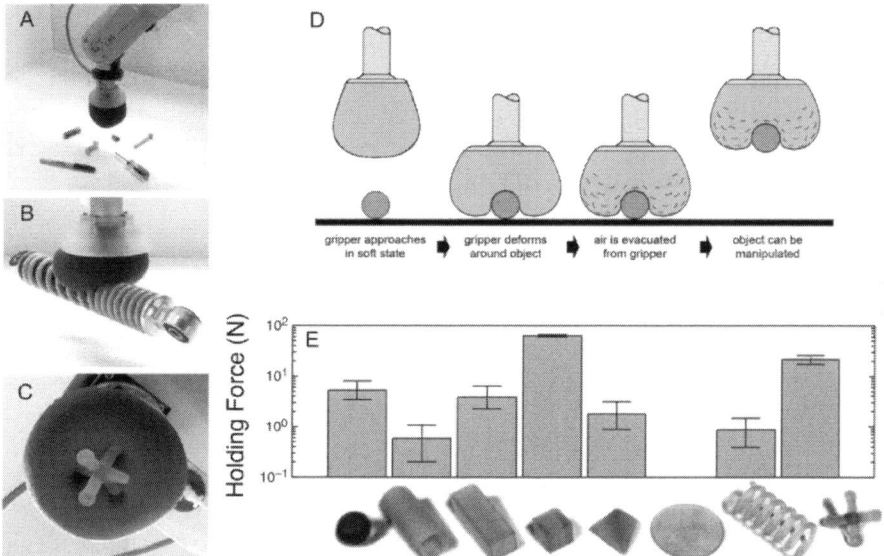

Fig. 4. **Jamming-based grippers for picking up a wide range of objects without the need for active feedback**. (A) Attached to a fixed-base robot arm. (B) Picking up a shock absorber coil. (C) View from the underside. (D) Schematic of operation. (E) Holding force Fh for several three-dimensional-printed test shapes (the diameter of the sphere shown on the very left, 2r = 25.4 mm, can be used for size comparison). The thin disk could not be picked up at all (from Brown et al., 2010, courtesy John Amend of Cornell University).

Information Theoretic Implications of Embodiment in Grasping

As we have seen, and similarly to the locomotion case, morphology and material properties can take over a significant part of a grasping task. However, in more complex scenarios, mechanical 'intelligence' has to be aided by software or control. In order for a controller to be able to take the right decisions and issue proper motor commands, it needs to perceive the relevant information regarding the agent's interaction with the environment. Our goal in this section is to emphasize that the body morphology is as important for the perception task, as it is for taking actions. We have picked slippage sensing for our case study — a prerequisite for stable grasping and fine object manipulation — and we will show how the particular shape and material properties of an artificial skin can facilitate perception.

Slippage detection. In humans, the ridged skin structure not only improves the mechanics of grasping as mentioned above, but also magnifies the pressure (which can be perceived) exerted by the manipulated object (Fearing & Hollerbach, 1984), and acts as a frequency filter for specific skin mechanoreceptors (Scheibert et al., 2009). Similar properties are desirable in robotic or prosthetic hands. A wide range of tactile sensors have been developed for slippage detection which use different transduction principles: piezoelectric sensors sensitive to vibrations, skin with round ridges and strain sensors, vibrating nibs on the skin surface sensed by accelerometers, or brushes on top of capacitive membranes (see the references in Damian et al., 2010). The morphology and material properties are significantly involved in all of those designs. In what follows, we want to look in detail into yet another solution where morphology maximizes the information that can be acquired about a slippage event.

Damian et al. (2010) devised a tactile sensor consisting of a silicone skin layer with ridges a few millimeters apart which transduces surface events to a force sensing resistor beneath (Fig. 5, A). Whereas a flat skin

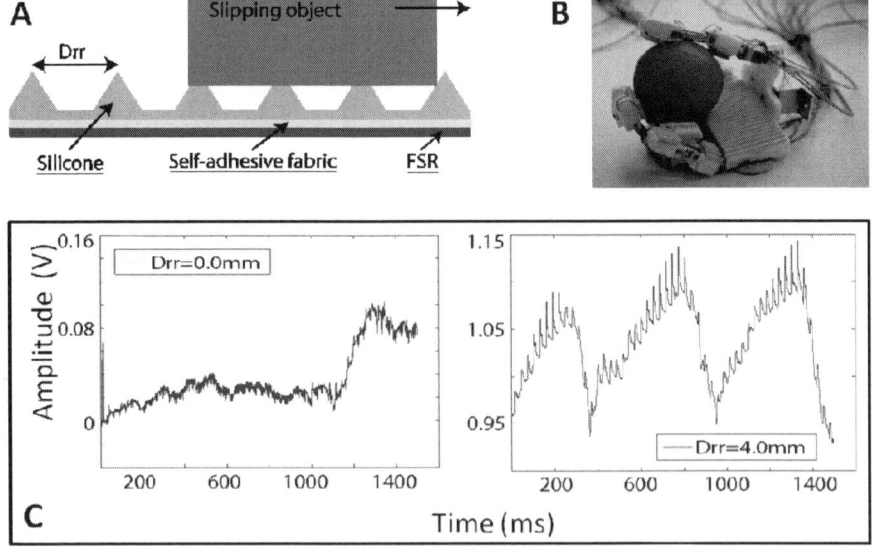

Fig. 5: **Slippage detection through ridged skin.** (A) Schematics of the artificial skin. Silicone skin with evenly spaced ridges is glued over a Force Sensing Resistor (FSR). (B) Robotic hand equipped with artificial ridged skin. (C) Signal generated by an object sliding over a skin without ridges (left), and with ridges 4 mm apart (right). The ridged skin provides a stronger signal with higher amplitude. In addition a clear periodic pattern allows for detection of slippage speed. (Damian et al., 2010)

without ridges, which was used as a reference, fails to detect an object sliding over it, ridged skin gives rise to peaks in the pressure sensor readings. Moreover, the frequency of the pressure signal obtained is directly proportional to the slippage speed and inversely proportional to the distance between ridges. The inter-ridge distance itself was found to further influence the quality of frequency encoded information. Among all skins, the one with a 4 mm spacing between ridges yielded discriminatory peak frequencies for each velocity (Fig. 5, C). The skin was afterwards employed in a robotic hand to stabilize grip. In summary, in this study, much of the electronic and algorithmic complexity present in other tactile sensing approaches has been successfully off-loaded to the morphology and allowed to detect slippage and gauge its speed with theoretically a single force sensor.

Visual Perception Case Studies

Unlike walking or grasping, seeing seems to be concerned exclusively with perception rather than action. The goal is to acquire useful information from the environment that can be used to perform various tasks. Nevertheless, embodiment plays a key role in the information that can be acquired and such information theoretic implications of embodiment for visual perception will be the topic of this section.

A prominent theory of visual perception was proposed by David Marr (1982): vision was treated as a stage-like computational process proceeding from a two-dimensional visual array (retina/camera image) to a three-dimensional description of the world as output. Whereas this approach has lead to many successes in computer vision, robots still fall short of the capabilities that humans and animals demonstrate in object recognition, identification, and scene understanding in unstructured environments.

An alternative, and perhaps a remedy to the shortcomings of the treatment of visual perception as image processing, can be provided by embodiment. The scope of the investigation of visual perception has to be broadened to the generation of raw input image. The amount of information present in the input flow is shaped by two factors: (1) morphology of the sensory apparatus; and (2) active generation of information through sensory-motor coordination. We will address these factors separately in the sections below, but we want to stress that they always act concurrently.

Thus far, we have been referring to the information theoretic implications of embodiment in a mostly informal sense. However, the information content or structure present in the sensory and motor modalities can be quantified. Lungarella & Sporns (2006) presented several methods for measuring the (undirected) information present in sensory modalities

(Shannon entropy, mutual information, integration, and complexity). To extract directed, or causal, relationships, such as from sensors to motors or vice versa, they employed transfer entropy; however, other measures are also available, as analyzed in Lungarella et al., 2007). Polani and colleagues have devised a different measure, empowerment, which measures how much influence an agent has on its environment, but only that influence that can be sensed by the agent's own sensors (see e.g., Jung et al., 2011). Yet another embodiment quantification method was presented recently by Thornton (2010), testifying the recent attention given to this subject. One of his case studies features a passive dynamic walker that we have (less formally) analyzed in the section on locomotion. Although such analysis tools are equally suited for animals and robots engaged in behavior, robots, as we have already discussed, are significantly easier to monitor and manipulate. Following the synthetic modeling approach, we will thus emphasize case studies on robots.

The Role of Eye Morphology in Visual Perception

Human eye. The retina of a human eye is a variable resolution sensor: the distribution of photoreceptors is non-homogeneous. The density of cones, which are used for high acuity vision, is greatest in the center (fovea) (e.g., Curcio et al., 1990). Through this morphological arrangement, a limited number of sensing and processing elements can provide both high acuity in the center of the visual field, and a wide field of view. In robots, the retinal morphology can be emulated by the log-polar transformation (e.g., Sandini & Metta, 2002), and the degree of variable resolution can be scaled arbitrarily. Martinez et al. (2010a) investigated this effect in a robot with two eyes performing vergence behavior (simultaneous movement of both eyes in opposite directions to obtain single binocular vision). The sensor morphology as represented by the log-polar transform clearly manifests itself in the information structure calculated on a sequence of images obtained from the robot. A similar phenomenon was observed by Lungarella & Sporns (2006). There, a simulated wheeled robot (but with a human-inspired eye) was driving around colored objects and foveated on them.

Insect eye[6]. It has been shown that for many objectives (e.g. obstacle avoidance) motion detection is all that is required. Motion detection can often be simplified if the light-sensitive cells are not spaced evenly, but if there is a non-homogeneous arrangement. For instance, Franceschini and co-workers (1992) found that in the compound eye of the house fly the spacing of the facets is denser toward the front of the animal. This non-homogeneous arrangement, in a sense, compensates for the phenomenon

---

[6] This case study has been adapted from Pfeifer & Gomez, 2009.

of motion parallax, i.e. the fact that at constant speed, objects on the side travel faster across the visual field than objects towards the front: it performs the 'morphological computation', so to speak. Allowing for some idealization, this implies that under the condition of straight flight, the same motion detection circuitry — the elementary motion detectors, or EMDs — can be employed for motion detection for the entire eye, a principle that has also been applied to the construction of navigating robots (e.g., Hoshino et al., 2000). In experiments with artificial evolution on real robots, it has been shown that certain aims, e.g. keeping a constant lateral distance to an obstacle, can be solved by proper morphological arrangement of the ommatidia, i.e. denser frontally than laterally without changing anything inside the neural controller (Lichtensteiger, 2004; Fig. 6). Because the sensory stimulation is only induced when the robot (or the insect) moves in a particular way, this is also called information self-structuring (or more precisely, self-structuring of the sensory stimulation), which leads us to the next section.

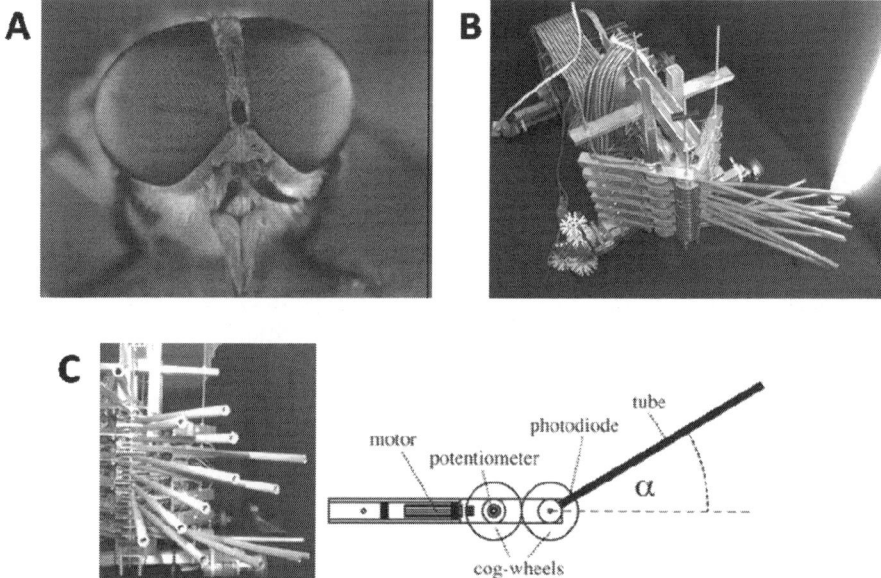

Fig. 6. Morphological computation through sensor morphology — the Eyebot. The specific non-homogeneous arrangement of the facets compensates for motion parallax, thereby facilitating neural processing. (A) Insect eye. (B) Picture of the Eyebot. (C) Front view: the Eyebot consists of a chassis, an on-board controller, and sixteen independently-controllable facet units, which are all mounted on a common vertical axis. A schematic drawing of the facet is shown on the right. Each facet unit consists of a motor, a potentiometer, two cog-wheels and a thin tube containing a sensor (a photo diode) at the inner end. These tubes are the primitive equivalent of the facets.

Active Vision

The previous section has demonstrated how a particular sensor morphology affects the information structure of the raw data that reaches the sensor and that enters subsequent processing afterwards. However, the sensory stimulation is not passively received, but rather actively generated. The point we want to make was beautifully expressed by John Dewey already in 1896 (Dewey, 1896):

> We begin not with a sensory stimulus, but with a sensory-motor coordination [...] In a certain sense it is the movement which is primary, and the sensation which is secondary, the movement of the body, head, and eye muscles determining the quality of what is experienced. In other words, the real beginning is with the act of seeing; it is looking, and not a sensation of light.

Only much later was Dewey's visionary observation picked up by research in active perception (e.g. Bajcsy, 1988; Churchland et al., 1994; Gibson, 1979; Noe, 2004).

Again, we will pick a robotic case study to illustrate this point. Lungarella & Sporns (2006) used an upper torso humanoid robot (Fig. 7, A) to evaluate the contribution of sensory-motor coupling to different informational measures by comparing two experimental conditions. In both conditions, the robot arm was following a preprogrammed trajectory. The movement of the ball results in a displacement of the ball relative to the head and leads to physical stimulation in the head-mounted camera. In the first condition, which we will refer to as 'fov', the sensory feedback is exploited by the controller of the robot head with camera to track the end-effector (orange ball). In other words, the sensory-motor loop (Fig. 7, B) was ensuring the orange ball stays at the center of the visual field — the fovea. In the second condition, 'rnd', the movement of the camera is unrelated to the movement of the ball (sensory-motor coupling is disrupted). The amount of information in the sequence of camera images was measured for both conditions (Fig. 7, C). As can be seen, there is more information structure in the case of the foveation condition for all measures; for example, the dark region in the center of the entropy panel indicates that entropy is clearly diminished in the center of the visual field (disorder has been reduced, or in other words, information structure has been induced), which is due to foveation being a sensory-motor coordinated behavior. Similar results were reported by Martinez et al. (2010a), who used a head with two cameras. In their case, coordinated behavior consisted in vergence, i.e. both eyes tracking salient objects. Moreover, Martinez et al. (2010a) also showed that it is not arbitrary coordinated behavior that generates information structure. A different behavior, one eye tracking the object and the other following its movements, i.e. without vergence, did not generate more information structure than random behavior. Although this behavior may seem sensory-motor coordinated to the outside observer, it does not match the robot's morphology, in this case the sensory apparatus. This illustrates the point that morphology and active perception cannot be considered in isolation.

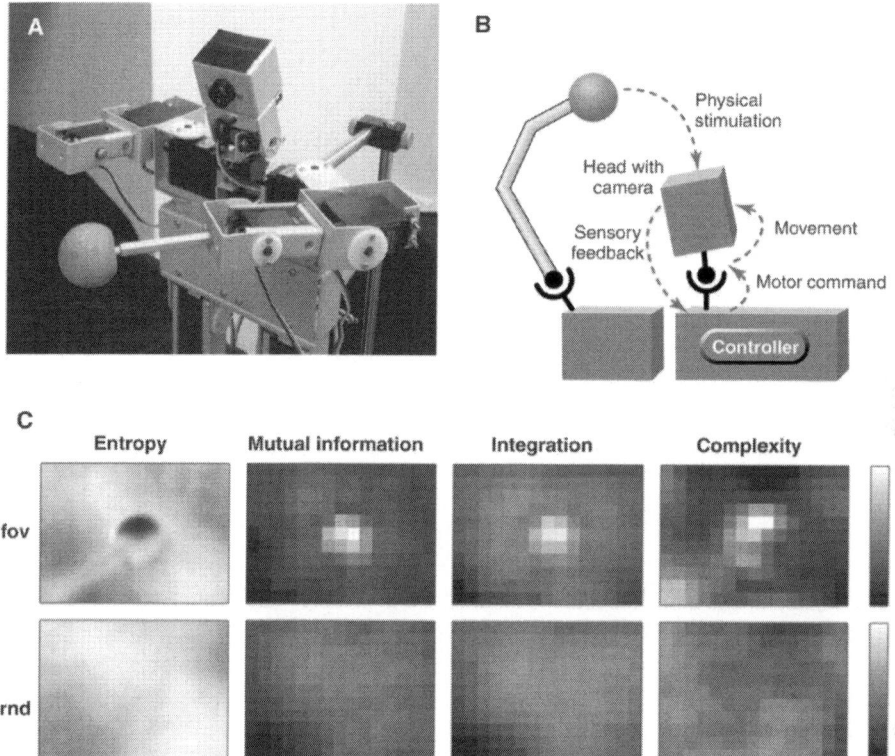

Fig. 7. Information self-structuring. (A) Picture of the robot, a small humanoid with a pan-tilt head equipped with a camera. (B) Schematic representation of the experimental setup. (C) Various measures to capture information structure: entropy (the amount of disorder in the system), mutual information (the extent to which the activity of one pixel can be predicted from the combined activities of neighboring pixels), integration (a measure of global coherence), and complexity (a measure that captures global coherence and local variation). The measures are applied to the camera image in the case of the foveation condition (top) and random condition (bottom). (From Pfeifer et al., 2007; there adapted from Lungarella & Sporns, 2006)

Information structure in individual sensory modalities, such as in the visual modality as shown above, is definitely a prerequisite for subsequent processing. However, for effective control of behavior we are also interested in relations between modalities, and in relations in time. In particular, we are interested in directed relations in time, such as the ones between motor and sensory modalities, which may indicate causal relations. Sensory-motor coordinated behavior increases the directed information flow, as measured using transfer entropy (Lungarella & Sporns, 2006; Martinez et al., 2010b). Such relations can be further exploited by the agent to learn to predict the consequences of its behavior. Moreover, predictability in the sensory-motor loop can be used to drive development (e.g., Oudeyer et al., 2007). Learning and representing the relations that exist between sensory and motor modalities constitute the first traces of cognition and will be the subject of the next section.

From Sensory-motor Interaction to Embodied Cognition

Thus far, we have been dealing with relatively low-level tasks such as locomotion, grasping, or simple visual perception. We have shown that such tasks can be performed without sophisticated cognitive processing, but rather through exploitation of body dynamics and interaction with the environment. While this research is interesting in itself, how does it relate to higher-level cognition? We will provide the link in this section.

Embodied Categorization[7]

For an autonomous embodied agent acting in the real world (e.g., an animal, a human, or a robot), perceptual categorization — the ability to make distinctions — is a hard problem (Harnad, 2005). First, based on the stimulation impinging on its sensory arrays (sensation) the agent has to rapidly determine and attend to what needs to be categorized. Second, the appearance and properties of objects or events in the environment being classified fluctuate continuously, for example owing to occlusions, or changes of distances and orientations with respect to the agent. And third, the environmental conditions (e.g., illumination, viewpoint, and background noise) vary considerably. There is much relevant work in computer vision that has been devoted to extracting scale- and translation-invariant low-level visual features and high-level multidimensional representations for the purpose of robust perceptual categorization (Riesenhuber & Poggio, 2002). Following this approach, however, categorization often turns out to be a very difficult if not an impossible computational feat, especially when sufficiently detailed information is lacking.

A solution that can only be pursued by embodied agents — but is not available when using a purely disembodied (i.e., computational) approach — is that through their interaction with the environment, agents generate the sensory stimulation required to perform the proper categorization and thus drastically simplify the problem of mapping sensory stimulation onto perceptual categories. The most typical and effective way is through a process of sensory-motor coordination. One demonstration of how sensory-motor coordination influences category formation

---

[7] This section has been adapted from Pfeifer et al., 2008.

can be found in the experiments by Pfeifer & Scheier (1997). These experiments show that mobile robots can reliably categorize big and small wooden cylinders only if their behavior is sensory-motor coordinated. A similar point is illustrated by the artificial evolution experiments of Beer (2003), where a simulated agent learns to discriminate between circular and diamond-shaped objects, or Nolfi (2002). The fittest agents, that is, those that most reliably categorized different kind of objects, were those engaging in sensory-motor coordinated behavior. Intuitively, in these examples, the interaction with the environment (a physical process) creates additional (i.e., previously absent) sensory stimulation, which is highly structured, thus facilitating subsequent information processing.

Let us compare the categories that we have just come across with categories as symbols as we know them from classical symbolic AI. Taking Beer's case study, if it was realized in a symbolic architecture, we should find a 'diamond' symbol, which represents the diamonds and onto which the instances of diamonds in the real world need to be mapped (a nontrivial task, as described above). Moreover, the pitfall of this approach is that cognitive processing becomes detached from real world interaction and from meaning for the agent (the notorious symbol grounding problem: Harnad, 1990). On the other hand, when one examines the control architectures used by Pfeifer & Scheier (1997) or by Beer (2003), it is not possible to identify a site where the categories (big vs. small cylinders, or circles vs. diamonds) reside. Beer's dynamical systems analysis of the behaving agent does not reveal clear neural correlates of 'circles' or 'diamonds' either. Rather than corresponding to 'labels' defined from the outside, the categories are in fact behaviors. A small cylinder can be grasped, whereas a big one cannot; a circle is caught by the agent, whereas a diamond is avoided. Thus, categories are intrinsically meaningful to the agent and they are emergent from complex system-environment dynamics (see also Kuniyoshi et al., 2004).

On the other hand, it is probably fair to say that the discrimination tasks the agents were engaged in were of limited complexity. The opponents therefore rightly raise the question of scalability (e.g., Edelman, 2003) and argue that clearly identifiable representations allowing for hierarchical abstractions are necessary to tackle more complex scenarios. However, the dynamical systems framework and the concept of attractors that we have witnessed in the section dealing with stability in locomotion can provide a solution here. Kuniyoshi et al. (2004) or Pfeifer & Bongard (2007, ch.5), explain how, adopting the dynamical systems perspective, discretely identifiable states emerge as attractors in the combined physical and neural system of an agent. For instance, such symbols (or proto-symbols) could be gaits in a running quadruped, or they can be 'categorizing behaviors'. On top of these proto-symbols, further, more cognitive but still grounded, processing can take place.[8]

Body Schema and Forward Models

As we have seen in the previous section, the distinction between cognitive and sensory-motor starts to blur. Categorization, perception, but even memory processes turn out to be directly coupled to sensory-motor processes and thus to embodiment (e.g., Edelman, 1987; Glenberg, 1997; Pfeifer & Scheier, 1999). What is the natural way in which an agent interacting with the world can gradually acquire cognition? We propose to follow a bottom-up and developmental pathway. Rather than starting from representations of objects or the world around the agent, we propose to start representing the very basis: the agent's body and its low-level interaction with the environment. In other words, as we have argued, any cognitive processing will always be mediated by the body and the sensory-motor loops. Therefore, these are the first candidates for an agent to learn about.

Concepts that are currently being studied, mainly in neuroscience and psychology, are 'body schema' (e.g., De Preester & Knockaert, 2005; Haggard & Wolpert, 2005; Higuchi et al., 2006; Maravita et al., 2003) and 'forward', or internal, models (Bays & Wolpert, 2007; Webb, 2004; Wolpert et al., 1998). Both concepts have also direct relevance for robotics (see e.g., Hoffmann et al., 2010, for a review). The body schema can be viewed as the sensory-motor 'representation' of the agent's body and its action possibilities. Forward models enable agents to predict the consequences of their actions and are related to anticipatory behavior (e.g., Pezzulo, 2007). In more concrete terms, for instance, in the (uncertain, dynamic, potentially hostile) world out there, it may be of advantage to: (i) predict the next sensory feedback in advance — for instance, during rapid locomotion, biological feedback is too slow; (ii) distinguish self-generated sensory information from sensory input generated by the environment, leading to detection of changes in the environment[9]; or (iii) simulate different courses of action and choose the one with the best consequences. Whereas it is not surprising that humans possess such capabilities, they have been discovered even in much simpler animals. For instance, prediction is demonstrated in the motor preparation of the prey-catching behavior of the jumping spider (Schomaker, 2004). As another example, rats are able to compare alternative paths in a T-maze before actually acting, thus 'planning in simulation' (Hesslow, 2002).

As discussed by Clark & Grush (1999), forward models are the

---

[8] Maass et al., 2004 provide a neurally inspired computational model of a two-tiered architecture that could be used to implement such a processing hierarchy.

[9] For instance, it feels different when we move our eyes than when the world moves, although on the retina it may look the same.

simplest instances of circuitry that emulates the world outside and thus stands for something that is not currently present in the sensory and motor states. Thus, we may want to attribute representation to such circuitry. A 'decoupled' forward model that is not just a few steps ahead of the sensory-motor reality but that can be executed independently, in the brain only, can then be viewed as emulation/simulation of the interaction with the world, or world model. Interestingly, such a forward model can also be exploited to exercise embodied categorization, which we have presented in the previous section, in simulation. In other words, if the agent can predict the sensory consequences of its actions, it can also 'imagine' catching a circle or diamond, or grasping a cylinder. The outcome of such internal simulation can be used to derive a perceptual judgment that would otherwise not have been possible. This is demonstrated by the agent of H. Hoffmann (2007), which uses such a 'mental' rehearsal of driving in its environment to discriminate passages and dead ends.

Let us now wrap up the nature of representations and cognition that we are acquiring. Rather than representing static features (such as objects), dynamic interaction patterns, which involve the robot acting in the environment, are represented. Such representations are best viewed as motor-based. They are action-oriented, originate in the sensory-motor apparatus and remain intimately related with it (Clark & Grush, 1999; Pezzulo, 2007)[10]. Whether we want to call these phenomena 'cognitive' depends on our definition of cognition. Some views reject the cognitive/non-cognitive divide altogether, some include into the cognitive realm all kinds of adaptively valuable organism/ environment coupling (e.g., Thelen & Smith, 1994). While we consider these views equally legitimate, the view proposed by Clark & Grush (1999), among others, is that cognizers must display the capacity for environmentally decoupled thought and contemplation of options. This is exactly what a decoupled forward model provides: simulation of the world, or 'mental imagery'. This phenomenon is believed to be at the core of grounded cognition (Barsalou, 2008; Gallese & Lakoff, 2005).

Discussion and Conclusion

We have seen a large variety of case studies. The question that immediately arises is whether there are general overarching principles governing all of them. A recently published scheme (Pfeifer et al., 2007) shows a potential way of integrating all of these ideas.

We will use Fig. 8 to summarize the most important implications of embodiment and to embed our case studies into a theoretical context.

---

[10] As opposed to symbolic AI representations that are world-centered.

Driven by motor commands, the musculoskeletal system (mechanical system) of the agent acts on the external environment (task environment or ecological niche). The action leads to rapid mechanical feedback characterized by pressure on the bones, torques in the joints, and passive deformation of skin tissue. In parallel, external stimuli (pressure, temperature, and electromagnetic fields) and internal physical stimuli (forces and torques developed in the muscles and joint-supporting ligaments, as well as accelerations) impinge on the sensory receptors (sensory system). The patterns induced thus depend on the physical characteristics and morphology of the sensory systems and on the motor commands. Especially if the interaction is sensory-motor coordinated, as in foveation, reaching, or grasping movements, information structure is generated. The effect of the motor command strongly depends on the tunable morphological and material properties of the musculoskeletal system, where by tunable we mean that properties such as shape and compliance can be changed dynamically. All parts of this diagram are crucial for the agent to function properly, but only one part concerns the controller or the central nervous system. The rest can be seen as 'morphological computation'.

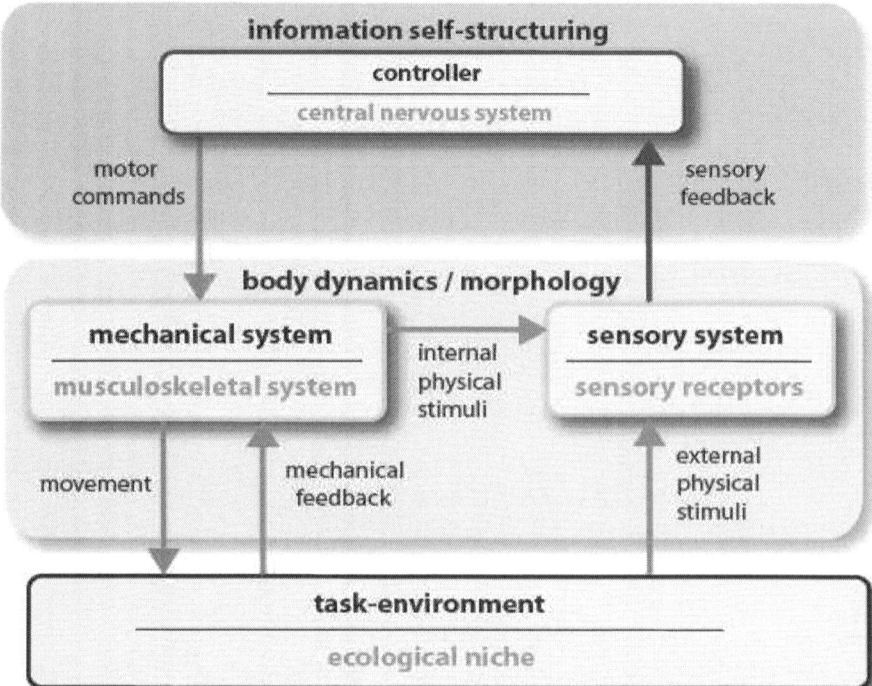

Fig. 8: Overview of the implications of embodiment — the interplay of information and physical processes (from Pfeifer et al., 2007; see text for details).

Let us now go through the case studies we have presented and locate them in Fig. 8. The passive dynamic walker is an instance of an interaction of the mechanical system with the environment solely — controller and sensory system are completely absent. Stabilization is achieved through the mechanical feedback loop shown in the lower left of the figure; in this case, the feedback is generated through ground reaction forces[11]. This scheme can be amended by a feed-forward controller that blindly sends motor commands to the mechanical system. That is the case for the monopod in Fig. 2 or for the hexapod RHex. As there is still no sensory system, these robots can function in the real world only thanks to mechanical self-stabilization. The 'cheap grasping' case studies illustrate a similar concept. This time, the material and morphology of the hand/gripper serve to stabilize a grasp without sensing. By contrast, the passive dynamic based walkers feature a complete scheme already — there is a sensory system and a feedback path to the controller. However, the control is rudimentary and it is still the intrinsic dynamics of the body that plays a dominant role. As a consequence of this — the intrinsic body dynamics is exploited rather than overridden — the robots also demonstrate unprecedented energy efficiency.

The study on leg coordination in insect walking provides a bridge from the physical implications of embodiment (that we have reviewed in the previous paragraph) to the information theoretic ones. Insects, when walking, also exploit mechanical feedback generated through ground reaction forces, but rather than exploiting it for gait stabilization, they capitalize on exploiting the internal sensory stimulation generated in the joint angles as one leg pushes back (thus inducing changes in the joint angles of all the other legs that are standing on the ground). This process corresponds to the lower left part of Fig. 8 and the arrow pointing from the mechanical system to the sensory system. This information can then be used for local control of individual legs. The study on slippage detection in grasping illustrates the role of the morphology of the sensory system. The particular shape of the skin — its surface is covered by ridges — magnifies the pressure exerted by objects that are grasped, and at the same time acts as a frequency filter, allowing for simply slippage speed calculation.

The case studies dealing with vision illustrate the effect of sensory morphology *and* sensory-motor coordination on the information structure that reaches a sensor. In the Eyebot, the 'insect eye' case study, given a certain behavioral pattern, e.g. moving straight, the robot induces sensory stimulation which has to be subsequently processed, for instance to achieve obstacle avoidance. The study shows that evolving a specific

---

[11] Note that the fact that the robot has no sensors and thus does not know anything about this mechanical feedback does not imply that there is no such feedback.

morphology of the facet distribution can take over a significant part of the 'processing', producing already highly structured and easy to process information for the nervous system. This process corresponds to the outer loop from the controller via mechanical system to task environment, back to sensory system and controller. The active vision case studies demonstrate the effect of action on the quality of subsequent perception, highlighting the need to treat perception as an intrinsically active process. We have also shown that the amount of sensory information can be measured quantitatively and that sensor morphology and sensory-motor coordination always go hand in hand and have to match.

There are two main conclusions that can be drawn from these case studies. First, it is important to exploit the dynamics in order to achieve energy-efficient and natural kinds of movements. The term 'natural' not only applies to biological systems, but artificial systems also have their intrinsic natural dynamics. Second, there is a kind of trade-off or balance: the better the exploitation of the dynamics, the simpler the control, the less neural processing will be required. Note that all this only works, if the agent is actually behaving in the real world and therefore is generating sensory stimulation. Once again, we see the importance of the motor system for the generation of sensory signals, or more generally for perception. It should also be noted that motor actions are physical processes, not computational ones, but they are computationally relevant, or put differently, relevant for neural processing, which is why we use the term 'morphological computation'.

Having said all this, it should be mentioned that there is an additional trade-off. The more the specific environmental conditions are exploited — and the passive dynamic walker is an extreme case — the more the agent's success will be contingent upon them. Thus, if we really want to achieve brain-like intelligence, the brain (or the controller) must have the ability to quickly switch to different kinds of exploitation schemes either neurally, or mechanically through morphological change.

Finally, we have sketched a pathway how cognition can naturally emerge on top of the low-level sensory-motor processes the body is engaged in. It is the body and the interaction with the environment that are the natural candidates for first primitive representations. We want to point out that cognition is in the service of behavior here. That is, these first representations or models have to bring behavioral advantage. We have shown how this is indeed the case in simple situations where a forward model can provide an estimate of the future consequences of an action. As these simple predictive mechanisms become progressively more decoupled and autonomous, and as perhaps other processes start operating on top of them, a natural transition toward cognitive processes, which are still grounded and meaningful for the agent, has been accomplished. Therefore, unlike the original radical thesis of Brooks

(1991), an embodied approach need not be anticomputationalist or anti-representationalist (Clark, 1997). Only, our view of computation and representation may have to be broadened.

Acknowledgments

We would like to thank Dana Damian and Harold Martinez for their kind help with the preparation of the sections on grasping and visual perception respectively. We would also like to thank Igor Farkas and Keith Gunura for reviewing an earlier version of this manuscript. M. H. was supported by the Swiss National Science Foundation project "From locomotion to cognition", under Grant 200020-122279/1.

References

Bajcsy R. (1988). Active perception. *Proc. IEEE, 76*, 966–1005.
Barsalou L. (2008). Grounded cognition. *Annual Review of Psychology, 59*, 617–45.
Bays P. M. & Wolpert D. M. (2007). Computational principles of sensorimotor control that minimize uncertainty and variability. *Journal of Physiology, 578*, 387–96.
Beer, R. (2003). The dynamics of active categorical perception in an evolved model agent. *Adaptive Behavior* 11, 209–43.
Blickhan R., Seyfarth A., Geyer H., Grimmer S., Wagner H., & Guenther M. (2007). Intelligence by mechanics. *Phil Trans R Soc Lond A, 365*, 199–220.
Borst C., Fischer M., & Hirzinger G. (2002). Calculating hand configurations for precision and pinch grasps, *in* 'Proc. IEEE/RSJ Int. Conf. Intelligent Robots and Systems (IROS)'.
Brooks R. A. (1991). Intelligence without representation. *Artificial Intelligence Journal, 47*, 139–59.
Brown E., Rodenberg N., Amend J., Mozeika A., Steltz E., Zakin M. R., Lipson H. & Jaeger H. M. (2010). From the cover: Universal robotic gripper based on the jamming of granular material. *Proc Natl Acad Sci USA, 107*, 18809–14. http://dx.doi.org/10.1073/pnas.1003250107
Buchli J. & Ijspeert A. J. (2008). Self-organized adaptive legged locomotion in a compliant quadruped robot. *Autonomous Robots, 25*, 331–47.
Cartmill M. (1979). The volar skin of primates: its frictional characteristics and their functional significance. *Amer J Physical Anthropology, 50*, 497–510.
Churchland P. S., Ramachandran V., & Sejnowski T. (1994). *Large-scale neuronal theories of the brain*. Cambridge: MIT Press, chapter A critique of pure vision.
Clark A. (1997). *Being there: putting brain, body and world together again* Cambridge: MIT Press.
Clark A. & Grush R. (1999). Towards cognitive robotics. *Adaptive Behaviour, 7*, 5–16.
Coleman M., Chatterjee A., & Ruina A. (1997). Motions of a rimless spoked wheel: a simple 3d system with impacts. *Dynamics and Stability of Systems, 12*, 139–60.
Collins S. H., Wisse M., & Ruina A. (2001). A three-dimentional passive-dynamic walking robot with two legs and knees. *International Journal of Robotics Research, 20*, 607–15.
Collins S., Ruina A., Tedrake R., & Wisse M. (2005). Efficient bipedal robots based on passive dynamic walkers. *Science, 307*, 1082–5.
Cruse H. (1990). What mechanisms coordinate leg movement in walking arthropods? *Trends in Neurosciences, 13*, 15–21.

Cruse H., Dean J., Durr V., Kindermann T., Schmitz J., & Schumm M. (2002). *Neurotechnology for biomimetic robots*. Cambridge: MIT Press, chapter A decentralized, biologically based network for autonomous control of (hexapod) walking (pp. 384–400).

Curcio A. C., Kenneth R. S., & Robert E. K. (1990). Human receptor topography. *J Comp Neurol, 292*, 497–523.

Damian D., Martinez H., Dermitzakis K., Hernandez Arieta A., & Pfeifer R. (2010). Artificial ridged skin for slippage speed detection in prosthetic hand applications, in 'Proc. IEEE/RSJ Int. Conf. Intelligent Robots and Systems (IROS)'.

De Preester H. & Knockaert K. (2005). *Body Image and Body Schema – interdisciplinary perspectives on the body*. Amsterdam: John Benjamins.

Dewey J. (1896). The reflex arc concept in psychology. *Psychological Review, 3*, 357–70.

Dur V., Krause A. F., Schitz J., & Cruse H. (2003). Neuroethological concepts and their transfer to walking machines. *Int J Robotics Research, 22*, 151–67.

Edelman G. E. (1987). *Neural Darwinism. The theory of neuronal group selection*. New York: Basic Books.

Edelman S. (2003). But will it scale up? not without representations. *Adaptive Behavior, 11*, 273–5.

Fearing R. & Hollerbach J. (1984). Basic solid mechanics for tactile sensing. *Int J Robotics Research, 1*, 266–75.

Franceschini N., Pichon J. & Blanes C. (1992). From insect vision to robot vision. *Trans R Soc London B, 337*, 283–94.

Gallese V. & Lakoff G. (2005). The brain's concepts: The role of the sensory-motor system in conceptual knowledge. *Cognitive Neuropsychology, 21*, 455–79.

Gibson J. (1979). *The ecological approach to visual perception*. Boston: Houghton Mifflin.

Glenberg A. M. (1997). What memory is for?. *Behavioral and Brain Sciences, 20*, 1–56.

Haggard P. & Wolpert D. M. (2005). *Higher-order motor disorders*. Oxford: Oxford University Press, chapter Disorders of body scheme.

Harnad S. (1990). The symbol grounding problem. *Physica D, 42*, 335–46.

Harnad S. (2005). *Handbook of categorization in cognitive science*. Oxford: Elsevier, chapter Cognition is categorization.

Hernandez Arieta A., Katoh R., Yokoi H. & Yu W. (2006). Development of a multi-DOF electromyography prosthetic system using the adaptive joint mechanism. *Applied Bionics and Biomechanics, 3*, 101–12.

Hesslow G. (2002). Conscious thought as simulation of behaviour and perception. *Trends in Cognitive Sciences, 6*, 242–7.

Higuchi T., Imanaka K., & Patla A. E. (2006). Action-oriented representation of peripersonal and extrapersonal space: Insights from manual and locomotor actions. *Japanese Psychological Research, 48*, 126–40.

Hoffmann H. (2007). Perception through visuomotor anticipation in a mobile robot. *Neural Networks, 20*, 22–33.

Hoffmann M., Marques, H., Hernandez Arieta, A., Sumioka, H., Lungarella, M. & Pfeifer, R. (2010). Body schema in robotics: a review. *IEEE Trans Auton Mental Develop, 2*, 304-324.

Hoshino K., Mura F., & Shimoyama I. (2000). Design and performance of a micro-sized biomorphic compound eye with a scanning retina. *J Microelectromech Syst, 9*, 32–7.

Iida F. & Pfeifer R. (2006). Sensing through body dynamics. *Robotics and Autonomous Systems, 54*, 631–40.

Jung T., Polani D., & Stone P. (in press). Empowerment for Continuous Agent-Environment Systems. *Adaptive Behavior*.

Koditschek D. E., Full R. J., & Buehler M. (2004). Mechanical aspects of legged locomotion control. *Arthropod structure and development, 33*, 251–72.

Kubow T. M. & Full R. J. (1999). The role of the mechanical system in control: a hypothesis of self-stabilization in hexapedal runners. *Phil Trans R Soc Lond B, 354*, 849–61.

Kuniyoshi Y., Yorozu Y., Ohmura Y., Terada K., Otani T., Nagakubo A., & Yamamoto T. (2004). From humanoid embodiment to theory of mind. In F. Iida, R. Pfeifer, L. Steels, & Y. Kuniyoshi (eds.), *Embodied Artificial Intelligence* (pp. 202–18). Springer: Berlin.

Lichtensteiger L. (2004). On the interdependence of morphology and control for intelligent behavior, PhD thesis, University of Zurich.

Lungarella M., Ishiguro, K., Kuniyoshi, Y. & Otsu, N. (2007). Methods for quantifying the causal structure of bivariate time series. *Int J of Bifurcation and Chaos, 17*, 903–21.

Lungarella M. & Sporns O. (2006). Mapping information flow in sensorimotor networks. *PLoS Comput Biol, 2*, 1301–12.

Maass W., Natschlaeger T., & Markram H. (2004). *Computational Neuroscience: A Comprehensive Approach*, Chapman & Hall/CRC, chapter Computational models for generic cortical microcircuits, pp. 575–605.

Maravita A., Spence C., & Driver J. (2003). Multisensory integration and the body schema: close to hand and within reach. *Curr Biol, 13*, R531–9.

Markram H. (2006). The blue brain project. *Nature Reviews Neuroscience, 1*, 153–9.

Marr D. (1982). *Vision: A Computational Investigation into the Human Representation and Processing of Visual Information.* Cambridge: MIT Press.

Martinez H., Lungarella M., & Pfeifer R. (2010a). On the influence of sensor morphology on eye motion coordination, *in* 'Proc. Int. Conf. Development and Learning (ICDL)'.

Martinez H., Sumioka H., Lungarella M., & Pfeifer R. (2010b). On the influence of sensor morphology on vergence. In S. Doncieux, B. Girard, A. Guillot, J. Hallam, J.-A. Meyer, & J.-B. Mouret (eds.), *From Animal to Animats 11, Proc Int Conf Sim Adaptive Beh* (pp. 146-55). Berlin: Springer.

Marzke M. & Marzke R. (2000). Evolution of the human hand: approaches to acquiring, analyzing and interpreting the anatomical evidence. *J Anat, 197*, 121-40.

McGeer T. (1990). Passive dynamic walking. *The International Journal of Robotics Research, 9*, 62–82.

Molina-Vilaplana J., Feliu-Batlle J., & Lopez-Coronado J. (2007). A modular neural network architecture for step-wise learning of grasping tasks. *Neural Networks, 20*, 631–45.

Noe A. (2004). *Action in perception.* Cambridge: MIT Press.

Nolfi S. (2002). Power and limit of reactive agents. *Neurocomputing, 49*, 119–45.

Oudeyer P.-Y., Kaplan F. & Hafner V. (2007). Intrinsic motivation systems for autonomous mental development. *IEEE Trans on Evol Comp, 11*, 265–86.

Pezzulo G. (2007). Anticipation and Future-Oriented Capabilities in Natural and Artificial Cognition. In M. Lungarella, F. Iida, J. C. Bongard, & R. Pfeifer (eds.), *50 Years of AI, Festschrift* (pp. 258-71). Berlin: Springer.

Pfeifer R. & Bongard J. C. (2007). *How the body shapes the way we think: a new view of intelligence.* Cambridge: MIT Press.

Pfeifer R. & Gomez G. (2009). Morphological computation - connecting brain, body, and environment. In B. Sendhoff, O. Sporns, E. Körner, H. Ritter, & K. Doya, K. (eds.), *Creating Brain-like Intelligence: From Basic Principles to Complex Intelligent Systems* (pp.66-83). Berlin: Springer.

Pfeifer R., Lungarella M., & Iida F. (2007). Self-organization, embodiment, and biologically inspired robotics. *Science, 318*, 1088–93.

Pfeifer R., Lungarella M., & Sporns O. (2008). The synthetic approach to embodied cognition: a primer. In O. Calvo & A. Gomila (eds.), *Handbook of Cognitive Science*

(pp. 121–37). Amsterdam: Elsevier.
Pfeifer R. & Scheier C. (1997). Sensory-motor coordination: The metaphor and beyond. *Robotics and Autonomous Systems, 20*, 157–78.
Pfeifer R. & Scheier C. (1999). *Understanding Intelligence.* Cambridge: MIT Press.
Poulakakis I., Papadopoulos E., & Buehler M. (2006). On the stability of the passive dynamics of quadrupedal running with a bounding gait. *International Journal of Robotics Research, 25*, 669–87.
Pylyshyn Z. (1987). *The robot's dilemma: The frame problem in artificial intelligence.* Norwood: Ablex.
Riesenhuber M. & Poggio T. (2002). Neural mechanisms of object recognition. *Current Opinion in Neurobiology, 22*, 162–8.
Ringrose R. (1997). Self-stabilizing running. In N. Kanayama, M. Kaneko, & T. Tsuji (eds.), *Proc IEEE Int Conf Robotics and Automation (ICRA)* (pp. 487-93). Albuquerque.
Sandini G. & Metta G. (2002). Retina-like sensors: Motivations, technology and applications. In F. G. Barth, J. A. C. Humphrey, & T. W. Secomb (eds.), *Sensors and sensing in biology and engineering* (pp. 379–92). Wien: Springer.
Saranli U., Buehler M., & Koditschek D. (2001). Rhex: a simple and highly mobile hexapod robot. *Int J Robotics Research, 20*, 616–31.
Scheibert J., Leurent S., Prevost A., & Debregas G. (2009). The role of fingerprints in the coding of tactile information probed with a biomimetic sensor. *Science, 13*, 1503–6.
Schomaker L. (2004). Anticipation in cybernetic systems: a case against mindless anti-representationalism. In W. Thissen, P. Wieringa, M. Pantic, & M. Ludema, (eds.), *Proc Int Conf Systems, Man and Cybernetics. Vol. 2* (pp. 2037–45). Den Haag.
Thelen E. & Smith L. (1994). *A Dynamic systems approach to the development of cognition and action* Cambridge: MIT Press.
Thornton C. (2010). Gauging the value of good data: Informational embodiment quantification. *Adaptive Behavior, 18*, 389-99.
Verdaasdonk B., Koopman H. & van der Helm F. (2009). Energy efficient walking with central pattern generators: from passive dynamic walking to biologically inspired control. *Biol Cybern, 101*, 49–61.
Vukobratovic M. & Vorovac B. (2004). Zero-moment point – thirty five years of its life. *International Journal of Humanoid Robotics, 1*, 157–73.
Webb B. (2004). Neural mechanisms for prediction: do insects have forward models?. *Trends in Neurosciences, 27*, 278–82.
Webb M. (2001). Can robots make good models of biological behaviour?. *Behavioral and brain sciences, 24*, 1033–50.
Wolpert D. M., Miall R. C., & Kawato M. (1998). Internal models in the cerebellum. *Trends in Cognitive Sciences, 2*, 338–47.
Yokoi H., Hernandez-Arieta A., Katoh R., Yu W., Watanabe I., & Maruishi M. (2004). Mutual adaptation in a prosthetics application. In F. Iida, R. Pfeifer, L. Steels, & Y. Kuniyoshi (eds.), *Embodied Artificial Intelligence* (pp. 147-59). Berlin: Springer.
Yu W., Yokoi H., & Kakazu Y. (2006). An interaction based learning method for assistive device systems. In J. X. Liu (ed.), *Focus on Robotics Research* (pp. 123–59). New York: Nova Publishers.

Interpretations of Embodied Cognition[1]

Shaun Gallagher

Philosophy and Cognitive Sciences, Institute of Simulation and Training,
University of Central Florida (USA)
School of Humanities, University of Hertfordshire (UK)
gallaghr@mail.ucf.edu

The concept of embodied cognition (EC) is not a settled one. A variety of theorists have attempted to outline different approaches and meanings related to this concept. They range from radical embodiment to minimal embodiment, and a number of positions in between. In addition, a variety of approaches to the study of cognition have been closely associated with the notion of embodiment — including enactive, embedded, and extended or distributed cognition approaches. Within these different perspectives there is no strong consensus on what weight to give to the concept of embodiment. Moreover, contrary to what some may think, not all EC approaches share a common opposition to the classical computational model of cognition. In this chapter I want to map out the landscape of these various senses of embodied cognition.

Minimal embodiment

One recent account of how embodiment figures into explanations of cognition takes social cognition as a focus. What Goldman & de Vignemont (2009) say about social cognition, however, can be applied to cognition generally. They place strict constraints on how we are to understand embodiment. So much so that most embodied theorists would likely fail to recognize what they describe as a case of embodied cognition and take it more as a dismissal of the importance of the body. Their starting point assumes that almost everything of importance for human cognition happens in the brain, "the seat of most, if not all, mental events" (2009, p. 154). Accordingly, the notion of embodied cognition seems all the more problematic if one defines the body as not including the brain, which is what they do: "Embodiment theorists want to elevate the importance of the body in explaining cognitive activities. What is meant by 'body' here? It ought to mean: the whole physical body minus the brain. Letting the brain qualify as part of the body would trivialize the claim that the body

---

[1] My research on this project was supported by a CNRS research grant as Visiting Researcher, Centre de Recherche en Epistémelogie Appliquée, École Polytechnique, Paris (2009-2010), and connects with my participation in the project on Embodied Virtues and Expertise. Australian Research Council. Project number/ID: DP1095109

is crucial to mental life" (p. 154). In addition to removing the brain from the body, Goldman & de Vignemont remove the body from the environment: they want to understand the contribution of "the body (understood literally), not [as it is related] to the situation or environment in which the body is embedded" (p. 154). A core claim in EC, however, is that the body *cannot be uncoupled from its environment*.[2] It would be difficult to find any EC theory that defines the body as this 'literal', and literally dead, brainless thing.

Goldman & de Vignemont further rule out anatomy and body activity (actions and postures) as trivial rather than important or constitutive contributors to cognitive processes. They are thus left with, as they put it, 'sanitized' body representations. They regard the concept of body-formatted representations ('B-formats') as "the most promising" concept for promoting an EC approach (p. 155). Unfortunately, they explain, there is no consensus about what B-formats are and their role in cognition is still under debate. It seems clear, however, that Goldman & de Vignemont consider B-formatted representations to be brain states (in the context of social cognition they involve mirror neuron activation [p. 156]), and as such, they do what many theorists do: they reduce embodiment to a set of neuronal processes. Although it's not clear how the reduction of the body to a set of brain processes remains consistent with their earlier elimination of the brain as part of what embodiment means, this strategy really brings us back to a model that is not inconsistent with the classical computational (CC) one that EC opposes, or at the very least it gives us an internalist view that is not inconsistent with the bodiless brain-in-a-vat conception of cognition.

Goldman & de Vignemont thus define embodiment and frame the problem in a way that precludes any significant contribution from the body. In doing so, they ignore the fact that EC challenges the very framework that they adopt. Goldman & de Vignemont nonetheless present a clear challenge to EC, and they make it specific by providing a list of questions that EC theorists should answer in order to clarify their claims, and to help those who are not quite sure. Here is their list.

1. Which interpretation of embodiment do they have in mind?
2. Which sectors of cognition, or which cognitive tasks, do they say are embodied; and how fully does each task involve embodiment?
3. How does the empirical evidence support the specific embodiment claims under the selected interpretation(s)?
4. How do the proffered claims depart substantially from CC?

(Goldman & de Vignemont, 2009, p. 158)

---

[2] E.g., "Given that bodies and nervous systems co-evolve with their environments, and only the behavior of complete animals is subjected to selection, the need for ... a tightly coupled perspective should not be surprising" (Beer, 2000). Also see Brooks (1991); Chemero (2009); Chiel & Beer (1997).

Interpretations of Embodied Cognition

Since a number of versions of EC reject representationalist theories of cognition, we can add a fifth question, closely related to (4).

5. Do mental representations play a role in this version of EC?

We can use these questions to guide our topographical survey, and we can start by asking them of Goldman & de Vignemont's 'most promising' but minimal conception of EC. (1) They suggest a minimal interpretation which frames embodiment in terms of sanitized brain processes. (2) Accordingly, they suggest it applies to some (but not all) aspects of social cognition, and not much else. As they say, "It is doubtful, however, that such a thesis can be generalized" (p. 158). On their view, B-formatted representations (perhaps mirror neuron activation) may feed a cognitive simulation process. (3) The empirical evidence is tied to mirror neuron research, and evidence that lesions that affect B-formatted representations "interfere with action and emotion recognition" (p. 156). (4) Although this minimal version of EC seems relatively consistent with CC, since social cognition is not 'pervasively embodied', Goldman & de Vignemont suggest that CC never anticipated the 'low-level nature' of B-representations. (5) This version of EC is strongly representational.

Biological embodiment: anatomy, chemistry, and movement

In contrast to Goldman & de Vignemont, who rule out anatomy and bodily movement as important, non-trivial factors for cognition, other theorists suggest that anatomy and movement are important contributors to the shaping of cognition prior to brain processing (pre-processing) and subsequent to brain processing (post-processing) of information in the cognitive system (e.g., Chiel & Beer, 1997; Shapiro, 2004; Straus, 1966; Hoffmann & Pfeifer, this volume; see Gallagher, 2005a). Embodiment in this case means that extra-neural structural features of the body shape our cognitive experience. For example, the fact that we have two eyes, positioned as they are, delivers binocular vision and allows us to see the relative depth of things. Similar things can be said about the position of our ears and our ability to tell the direction of sound. As Shapiro puts it, "the point is not simply [or trivially] that perceptual processes fit bodily structure. Perceptual processes *depend on and include* bodily structures" (2004, p. 190).

Our sensory experience also depends on the way our head and body move, as we see in the case of parallax (Churchland et al., 1994; Shapiro, 2004). Furthermore, our motor responses, rather than fully determined at brain-level, are mediated by the design of muscles and tendons, their degrees of flexibility, their geometric relationships to other muscles and joints, and their prior history of activation (Zajac, 1993). Movement is not always centrally planned; it is based on a competitive system that requires what Andy Clark terms 'soft assembly'. The nervous system learns "to modulate parameters (such as stiffness [of limb or joint]) which will then *interact* with intrinsic bodily and environmental constraints so as to yield desired outcomes" (Clark 1997, p. 45).

Many of these insights are still cast in terms of information processing, and as such may be consistent with the general principles of classical cognitivism. As Shapiro notes: "steps in a cognitive process that a traditionalist would attribute to symbol manipulation might, from the perspective of EC, emerge from the physical attributes of the body" (2007, p. 340). In addition, even if the body is doing some of the work, cognitivists could easily claim that pre-processing is in fact feeding the more central processing that is certainly more constitutive of cognition, just as post-processing is to some degree determined by instructions from the brain as central processor.

More holistic, proprioceptive and emotion-related processes, however, may be more challenging to the classical conception. There is good empirical evidence that they have a profound effect on perception and thinking. For example, vibration-induced proprioceptive patterns that change the posture of the whole body are interpreted as changes in the perceived environment (Roll & Roll 1988, p. 162). Proprioceptive adjustments of the body schema can help to resolve perceptual conflicts (Harris, 1965, p. 419; Rock & Harris, 1967). Experimental alterations of the postural schema lead to alterations in space perception and perceptual shifts in external vertical and horizontal planes (Bauermeister, 1964; Wapner & Werner, 1965). Likewise hormonal changes — changes in body chemistry — as well as visceral and musculoskeletal processes, can bias perception, memory, attention, and decision-making (Damasio, 1994; Bechara et al., 1997; Gallagher, 2005; Shapiro, 2004). The regulation of body chemistry is not autonomous from cognitive processes, and vice versa. "Body regulation, survival, and mind are intimately interwoven" (Damasio, 1994, p. 123).

On this reading of EC, the classic computational/functionalist thought experiment of the brain-in-the-vat completely fails. The claim that cognitive function and experience would be the same, or even similar to a fully embodied subject, if the appropriate inputs were delivered to a disembodied brain in a vat fails to take into consideration the contributions of body performances. As pointed out by a number of theorists, the experimenters would have to replicate everything that the biological body delivers in terms of pre- and post-processing, hormonal and neurotransmitter chemistry, and emotional life. Thus, as Damasio suggests, this would require the creation of a body surrogate "and thus confirm that 'body-type inputs' are required for a normally minded brain after all" (1994, p. 228; also see Gallagher, 2005b; Cosmelli & Thompson, 2007).

The body as semantic engine

Not only does the structure, composition, and motor abilities of the body determine how we experience things, they also determine what we experience, and how we understand the world. Various experiments show that how we are moving or posturing ourselves (e.g., pushing away vs. pulling toward) will affect our evaluations of target objects (e.g., Cacioppo et al., 1993; Chen & Bargh, 1999; Koch, this volume). Shapiro builds on observations made by French (1990) about the kind of cognitive associations we might make if our bodies were different. If our eyes were located on our knees, for example, it would not only change our spatial perspectives, it would create differences in our conceptual associations. We might associate crawling on the floor with torture (Shapiro 2004, p. 195).

Lakoff & Johnson, drawing primarily on cognitive and experimental linguistics and cultural anthropology, but also citing psychological, neuroscientific, and cognitive science research on mental rotation, mental imagery, gestures, and sign language, have famously argued that our conceptual life begins in spatial and motor behaviors and derives meaning from bodily experience (Johnson, 2010; Lakoff, in press). Accordingly, the "peculiar nature of our bodies shapes our very possibilities for conceptualization and categorization" (Lakoff & Johnson, 1999, p. 19). For them, the specific mechanism that bridges embodied experience and conceptual thought is metaphor.

Metaphors are built on basic and recurring image-schemas such as front-back, in-out, near-far, pushing, pulling, supporting, balance, etc., and the basic image-schemas are built on bodily experience (1999, p. 36). Thus, "the concepts of *front* and *back* are body-based. They make sense only for beings with fronts and back. If all beings on this planet were uniform stationary spheres floating in some medium and perceiving equally in all directions, they would have no concepts of *front* and *back*" (1999, p. 34). Similar things can be said for *up-down*, and so forth. These basic image-schemas then shape, metaphorically, our abstract conceptual thought in relation to planning and decision-making, for example. Thus, justice is conceived in terms of balance; virtue is conceived in terms of being upright; planning for the future is conceived in terms of up and forward — "What's up?" "What's coming up this week?" The *in* and *out* body-schema, and the containment metaphor, for example, range over a vast set of metaphors and concepts, from the close to literal: "John went out of the room", to the abstract: "She finally came out of her depression", or "I don't want to leave any relevant data out of my argument", to the logically abstract, such as the law of the excluded middle in logic (Johnson, 1987). This view has been extended to explanations of mathematical concepts as well (Lakoff & Núñez, 2000).

At least in some respects, the embodied view taken up by Lakoff and Johnson involves neural embodiment. "An embodied concept is a neural structure that is part of, or makes use of the sensorimotor system of our brains. Much of conceptual inference is, therefore, sensorimotor inference" (1999, p. 20). Although generally the Lakoff-Johnson view is taken to be consistent with a connectionist view, on at least one interpretation (Zlatev, 2010) their position is not inconsistent with classical cognitivism. Yet, consistent with more enactive views of cognition, they eschew strong representationalism.

> As we said in *Philosophy in the Flesh*, the only workable theory of representations is one in which a representation is a flexible pattern of organism-environment interactions, and not some inner mental entity that somehow gets hooked up with parts of the external world by a strange relation called 'reference'. We reject such classical notions of representation, along with the views of meaning and reference that are built on then. Representation is a term that we try carefully to avoid. (Johnson & Lakoff, 2002, p. 249-250)

Embodied functionalism

In some regards the notion of an embodied functionalism is either trite, since even functionalist systems need to be physically embodied, or contradictory, since one hallmark of functionalism is a certain indifference to the physicality that sustains the system (body neutrality, multiple realizability). The idea that functionalists should take notions of embodiment seriously, however, can be found in some discussions of the extended mind, e.g., Andy Clark (2008a), Wheeler (2005), Rowlands (2006; 2010). I'll focus on Clark as the main proponent of this view. On the one hand, Clark argues for a step back towards the idea of a minimal embodiment in the sense that he considers factors associated with anatomical determination and embodied semantics to be "trivial and uninteresting" rather than deeply "special" (2008b, p. 38). On the other hand, he defends the notion that the body plays an important role as part of the extended mechanisms of cognition. In this regard, the physical body functions as a non-neural vehicle for cognitive processes, in much the same general way that the physical processes of neurons do. The body is part of an extended cognitive system that starts with the brain and includes body and environment. As he puts it, "the larger systemic wholes, incorporating brains, bodies, the motion of sense organs, and (under some conditions) the information-bearing states of non-biological props and aids, may sometimes constitute the *mechanistic supervenience base* for mental states and processes" (2008b, p. 38).

This view is not to be confused with the idea that the (human) body offers certain determining constraints (sensory-motor contingencies) that make (human) experience unique, an idea associated with O'Regan &

Interpretations of Embodied Cognition

Noë's (2001) theory of enactive perception. Clark is not convinced that an animal with a very different body could not experience certain aspects of the spatial environment in exactly the same way. Rather, different bodies can compute or process information differently but still produce the same experience. The important thing for Clark (citing as evidence experiments by Ballard et al., 1997) is that part of the computing mechanism can include the body. In accomplishing certain tasks, for example, we could store task-relevant information in our brain-based memory system and consult the information in that store; alternatively, we could leave it the information in the environment where it is and simply use our bodies to perceptually consult it when needed. In the latter case, consistent with Rob Wilson's (1994) notion of 'exploitative representation' and 'wide computing', the perceiving body is playing a certain computational role that could be done fully 'in the head'; the body does this sort of thing frequently, and in effect operates as an 'external' vehicle for cognition. As Clark (2007) makes clear, this view of an embodied extension of cognition (he calls it 'simple embodiment' [Clark, 1999]) is also consistent with a robust representationalism for higher cognitive processes, as well as with a minimal representationalism (involving action-oriented representations) for action (see Clark & Grush, 1999).

One way to split the difference between those who would argue for a special and essential role for embodiment and those who would give the body only a 'simple' functional role, is to suggest that embodiment especially matters for phenomenal consciousness, but not for cognition. The same cognitive results supervening on specifically embodied processes may feel different or register differently in experience, while still being functionally equivalent in regard to cognitive state.

Clark hesitates to accept this kind of division of labor. He argues that even for experience one should allow the possibility that the cognitive system will provide "compensatory downstream adjustments" that would, so to speak, even out differences in the experiential aspects that accompany cognition (Clark, 2007). While there seems no strong reason to think this is the case (Clark cites no evidence to support this view), or even to think that it should be the case (after all, why should it matter that a frog's consciousness have the same phenomenal feel as a human's consciousness), there is some evidence against it. Wearing prism goggles changes visual experience by altering the angle of perspective on the visual field. A set of prism goggles may shift the visual field to the right by 40 degrees, or may even invert the visual field. It was once thought that the perceptual system eventually corrects for this distortion and the subject, who is initially disoriented, starts to experience the world and act in it as if she were not wearing the goggles. That would mean that the visual system makes compensatory downstream adjustments at brain level to restore visual-motor experience to our normal parameters. But this has been shown not to be the case (Linden et al., 1999). Subjects make important adjustments in their motor behavior, but their visual experience remains distorted. Prism glasses basically change the normal visual system at the basic bodily level (that is, the normal workings of the physical eye, plus the prism glasses, would be equivalent to a different eye structure). Brain-based processes that may allow us to adjust motor behavior to cope with this different visual experience, however, do not allow for a compensatory downstream adjustments that would restore upright visual experience. Even if this suggests that Clark might be wrong about the idea of compensatory effects with respect to experience, restoring the compromise division of labor (functionalist cognition vs embodied consciousness) it was meant to challenge, is hardly consistent with stronger versions of EC.

Radical embodiment

Enactive views on embodied cognition emphasize the idea that perception is *for action*, and that this action-orientation shapes most cognitive processes. This approach often comes with strong calls to radically change our ways of thinking about the mind and doing cognitive science (e.g., Gallagher & Varela, 2003; Thompson, 2007; Thompson & Varela, 2001; Varela et al., 2001). Thompson & Varela (2001) agree on Clark's (1999) three-point summary of the enactive view:

1. understanding the complex interplay of brain, body and world requires the tools and methods of nonlinear dynamical systems theory;
2. traditional notions of representation and computation are inadequate;
3. traditional decompositions of the cognitive system into inner functional subsystems or modules ('boxology') are misleading, and blind us to arguably better decompositions into dynamical systems that cut across the brain–body–world divisions.

(Thompson & Varela, 2001, p. 418; also see Chemero, 2009, p. 29).

Similar to Clark and the idea of extended cognition, enactive approaches argue that cognition is not entirely 'in the head', but distributed across brain, body, and environment. In contrast to Clark's functionalist view, however, enactive theorists claim that the (human) bodily processes shape and contribute to the constitution of consciousness and cognition in an irreducible and irreplaceable way. Specifically, on the enactive view, biological aspects of bodily life, including organismic and emotion regulation of the entire body, have a permeating effect on cognition, as do processes of sensori-motor coupling between organism and environment. Noë (2004; also see O'Regan & Noë, 2001; Hurley, 1998) developed a detailed account of enactive perception where sensory-motor contingencies and environmental affordances take over the work that had been attributed to neural computations and mental representations.

Thompson and Varela (2001) and Gallagher (2001; 2005a) add to this the dimension of intersubjective interaction, which, they regard, in contrast to Goldman & de Vignemont, as involving fully embodied processes that involve facial expression, posture, movement, gestures, and distinct forms of sensory-motor couplings. This is supported by developmental studies that suggest infants engage in embodied intersubjective practices from birth. Mirror neurons may contribute to "primary intersubjective" processes (Trevarthen, 1979), understood as part of the neural underpinnings of enactive social perception of motor intentions and response preparation rather than a simulation or simple mirroring of mental states (Gallagher, 2007). Context and social environment also contribute to "secondary intersubjective" (Trevarthen & Hubley, 1978) practices starting at 9-12 months of age. In the intersubjective context, perception is often *for inter-action* with others, where perceptually-guided interaction becomes a principle of social cognition and generates meaning in a process of 'participatory sense-making' (De Jaegher & Di Paulo, 2007; De Jaegher, Di Paulo & Gallagher, in press; Gallagher, 2009).

Conclusion

It is often thought that EC approaches, even if they differ among themselves, are united in their opposition to traditional versions of computationalism and representationalism, but this is clearly not the case. Indeed, disagreements within the EC camp are primarily disagreements about just these issues (see Table 1 for an overview). But perhaps one important outcome of the EC approaches is that they have moved the issues about computationalism and representationalism front and center, even in the minds of those who have taken less-embodied approaches. Thus there have been recent wholesale investigations into the concept of representation (e.g., Chemero, 2009; Hutto, 2008; Gallagher, 2008; Ramsey, 2007), as well as careful and somewhat defensive explanations of what representation means in analytic philosophy of mind (e.g., Burge, 2010; and see Crane, 2008 for a similar analysis). On the EC side, it seems incumbent to deliver on some promissory notes. As Chemero (2009) makes clear, it will be important to 'scale up' dynamic systems approaches from the analysis of action and perception to higher cognitive performance in what are considered to be 'representation-hungry' tasks (Clark & Toribio, 1994). "It is still an open-question how far beyond minimally cognitive behaviors radical embodied cognitive science can get" (Chemero, 2009, p. 43). Accordingly, within EC one of the most important and interesting debates is that between functionalist and radical versions, the first appealing to representations and eschewing any essentialist view of the body, the second dismissing representations and insisting on the ineliminable nature of the body. One of the leading theoretical questions in this field is whether it's possible to integrate these views (see Menary, 2007) or to defend a non-functionalist and enactive version of the extended mind hypothesis (Gallagher, in press).

What is clear, however, in contrast to Goldman & de Vignemont's critical suggestions, is that embodied approaches to cognition are not brainless; the proper explanatory unit is brain-body-environment rather than the 'body (understood literally)." Furthermore, EC is supported by good scientific evidence from a variety of disciplines, including brain science. Understood broadly, EC is also able to address multiple sectors of cognition, from action and perception, to social cognition, and more abstract, higher-level cognition. Goldman & de Vignemont (2009) begin their essay dramatically by suggesting that "a specter is haunting the laboratories of cognitive science" — the EC reply can only be "*Bodies of the world unite ... with your brains and your environments!*"

Table 1. Different theories of embodiment

Interpretation	Minimal embodiment	Embodied functionalism	Biological embodiment	Embodied semantics	Radical (enactive) embodiment
Sectors of cognition	Social cognition	Perception/ action & higher-level cognition	Perception/ action	Higher-level cognition	Perception/ action, social cognition
Empirical evidence	Neuroscience (mirror neurons, lesions)	Experimental psychology, robotics, engineering	Biology, experimental psychology	Linguistics, psychology, neuroscience, cultural anthropology	Developmental psychology, neuroscience, empirical psychology
Consistent with CC	Yes	Yes	Neutral	Neutral	No
Representations	Strong yes	Yes for 'representation hungry' processes and minimal representations for action	Weak	Weak	No
Representatives	Goldman & de Vignemont	Clark, Wheeler, Rowlands	Shapiro, Beers	Johnson, Lakoff, Nuñez	Varela, Thompson, Noë, Gallagher, Hutto

References

Ballard D. H., Hayhoe M. M., Pook P. K., & Rao R. P. N. (1997). Deictic codes for the embodiment of cognition. *Behavioral and Brain Sciences, 20,* 723-67.

Bauermeister M. (1964). The effect of body tilt on apparent verticality, apparent body position and their relation. *Journal of Experimental Psychology, 67,* 142-7.

Bechara A., Damasio H., Tranel D., & Damasio A. R. (1997). Deciding advantageously before knowing the advantageous strategy. *Science, 275,* 1293-5.

Beer R. (2000). Dynamical approaches to cognitive science. *Trends in Cognitive Sciences, 4,* 91-9.

Brooks R. (1991). Intelligence without representation. *Artificial Intelligence, 47,* 139-59.

Burge T. (2010). Origins of perception. Paper presented as the *First 2010 Jean Nicod Prize Lecture*. Paris 14 June 2010.

Cacioppo J. T., Priester J. R., & Bernston G. G. (1993). Rudimentary determination of attitudes: II. Arm flexion and extension have differential effects on attitudes. *Journal of Personality and Social Psychology, 65,* 5-17.

Chen S. & Bargh J. A. (1999). Consequences of automatic evaluation: Immediate behavior predispositions to approach or avoid the stimulus. *Personality and Social Psychology Bulletin, 25,* 215-24.

Chemero A. (2009). *Radical Embodied Cognitive Science.* Cambridge: MIT Press.

Chiel H. & Beer R. (1997). The brain has a body: Adaptive behavior emerges from interactions of nervous system, body and environment. *Trends in Neuroscience, 20,* 553-7.

Cosmelli D. & Thompson E. (2007). Embodiment or envatment? Reflections on the bodily basis of consciousness. In J. Stewart, O. Gapenne, & E. di Paolo (eds.), *Enaction: Towards a New Paradigm for Cognitive Science.* Cambridge: MIT Press.

Churchland P. S. Ramachandran V. S., & Sejnowski T. J. (1994). A critique of pure vision. In C. Koch and J. L. Davis (eds.), *Large-scale Neuronal Theories of the Brain.* Cambridge: MIT Press.

Clark A. (2008a). *Supersizing the Mind: Reflections on Embodiment, Action, and Cognitive Extension.* Oxford: Oxford University Press.

Clark A. (2008b). Pressing the flesh: A tension on the study of the embodied, embedded mind. *Philosophy and Phenomenological Research, 76,* 37-59.

Clark A. (1999). An embodied cognitive science? *Trends in Cognitive Sciences, 3,* 345-51.

Clark A. (1997). *Being There.* Cambridge: MIT Press.

Clark A. & Grush R. (1999). Towards a cognitive robotics. *Adaptive Behavior, 7,* 5-16.

Clark A. & Toribio J. (1994). Doing without representing? *Synthese, 101,* 401-31.

Crane T. (2008). Is perception a propositional attitude? *Philosophical Quarterly, 59,* 452-69.

Damasio A. (1994). *Descartes Error: Emotion, Reason, and the Human Brain.* New York: G. P. Putnam.

De Jaegher H. & Di Paolo E. (2007). Participatory Sense-Making: An enactive approach to social cognition. *Phenomenology and the Cognitive Sciences, 6,* 485-507

De Jaegher H., Di Paulo E., & Gallagher S. (2010). Can social interaction constitute social cognition? *Trends in Cognitive Sciences, 14,* 441-7.

French R. (1990). Subcognition and the limits of the Turing test. *Mind, 99,* 53-65.

Gallagher S. (in press). The overextended mind. *Versus: Quaderni di studi semiotici.*

Gallagher S. (2009). Two problems of intersubjectivity. *Journal of Consciousness Studies, 16,* 298-308

Gallagher S. (2008). Are minimal representations still representations? *International Journal of Philosophical Studies, 16,* 351-69.

Gallagher S. (2007). Simulation trouble. *Social Neuroscience, 2*, 353-65.
Gallagher S. (2005a). *How the Body Shapes the Mind*. Oxford: Oxford University Press.
Gallagher S. (2005b). Metzinger's matrix: Living the virtual life with a real body. *Psyche: An interdisciplinary journal of research on consciousness*.
(http://psyche.cs.monash.edu.au/symposia/metzinger/Gallagher.pdf)
Gallagher S. (2001). The practice of mind: Theory, simulation, or interaction? *Journal of Consciousness Studies, 8*, 83–107
Gallagher S. & Varela F. (2003). Redrawing the map and resetting the time: Phenomenology and the cognitive sciences. *Canadian Journal of Philosophy, Suppl, 29*, 93-132.
Goldman A. & De Vignemont F. (2009). Is social cognition embodied? *Trends in Cognitive Sciences, 13*, 154-59.
Harris C. S. (1965). Perceptual adaptation to inverted, reversed, and displaced vision. *Psychological Review, 72*, 419-44.
Hurley S. (1998). *Consciousness in Action*. Cambridge: Harvard University Press.
Hutto D. (2008). *Folk Psychological Narratives The Sociocultural Basis of Understanding Reasons*. Cambridge: MIT Press.
Johnson M. (2010). Metaphors and cognition. In S. Gallagher & M. Schmicking (eds.), *Handbook of Phenomenology and Cognitive Science*. Dordrecht: Springer.
Johnson M. (1987). *The Body in the Mind: The Bodily Basis of Meaning, Imagination, and Reason*. Chicago: University of Chicago Press.
Johnson M. & Lakoff G. (2002). Why cognitive linguistics requires embodied realism. *Cognitive Linguistics, 13*, 245-63.
Lakoff G. (2008). The neural theory of metaphor. In R. Gibbs (ed.), *The Cambridge Handbook of Metaphor and Thought* (pp. 17-38). Cambridge: Cambridge University Press.
Lakoff G. & Johnson M. (1999). *Philosophy in the Flesh: The Embodied Mind and its Challenge to Western Thought*. New York: Basic Books.
Lakoff G. & Núñez R. (2000). *Where Mathematics Comes From*. New York: Basic Books.
Linden D. E. J., Kallenbach U., Heineckeô A., Singer W., & Goebel R. (1999). The myth of upright vision. A psychophysical and functional imaging study of adaptation to inverting spectacles. *Perception, 28*, 469-81.
Menary R. (2007). *Cognitive Integration: Mind and Cognition Unbounded*. Basingstoke: Palgrave Macmillan.
Noë A. (2004). *Action in Perception*. Cambridge: MIT Press.
O'Regan K. & Noë A. (2001). A sensorimotor account of vision and visual consciousness. *Behavioral and Brain Sciences, 23*, 939–973.
Ramsey W. (2007). *Representation Reconsidered*. Cambridge: Cambridge University Press.
Rock I. & Harris C. S. (1967). Vision and touch. *Scientific American, 216*, 96-104.
Rowlands M. (2010). *The New Science of the Mind*. Cambridge: MIT Press.
Rowlands M. (2006). *Body Language*. Cambridge: MIT Press.
Roll J-P. & Roll R. (1988). From eye to foot: A proprioceptive chain involved in postural control. In G. Amblard, A. Berthoz, & F. Clarac (eds.), *Posture and Gait: Development, Adaptation, and Modulation* (pp. 155-164). Amsterdam: Excerpta Medica.
Wapner S. & Werner H. (1965). An experimental approach to body perception from the organismic developmental point of view. In S. Wapner & H. Werner (eds.), *The Body Percept* (pp. 9–25). New York: Random House.
Shapiro L. A. (2004). *The Mind Incarnate*. Cambridge: MIT Press.
Shapiro L. A. (2007). The embodied cognition research programme. *Philosophy Compass, 2*, 338–46.
Straus E. (1966). *Philosophical Psychology*. New York: Basic Books.
Thompson E. (2007). *Mind in Life: Biology, Phenomenology and the Sciences of Mind*. Cambridge: Harvard University Press.

Thompson E. & Varela F. (2001). Radical embodiment: Neural dynamics and consciousness. *Trends in Cognitive Sciences, 5,* 418-25
Trevarthen C. B. (1979). Communication and cooperation in early infancy: A description of primary intersubjectivity. In M. Bullowa (ed.), *Before Speech* (pp. 321-47). Cambridge: Cambridge University Press.
Trevarthen C. & Hubley P. (1978). Secondary intersubjectivity: Confidence, confiding and acts of meaning in the first year. In A. Lock (ed.), *Action, Gesture and Symbol: The Emergence of Language* (pp. 183-229). London: Academic Press.
Varela F. J., Thompson E., & Rosch E. (1991). *The Embodied Mind: Cognitive Science and Human Experience.* Cambridge: MIT Press.
Wilson R. A. (1994). Wide computationalism. *Mind, 103,* 351-72.
Wheeler M. (2005). *Reconstructing the Cognitive World.* Cambridge: MIT Press.
Zajac F. E. (1993). Muscle coordination of movement: A perspective. *Journal of Biomechanics, 26, suppl 1,* 109-24.
Zlatev J. (2010). Phenomenology and Cognitive Linguistics. In S. Gallagher & D. Schmicking (eds.), *Handbook of Phenomenology and Cognitive Science.* Dordrecht: Springer.

Section 2

Embodiment: Formal Approaches

The Transfer of Principles of Non-Equilibrium Physics to Embodied Cognition

Hermann Haken* and Wolfgang Tschacher**

*Institute for Theoretical Physics, University of Stuttgart, Germany
cos@itp1.uni-stuttgart.de
**University Hospital of Psychiatry, University of Bern, Switzerland
wolfgang.tschacher@spk.unibe.ch

1. Towards a general formulation of self-organization

In this chapter, we wish to study embodied cognition on the basis of self-organized pattern formation. We will interpret pattern formation in a rather wide sense: one may think of spatial, temporal, spatio-temporal, or behavioral patterns. We will introduce the idea of pattern formation by means of a few examples taken from various fields of science.

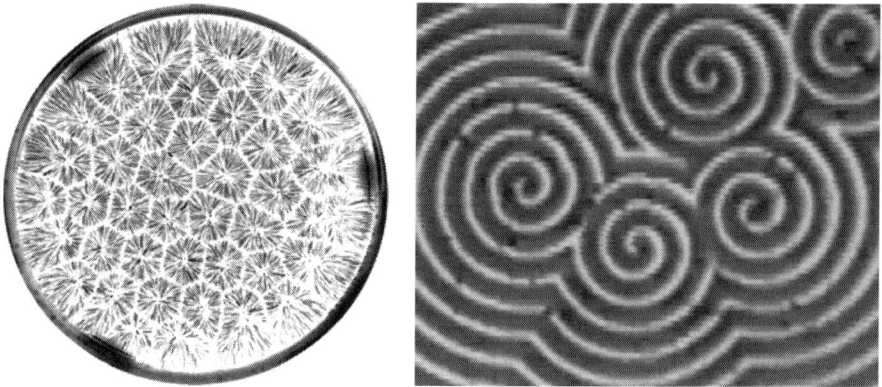

Fig. 1: Examples of pattern formation. Left: Bénard cells in a Petri dish viewed from above. Right: Belousov-Zhabotinsky reaction

In physics, a fluid in a container heated from below may spontaneously form hexagonal cells (establishing the so-called Bénard convection, Fig. 1 left). In each cell, a fluid compartment rises due to the heating, cools at the upper surface of the container, and eventually sinks down at the borders of the rising compartment. This revolving conical pattern is dynamical in nature. An example of pattern formation in optics is the laser, which has become a paradigmatic system for synergetics; we will elaborate it below. Well-known further examples of self-organizing dynamics come from chemistry: specific substances, when poured together, may spontaneously form rotating spirals or concentric waves that run outwards (the

Belousov-Zhabotinsky reaction, Fig. 1 right). In biology, we observe the growth of organisms with their highly sophisticated structures, which may also be conceived as patterns. Finally, one may think of behavioral patterns, the simplest ones perhaps occurring in movement coordination such as the gaits of quadrupeds or hand movements (Haken et al., 1985). An important aspect of all such pattern formation is the fact that these patterns arise spontaneously, i.e. there is no ordering hand that creates them like a sculptor would do.

Some 40 years ago, one of us initiated an interdisciplinary field of research that aimed at studying the self-organized formation of patterns from a unifying point of view. We called it synergetics, signifying a science of cooperation (Haken, 1977). Synergetics combined methods of dynamical systems theory (which it developed even further) with methods of statistical physics (thereby taking into account the important role of fluctuations, i.e. of chance events). Synergetics is focused especially on those situations where new patterns arise. Initially, in order to express the synergetic approach as clearly as possible, we chose examples from physics, especially the light source laser, as paradigmatic systems. As an interdisciplinary field, however, applications of the synergetic principles have ranged from physical to social to psychological and neuronal dynamics. This was the agenda of a series of international interdisciplinary symposia starting in 1972[1]. The field has generated numerous publications and a book series with proceedings, monographs and edited volumes (the Series on Synergetics, published by Springer Verlag, Berlin).

A major goal within synergetics was to base brain functioning on abstract assumptions, which can be formulated independently of a specific physical substrate. One of us (Haken, 1996) has suggested to treat the brain as an open physical system, which on the one hand obeys the fundamental laws of physics, but is also subject to laws at the superordinate level of synergetics. We may thus say that the brain is an open and complex physical system, to which the mathematical tools and concepts of synergetics may be applied. The corresponding systems concept can be summarized as follows: A system is conceived of as an ensemble of individual components interacting with each other; at the same time, the system is embedded in an environment, with which it may exchange energy, matter and/or information. Open systems are those, which are maintained in their ordered dynamical state by an influx of energy, matter or information with a corresponding outflux of degraded energy or matter (on this degradation process focuses the free-energy principle: See Friston, this volume). In mathematical terms, the level or amount of such influx serves as control parameter(s) of the system. Additionally, the individual components of the system are subject to continuous stochastic

---

[1] for a list see www.upd.unibe.ch

fluctuations, which may be of internal or external origin. Such stochasticity has turned out to be quite essential for the initiation of ordering processes.

When a control parameter exceeds a critical value, fluctuations may trigger the establishment of a variety of spatial, temporal or behavioral patterns. In many cases, the single potential patterns are mutually exclusive, i.e. in general they appear to 'compete' with one another. In these cases, one specific pattern wins the competition and consequently acts as order parameter. In some cases, several order parameters may result from the competition, which then govern a coexistence of different patterns. While the order parameters are brought about by the cooperation of the individual components, they in turn prescribe the behavior of the latter parts, or in other words, they enslave the components ('slaving principle'). The slaving principle is an example of circular causality.

Of particular interest to us are so-called transients close to the critical values of the system. Transient dynamics occurs during the buildup of a pattern; as soon as the control parameter is switched off the pattern decreases. Thus we may distinguish three phases:

Phase 1: Buildup of a highly ordered coherent state by means of the recruitment of components;

Phase 2: Fully developed pattern of the coherent state;

Phase 3: Decay of that pattern.

A paradigmatic model of the spontaneous formation of ordered states is a gas laser (Fig. 2). The gas, composed of atoms, is enclosed in a glass cylinder. At its end faces, mirrors are mounted that serve to reflect light running in axial direction, so that it can stay comparatively long inside this device before it eventually exits through one of the half-silvered mirrors. The laser allows us to exemplify the various aspects of the buildup of self-organization mentioned above.

The laser system is composed of atoms as well as of light waves emitted by the atoms. The environment contributes to self-organization in two ways. First, there is a static environmental contribution: The glass tube provides confinement of the atoms; the mirrors at the end faces serve for a pre-selection of permitted light waves. Second, the environment contributes dynamically: An electric current, generated by a battery as an energy source, is sent through the device. This free energy lifts atoms from their resting states to excited (energy-richer) states. The control parameter here is the strength of the electric current — if strong enough, it can generate a sufficiently large number of excited atoms. As soon as this number is larger than that of the atoms in the resting state, laser physics speaks of an 'inversion'.

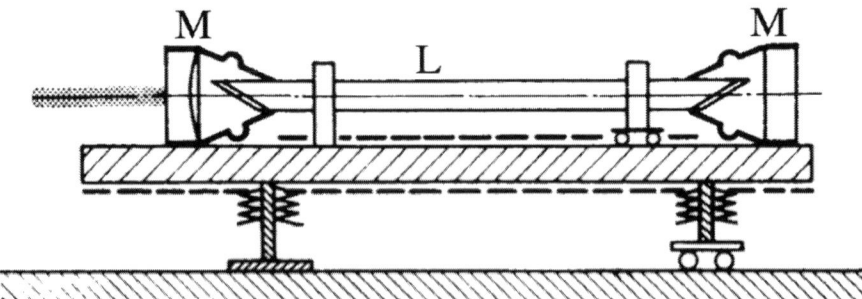

Fig. 2: Schema of a gas laser. L, discharge tube; M, mirrors. Laser is mounted so as to avoid vibrations (Haken, 1985)

Fluctuations are provided by the spontaneous emission of light wave tracks that are rather short, e.g. of one meter length. At this point in Phase 1, competition sets in: When a positive inversion is reached, avalanches of light waves may be formed. That means, a light wave impinging on an excited atom forces the latter to enhance this wave. This process, when continued, leads to the avalanche. There are different kinds of avalanches of different wave lengths that compete with each other. The most efficient avalanche 'wins' and becomes the order parameter of the laser system. This is a wave that is practically infinitely long. Laser action does evolve only if the inversion is kept sufficiently high by means of the electric current. The order parameter then emerges as a macroscopic wave of high amplitude (Phase 2). According to the slaving principle, the order parameter forces the individual atoms to behave in such a way that they maintain its existence, by the mechanism of circular causality (Tschacher & Haken, 2007). Through the ongoing laser process, however, the inversion is continuously depleted: Stronger order parameters entail faster depletion. This can be shown both mathematically as well as empirically when the electric current through the glass tube is suddenly switched off (Phase 3). This fast depletion of inversion is achieved by the coordinated action of the atoms of the gas. In other words, depletion is achieved by the action of the order parameter until, eventually, the resting state of all atoms is again realized.

We have now arrived at a picture, that of a transient system, needed to illustrate our approach to embodied cognition. To summarize this process in the laser: By means of a strong enough electric current suddenly a critical, sufficiently high inversion is reached. Then in Phase 1, by means of fluctuations, a competition of initiated patterns sets in. In Phase 2 a coherent wave, the order parameter, emerges. Phase 3 is reached when the coherent wave decays as a consequence of the inversion being lowered by the action of the wave.

2. Embodied cognition, not only computation

In this section we will describe the shift of paradigm that has occurred in cognitive science during recent decades. This shift has resulted in a general focus on the embodiment of most, if not all cognitive acts. In its general form, the concept 'embodied cognition' conveys the idea that cognition must always be viewed in context. A shared conviction has emerged in the cognitive science community as well as in cognitive psychology that one should address more deeply the intrinsic relationship between cognition and its environment. Due to the embodiment perspective, the ecology of cognition deserves more profound and careful investigation.

The increasing appeal of embodiment derives from a confluence of different fields of cognition research. To begin with, there is a continuous line of philosophical thinking, that of phenomenology, which has always emphasized the role of the body for the mind (Heidegger, 1927). Another important origin goes back to the quite distant field of informatics and computer science, which has encountered a large-scale engineering fiasco in the last century: Despite the work of decades, the creation of artificial intelligence (AI) has been largely unsuccessful. The consequence drawn by a majority of AI researchers and cognitive scientists has been to move into the field of embodied agents and robotics (Brooks, 1991; Hoffmann & Pfeifer, this volume). It is widely recognized today that intelligent cognition on the basis of symbol manipulation alone is unattainable; one must therefore regard classical AI as a failed paradigm and contemplate the reasons of its failure (Dreyfus, 1992).

This changing of perspectives in informatics has entailed marked reverberations in cognitive psychology. Why especially in psychology? — in the 1960s, after decades of behaviorism, psychologists were actively searching for a justification to scientifically investigate (again) cognition and thinking. Cognition has attributes that appeared elusive to scientific study (it is a largely subjective phenomenon; unlike physical processes, it is intentional in the sense of Brentano, 1874). In a strictly behaviorist scientific framework, the promise that intelligent and conscious computers would be a reality well before the end of the 20th century (Minsky, cited in Dreyfus, 1992) was perceived as a great relief by psychologists. Their conclusion was that, if even machines can be developed to become thinking machines, it should be well justified to again explore thinking in humans. Important implications followed from this, especially that human cognition should be conceptualized along the lines of *computation*, of computer-like information processing and manipulation of symbols. In the computational framework, these symbols are conceived as (per se) meaningless tokens, as mere stand-ins for items of the outside world, which they represent internally. The methodology to describe (and maybe eventually synthesize) cognition was derived from propositional logic, predicate logic and set theory.

When the classical concept of AI finally failed, however, and the new research program of embodied agents was gradually instantiated (Brooks, 1991), the message for cognitive psychology was modified once more: Psychology likewise developed in the direction of embodied cognition. This road was additionally paved by experimental findings in social psychology, which had shown over the years to what extent social cognition was influenced by motor behavior and posture (e.g., Strack et al., 1988). The conclusion of abandoning pure computation in favor of embodied cognition was supported by a further development: The rise of neurobiology. To a biologist, cognition is a natural product of the body, especially of the activity of neurons. Embodiment is not synonymous with neuroscience; yet the 'decade of the brain' (proclaimed by a US president in 1990 and now entering its 21st year) likely provided an additional boost for the research program of embodied cognition.

3. Embodiment: The ecology of cognition

Our argument in this section will be that, since the metaphor of cognition as computation has been largely abandoned, the concept of cognition (as embodied cognition) needs a new formalism. We think that the framework and principles of synergetics can provide such a new formalism.

To align our proposal with the development of psychology, let us consider Kurt Lewin's topological psychology, an early realization of a dynamical systems theory in psychology (Tschacher & Dauwalder, 1999a; Tschacher, 1997). Lewin (1936) defined the ensemble of all psychologically active variables as 'life space' (*Lebensraum*). Life space consists of a person P together with this person's psychological environment U. Any behavior V (i.e. any reorganization of life space) was regarded as depending on the state of life space itself at a given moment in time, and was described by Lewin simply as a function of P and U:

$$V = f(P,U) \tag{1}$$

Life space is itself embedded in a 'foreign hull' of non-psychological variables (e.g., the architectural environment). This hull comprises the static environmental contribution mentioned in section 1. The explicit consideration of the environment as a set of psychological variables U on the one hand and as a hull of behavior on the other was among the concepts that stimulated the psychological field of ecological psychology (Barker, 1968).

Life space is in itself not a dynamical construct; therefore, a dynamic environmental contribution is needed to understand how change comes about. In psychology this influence is called 'motivational'. Therefore,

Lewin introduced the concept of valence, which imposes a psychological vector field onto life space. Valence consequently became the focal concept in Gibson's (1979) theory of ecological perception (then termed 'affordance'): "...affordances and only the relative availability (or nonavailability) of affordances create selection pressure on the behavior of individual organisms; hence, behavior is regulated with respect to the affordances of the environment of a given animal." (Reed, 1996, p. 18).

Affordances may be conceived of as environmental resources encountered by an agent. Thus, affordances exist as properties of environmental niches, independent of an agent. Reed (1996) rejected the mutualist position that affordances exist only through the interaction of a specific environment with an agent. For example, a barstool affords sitting for most adult humans. It does not afford sitting for an elephant or a human infant simply because they could not realize the chair's affordance, even though it exists. In other words, in the view of ecological psychology, agent and environment are connected by affordances, which are environmental properties. Affordances are simply there to be 'picked up' or utilized. The notion of a pick-up of information constitutes the Gibsonian view of direct perception (Gibson, 1979; Greeno & Moore, 1993). In its emphasis on ecological perception, the notion of a pick-up of information conforms with a Darwinistic, functional view: The functionality of an object, its resourcefulness and *Zuhandenheit* (Heidegger, 1927), are perceived primarily, the 'ontological' object-per-se is represented in second line (if at all).

This ecological perspective can be easily developed towards a unified concept of 'situated cognition' (see Tschacher & Dauwalder, 1999a). But how about embodied cognition? Situatedness and embodiment are closely linked in that they both point to the mechanisms by which variables afford behavior of an agent. Situative and bodily variables both comprise the environment of the agent.

4. A model of embodied cognition

There is agreement in the dynamics community that cognitive pattern is not pre-programmed but is 'soft-assembled' by pattern formation and self-organization (Thelen & Smith, 1994; Tschacher & Dauwalder, 2003). This assumption was introduced into neurocognitive science by synergetics and complexity theory (e.g., Haken, 1996; Kelso, 1995) in continuation of previous cognitive theory in Gestalt psychology, especially by Köhler (1920) and Lewin (1936). The alignment of synergetics and Gestalt psychology was motivated by evident and deep similarities between the properties of dynamical attractors and those of Gestalt perception (e.g. Haken & Stadler, 1990).

The computational paradigm in classical cognitive science has shown an inclination to address 'higher' cognitive functions. Given the developments and problems that we have outlined in the previous section, it was wise to put cognitive theory back on its feet again. Accordingly, dynamics would start in a bottom-up fashion at the sensorimotor level, considering perception-action loops (Clark, 1997) and the ecological embeddings in which these loops occur. Thus cognition can be grounded by an embodied and situated approach. Several of the hotly debated problems consequently appear in a different light: The dynamical view would not investigate 'symbol grounding', but rather the emergence of symbols as pattern formation. The dynamical view would not regard mental representation as primary, but rather how perception-action loops are evoked in their valent environment.

One of us (Tschacher, 1997) has conceptualized agent-environment coupling starting from Lewin's life-space treatment. In this model, self-organizational processes in agent-environment interaction can be illustrated. According to Lewin, temporal progression of behavior takes place 'contemporally', without causal dependence on past or future states of the life space (see equation (1)). Instead, behavioral change was represented in his model by vectors and force fields (the dynamical components of life space), which attach to the objects in life space supplying temporal causation. For our present purposes, we prefer to avoid Lewin's notion of contemporality, and 'dynamise' life space (1) by:

$$\frac{dP}{dt} = f_1(P, U, \nabla) + \varepsilon_t \tag{2}$$

$$\frac{dU}{dt} = f_2(P, U, \nabla) + \varepsilon_t \tag{3}$$

This dynamical and recursive reformulation of (1) is in the spirit of dynamical systems theory. The motivational terms of Lewin's vector psychology are substituted by the differentials (i.e. changes) of agent/person P and environment U. P denotes the state of a person in m-dimensional person space, comprising cognitive and emotional variables needed to describe the person. U denotes the state of the environment in n-dimensional environment space. U contains all further variables that can affect the cognitive and emotional variables of P, such as bodily states of P and objects perceived by P. ∇ is an operator for partial derivatives (to deal with possible inhomogeneities of life space), ε_t stands for stochastic noise. Expressed in Piagetian terminology, (2) addresses the processes of accommodation (i.e. how cognitive schemata adapt to environmental facts), and (3) those of assimilation.

For reasons of simplicity, we assume that the environment U is constant over the time scales that are of interest here, i.e. we focus on a person's accommodation. Equation (3) then collapses into a set of parameters μ, which act as environmental control parameters of the person's change. Note that we thus imply that bodily variables of P are a part of the environment of the person. Consequently, the system (2), (3) can be written as:

$$\frac{dP}{dt} = f_\mu(P, \nabla) + \varepsilon_t \qquad (4)$$

This formulation has significance for the empirical analysis of multivariate time series, e.g. in psychotherapy research. It means that the change of a person is a function of previous states of the person. With some assumptions (ergodicity, linearity) this can be translated to a simpler approach, which is accessible for vector autoregression (VAR) modelling (Tschacher & Ramseyer, 2009).

(4) can be examined by linear stability analysis (see Haken, 1988, p. 46f; Haken & Wunderlin, 1991, p. 219ff) to check the stability of a point attractor, which is given by

$$\frac{dP_0}{dt} = f_\mu(P_0, \nabla) + \varepsilon_t = 0 \qquad (5)$$

P_0 is the state of the person at some stable point induced by environmental (including embodied) constraints μ_0. This stable point attractor in state space is continuously challenged by the fluctuations ε_t, which add small perturbations ∂P to the person's state P_0. Thus, the solution for $\frac{d(P_0 + \partial P)}{dt}$ is required which can be written as

$$\frac{d(P_0)}{dt} + \frac{d(\partial P)}{dt} = f_\mu(P_0 + \partial P, \nabla) \qquad (6)$$

The right hand side of (6) can be expanded in a Taylor series in ∂P: $f_\mu(P_0, \nabla) + l_\mu(P_0, \nabla)\partial P + l_\mu(P_0, \nabla)(\partial P)^2 + \ldots$. The first term of the series is identical to the first term on the left side of (6) and can therefore be eliminated. Squares and higher powers may be neglected if ∂P is very small. Thus, a solvable linearized equation remains where eigenvalues λ_i can be computed. The eigenvalues characterize the stability of a state P_0 of a person.

$$\frac{d(\partial P)}{dt} = l_\mu(P_0, \nabla)\partial P \qquad (7)$$

This formalization shows that attractors in the life space of a person exist and demonstrates, in principle, how they can be found. Such attractors at P_0 may be realized as cognitive schemata or emotional states.

We would generally assume P to consist of a large number of variables. Thus, P_0 denotes a complex, i.e. a very high-dimensional state. Correspondingly, the number of characterizing λ_i would be high. At this point the core of synergetic theory comes to bear, i.e. the mathematical formulation of the 'slaving principle'. Haken (e.g., 1988, p. 48f) demonstrated that the number of degrees of freedom may be drastically reduced. He showed that one or a few variables P_u — those variables with index u that become unstable at critical values of control parameters μ — succeed in entraining and synchronizing all remaining variables. This was described by the examples of section 1. These variables are called the order parameters of the system P. They reduce the dimensionality of P_0 enormously by application of the slaving principle to all stable components of P_0.

We have used the formalization in this section to demonstrate that, building on Lewin's psychological assumptions, the principles of synergetics can be applied to life space, a complex psychological system. Cognitive or emotional attractor states of a person are conceived of as being affected by environmental constraints, including constraints due to bodily variables. Such attractors are therefore examples of embodied cognition. In terms of ecological psychology, the body creates affordances that then shape cognition. The mathematics used here is of course tautological, reflecting predominantly our theoretical assumptions. Tautologies do not prove or disprove hypotheses, but they demonstrate that the frameworks that we have combined — ecological psychology, dynamical systems theory and synergetics — provide a consistent picture for embodied cognition. Ensuingly, it is the task of empirical studies to support the various predictions that result from our theoretical platform.

5. Discussion and implications for empirical work

Efficiency and intentionality

The synergetic model addresses the three phases of a transient system as described in section 1. In Phase 1, the buildup of pattern is initiated. In a competition between components of the system, one of many potential internal states P_u of the person eventually prevails. Hence, which features are specific for the successful component P_u?

Although fluctuations ∂P play a decisive role in the emergence of a stable state of embodied cognition, the resulting P_u, however, is definitely not arbitrary. This can be easily shown in any of the paradigmatic self-organizing systems mentioned in the introduction: When the buildup of pattern in Phase 1 is repeated in different runs of an experiment, the same pattern (i.e. the same order parameter) is generated if the conditions (control parameters and the static environment) are equal (we disregard bistability here, as in clockwise vs. counterclockwise rotation of Bénard cells, because it has no influence on the efficacy of a pattern).

We have proposed previously that those patterns are established which are 'efficient' or 'optimal' (Tschacher, 1997; Tschacher & Haken, 2007; Haken & Tschacher, 2010). This proposal must obviously specify the reference, quasi the 'purpose', of efficiency or optimality: Self-organizing systems show pattern formation *about what*? We have suggested that this reference relates specifically to the control parameters of the system: These are always reduced by the coordinated action. In the case of the laser system, the inversion is continuously depleted by the coordinated laser light (the order parameter): The stronger the order parameter, the faster the depletion. Laser action dies out as soon as the inversion drops below a critical level (Phase 3). Below that level, only incoherent waves and eventually no waves are emitted any more. If, as in many applications of laser physics, continuous laser action is desired, then the depletion of inversion must be counteracted by a continuous electric current.

It is true that the buildup of laser action in Phase 1 is afforded (to use Gibson's terminology) by the electric current that caused the inversion. The depletion of inversion by laser action in Phase 3 is thus the flip-side of Phase 1 buildup, but depletion is of specific interest with respect to efficiency: It gives us a clue that laser action *is about* the reduction of its control parameter. The same dynamics occurs in any self-organizing system: The pattern reduces the free energy influx, which is described by the control parameters, in an efficient and targeted manner.

Why is this meaningful? The aboutness of self-organized action apparently provides us with a physical analog for aboutness in the philosophy of mind: Intentionality (Tschacher, 2009). Intentionality has been proposed as a characterizing property of mental acts, as the distinguishing feature of a process being mental (Brentano, 1874). It is intriguing to consider that material and mental dynamics may not be categorically different with respect to intentional behavior. Hence self-organizing systems may be those physical systems that can mimic intentional behavior of the mind to a certain degree. This is likely the way how the brain can host the mind (this admittedly expressed in dualistic language). Quite evidently, the mind-body problem is concerned here. According to the interpretation suggested by synergetics (Haken, 1996) we may also be dealing with mind and body as identical, like two sides of the same medal, the medal being the order parameter.

Efficient embodied agents

One goal is to understand intelligent behavior, a further goal is to synthesize it. The synthetic goal has been the main entry on the agenda of the Artificial Intelligence (AI) research program, which has come to a standstill in the so-called 'AI winter'. It would be too complicated here to diagnose the reasons that have led AI into this state of affairs. Nevertheless, as indicated above, such explanations can be highly illuminating for understanding intelligent behavior, i.e. both for the philosophy of mind and for psychology.

It is our impression, from a synergetic point of view, that AI has neglected two aspects of intelligence: First, embodiment variables have not been considered as control parameters of cognition; second, the property of intentionality was insufficiently covered in the propositional framework. Let us briefly discuss these two shortcomings. The problem of lacking embodiment has been remedied largely in recent years, at least theoretically (Pfeifer & Scheier, 1999; Tschacher & Dauwalder, 1999b). In the meanwhile, embodied autonomous agents rank high in contemporary robotics research.

We assume that especially the second point needs closer attention. In order to synthesize intelligent agents one must focus on the prerequisites of intentional or intentional-like systems. How can these prerequisites be created? It has proven dysfunctional to prewire intelligent cognition in computational architectures. A complex driven system is needed, in which patterns are allowed to emerge spontaneously; these same patterns must then be used by the system to perceive and categorize events. In other words, perception and action should be engineered in a complementary fashion, as sensorimotor couplings (Jordan, 2003), treating perception and action as a unity described, in terms of synergetics, by a single order parameter. Complexity is a trivial yet necessary further prerequisite for self-organized patterns to emerge: All Darwinistic, competitive processes demand a large number of components upon which selection pressure can be applied. Complexity is a condition for intelligent processes to come to the fore – there can be no intelligence in non-complex circumstances, unless an intelligent agent is already present. Given that intentionality is necessary for autonomous intelligent agents, is embodiment likewise a necessary condition? The only known types of intelligence, i.e. animals, are definitely embodied, suggesting that embodied cognition is required. This is only an induction, not ruling out the feasibility of disembodied intelligence: But neither AI nor metaphysics have as yet provided support for this hypothesis.

References

Barker R. G. (1968). *Ecological psychology.* Stanford: Stanford University Press.

Brentano F. (1874). *Psychologie vom empirischen Standpunkte.* Leipzig: Duncker & Humblot.

Brooks R. A. (1991). Intelligence without representation. *Artificial Intelligence, 47,* 139-59.

Clark A. (1997). *Being there: Putting brain, body, and world together again.* Cambridge: MIT Press.

Dreyfus H. L. (1992) *What computers still can't do. A critique of artificial reason.* Cambridge: MIT Press.

Gibson J. J. (1979). *The ecological approach to visual perception.* Boston: Houghton Mifflin.

Greeno J. G. & Moore J. L. (1993). Situativity and symbols: Response to Vera and Simon. *Cognitive Science, 17,* 49-59.

Haken H. (1977). *Synergetics – An introduction. Nonequilibrium phase-transitions and self-organization in physics, chemistry and biology.* Berlin: Springer.

Haken H. (1985). *Laser light dynamics.* Amsterdam: North-Holland.

Haken H. (1988). *Information and self-organization (A macroscopic approach to complex systems).* Berlin: Springer.

Haken H. (1996). *Principles of brain functioning: A synergetic approach to brain activity, behavior, and cognition.* Berlin: Springer.

Haken H. & Stadler M. (1990). *Synergetics of cognition.* Berlin: Springer.

Haken H. & Wunderlin A. (1991). *Die Selbststrukturierung der Materie.* Braunschweig: Vieweg.

Haken H., Kelso J. A. S., & Bunz H. (1985). A theoretical model of phase transitions in human hand movements. *Biological Cybernetics, 51,* 347-56.

Haken H. & Tschacher W. (2010). A theoretical model of intentionality with an application to neural dynamics. *Mind and Matter, 8,* 7-18.

Heidegger M. (1927). *Sein und Zeit.* Tübingen: Max Niemeyer.

Jordan S. (2003). The embodiment of intentionality. In Tschacher W. & Dauwalder J.-P. (eds.), *The dynamical systems approach to cognition* (pp. 201-28). Singapore: World Scientific.

Kelso J. A. S. (1995). *Dynamic patterns: The self-organization of brain and behavior.* Cambridge: MIT Press.

Köhler W. (1920). *Die physischen Gestalten in Ruhe und in stationärem Zustand.* Braunschweig: Vieweg.

Lewin K. (1936). *Principles of topological psychology.* New York: McGraw-Hill. (German: Grundzüge der topologischen Psychologie. Bern: Huber, 1969).

Pfeifer R. & Scheier C. (1999). *Understanding intelligence.* Cambridge: MIT Press.

Reed E. S. (1996). *Encountering the world: Toward an ecological psychology.* Oxford: Oxford University Press.

Strack F., Martin, L. L., & Stepper S. (1988). Inhibiting and facilitating conditions of the human smile: A nonobtrusive test of the facial feedback hypothesis. *J Pers Soc Psychol, 54,* 768-77.

Thelen E. & Smith L. B. (1994). *A dynamic systems approach to the development of cognition and action.* Cambridge: MIT Press.

Tschacher W. (1997). *Prozessgestalten – Die Anwendung der Selbstorganisationstheorie und der Theorie dynamischer Systeme auf Probleme der Psychologie.* Göttingen: Hogrefe.

Tschacher W. (2009). Intentionality: A naturalization proposal on the basis of complex dynamical systems. *Springer Encyclopedia of Complexity and Systems Science,* 4893-902.

Tschacher W. & Dauwalder J.-P. (1999a). Situated cognition, ecological perception, and synergetics: A novel perspective for cognitive psychology? In Tschacher W. & Dauwalder J.-P. (eds.), *Dynamics, synergetics, autonomous agents* (pp. 83-104). Singapore: World Scientific.

Tschacher W. & Dauwalder J.-P. (eds.)(1999b). *Dynamics, synergetics, autonomous agents*. Singapore: World Scientific.

Tschacher W. & Dauwalder J.-P. (2003). *The dynamical systems approach to cognition*. Singapore: World Scientific.

Tschacher W. & Haken H. (2007). Intentionality in non-equilibrium systems? The functional aspects of self-organized pattern formation. *New Ideas in Psychology, 25*, 1-15.

Tschacher W. & Ramseyer F. (2009). Modeling psychotherapy process by time-series panel analysis (TSPA). *Psychotherapy Research, 19*, 469-81.

Embodied Inference: or "I think therefore I am, if I am what I think"

Karl Friston

Wellcome Trust Centre for Neuroimaging, London,
Institute of Neurology, University College of London, United Kingdom
k.friston@fil.ion.ucl.ac.uk

Introduction

This chapter considers situated and embodied cognition in terms of the free-energy principle. The free-energy formulation starts with the premise that biological agents must actively resist a natural tendency to disorder. It appeals to the idea that agents are essentially inference machines that model their sensorium to make predictions, which action then fulfils. The notion of an inference machine was articulated most clearly by Helmholtz[1] and developed in psychophysics by Gregory[2,3]. The basic premise is that agents, and in particular their brains, entail a model of how their sensory data are generated. Optimization of this model's parameters corresponds to perceptual inference and learning on a moment to moment basis; while optimization of the model *per se* rests on changes in the form or configuration of the phenotype at neurodevelopmental or evolutionary timescales. The free-energy formulation generalises the concept of agents as inference machines and considers each agent as a statistical model of its environmental niche (econiche). In brief, the free-energy principle takes the existence of agents as its starting point and concludes that each phenotype or agent *embodies* an optimal model of its econiche. This optimality is achieved by minimizing free-energy, which bounds the evidence for each agent (model), afforded by sensory interactions with the world. In this sense, each agent distils and embodies causal structure in its local environment. However, the key role of embodiment also emerges in a slightly deeper and more subtle argument: Not only does the agent embody the environment but the environment embodies the agent. This is true in the sense that the physical states of the agent (its internal milieu) are part of the environment. In other words, the statistical model entailed by each agent includes a model of itself as part of that environment. This model rests upon prior expectations about how environmental states unfold over time. Crucially, for an agent to exist, its model must include the prior expectation that its form and internal (embodied) states are contained within some invariant set. This is easy to see by considering the alternative: If the agent (model) entailed prior expectations that it will change irreversibly, then (as an optimal model of itself), it will cease to exist in its present state. Therefore, if the agent (model) exists, it must *a priori* expect to occupy an invariant set of bounded states (cf., homeostasis). Heuristically, if I am a model of my environment and my environment includes me, then I model myself as existing. But I will only exist iff (sic) I am a veridical model of my environment. Put even more simply; "I think therefore I am,[4] iff I am what I think". This tautology is at the heart of the free-energy principle and celebrates the circular causality that underpins much of embodied cognition.

Under this view, each organism represents a hypothesis or model that contains a different set of prior expectations about the environment it inhabits. Interactions with the environment can be seen as hypothesis testing or model optimisation, using the free-energy as a measure of how good its model is. Phenotypes or species that attain a low free-energy (i.e., maximise the evidence for their model) represent optimal solutions in a free-energy or fitness landscape, where exchanges with the environment are consistent with their prior expectations. The characteristic of biological agents is that they *a priori* expect their physical states to possess key invariance properties. These priors are mandated by the very existence of agents and lead naturally to phenomena like homeostasis, and preclude surprising exchanges with the world. It can be seen that the role of prior expectations is crucial in this formulation: If each agent is a hypothesis that includes prior expectations, then these expectations must include the prior that the agent occupies an invariant (attracting) set of physical states. However, this is only a hypothesis, which the agent must test using sensory samples from the environment. Iff its hypothesis is correct, the agent will retain its priors and maintain its states within physiological bounds. This highlights the key role of priors and their intimate relationship to the structural form of phenotypes. It also suggests that simple prior expectations about homeostasis may be heritable and places the free-energy formulation (at least potentially) in an evolutionary setting. These arguments appeal to embodied cognition in that cognition and perception can be regarded as hypothesis testing about the environment in which the agent is situated, and which embodies the agent *per se*.

In summary, embodiment plays a fundamental and bilateral role in the free-energy formulation. On the one hand, agents embody (model) causal structure in the environment. On the other hand, the physical instantiation of this model is embodied in the environment. Only when the two are mutually compatible can the agent exist. This necessarily implies a low free-energy, which bounds the evidence for a model or hypothesis about an agent's milieu. As the long-term average of negative log-evidence is the entropy of an agent's sensory states, these low free-energy solutions implicitly resist a tendency to disorder and enable organisms to violate the second law of thermodynamics.

In what follows, we will go through these arguments in more detail and try to connect them to established theories about perception, cognition and behaviour. This chapter comprises three sections. The first provides a heuristic overview of the free-energy formulation and its conceptual underpinnings. This formulation is inherently mathematical (drawing from statistical physics, dynamical systems and information theory). However, the basic ideas are intuitive and will be presented as such. For more technical readers, formal details (e.g., mathematical equations) can be found in the figures and their legends. In the second section, we examine these ideas in the light of existing theories about how the brain works. In the final section, we will look more closely at the role of prior expectations as policies for negotiating with the environment and try to link policies to itinerancy and related concepts from synergetics.

1. The Free-Energy Principle

In recent years, there has been growing interest in applying free-energy principles to the brain[5], not just in the neuroscience community, where it has caused some puzzlement[6] but from fields as far apart as psychotherapy[7] and social politics[8]. The free-energy principle has been described as a unified brain theory[9] and yet may have broader implications that speak to the way that any biological system interacts with its environment. This section describes the origin of the free-energy formulation, its underlying premises and the implications for how we represent and interact with our world.

The free-energy principle is a simple postulate that has complicated ramifications. It says that self-organising systems (like us) that are at equilibrium with their environment must minimise their free-energy[10]. This postulate is as simple and fundamental as Hamilton's law of Least Action and the celebrated H-theorems in statistical physics. The principle was originally formulated as a computational account of perception that borrows heavily from statistical physics and machine learning. However, it quickly became apparent that its explanatory scope included action and behaviour and was linked to our very existence: In brief, the free-energy principle takes well-known statistical ideas and applies them to deep problems in population (ensemble) dynamics and self-organisation. In applying these ideas, many aspects of our brains, how we perceive and the way we act become understandable as necessary and self-evident attributes of biological systems.

The principle is essentially a mathematical formulation of how adaptive systems (i.e., biological agents, like animals or brains) resist a natural tendency to disorder[11-14]. What follows is a non-mathematical treatment of its motivation and implications. We will see that although the motivation is quite straightforward, the implications are complicated and diverse. This diversity allows the principle to account for many aspects of brain structure and function and lends it the potential to unify different perspectives on how the brain works. In the next section, we will see how the principle can be applied to neuronal systems, as viewed from these perspectives. This section is rather abstract and technical but the next section tries to unpack the basic idea in more familiar terms.

1.1 Resisting a tendency to disorder

The defining characteristic of biological systems is that they maintain their states and form in the face of a constantly changing environment[11-14]. From the point of view of the brain, the environment includes both the external and internal milieu. This maintenance of order is seen at many levels and distinguishes biological from other self-organising systems. Indeed, the physiology of biological systems can be reduced almost entirely to their homeostasis (the maintenance of physiological states within certain bounds[15]). More precisely, the repertoire of physiological and sensory states an organism can be in is limited, where those states define the organism's phenotype. Mathematically, this means that the probability distribution of the agent's (interoceptive and exteroceptive) sensory states must have low entropy. Low entropy just means that there is a high probability that a system will be in one of a small number of states, and a low probability that it will be in the remaining states. Entropy is also the average self-information. Self-information is the 'surprise' or improbability of something happening[16] or, more formally, its negative log-probability. Here, 'a fish out of water' would be in a surprising state (both emotionally and mathematically). Note that both entropy and surprise depend on the agent; what is surprising for one agent (e.g., being out of water) may not be surprising for another. Biological agents must therefore minimise the long-term average of surprise to ensure that their sensory entropy remains low. In other words, biological systems somehow manage to violate the Fluctuation Theorem, which says the entropy of (non-adaptive) systems can fall but the probability of entropy falling vanishes exponentially as the observation time increases[17].

In short, the long-term (distal) imperative, of maintaining states within physiological bounds, translates into a short-term (proximal) suppression of surprise. The sort of surprise we are talking about here is associated with unpredicted or shocking events (e.g., tripping and falling in the street or the death of a loved one). Surprise is not just about the current state (which cannot be changed) but also about the movement or transition from one state to another (which can). This motion can be very complicated and itinerant (wandering) provided it revisits a small set of states (called a global random attractor[18]) that are compatible with survival (e.g., driving a car within a small margin of error). It is this motion or these state-transitions that the free-energy principle optimises.

So far, all we have said is that biological agents must avoid surprises to ensure that their exchanges with the environment remain within bounds. But how do they do this? A system cannot know whether its sensations are surprising or avoid them even if it did know. This is where free-energy comes in: Free-energy is an upper bound on surprise, which means that if agents minimise free-energy they implicitly minimise surprise. Crucially, free-energy can be evaluated because it is a function of two things the agent has access to: its sensory states and a recognition density encoded by its internal states (e.g., neuronal activity and connection strengths). The recognition density is a probability distribution of putative environmental causes of sensory input; i.e., a probabilistic representation of what caused sensations. These causes can range from the presence of an object in the field of view that causes sensory impressions on the eye, to physiological states like blood pressure that cause interoceptive signals. The (variational) free-energy construct was introduced into statistical physics to convert difficult probability density integration problems into easier optimisation problems[19]. It is an information theoretic quantity (like surprise) as opposed to a thermodynamic energy. Variational free-energy has been exploited in machine learning and statistics to solve many inference and learning problems[20-22]. In this setting, surprise is called the (negative) model log-evidence (i.e., the log-probability of getting some sensory data, given it was generated by a particular model). In our case, the model is entailed by the agent. This means minimising surprise is the same as maximising the sensory evidence for a model or agent. In the present context, free-energy provides the answer to a fundamental question: How do self-organising adaptive systems avoid surprising states? They can do this by minimising their free-energy. So what does this involve?

1.2 Action and perception

In brief, agents can suppress free-energy by changing the two things free-energy depends on. They can change sensory input by acting on the world or they can change their recognition density by changing their internal states. This distinction maps nicely onto action and perception. One can understand this in more detail by considering three mathematically equivalent formulations of free-energy (see Fig. 1 and ref [5]; Supplementary material, for a more formal treatment). The free-energy bound on surprise is constructed by simply adding a non-negative term to surprise. This term is a function of the recognition density encoded by the agent's internal states. We will refer to this term as a posterior divergence. Creating the free-energy bound in this way leads to the first formulation:

1.2.1 Free-energy as posterior divergence plus surprise

The posterior divergence is a Kullback-Leibler divergence (cross entropy) and is just the difference between the recognition density and the posterior or conditional density on the causes of sensory signals. This conditional density represents the best possible guess about the true causes. The difference between the two densities is always non-negative and free-energy is therefore an upper bound on surprise. This is the clever part of the free-energy formulation; because minimising free-energy by changing the recognition density (without changing sensory data) reduces the difference, making the recognition density a good approximation to the conditional density and the free-energy a good approximation to surprise. The recognition density is specified by its sufficient statistics, which are the agent's internal states. This means an agent can reduce posterior divergence (i.e. free-energy) by changing its internal states. This is essentially perception and renders an agent's internal states representations of the causes of its sensations.

1.2.2 Free-energy as prior divergence minus accuracy

The second formulation expresses free-energy as prior divergence minus accuracy. In the model comparison literature, prior divergence is called 'complexity'. Complexity is the difference between the recognition density and the prior density on causes encoding beliefs about the state of the world before observing sensory data (this is also known as Bayesian surprise[23]). Accuracy is simply the surprise about sensations expected under the recognition density. This formulation shows that minimising free-energy by changing sensory data (without changing the recognition density) must increase the accuracy of an agent's predictions. In short, the agent will selectively sample the sensory inputs that it expects. This is known as active inference[24]. An intuitive example of this process (when it is raised into consciousness) would be feeling our way in darkness; anticipating what we might touch next and then trying to confirm those expectations. In short, agents can act on the world to minimise free-energy by increasing the accuracy of their predictions through selective sampling of the environment.

1.2.3 Free-energy as expected energy minus entropy

The final formulation expresses free-energy as an expected energy minus entropy. This formulation is important for three reasons. First, it connects the concept of free-energy as used in information theory with homologous concepts used in statistical thermodynamics. Second, it shows that the free-energy can be evaluated by an agent because the expected energy is the surprise about the joint occurrence of sensations and their perceived causes, while the entropy is simply the entropy of its recognition density. Third, it shows that free-energy rests upon a generative model of the world; which is expressed in terms of the joint probability of a sensation and its causes occurring together. This means that an agent must have an implicit generative model of how causes conspire to produce sensory data. It is this model that defines both the nature of the agent and the quality of the free-energy bound on surprise.

1.3 Generative models in the brain

We have just seen that one needs a generative model (denoted by $p(\tilde{s}, \vartheta \mid m)$ in the figures) of how the sensorium is caused to evaluate free-energy. These models combine the likelihood of getting some data, given their causes and prior beliefs about these causes. These models have to explain complicated dynamics on continuous states with hierarchical or deep causal structure. Many biological systems, including the brain, may use models with the form shown in Fig. 2. These are hierarchical dynamic models and provide a very general description of states in the world. They are general in the sense that they allow for cascades or hierarchies of nonlinear dynamics to influence each other. They comprise equations of motion and static nonlinear functions that mediate the influence of one hierarchical level on the next. Crucially, these equations include random fluctuations on the states and their motion, which play the role of observation noise at the sensory level and state-noise at higher levels. These random fluctuations induce uncertainty about states of the world and the parameters of the model. In these models, states are divided into *causal states*, which link states in different hierarchical levels and *hidden states*, which link states over time and lend the model memory. Gaussian assumptions about the random fluctuations furnish the likelihood and (empirical) priors on predicted motion that constitute a probabilistic generative model. These assumptions about random effects are encoded by their (unknown) precision, or inverse variance. See Fig. 2 for details. We will appeal to this sort of model below, when trying to understand how the brain complies with the free-energy principle, in terms of its architecture and dynamics.

In summary, the free-energy induces a probabilistic model of how sensory data are generated and a recognition density on the model's parameters (i.e., sensory causes). Free-energy can only be reduced by changing the recognition density to change conditional expectations about what is sampled or by changing sensory samples (i.e. sensory input) so that they conform to expectations. This corresponds to perception and action respectively. We will see later that minimising free-energy corresponds to minimising prediction errors. It then becomes almost self-evident that biological agents can suppress prediction errors by changing predictions (perception) or what is predicted (action): see Fig. 2. In the next section, we consider the implications of this formulation in light of some key theories about the brain.

K. Friston

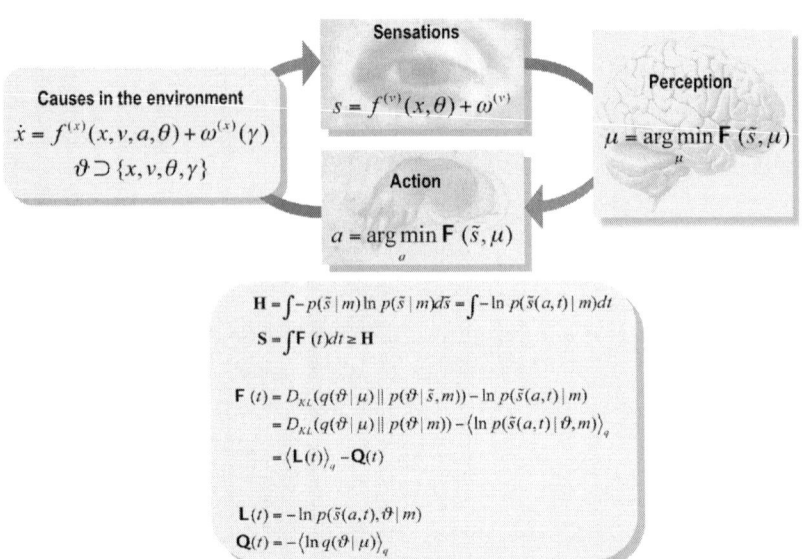

Fig. 1: The free-energy principle. This schematic shows the dependencies among the quantities that define the free-energy of an agent or brain, denoted by m. These include, its internal states μ(t), generalised sensory signals (i.e., position, velocity, acceleration etc.) $\tilde{s}$ (t) = [s, s', s'', ...]^T and action a(t). The environment is described by equations, which specify the motion of its states {x(t), v(t)}. Both internal brain states and action minimise free-energy $F(\tilde{s}, \mu)$, which is a function of sensory input and the internal states. These states encode a recognition density q(ϑ | μ) on the causes $\vartheta \supset \{x, v, \theta, \gamma\}$ of sensory input. These comprise states of the world $u(t) : u \in x, v$ and parameters $\varphi \in \theta, \gamma$ controlling the equations of motion and the amplitude of the random fluctuations $\omega^{(u)} : u \in x, v$ on the hidden states and sensory input. The lower panel provides the key equations behind the free-energy formulation. The first pair says that the path integral of free-energy (free-action; **S**) is an upper bound on the entropy of sensory states, **H**. This entropy is average surprise, which (under ergodic assumptions) is the long-term average or path integral of surprise. The free-energy per se $F(t) := F(\tilde{s}, \mu)$ is then expressed in three ways to show what its minimisation means. The first equality shows that optimising brain states, with respect to the internal states, makes the recognition density an approximate conditional density on the causes of sensory input. Furthermore, it shows that free-energy is an upper bound on surprise. This enables action to avoid surprising sensory encounters. The second equality shows that action can only reduce free-energy by selectively sampling data that are predicted by under the recognition density. The final equality expresses free-energy in terms of an expected energy $L(t)$ based on a generative model and the entropy Q(t) of the recognition density. In this figure, < · >$_q$ denotes expectation or average, under the recognition density and $D_{KL}(\cdot \| \cdot)$ is a non-negative Kullback-Leibler divergence (i.e., difference between two probability densities). In summary, free-energy rests on two probability densities; one that generates sensory samples and their causes, $p(\tilde{s}, \vartheta | m)$ and the recognition density, $q(\vartheta | \mu)$. The first is a probabilistic generative model, whose form is entailed by the agent or brain (denoted by m), while the second represents the best probabilistic estimate of the causes and is encoded by internal states. The free-energy principle states that all quantities that can change (sufficient statistics and action) minimise free-energy.

Fig. 2 (next page): Action and perception. This schematic illustrates the bilateral role of free-energy (i.e., prediction error) in driving action and perception: Action: Acting on the environment by minimising free-energy enforces a sampling of sensory data that is consistent with the current representation (i.e., changing sensations to minimise prediction error). This is because free-energy is a mixture of complexity and accuracy (the second expression for free-energy in Fig. 1). Crucially, action can only affect accuracy. This means the brain will reconfigure its sensory epithelia to sample inputs that are predicted by its representations; in other words, to minimise prediction errors. The equation above action simply states that action performs a gradient decent on (i.e., minimises) free-energy (see ref [10] for details). Perception: Optimizing free-energy by changing the internal states that encode the recognition density makes it an approximate posterior or conditional density on the causes of sensations. This follows because free-energy is surprise plus a Kullback-Leibler divergence between the recognition and conditional densities (the first expression for free-energy in Fig. 1). Because this difference is non-negative, minimising free-energy makes the recognition density an approximate posterior probability. This means the agent implicitly infers or represents the causes of its sensory samples in a Bayes-optimal fashion. At the same time, the free-energy becomes a tight bound on surprise that is minimised through action. The equation above perception simply states that internal states perform a gradient decent on (i.e., minimise) free-energy. This gradient decent is in a moving frame of reference for generalised states and accumulates gradients over time for the parameters (see ref [5] for details). Prediction error: Prediction error is simply the difference between predicted and observed sensory states. The equations show that the free-energy comprises the expected energy L (t), which is effectively the (precision weighted) sum of squared error. This error contains the sensory prediction error and other differences that mediate empirical priors on the motion of hidden states and the parameters. The predictions rest on a generative model of how sensations are caused. These models have to explain complicated dynamics on continuous states with hierarchical or deep causal structure. An example of one such generic model is shown on the right. Generative model: Here $f^{(i,u)} : u \in x, v$ are continuous nonlinear functions of (hidden and causal) states, parameterised by $\theta \subset \vartheta$ at the i-th level of a hierarchical dynamic model. The random fluctuations $\omega^{(u)} : u \in x, v$ play the role of observation noise at the sensory level and state-noise at higher levels. Causal states $v^{(i)} \subset \vartheta$ link hierarchical levels, where the output of one level provides input to the next. Hidden states $x^{(i)} \subset \vartheta$ link dynamics over time and lend the model memory. Gaussian assumptions about the random fluctuations specify the likelihood and furnish empirical priors in terms of predicted motion. These assumptions are encoded by their or precision or inverse variance $\Pi^{(i,u)} : u \in x, v$, which depend on precision parameters $\gamma \subset \vartheta$. The associated message-passing scheme implementing perception is shown in the next figure. In this and subsequent figures, subscripts denote differentiation, D is a temporal derivative operator that acts on generalised states and κ is a large positive constant (see ref [48] for details).

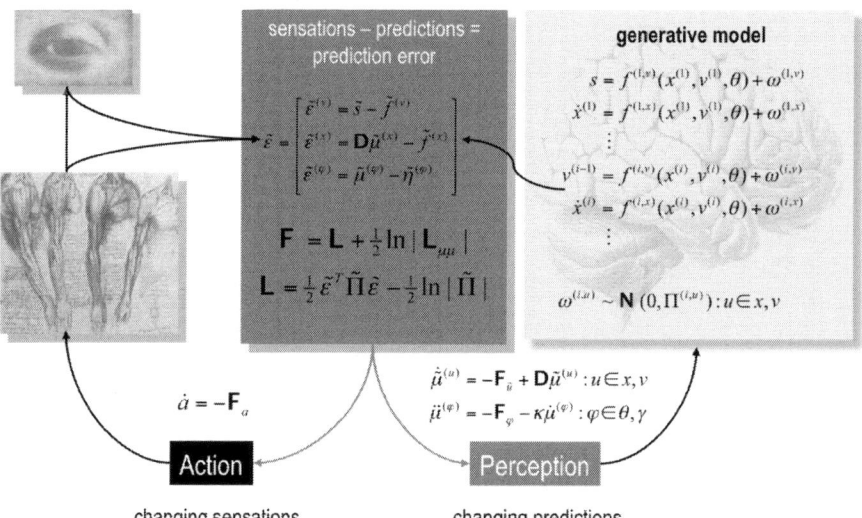

THE BAYESIAN BRAIN AND OTHER THEORIES

This section attempts to place some key brain theories within the free-energy framework, in the hope of identifying common themes. It reprises and extends the review in ref [5]. We will consider a range of theories that derive from both the biological and physical sciences (e.g., neural Darwinism, information theory and optimal control). Crucially, one key theme runs throughout these theories; namely, optimization. Furthermore, if we look closely at what is optimized, the same quantity keeps emerging, namely value, expected reward, expected utility; or its complement: surprise, prediction-error or expected cost. We will see that this quantity is effectively free-energy.

2.1 The Bayesian brain hypothesis

The Bayesian brain hypothesis[25] uses Bayesian probability theory to formulate perception as a constructive process based on internal or generative models. The underlying idea is that the brain has a model of the world[1-3] that it tries to optimise using sensory inputs[28-33]. This idea is related to analysis by synthesis[27] and epistemological automata[26]. In other words, the brain is an inference machine that actively predicts and explains its sensations[1,3,30]. Central to this hypothesis is a probabilistic model that can generate predictions, against which sensory samples are tested to update beliefs about their causes. In Bayesian treatments, this generative model decomposes into the likelihood (the probability of sensory data, given their causes) and a prior (the *a priori* probability of those causes). Perception then becomes the inversion of the likelihood model (mapping from causes to sensations) to access the posterior probability of the causes, given sensory data (mapping from sensations to causes). This inversion is exactly the same as minimising the difference between the recognition and posterior densities (posterior divergence) to suppress free-energy. Indeed, the free-energy formulation was developed to finesse the difficult problem of exact inference by converting it into an easier optimisation problem[19-22]. This has furnished some powerful approximation techniques for model identification and comparison (e.g., variational Bayes or ensemble learning[34]). There are many interesting issues that attend the Bayesian brain hypothesis; we will focus on two.

The first is the form of the generative model and how it manifests in the brain. One criticism of Bayesian treatments is that they ignore the question of how prior beliefs, which are necessary for inference, are formed[32]. However, this criticism disappears under hierarchical generative models, in which the priors themselves are optimised[31,33]. In hierarchical models (cf, the right panel in Fig. 2), causes in one level of a model generate subordinate causes in a lower level, while the sensory data *per se* are generated at the lowest level. Minimising the free-energy of representations effectively optimises empirical priors (i.e., the probability of causes at one level, given those in the level above). Crucially, because empirical priors are linked hierarchically, they are informed by sensory data, enabling the brain to optimise its prior expectations online. This optimisation makes every level in the hierarchy accountable to others, furnishing an internally consistent representation of sensory causes, at multiple levels of description. Not only do hierarchical models have a key role in statistics (e.g., random effects models and parametric empirical Bayes[35,36]), they may also be an important metaphor for the brain, given the hierarchical arrangement of its cortical sensory areas[37-39].

The second issue is the form of the recognition density. This has to be encoded by physical attributes (i.e., internal states) of the brain, such as synaptic activity, efficacy and gain. In general, any density is encoded by its sufficient statistics (for example, the mean and variance of a Gaussian density). The way the brain encodes these statistics places important constraints on the sorts of schemes that underlie recognition. The differences between these schemes can usually be reduced to differences in the form of the recognition density. They range from free-form schemes, which use a vast number of sufficient statistics (e.g., particle filtering[31] and probabilistic population codes[40-43]) to simpler forms, which make stronger assumptions about the shape of the recognition density. These assumptions mean that the recognition density can be encoded with a small number of sufficient statistics. The simplest assumed form is Gaussian, which only requires the conditional mean or expectation. This is also known as the Laplace assumption [44], under which the free-energy reduces to the sum of squared prediction error at each level of the model (in fact, this assumption gives exact inference under some common models, such as factor analysis[45]). Minimising free-energy then corresponds to explaining away the prediction error (Fig. 2). This is known as predictive coding and has become a popular framework for understanding neuronal message-passing among different levels of sensory cortical hierarchies[46]. In this scheme, prediction error units compare conditional expectations with top-down predictions to elaborate a prediction error. This is passed forward to drive the units in the level above that encode conditional expectations and optimise top-down predictions to explain (i.e., reduce) prediction error in the level below. This just means countering excitatory bottom-up inputs to a prediction error neuron with inhibitory synaptic inputs that are driven by top-down predictions. See Fig. 3 and refs [47] and [48] for a detailed discussion. The reciprocal exchange of bottom-up prediction errors and top-down predictions proceeds until prediction error is minimised at all levels and conditional expectations are optimised. This scheme has been invoked to explain many features of early visual responses [46,49] and provides a plausible account of repetition suppression and mismatch responses in electrophysiology[50]. Fig. 4 provides an example of perceptual categorisation that uses this scheme. Message-passing of this sort is consistent with known functional asymmetries in real cortical hierarchies [51], where forward connections (which convey prediction errors) are driving and backwards connections (that model the nonlinear generation of sensory input) show both driving and modulatory characteristics [52]. This asymmetric message-passing is also a characteristic feature of adaptive resonance theory[53,54], which shares formal similarities with predictive coding.

In summary, the theme underlying the Bayesian brain and predictive coding is that the brain is an inference engine that is trying to optimise probabilistic representations of what caused its sensory input. This optimisation can be finessed using a (variational free-energy) bound on surprise. In machine learning and statistics, surprise is known as the (negative) log-evidence or marginal likelihood of some data, given a model. In this sense, the free-energy principle subsumes the Bayesian brain hypothesis and can be implemented by the many schemes considered in this field. Almost invariably, these involve some form of message-passing or belief propagation among brain areas or units. We have focused on one of the simplest schemes, namely predictive coding, which lends itself to a neurobiologically plausible implementation. Furthermore, it allows us to connect to another principled approach to sensory processing, namely information theory:

2.2 The principle of efficient coding

This principle suggests that the brain optimises the mutual information (i.e., mutual predictability) between the sensorium and its internal representation, under constraints on the efficiency of those representations. This line of thinking was articulated by Barlow[55] in terms of a redundancy reduction principle (or principle of efficient coding) and formalised later in terms of the infomax principle[56]. It has been applied in machine learning[57], leading to things like independent component analysis[58], and in neurobiology, to understand the nature of neuronal responses[59-62]. This principle is extremely effective in predicting the empirical characteristics of classical receptive fields[59] and provides a formal explanation for sparse coding[61] and the segregation of processing streams in visual hierarchies[63]. It has been extended to cover dynamics and motion trajectories[64,65] and even used to infer the metabolic constraints on neuronal processing[66]. At its simplest, it says that neuronal activity should encode sensory information in an efficient and parsimonious fashion. It considers the mapping between one set of variables (sensory states) and another (variables representing those states). At first glance, this seems to preclude a probabilistic representation, because this would involve a mapping between sensory states and a probability density. However, the infomax principle can be applied to the sufficient statistics of a recognition density. In this context, the infomax principle suggests that conditional expectations should afford an accurate but parsimonious prediction of sensory signals.

Crucially, the infomax principle is a special case of the free-energy principle, which arises when we ignore uncertainty in probabilistic representations (and when there is no action, see Fig. 5 and ref [5]; supplementary material for mathematical details). This is easy to see by noting that sensory signals are generated by causes. This means it is sufficient to represent the causes to predict these signals. More formally, the infomax principle can be understood in terms of the decomposition of free-energy into complexity and accuracy: Mutual information is optimised when conditional expectations maximise accuracy (or minimise prediction error), while efficiency is assured by minimising complexity (the prior divergence). This ensures that the generative model is not over-parameterised and leads to a parsimonious representation of sensory data that conforms to prior constraints on their causes. It is interesting that advanced model optimisation techniques use free-energy optimisation to eliminate redundant model parameters[67]. This might provide a nice explanation for synaptic pruning and homeostasis in the brain during neurodevelopment[68] and sleep[69].

The infomax principle pertains to a forward mapping from sensory input to representations. How does this relate to optimising generative models, which map from causes to sensory inputs? These perspectives can be reconciled by noting that all recognition schemes based on infomax can be cast as optimising the parameters of a generative model[70]. For example, in sparse coding models[61], the implicit priors posit independent causes that are sampled from a heavy tailed or sparse distribution[48]. The fact that these models predict empirically observed receptive fields so well, suggests that we are endowed with (or acquire) prior expectations that the causes of our sensations are largely independent and sparse.

Bayesian surprise was invoked recently to explain sampling in models of visual search and salience[23]. Bayesian surprise is the difference between the posterior and prior densities on the causes of sensory input and is formally identical to complexity. It is interesting because it appears to contradict the principle of efficient coding; in that maximising Bayesian surprise increases complexity. However, this apparent paradox is resolved easily by noting that any change to the posterior (or recognition) density that increases accuracy will incur a complexity cost and increase Bayesian surprise. However, under the free-energy formulation, Bayesian surprise *per se* is not optimised; it should be *minimised* in the absence of a recognisable stimulus. It might be interesting to test this prediction empirically.

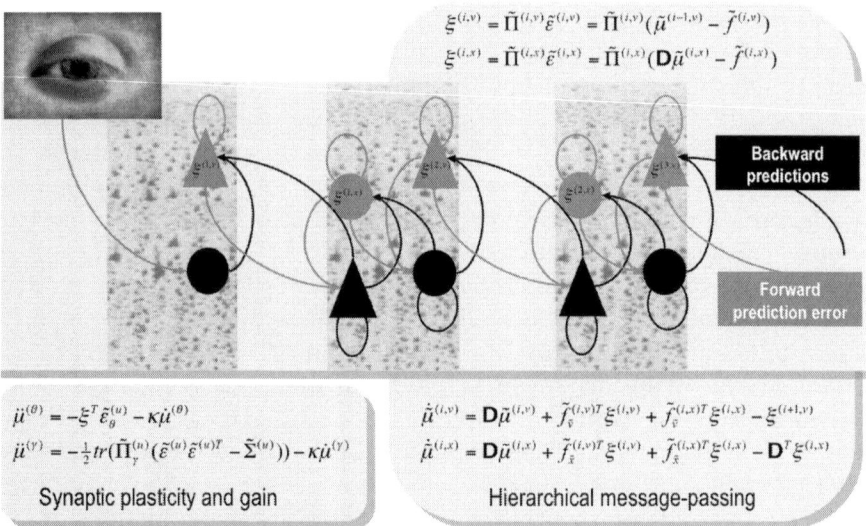

Fig. 3: Hierarchical message-passing in the brain. The schematic details a neuronal architecture that optimises the conditional expectations of causes in hierarchical models of sensory input of the sort illustrated in the previous figure. It shows the putative cells of origin of forward driving connections that convey prediction-error from a lower area to a higher area (grey arrows) and nonlinear backward connections (black arrows) that construct predictions [47]. These predictions try to explain away prediction-error in lower levels. In this scheme, the sources of forward and backward connections are superficial and deep pyramidal cells (triangles) respectively, where state-units are black and error-units are grey. The equations represent a gradient descent on free-energy using the generative model of the previous figure. Predictions and prediction-error: If we assume that neuronal activity encodes the conditional expectation of states, then recognition can be formulated as a gradient descent on free-energy. Under Gaussian assumptions, these recognition dynamics can be expressed compactly in terms of precision weighted prediction-errors $\xi^{(i,u)} : u \in x, v$ on the causal states and motion of hidden states. The ensuing equations suggest two neuronal populations that exchange messages; causal or hidden state-units encoding expected states and error-units encoding prediction-error. Under hierarchical models, error-units receive messages from the state-units in the same level and the level above; whereas state-units are driven by error-units in the same level and the level below. These provide bottom-up messages that drive conditional expectations $\mu^{(i,u)} : u \in x, v$ towards better predictions to explain away prediction-error. These top-down predictions correspond to $f^{(i,u)} : u \in x, v$. This scheme suggests the only connections that link levels are forward connections conveying prediction-error to state-units and reciprocal backward connections that mediate predictions. Note that the prediction errors that are passed forward are weighted by their precision. This tells us that precision may be encoded by the postsynaptic gain or sensitivity of error units, which also has to be optimised: Synaptic plasticity and gain: The corresponding equations for changes in the conditional expectation of the parameters of the model and the precisions of random fluctuations are related to formal models of associative plasticity and reinforcement learning: see refs [48] and [146] for further details.

Fig. 4 (next page): Birdsongs and perceptual categorisation. Left: The generative model of birdsong used in this simulation comprises a Lorenz attractor, whose shape is determined by two causal states (v_1, v_2). Two of the attractor's hidden states are used to modulate the amplitude and frequency of stimuli generated by a synthetic syrinx (an example is shown as a sonogram). The ensuing stimuli were then presented to a synthetic bird to see if it could recover the causal states (v_1, v_2) that categorise the chirp in a two-dimensional perceptual space. This involves minimising free-energy by changing the internal representation ($\mu_1^{(v)}, \mu_2^{(v)}$) of the causes. Examples of this perceptual inference or categorisation are shown on the right. Right: Three simulated songs are shown (upper panels) in sonogram format. Each comprises a series of chirps whose frequency and number fall progressively (from a to c), as a causal state (known as the Raleigh number; v_1 on the left) is decreased. Lower left: This graph depicts the conditional expectations of the causal states, shown as a function of peristimulus time for the three songs. It shows that the causes are identified after about 600 milliseconds with high conditional precision (90% confidence intervals are shown in grey). Lower right: This shows the conditional density on the causes shortly before the end of peristimulus time (i.e., the dotted line in the left panel). The small dots correspond to conditional expectations and the grey areas correspond to the 90% conditional confidence regions. Note that these encompass the true values (large dots) used to generate the songs. These results illustrate the nature of perceptual categorisation under the inference scheme in Fig. 3: Here, recognition corresponds to mapping from a continuously changing and chaotic sensory input to a fixed point in perceptual space.

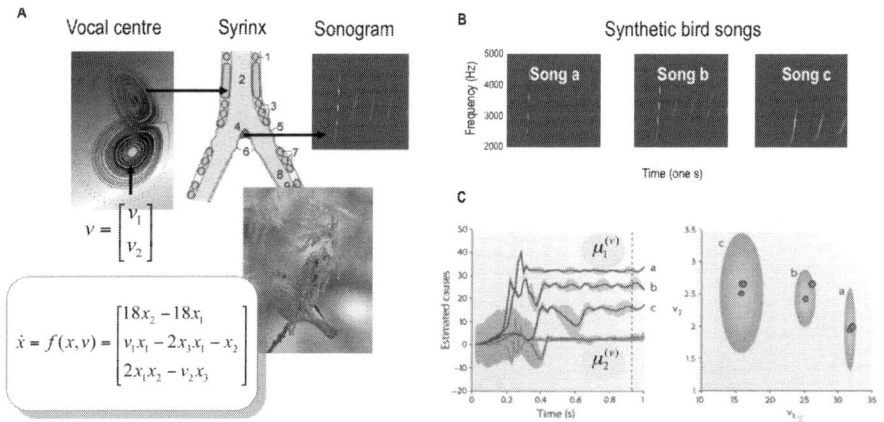

Perceptual inference and categorisation

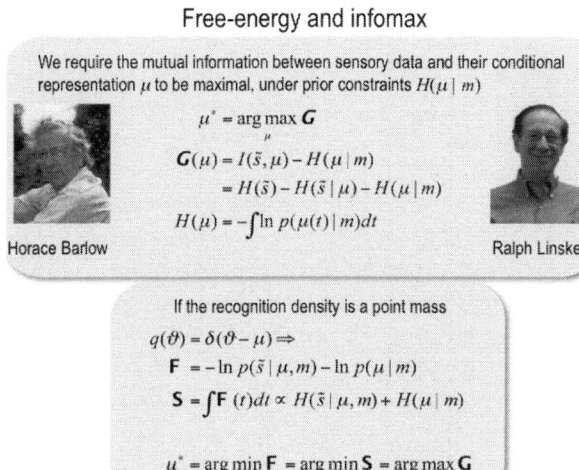

Fig. 5: Free-energy and infomax. This schematic provides the key equalities that show the infomax principle is a special case of the free-energy principle that obtains when we discount uncertainty and represent sensory data with point estimates of their causes. Alternatively, the free-energy is a generalization of the infomax principle that covers probability densities on the unknown causes of data. Horace Barlow and Ralph Linsker are two of the key people behind the principle of efficient coding and infomax.

In summary, the principle of efficient coding says the brain should optimise the mutual information between its sensory signals and some parsimonious neuronal representations. This is the same as optimising the parameters of a generative model to maximise the accuracy of predictions (i.e., to minimise prediction error), under complexity constraints. Both are mandated by the free-energy principle, which can be regarded as a probabilistic generalisation of the Infomax principle (see Fig. 5). We now turn to more biologically inspired ideas about brain function that focus on neuronal dynamics and plasticity. This takes us deeper into neurobiological mechanisms and implementation of theoretical principles above.

2.3 The cell assembly and correlation theory

The cell assembly theory was proposed by Hebb[71] and entails Hebbian — or associative — plasticity, which is a cornerstone of neural network theory and of the empirical study of use-dependent or experience-dependent plasticity[72]. There have been several elaborations of this theory; for example, the correlation theory of von der Malsburg[73,74] and formal refinements to Hebbian plasticity *per se*[75]. The cell assembly theory posits the formation of groups of interconnected neurons through a strengthening of their synaptic connections that depends on correlated pre- and post-synaptic activity; i.e., 'cells that fire together wire together'. This enables the brain to distil statistical regularities from the sensorium. The correlation theory considers the selective enabling of synaptic efficacy and their plasticity (cf. meta-plasticity[76]) by fast synchronous activity induced by different perceptual attributes of the same object (e.g., a red bus in motion). This resolves a putative deficiency of classical plasticity, which cannot ascribe a pre-synaptic input to a particular cause (i.e., redness of the bus)[73]. The correlation theory underpins theoretical treatments of synchronised brain activity and its role in associating or binding attributes to specific objects or causes[74,77]. Another important field that rests upon associative plasticity is the use of attractor networks as models of memory formation and retrieval[78-80]. So how do correlations and associative plasticity figure in the free-energy formulation?

Hitherto, we have considered only inference on states of the world that cause sensory signals, where conditional expectations about states are encoded by synaptic activity. However, the causes covered by the recognition density are not restricted to time-varying states (e.g., the motion of an object in the visual field); they also include time-invariant regularities that endow the world with causal structure (e.g., objects fall with constant acceleration). These regularities are parameters of the generative model and have to be inferred by the brain. The conditional expectations of these parameters may be encoded by synaptic efficacy (these expectations are $\mu^{(\theta)}$ in Fig. 3). Inference on parameters corresponds to optimising connection strengths in the brain; i.e., plasticity that underlines learning. So what form would this learning take? It transpires that a gradient descent on free-energy (i.e., changing connections to reduce free-energy) is formally identical to Hebbian plasticity[33,48] (see Fig. 3). This is because the parameters of the generative model determine how expected states (synaptic activity) are mixed to form predictions. Put simply, when the pre-synaptic predictions and post-synaptic prediction-errors are highly correlated, the connection strength increases, so that predictions can suppress prediction errors more efficiently. Fig. 6 shows a simple example of this sort of sensory learning, using an oddball paradigm to elicit repetition suppression.

In summary, the formation of cell assemblies reflects the encoding of causal regularities. This is just a restatement of cell assembly theory in the context of a specific implementation (predictive coding) of the free-energy principle. It should be acknowledged that the learning rule in predictive coding is really a delta rule, which rests on Hebbian mechanisms; however, Hebb's wider notions of cell assemblies were formulated from a non-statistical perspective. Modern reformulations suggest that both inference on states (i.e., perception) and inference on parameters (i.e., learning) minimise free-energy (i.e., minimise prediction error) and serve to bound surprising exchanges with the world. So what about synchronisation and the selective enabling of synapses?

2.4 Biased competition and attention

To understand what is represented by the modulation of synaptic efficacy — or synaptic gain — we have to consider a third sort of cause in the environment; namely, the amplitude of random fluctuations. Causal regularities encoded by synaptic efficacy control the deterministic evolution of states in the world. However, stochastic or random fluctuations in these states play an important part in generating sensory data. Their amplitude is usually parameterized as precision (i.e., inverse variance) that encodes the reliability of prediction errors. Precision is important, especially in hierarchical schemes, where it controls the relative influence of bottom-up prediction errors and top-down predictions. So how is precision encoded in the brain? In predictive coding, expected precision modulates the amplitude of prediction errors (these expectations are $\mu^{(\gamma)}$ in Fig. 3), so that prediction errors with high precision have a greater impact on units encoding conditional expectations. This means that precision corresponds to the synaptic gain of prediction error units. The most obvious candidates for controlling gain (and implicitly encoding precision) are classical neuromodulators like dopamine and acetylcholine, which provides a nice link to theories of attention and uncertainty[81-83]. Another candidate is fast synchronised pre-synaptic input that lowers effective post-synaptic membrane time constants and increases synchronous gain[84]. This fits comfortably with the correlation theory and speaks to recent ideas about the role of synchronous activity in mediating attentional gain[85,86].

In summary, the optimisation of expected precision in terms of synaptic gain links attention and uncertainty in perception (through balancing top-down and bottom-up effects on inference) to synaptic gain and synchronisation. This link is central to theories of attentional gain and biased competition[86-91], particularly in the context of neuromodulation[92,93]. Clearly, these arguments are heuristic but show how different perspectives can be linked by examining mechanistic theories of neuronal dynamics and plasticity under a unifying framework. Fig. 7 provides a summary of the various neuronal processes that may correspond to optimising conditional expectations about states, parameters and precisions; namely, optimising synaptic activity, efficacy and gain respectively. In cognitive terms, these processes map nicely onto perceptual inference, learning and attention. The theories considered so far have dealt only with perception. However, from the point of view of the free-energy principle, perception just makes free-energy a good proxy for surprise. To actually reduce surprise we need to act. In the next section, we retain a focus on cell assemblies but move to the selection and reinforcement of stimulus-response links.

2.5 Neural Darwinism and value-learning

In the theory of neuronal group selection[94], the emergence of neuronal assemblies or groups is considered in the light of selective pressure. The theory has four elements: Epigenetic mechanisms create a primary repertoire of neuronal connections, which are refined by experience-dependent plasticity to produce a secondary repertoire of neuronal groups. These are selected and maintained through reentrant signalling (the recursive exchange of signals among neuronal groups). As in cell assembly theory, plasticity rests on correlated pre and post-synaptic activity but here it is modulated by value. Value is signalled by ascending neuromodulatory transmitter systems and controls which neuronal groups are selected and which are not. The beauty of neural Darwinism is that it nests selective processes within each other. In other words, it eschews a single unit of selection and exploits the notion of meta-selection (the selection of selective mechanisms; e.g. ref [95]). In this context, value confers adaptive fitness by selecting neuronal groups that meditate adaptive stimulus-stimulus associations and stimulus-response links. The capacity of value to do this is assured by natural selection; in the sense that neuronal systems reporting value are themselves subject to selective pressure.

This theory, particularly value-dependent learning[96], has deep connections with reinforcement learning and related approaches in engineering such as dynamic programming and temporal difference models[97,98] (see below). This is because neuronal systems detecting valuable states reinforce connections to themselves, thereby enabling the brain to label a sensory state as valuable iff it leads to another valuable state. This ensures that agents move through a succession of states that have acquired value to access states (rewards) with genetically specified (innate) value. In short, the brain maximises value, which may be reflected in the discharge of dedicated neuronal systems (e.g., dopaminergic systems[98-102]). So how does this relate to the optimisation of free-energy?

The answer is simple: value is inversely proportional to surprise, in the sense that the probability that a phenotype is in a particular state increases with the value of that state. More formally $V = -\Gamma \ln p(\tilde{s} \mid m)$, where Γ encodes the amplitude of random fluctuations (see ref [5]; supplementary material). This means the adaptive fitness of a phenotype is the negative surprise averaged over all the states it experiences, which is simply its negative entropy. Indeed, the whole point of minimising free-energy (and implicitly entropy) is to ensure agents spend most of their time in a small number of valuable states. In short, that free-energy is (a bound on) the complement of value and its long-term average is (a bound) on the complement of adaptive fitness. But how do agents know what is valuable? In other words, how does one generation tell the next which states have value (i.e., are unsurprising). Value or surprise is determined by the agent's generative model and its implicit expectations — these specify the value of sensory states and, crucially, are heritable. This means prior expectations that are specified epigenetically can prescribe an attractive state. In turn, this enables natural selection to optimise prior expectations and ensure they are consistent with the agent's phenotype. Put simply, valuable states are just states the agent expects to frequent. These expectations are constrained by the form of its generative model, which is specified genetically and fulfilled behaviourally, under active inference. It is important to appreciate that prior expectations include not just what will be sampled from the world but how the world sampled. This means natural selection may equip agents with the prior expectation they will explore their environment, until attractive states are encountered. We will look at this more closely in the next section, where priors on motion through state-space are cast in terms of policies in reinforcement learning.

In summary, neuronal group selection rests on value, which depends on prior expectations about what agents expect to encounter. These expectations are sensitive to selective pressure at an evolutionary timescale and are fulfilled as action minimises free-energy. Both Neural Darwinism and the free-energy principle try to understand somatic changes in an individual in the context of evolution: Neuronal Darwinism appeals to selective processes, while the free-energy formulation considers the optimisation of ensemble or population dynamics in terms of entropy and surprise. The key theme that emerges here is that (heritable) prior expectations can label things as innately valuable (unsurprising); but how does labelling states lead to adaptive behaviour? In the final section, we return to reinforcement learning and related formulations of action that try to explain adaptive behaviour in terms of policies and cost-functions.

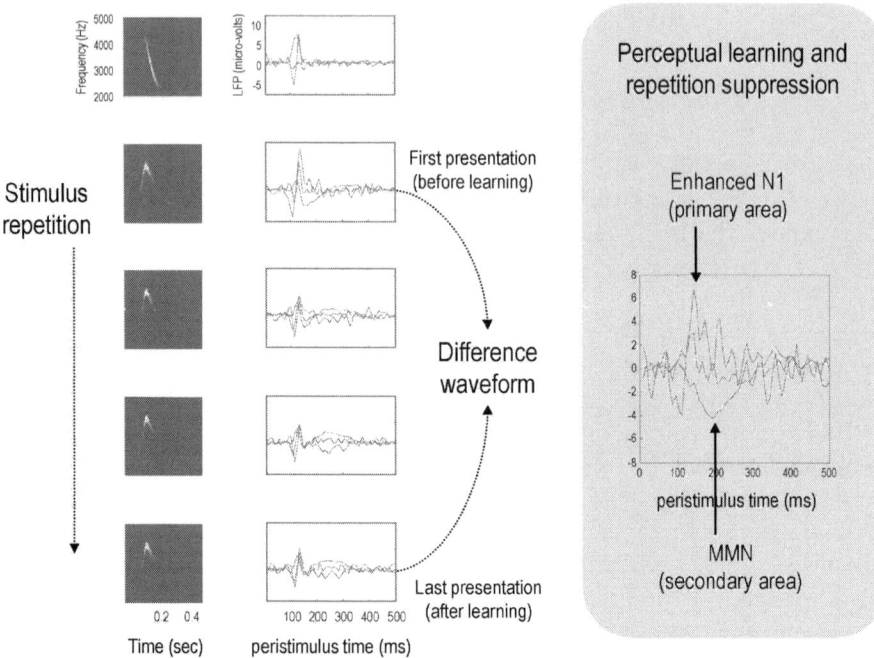

fig. 6: A demonstration of perceptual learning. This figure shows the results of a simulated roving oddball paradigm, in which a stimulus is changed sporadically to elicit an oddball (i.e., deviant) response. The stimuli used here are chirps of the same sort as those used in Fig. 4. Left panels: The left column shows the percepts elicited in sonogram format. These are simply the predictions of sensory input, based on their inferred causes (i.e., the expectations about hidden states). The right column shows the evolution of prediction error at the first (dotted lines) and second (solid line) levels of a simple linear convolution model (in which a causal state produces time-dependent amplitude and frequency modulations). The results are shown for one learned chirp (top graph) and the first four responses to a new chirp (lower graphs). The new chirp was generated by changing the parameters of the underlying equations of motion. It can be seen that following the first oddball stimulus, the prediction errors show repetition suppression (i.e., the amplitudes of the traces get smaller). This is due to learning the model parameters over trials (see synaptic plasticity and gain in Fig. 3). Of particular interest is the difference in responses to the first and last presentations of the new stimulus: these correspond to the deviant and standard responses, respectively. Right panel: This shows the difference between standard and oddball responses, with an enhanced negativity at the first level early in peristimulus time (dotted lines for inferred amplitude and frequency), and a later negativity at the higher or second level (solid line for the causal state). These differences could correspond to phenomena like enhanced N1 effects and the mismatch negativity (MMN) found in empirical difference waveforms. Note that superficial pyramidal cells (see Fig. 3) dominate event related potentials and that these cells may encode prediction error[47,146].

Embodied Inference: or "I think therefore I am, if I am what I think"

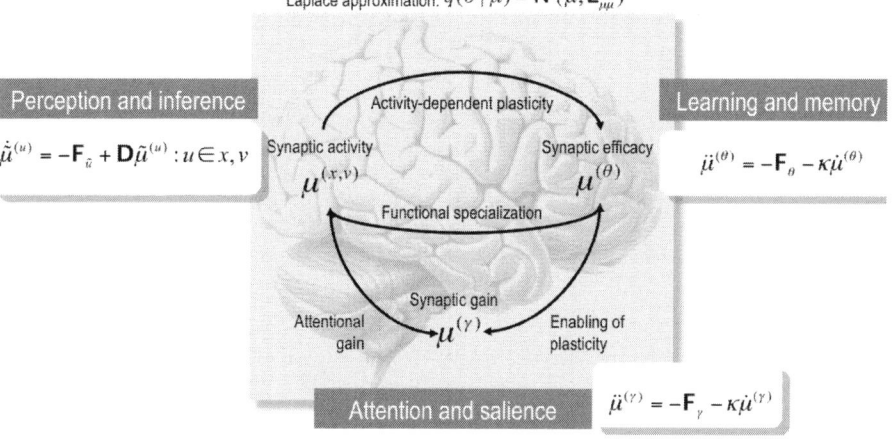

Fig. 7: The recognition density and its sufficient statistics. This schematic maps free-energy optimisation of the recognition density to putative processes in the brain: Under the Laplace assumption, the sufficient statistics of the recognition density (encoded by internal states) reduce to the conditional expectations (i.e., means). This is because the conditional precision is the curvature of the energy evaluated at the mean. Optimizing the conditional means of states of the world may correspond to optimising synaptic activity that mediates hierarchical message passing. Optimising the conditional means of parameters encoding causal structure may be implemented by associative mechanisms implementing synaptic plasticity and, finally, optimizing the conditional precisions may correspond to optimising synaptic gain (see Fig. 3).

POLICIES AND PRIORS

So far, we have established a fundamental role for generative models in furnishing a free-energy bound on surprise (or the value of attracting states an agent occupies). We have considered general (hierarchical and dynamic) forms for this model that prescribe predictions about how an agent will move through its state-space: in other words the state-transitions it expects. This expected motion corresponds to a *policy* that action is enslaved to pursue. However, we have not considered the form of this policy; i.e., the form of the equations of motion. In this section, we will look at universal forms for policies that define an agent's generative model. Because policies are framed in terms of equations of motion they manifest as (empirical) priors on the state-transitions an agent expects to make. This means that policies and priors are the same thing (under active inference) and both rest on the form of generative models embodied by agents. We first consider universal forms based on optimal control theory and reinforcement learning. These policies use an explicit representation of value to guide motion, under simplifying assumptions about state-transitions. Although useful heuristics these policies do not generalise to dynamical settings. This is because they only lead to fixed (low-cost) states (i.e., fixed-point attractors). Although this is fine for plant control in engineering or psychology experiments with paradigmatic end-points, fixed-point policies are not viable solutions for real agents (unless they aspire to be petrified or dead). We will then move on to wandering or itinerant policies that lead to invariant sets of attracting states. Itinerant policies may offer universal policies and implicitly, universal forms for generative models.

From the previous section, policies (equations of motion in Fig. 2) have to satisfy constraints that are hereditable. In other words, they have to be elaborated given only sparsely encoded information about what states are innately attractive or costly, given the nature of the agent's phenotype. We will accommodate this with the notion of cost-functions. Cost-functions can be thought of as standing in for the genetic specification of attractive states but they also allow us to connect to another important perspective on policies from engineering and behavioural economics:

3.1 Optimal control and Game Theory

Value is central to theories of brain function that are based on reinforcement learning and optimum control. The basic notion that underpins these treatments is that the brain optimises value, which is expected reward or utility (or its complement, expected loss or cost). This is seen in behavioural psychology as reinforcement learning[103], in computational neuroscience and machine-learning, as variants of dynamic programming such as temporal difference learning[104-106], and in economics, as expected utility theory[107]. The notion of an expected reward or cost is crucial here; it is the cost expected over future states, given a particular policy that prescribes action or choices. A policy specifies the states an agent will move to from any given state (or motion through state-space in continuous time). This policy has to access sparse rewarding states given only a cost-function, which labels states as costly or not. The problem of optimising the policy is formalised in optimal control theory as the Bellman equation and its variants [104], which expresses value as a function of the optimal policy and a cost-function. If one can solve the Bellman equation, one can associate each sensory state with a value and optimise the policy by ensuring the next state is the most valuable of the available states. In general, it is impossible to solve the Bellman equation exactly but a number of approximations exist, ranging from simple Rescorla-Wagner models[103] to more comprehensive formulations like Q-learning[105]. Cost also has a key role in Bayesian decision theory, where optimal decisions minimise expected cost, not over time but in the context of uncertainty about outcomes; this is central to optimal decision (game) theory and behavioural economics[107-109].

So what does free-energy bring to the table? If value is inversely proportional to surprise (see above), then free-energy is (an upper bound on) expected future cost. This makes sense, because optimal control theory assumes that action minimises expected cost, whereas the free-energy principle states that it minimises free-energy. Furthermore, the dynamical perspective provides a mechanistic insight into how policies are specified in the brain: Under the Principle of Optimality[104] cost is the rate of change of value, which depends on changes in sensory states. This suggests that optimal policies can be prescribed by prior expectations about the motion of sensory states. Put simply, if priors induce a fixed-point attractor, when the states arrive at the fixed point, value will stop changing and cost will be minimised. A simple example is shown in Fig. 8, in which a cued arm movement is simulated using only prior expectations that the arm will be drawn to a fixed point (the target). This figure illustrates how computational motor control[110-114] can be formulated in terms of priors and the suppression of sensory prediction errors[115]. More generally, it shows how rewards and goals can be considered as prior expectations that action is obliged to fulfil[24] (see also ref [116]).

However, fixed-point policies based on maximising value (minimising surprise) explicitly are flawed in two respects. First, they lead to fixed-point attractors, which are not viable solutions for agents immersed in environments with autonomous and dissipative dynamics. The second and slightly more subtle problem with optimal control and its ethological variants is that they assume the existence of a policy (flow though state-space) that always increases value. Mathematically, this assumes value is 'Lyapunov function' of the policy. Unfortunately, these policies do not necessarily exist. Technically, value is proportional to (log) eigensolution to the Fokker-Planck equation describing the density dynamics of an infinite number of agents pursuing the same policy under random fluctuations. This eigensolution is the equilibrium density and is a function of the policy. However, this does not imply that the policy or flow always increases value: According to the Helmholtz decomposition (also known as the fundamental lemma of vector calculus) flow can always be decomposed into two components: an irrotational (curl-free) flow and a solenoidal (divergence-free) flow. When these components are orthogonal it is relatively easy to show that value is a Lyapunov function of the flow. However, there is no lemma or requirement for this orthogonality to exist and the Principle of Optimality[104] is not guaranteed. In summary, although value can (in principle) be derived from the policy, the policy cannot (in general) be derived from the flow. So where does that leave us in a search for universal policies? We turn for an answer to itinerant policies that are emerging as a new perspective on behaviour and purposeful self-organisation.

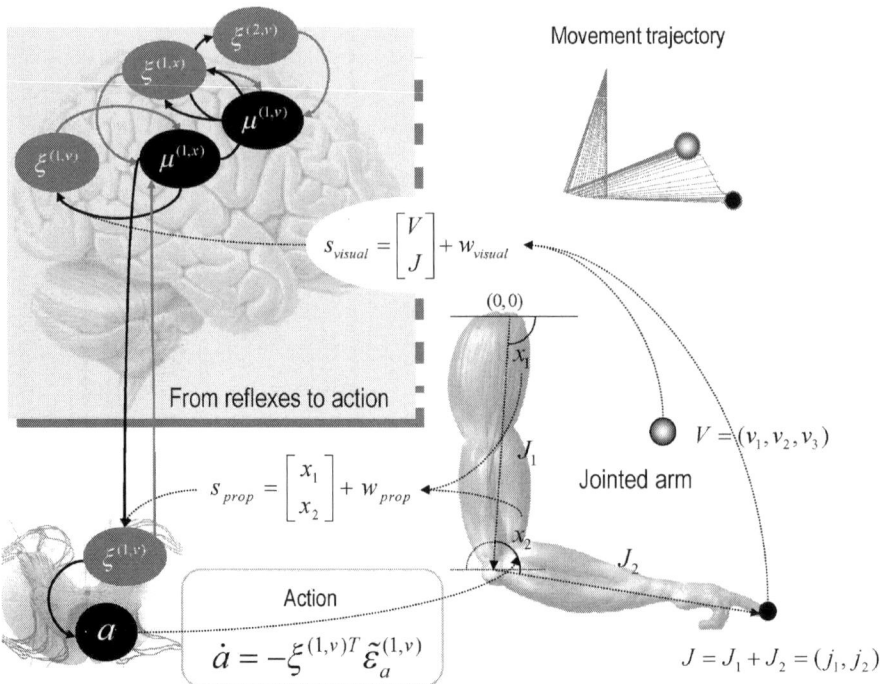

Fig. 8: A demonstration of cued-reaching movements. Lower right: motor plant, comprising a two-jointed arm with two hidden states, each of which corresponds to the angular position of joints. The position of the finger (black circle) is the sum of the vectors describing the location of each joint. Here, causal states in the world are the position and brightness of the target (grey sphere). The arm obeys Newtonian mechanics, specified in terms of angular inertia and friction. Left: The brain senses hidden states directly in terms of proprioceptive input (s_{prop}) that signals the angular positions (x_1, x_2) of the joints and indirectly, through seeing the location of the finger in space (j_1, j_2). In addition, the agent senses the target location (v_1, v_2) and brightness (v_3) through visual input (s_{visual}). Sensory prediction errors are passed to higher brain levels to optimise the conditional expectations of hidden states (i.e., the angular position of the joints) and causal (i.e., target) states. The ensuing predictions are sent back to suppress sensory prediction errors. At the same time, sensory prediction errors are also trying to suppress themselves by changing sensory input through action. The grey and black lines denote reciprocal message-passing among neuronal populations that encode prediction error and conditional expectations; this architecture is the same as that depicted in Fig. 3. The descending black line represents motor control signals (predictions) from sensory state-units. The agent's generative model includes priors on the motion of hidden states that effectively engage an invisible spring between the finger and target (when the target is illuminated). This induces a prior expectation that the finger will be drawn to the target, when cued appropriately. Insert (upper right): The ensuing movement trajectory caused by action. The black circles indicate the initial and final positions of the finger, which reaches the target (grey ball) quickly and smoothly.

3.2 Itinerant policies

This subsection considers attractive states that are not fixed-points but bounded sets that arise from itinerant (wandering or searching) dynamics. This speaks to optimising space-filling attractors that ensure low-cost equilibria. The importance of itinerancy has been articulated many times in the past (see ref [117]), particularly from the perspective of computation and autonomy (with a focus on Milnor attractors[118]). It has also been considered formally in relation to cognition (with a focus on attractor relics, ghosts or ruins[119]) and implicitly in ethology[120]. The ethological perspective is useful here because it suggests that some species are equipped with prior expectations that they will engage in exploratory or social play. For example, 'rough and tumble play' may be a fundamental form of play comprising a unique set of behaviours that can be distinguished from aggression and other childhood activities. Tani et al. [121] consider itinerant dynamics in terms of bifurcation parameters that generate multiple goal-directed actions on the behavioural side, and optimization of the same parameters when recognizing actions. They provide a series of elegant robotic simulations to show generalization by learning with this scheme. See also ref [122] for interesting simulations of itinerant exploration, using just prediction errors on sensory samples over time.

Although there may not be a universal form for itinerant policies, the principles upon which they are based may be universal. One principle (which we focus on here) is the vitiation or destruction of costly attractors. This idea appears in several guises and has found important applications in a number of domains. For example, it is closely related to the notion of autopoiesis and self-organisation in situated (embodied) cognition[123]. It is formally related to the destruction of gradients in synergetic treatments of intentionality[124]. Mathematically, it is finding a powerful application to universal optimisation schemes[125] and in models of perceptual categorization[126]. The dynamical phenomena, upon which these schemes rest, involve an itinerant wandering through state-space along heteroclinic channels (orbits connecting different fixed-points). Crucially, these attracting sets are weak (Milnor) attractors or attractor ruins that expel the state until it finds the next weak attractor or ruin. The result is a sequence of transitions through state-space that, in some instances, can be stable and repeating. The resulting stable heteroclinic channels have already been proposed as a metaphor for neuronal dynamics and underlying cognitive processing[127]. Furthermore, the notion of Milnor or ruined attractors underlies much of the technical and cognitive literature on itinerant dynamics. For example, Tyukin et al. [126] can explain "a range of phenomena in biological vision, such as mental rotation, visual search, and the presence of multiple time scales in adaptation" using the concept of weakly attracting sets.

To illustrate itinerant policies we will focus on the simplest of examples: An examination of the density dynamics, upon which the free-energy principle is based, suggests it is sufficient to keep moving until an *a priori* attractor is encountered (see ref [5]; supplementary material). This entails destroying unexpected (costly) fixed-points in the environment by making them unstable (like shifting to a new position when sitting uncomfortably). Mathematically, this reduces to adopting a policy that ensures a positive divergence in costly states (intuitively, this is like moving through a liquid with negative viscosity). Fig. 9 illustrates a solution to the classical mountain car problem using a simple prior that induces this sort of policy. This prior is on the motion of (i.e., changes in) states and enforces exploration until an attractive state is found. Priors of this sort may provide a principled way to understand the exploration-exploitation trade-off[128-130] and related issues in evolutionary biology [131]. The implicit use of priors to induce dynamical instability (i.e., autovitiation) also provides a key connection to dynamical systems theory approaches to the brain that emphasise the importance of itinerant dynamics, metastability, self-organised criticality and winner-less competition[127,132-139], which play a key role in synergetic and autopoietic accounts of adaptive behaviour[13,122,124].

The mountain car example (Fig. 9) provides a fairly abstract example of a very simple (if effective) itinerant policy. It may help to consider formally related policies in simple organisms whose genetic and cellular mechanisms are well understood: The bacterium Escherichia coli (E. coli) is an organism of choice for unravelling biochemical pathways, deciphering the genetic code and studying the molecular biology of behaviour[140,141]. E. coli is propelled in aqueous media by long thin helical filaments, each driven by a reversible rotary engine at its base. As peritrichous bacteria they alternately swim and tumble (thrash about with little forward progress), elaborating a random walk; with relatively straight swims interrupted by tumbles that reorient the bacterium. Bacteria such as E. coli cannot choose the direction in which they swim and are unable to swim in a straight line for more than a few seconds due to rotational diffusion. Given these limitations, it is remarkable that they can direct their motion to high concentrations of attractants (i.e., chemotaxis). If the bacterium senses that it is moving in the right direction (towards an attractant), it will keep swimming in a straight line for a longer time before tumbling. If it is moving in the wrong direction, it will tumble sooner and try a new direction. In short, by selective modulation of tumbling frequency, these bacteria show chemotaxis[140]. This is a nice example of an itinerant policy based on the prior expectation (endowed by natural selection) that the organism will only change its motion through state-space when it encounters unexpected (costly) generalised states (here, a decease in the concentration of attractants).

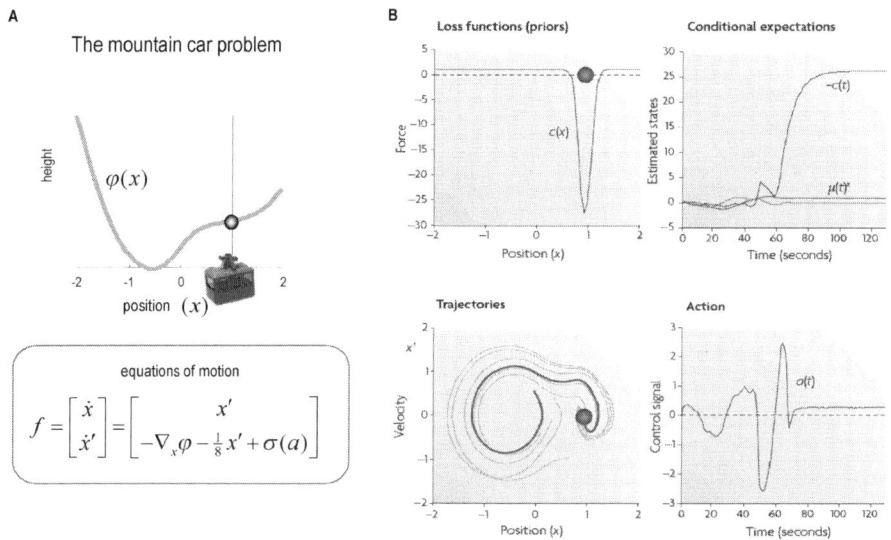

Fig. 9: Active inference and behavior. Solving the mountain car problem with prior expectations. This example shows how paradoxical but adaptive behaviour (e.g. moving away from a target to secure it later) emerges from simple priors on the motion of hidden states in the world. Panel A shows the landscape or potential energy function (with a minimum at $x = -0.5$) that exerts forces on the car. The car is shown at the target position on the hill at $x = 1$, indicated by the grey ball. The equations of motion of the car are shown below the figure. Crucially, at $x = 0$ the force on the car cannot be overcome by the agent, because a squashing function $-1 \leq \sigma(a) \leq 1$ is applied to action to prevent it being greater than one. This means that the agent can only access the target by starting halfway up the left hill to gain enough momentum to carry it up the other side. Panel B: The results of active inference under priors that destabilise fixed points outside the target domain. The priors are encoded in a cost-function $c(x)$ (lower left), which drives a hidden state corresponding to friction. When friction is negative the car expects to go faster (see ref [5], Supplementary material for details). The inferred hidden states (upper right: position, velocity and negative dissipation) show that the car explores its landscape until it encounters the target. At this point friction increases dramatically to prevent the car from escaping (i.e., falling down the hill). The ensuing trajectory is shown on the upper left. The paler lines provide exemplar trajectories from other trials, with different starting positions. In the real world friction is constant. However, the car expects friction to change with position, thus enforcing exploration or exploitation. These expectations are fulfilled by action (lower right).

In summary, the predictions afforded by generative models of the world oblige action to pursue policies specified in terms of equations of motion through state-space. Fixed-point policies, of the sort found in optimal control and decision (game) theory, start with the notion of cost or utility and try to construct value-functions of states, whose gradients guide the flow. Conversely, the free-energy formulation starts with (a bound on) the value of states, which is specified (via flow) by priors on the motion of hidden environmental states. These priors can incorporate cost-functions to vitiate costly states, leading to itinerant policies. In this view, the problem of finding sparse rewards in the environment is nature's solution to the problem of how to minimise the entropy (average surprise or free-energy) of an agent's states; by ensuring they occupy a limited invariant set of attracting (i.e., rewarding) states. These dynamics rest on the complementary self-construction (autopoiesis) and destruction (autovitiation) of attracting sets, which are mandated by the existence of agents that are at equilibrium with their environment.

DISCUSSION

Although contrived to highlight commonalities, the material reviewed in this chapter suggests that many global theories of brain function can be united under a Helmholtzian perspective on the brain as generative model of the world it inhabits[1,27,2,30]. Notable examples include the integration of the Bayesian brain and computational motor control, the objective functions shared by predictive coding and the infomax principle, hierarchical inference and theories of attention (e.g., biased competition), the embedding of perception in natural selection and the link between optimum control (i.e., reinforcement learning and dynamic programming) and more exotic phenomena in dynamical systems theory (i.e., attractors, winner-less competition and itinerancy). The constant theme in all these theories is that the brain optimises a (free-energy) bound on surprise or its complement, value. This manifests as perception (so as to change predictions), or action (so as to change the sensations that are predicted). Crucially, these predictions depend on prior expectations (that furnish policies), which are optimised at different (somatic and evolutionary) time scales and define what is valuable. See Fig. 10 for a schematic summary of free-energy optimisation at different scales.

What does the free-energy principle portend for the future? If its main contribution is to integrate established theories, then the answer is probably "not a lot". On the other hand, it may provide a framework in which current debates could be resolved; e.g., does dopamine encode reward prediction error or surprise[142,143]. This is particularly important for understanding things like addiction, Parkinson's disease and schizophrenia. Indeed the free-energy formulation has already been used to explain the positive symptoms of schizophrenia (i.e., hallucinations and delusions), in terms of false inference[144]. The free-energy formulation may also provide some new approaches to old problems that might call for a reappraisal of conventional notions (particularly in reinforcement learning and motor control; see the previous section). If the arguments underlying the free-energy principle hold, then the real challenge is to understand how it manifests in the brain. This speaks to a greater appreciation of hierarchical message-passing[47] and the functional role of specific neurons and microcircuits; and the dynamics they support (e.g., what is the relationship between predictive coding, attention and dynamic coordination in the brain?[145]). Beyond neuroscience, many exciting applications in engineering, robotics, embodied cognition and evolutionary biology suggest themselves; although fanciful, it is not difficult to imagine building little free-energy machines that garner and model sensory information (like our children) to maximise the evidence for their own existence.

CONCLUSION

The free-energy principle rests on a fundamental imperative for biological systems; namely, to select exchanges with the environment that ensure their physical states constitute an invariant bounded set. This precludes phase-transitions and underwrites the system's (agent's) longevity. In the introduction, we summarised this as "I think therefore I am, iff I am what I think". In other words, I model myself as embodied in my environment and harvest sensory evidence for that model. If I am what I model, then confirmatory evidence will be available. If I am not, then I will experience things that are incompatible with my (hypothetical) existence. And, after a short period, will cease to exist in my present form.

The implicit duality between 'being' and 'thinking' is not the Cartesian duality that preoccupies philosophers. It is a pragmatic duality between physical states and a probabilistic representation they entail. These entailed constructs are the generative and recognition densities in Figure 1. The free-energy is a functional (function of a function) of these densities and is therefore a function of their sufficient statistics (internal states). In principle, it should be possible to infer the functional form of the free-energy given the action and internal states of any organism. In short, the densities are well-defined (if not necessarily unique) mathematical constructs that are paired with (entailed by) the physical states of an agent. These constructs can be quantified and studied empirically. A simple example here is the duality between neuronal activity as a physiological process and as a conditional expectation about a hidden state of the world. This exemplifies one functional form for the free-energy. To establish that this is the right form, one would need to show that it is minimised by action and perception.

The free-energy perspective does not mean that we get up in the morning and set about minimising our free-energy; any more than E. coli are purposefully trying to minimise prediction error when tumbling through their milieu. We are saying that if biological systems attain equilibrium with their environment, their internal states must entail a generative model of their world, whose free-energy is minimised by action and perception. This is true whether you are an E. coli or an evangelist. Because free-energy is a function of sensations and internal states it is, in essence, an attribute of an embodied inference.

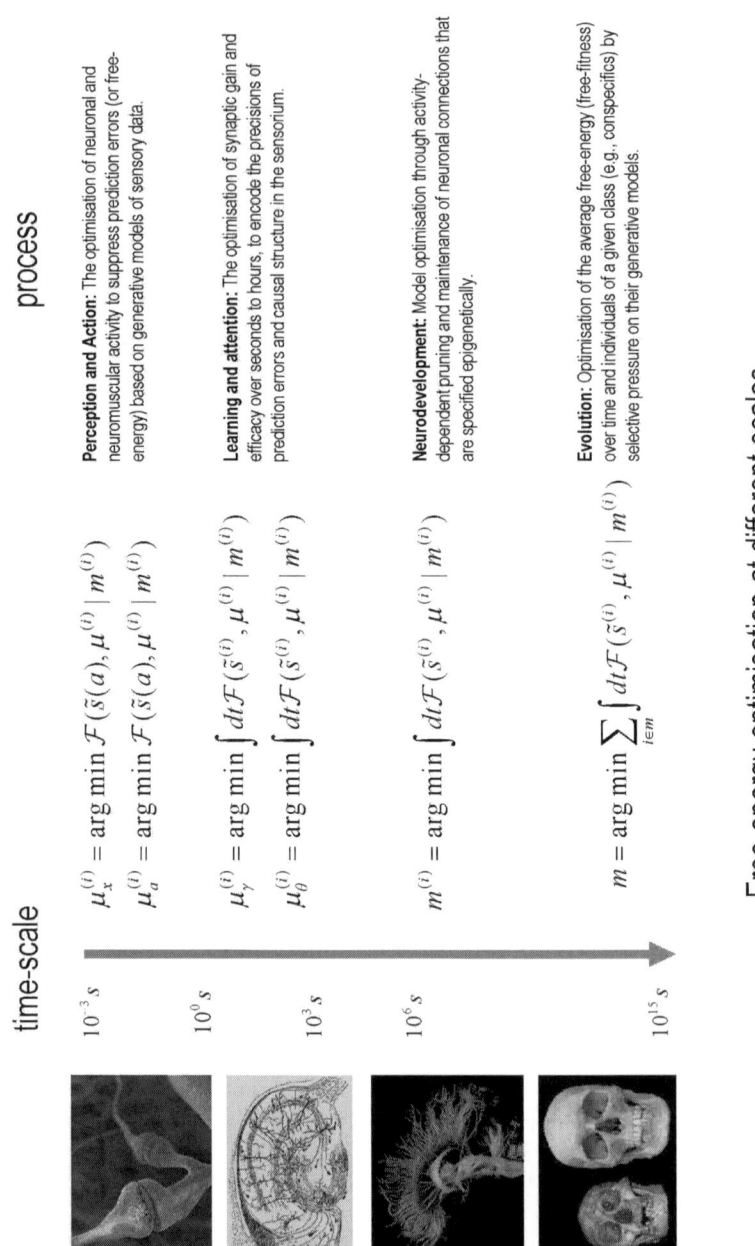

Fig. 10: Optimising free-energy over different time-scales. This schematic summarises the various time-scales over which minimisation of free-energy can be considered as optimising the state (perception), configuration (action), connectivity (learning and attention), anatomy (neuro-development) and the phenotype (evolution) of an agent. Here, F ($\tilde{s}, \mu^{(i)} \mid m^{(i)}$) is the free-energy of the sensory data (and its temporal derivatives) $\tilde{s}(a)$ and states μ of an agent $m^{(i)} \in m$ that belongs to class m, while action a determines the sampling of sensory data. The physical states of the phenotype μ encode an implicit recognition density. In the brain, these representations could correspond to synaptic activity, gain and strength.

Acknowledgments

This work was funded by the Wellcome Trust. I would like to thank my colleagues at the Wellcome trust Centre for Neuroimaging, The Institute of Cognitive Neuroscience and the Gatsby Computational Neuroscience Unit for invaluable collaborations and discussions. I would also like to thank the organisers and participants of the 15th Herbstakademie / Fall Academy: Embodied Cognition and Embodied Communication for insights and discussions.

References

1. Helmholtz H. von (1866). Concerning the perceptions in general. In *Treatise on physiological optics*, vol. III, 3rd edn (translated by J. P. C. Southall 1925 Opt. Soc. Am. Section 26, reprinted New York: Dover, 1962).
2. Gregory R. L. (1968). Perceptual illusions and brain models. *Proc R Soc Lond B, 171*, 179-96.
3. Gregory R. L. (1980). Perceptions as hypotheses. Phil. *Trans R Soc Lond B, 290*, 181-97.
4. Descartes R. (1637/1960). *Discourse on Method and Meditations*. L. J. Lafleur (transl.). New York: The Liberal Arts Press.
5. Friston K. (2010). The free-energy principle: a unified brain theory? *Nat Rev Neurosci, 11*, 127-38.
6. Thornton C. (2010). Some puzzles relating to the free-energy principle: comment on Friston. *Trends Cogn Sci, 14*, 53-4; author reply 54-5.
7. Carhart-Harris R. L. & Friston K. J. (2010). The default-mode, ego-functions and free-energy: A neurobiological account of Freudian ideas. *Brain, 133*, 1265-83.
8. Grist M. (2010). *Changing the Subject*. RSA. www.thesocialbrain.wordpress.com (pp. 74-80).
9. Huang G. (2008). Is this a Unified Theory of the Brain? *New Scientist, 2658*, 30-3.
10. Friston K., Kilner J., & Harrison L. (2006). A free-energy principle for the brain. *J Physiol Paris, 100*, 70-87.
11. Ashby W. R. (1947). Principles of the self-organising dynamic system. *J Gen Psychology, 37*, 125-8.
12. Nicolis G. & Prigogine I. (1977). *Self-organisation in non-equilibrium systems* (p. 24). New York: John Wiley.
13. Haken H. (1983). *Synergetics: An introduction. Non-equilibrium phase transition and self-organisation in physics, chemistry and biology* (3rd ed). Berlin: Springer.
14. Kauffman S. (1993). *The Origins of Order: Self-Organization and Selection in Evolution*. Oxford: Oxford University Press.
15. Bernard C. (1974). *Lectures on the phenomena common to animals and plants*. H. E. Hoff, R. Guillemin, & L. Guillemin (transl.). Springfield: Charles C Thomas.
16. Applebaum D. (2008). *Probability and Information: An Integrated Approach*. Cambridge: Cambridge University Press.
17. Evans D. J. (2003). A non-equilibrium free-energy theorem for deterministic systems. *Molecular Physics, 101*, 1551-4.
18. Crauel H. & Flandoli F. (1994). Attractors for random dynamical systems. *Probab Theory Relat Fields, 100*, 365-93.
19. Feynman R. P. (1972). *Statistical mechanics*. Reading: Benjamin.
20. Hinton G. E. & van Camp D. (1993). Keeping neural networks simple by minimising the description length of weights. *Proceedings of COLT-93* (pp. 5-13).

21. MacKay D. J. C. (1995). Free-energy minimisation algorithm for decoding and cryptoanalysis. *Electronics Letters, 31,* 445-7.
22. Neal R. M. & Hinton G. E. (1998). A view of the EM algorithm that justifies incremental, sparse, and other variants. In M. I. Jordan (ed.). *Learning in Graphical Models* (pp. 355-68). Dordrecht: Kluwer Academic Publishers.
23. Itti L. & Baldi P. (2009). Bayesian Surprise Attracts Human Attention. *Vision Res., 49,* 1295-306.
24. Friston K., Daunizeau J., & Kiebel S. (2009). Active inference or reinforcement learning? *PLoS-ONE, 4,* e6421.
25. Knill D. C. & Pouget A. (2004). The Bayesian brain: the role of uncertainty in neural coding and computation. *Trends Neurosci, 27,* 712-9.
26. MacKay D. M. (1956). The epistemological problem for automata. In C. E. Shannon & J. McCarthy (eds.), *Automata Studies* (pp. 235-51). Princeton: Princeton University Press.
27. Neisser U. (1967). *Cognitive Psychology.* New York: Appleton-Century-Crofts.
28. Ballard D. H., Hinton G. E., & Sejnowski T. J. (1983). Parallel visual computation. *Nature, 306,* 21-6.
29. Kawato M., Hayakawa H., & Inui T. (1993). A forward-inverse optics model of reciprocal connections between visual areas. Network. *Computation in Neural Systems, 4,* 415-22.
30. Dayan P., Hinton G. E., & Neal R. M. (1995). The Helmholtz machine. *Neural Computation, 7,* 889-904.
31. Lee T. S. & Mumford D. (2003). Hierarchical Bayesian inference in the visual cortex. *J Opt Soc Am Opt Image Sc Vis, 20,* 1434-48.
32. Kersten D., Mamassian P., & Yuille A. (2004). Object perception as Bayesian inference. *Annu Rev Psychol, 55,* 271-304.
33. Friston K. J. (2005). A theory of cortical responses. *Philos Trans R Soc Lond B Biol Sci, 360,* 815-36.
34. Beal M. J. (2003). *Variational Algorithms for Approximate Bayesian Inference.* PhD. Thesis, Gatsby Computational Neuroscience Unit, University College London.
35. Efron B. & Morris C. (1973). Stein's estimation rule and its competitors — an empirical Bayes approach. *J Am Statist Assoc, 68,* 117-30.
36. Kass R. E. & Steffey D. (1989). Approximate Bayesian inference in conditionally independent hierarchical models (parametric empirical Bayes models). *J Am Stat Assoc, 407,* 717-26.
37. Zeki S. & Shipp S. (1988). The functional logic of cortical connections. *Nature, 335,* 311-7.
38. Felleman D. J. & Van Essen D. C. (1991). Distributed hierarchical processing in the primate cerebral cortex. *Cerebral Cortex, 1,* 1-47.
39. Mesulam M. M. (1998). From sensation to cognition. *Brain, 121,* 1013-52.
40. Sanger T. (1996). Probability density estimation for the interpretation of neural population codes. *J Neurophysiol, 76,* 2790-3.
41. Zemel R., Dayan P., & Pouget A. (1998). Probabilistic interpretation of population code. *Neural Computat, 10,* 403-30.
42. Paulin M. G. (2005). Evolution of the cerebellum as a neuronal machine for Bayesian state estimation. *J Neural Eng, 2,* 219-34.
43. Ma W. J., Beck J. M., Latham P. E., & Pouget A. (2006). Bayesian inference with probabilistic population codes. *Nat Neurosci, 9,* 1432-8.
44. Friston K., Mattout J., Trujillo-Barreto N., Ashburner J., & Penny W. (2007). Variational free-energy and the Laplace approximation. *Neuroimage, 34,* 220-34.
45. Roweis S. & Ghahramani Z. (1999). A unifying review of linear Gaussian models. *Neural Computation, 11,* 305-45

46. Rao R. P. & Ballard D. H. (1998). Predictive coding in the visual cortex: A functional interpretation of some extra-classical receptive field effects. *Nature Neuroscience, 2,* 79-87.
47. Mumford D. (1992). On the computational architecture of the neocortex. II. The role of cortico-cortical loops. *Biol Cybern, 66,* 241-51.
48. Friston K. (2008). Hierarchical models in the brain. *PLoS Comput Biol, 4,* e1000211.
49. Murray S. O., Kersten D., Olshausen B. A., Schrater P., & Woods D. L. (2002). Shape perception reduces activity in human primary visual cortex. *Proc Natl Acad Sci USA, 99,* 15164-9.
50. Garrido M. I., Kilner J. M., Kiebel S. J., & Friston K. J. (2009). Dynamic causal modeling of the response to frequency deviants. *J Neurophysiol, 101,* 2620-31.
51. Sherman S. M. & Guillery R. W. (1998). On the actions that one nerve cell can have on another: distinguishing "drivers" from "modulators". *Proc Natl Acad Sci USA, 95,* 7121-6.
52. Angelucci A. & Bressloff P. C. (2006). Contribution of feedforward, lateral and feedback connections to the classical receptive field center and extra-classical receptive field surround of primate V1 neurons. *Prog Brain Res, 154,* 93-120.
53. Grossberg S. (2007). Towards a unified theory of neocortex: laminar cortical circuits for vision and cognition. *Prog Brain Res, 165,* 79-104.
54. Grossberg S. & Versace M. (2008). Spikes, synchrony, and attentive learning by laminar thalamocortical circuits. *Brain Res, 1218,* 278-312.
55. Barlow H. (1961). Possible principles underlying the transformations of sensory messages. In W. Rosenblith (ed.). *Sensory Communication* (pp. 217-234). Cambridge: MIT Press.
56. Linsker R. (1990). Perceptual neural organisation: some approaches based on network models and information theory. *Annu Rev Neurosci, 13,* 257-81.
57. Oja E. (1989). Neural networks, principle components, and subspaces. *Int J Neural Systems, 1,* 61-8.
58. Bell A. J. & Sejnowski T. J. (1995). An information maximisation approach to blind separation and blind de-convolution. *Neural computation, 7,* 1129-59.
59. Atick J. J. & Redlich A. N. (1992). What does the retina know about natural scenes? *Neural Computation, 4,* 196-210.
60. Optican L. & Richmond B. J. (1987). Temporal encoding of two-dimensional patterns by single units in primate inferior cortex. II Information theoretic analysis. *J Neurophysiol, 57,* 132-46.
61. Olshausen B. A. & Field D. J. (1996). Emergence of simple-cell receptive field properties by learning a sparse code for natural images. *Nature, 381,* 607-9.
62. Simoncelli E. P. & Olshausen B. A. (2001). Natural image statistics and neural representation. *Annu Rev Neurosci,* 24, 1193-216.
63. Friston K. J. (2000). The labile brain. III. Transients and spatio-temporal receptive fields. *Philos Trans R Soc Lond B Biol Sci, 355,* 253-65.
64. Bialek W., Nemenman I., Tishby N. (2001). Predictability, complexity, and learning. *Neural Comput, 13,* 2409-63.
65. Lewen G. D., Bialek W., & de Ruyter van Steveninck R. R. (2001). Neural coding of naturalistic motion stimuli. *Network, 12,* 317-29.
66. Laughlin S. B. (2001). Efficiency and complexity in neural coding. *Novartis Found Symp, 239,* 177-87
67. Tipping M. E. (2001). Sparse Bayesian learning and the Relevance Vector Machine. *J Machine Learning Research, 1,* 211-44.
68. Paus T., Keshavan M., & Giedd J. N. (2008). Why do many psychiatric disorders emerge during adolescence? *Nat Rev Neurosci, 9,* 947-57.

69. Gilestro G. F., Tononi G., & Cirelli C. (2009). Widespread changes in synaptic markers as a function of sleep and wakefulness in Drosophila. *Science, 324,* 109-12.
70. Roweis S. & Ghahramani Z. (1999). A unifying review of linear Gaussian models. *Neural Computation, 11,* 305-45.
71. Hebb D. O. (1949) *The organization of behaviour.* New York: Wiley.
72. Paulsen O. & Sejnowski T. J. (2000). Natural patterns of activity and long-term synaptic plasticity. *Current opinion in neurobiology, 10,* 172–9.
73. von der Malsburg C. (1981). *The Correlation Theory of Brain Function.* Internal Report 81-2, Dept. of Neurobiology, Max-Planck-Institute for Biophysical Chemistry, Gottingen.
74. Singer W. & Gray C. M. (1995). Visual feature integration and the temporal correlation hypothesis. *Annu Rev Neurosci, 18,* 555-86.
75. Bienenstock E. L., Cooper L. N., & Munro P. W. (1982). Theory for the development of neuron selectivity: orientation specificity and binocular interaction in visual cortex. *J Neurosci, 2,* 32-48.
76. Abraham W. C. & Bear M. F. (1996). Metaplasticity: the plasticity of synaptic plasticity. *Trends Neurosci, 19,* 126-30.
77. Pareti G. & De Palma A. (2004). Does the brain oscillate? The dispute on neuronal synchronization. *Neurol Sci, 5,* 41-7.
78. Leutgeb S., Leutgeb J. K., Moser M. B., & Moser E. I. (2005). Place cells, spatial maps and the population code for memory. *Curr Opin Neurobiol, 15,* 738-46.
79. Durstewitz D. & Seamans J. K. (2006). Beyond bistability: biophysics and temporal dynamics of working memory. *Neuroscience, 139,* 119-33.
80. Anishchenko A. & Treves A. (2006). Autoassociative memory retrieval and spontaneous activity bumps in small-world networks of integrate-and-fire neurons. *J Physiol Paris, 100,* 225-36.
81. Abbott L. F., Varela J. A., Sen K., & Nelson S. B. (1997). Synaptic depression and cortical gain control. *Science, 275,* 220-4.
82. Yu A. J. & Dayan P. (2005). Uncertainty, neuromodulation and attention. *Neuron, 46,* 681-92.
83. Doya K. (2002). Metalearning and neuromodulation. *Neural Netw, 15,* 495-506.
84. Chawla D., Lumer E. D., & Friston K. J. (1999). The relationship between synchronization among neuronal populations and their mean activity levels. *Neural Comput, 11,* 1389-411.
85. Fries P., Womelsdorf T., Oostenveld R., & Desimone R. (2008). The effects of visual stimulation and selective visual attention on rhythmic neuronal synchronization in macaque area V4. *J Neurosci, 28,* 4823-35.
86. Womelsdorf T. & Fries P. (2006). Neuronal coherence during selective attentional processing and sensory-motor integration. *J Physiol Paris, 100,* 182-93.
87. Desimone R. (1996). Neural mechanisms for visual memory and their role in attention. *Proc Natl Acad Sci USA, 93,* 13494-9.
88. Treisman A. (1998). Feature binding, attention and object perception. *Philosophical Transactions of the Royal Society of London Series B, 353,* 1295-306.
89. Maunsell J. H. & Treue S. (2006). Feature-based attention in visual cortex. *Trends in Neuroscience, 29,* 317-22.
90. Spratling M. W. (2008). Predictive-coding as a model of biased competition in visual attention. *Vision Research, 48,* 1391-408.
91. Reynolds J. H. & Heeger D. J. (2009). The normalization model of attention. *Neuron, 61,* 168-85.
92. Schroeder C. E., Mehta A. D., & Foxe J. J. (2001). Determinants and mechanisms of attentional modulation of neural processing. *Front Biosci, 6,* D672-84.

93. Hirayama J., Yoshimoto J., & Ishii S. (2004). Bayesian representation learning in the cortex regulated by acetylcholine. *Neural Netw, 17*, 1391-400.
94. Edelman G. M. (1993). Neural Darwinism: selection and reentrant signaling in higher brain function. *Neuron, 10*, 115-25.
95. Knobloch F. (2001). Altruism and the hypothesis of meta-selection in human evolution. *J Am Acad Psychoanal, 29*, 339-54.
96. Friston K. J., Tononi G., Reeke G. N. Jr, Sporns O., & Edelman G. M. (1994). Value-dependent selection in the brain: simulation in a synthetic neural model. *Neuroscience, 59*, 229-43.
97. Sutton R. S. & Barto A. G. (1981). Toward a modern theory of adaptive networks: expectation and prediction. *Psychol Rev, 88*, 135-70.
98. Montague P. R., Dayan P., Person C., & Sejnowski T. J. (1995). Bee foraging in uncertain environments using predictive Hebbian learning. *Nature, 377*, 725-8.
99. Schultz W. (1998). Predictive reward signal of dopamine neurons. *J Neurophysiol, 80*, 1-27.
100. Daw N. D. & Doya K. (2006). The computational neurobiology of learning and reward. *Curr Opin Neurobiol, 16*, 199-204.
101. Redgrave P. & Gurney K. (2006). The short-latency dopamine signal: A role in discovering novel actions? *Nature Reviews Neuroscience, 7*, 967-75.
102. Berridge K. C. (2007). The debate over dopamine's role in reward: the case for incentive salience. *Psychopharmacology (Berl), 191*, 391-431.
103. Rescorla R. A. & Wagner A. R. (1972). A theory of Pavlovian conditioning: variations in the effectiveness of reinforcement and nonreinforcement. In A. H. Black & W. F. Prokasy (eds.), *Classical Conditioning II: Current Research and Theory* (pp. 64-99). New York: Appleton Century Crofts.
104. Bellman R (1952). On the Theory of Dynamic Programming. *Proceedings of the National Academy, 38*, 716-9.
105. Watkins C. J. C. H. & Dayan P. (1992). Q-learning. *Machine Learning, 8*, 279-92.
106. Todorov E. (2006). Linearly-solvable Markov decision problems. In Scholkopf et al. (eds). *Advances in Neural Information Processing Systems 19* (pp. 1369-76). Cambridge: MIT Press.
107. Camerer C. F. (2003). Behavioural studies of strategic thinking in games. *Trends Cogn Sci, 7*, 225-31.
108. Smith J. M. & Price G. R. (1973). The logic of animal conflict, *Nature, 246*, 15-8.
109. Nash J. (1950). Equilibrium points in n-person games. *Proceedings of the National Academy of Sciences of the United States of America, 36*, 48-9.
110. Wolpert D. M. & Miall R. C. (1996). Forward Models for Physiological Motor Control. *Neural Netw, 9*, 1265-79.
111. Todorov E. & Jordan M. I. (1998). Smoothness maximization along a predefined path accurately predicts the speed profiles of complex arm movements. *J Neurophysiol, 80*, 696-714.
112. Tseng Y. W., Diedrichsen J., Krakauer J. W., Shadmehr R., & Bastian A. J. (2007). Sensory prediction-errors drive cerebellum-dependent adaptation of reaching. *J Neurophysiol, 98*, 54-62.
113. Bays P. M. & Wolpert D. M. (2007). Computational principles of sensorimotor control that minimize uncertainty and variability. *J Physiol, 578*, 387-96.
114. Shadmehr R. & Krakauer J. W. (2008). A computational neuroanatomy for motor control. *Exp Brain Res, 185*, 359-81.
115. Friston K. J., Daunizeau J., Kilner J., & Kiebel S. J. (2010). Action and behaviour: A free-energy formulation. *Biol Cybern, 102*, 227-60.
116. Verschure P. F., Voegtlin T., & Douglas R. J. (2003). Environmentally mediated synergy between perception and behaviour in mobile robots. *Nature, 425*, 620-4.

117. Nara S. (2003). Can potentially useful dynamics to solve complex problems emerge from constrained chaos and/or chaotic itinerancy? *Chaos, 13,* 1110-21.
118. van Leeuwen C. (2008). Chaos breeds autonomy: connectionist design between bias and baby-sitting. *Cogn Process, 9,* 83-92.
119. Gros C. (2009). Cognitive computation with autonomously active neural networks: an emerging field. *Cognitive Computation, 1,* 77-99.
120. Panksepp J., Siviy S., & Normansell L. (1984). The psychobiology of play: theoretical and methodological perspectives. *Neurosci Biobehav Rev., 8,* 465-92.
121. Tani J., Ito M., & Sugita Y. (2004). Self-organization of distributedly represented multiple behavior schemata in a mirror system: reviews of robot experiments using RNNPB. *Neural Networks, 17,* 1273-89.
122. Herrmann J. M., Pawelzik K., & Geisel T. (1999). Self-localization of autonomous robots by hidden representations. *Autonomous Robots, 7,* 31-40.
123. Maturana H. R. & Varela F. (1972). De máquinas y seres vivos. Santiago, Chile: Editorial Universitaria. English version: Autopoiesis: the organization of the living. In H. R. Maturana & F. G. Varela (eds.) (1980). *Autopoiesis and Cognition.* Dordrecht, Netherlands: Reidel
124. Tschacher W. & Haken H. (2007). Intentionality in non-equilibrium systems? The functional aspects of self-organised pattern formation. *New Ideas in Psychology, 25,* 1-15.
125. Tyukin I., van Leeuwen C., & Prokhorov D. (2003). Parameter estimation of sigmoid superpositions: dynamical system approach. *Neural Comput., 15,* 2419-55.
126. Tyukin I., Tyukina T., & van Leeuwen C. (2009). Invariant template matching in systems with spatiotemporal coding: A matter of instability. *Neural Netw, 22,* 425-49.
127. Rabinovich M., Huerta R., & Laurent G. (2008). Neuroscience. Transient dynamics for neural processing. *Science, 321,* 48-50.
128. Cohen J. D., McClure S. M., & Yu A. J. (2007). Should I stay or should I go? How the human brain manages the trade-off between exploitation and exploration. *Philos Trans R Soc Lond B Biol Sci, 362,* 933-42.
129. Ishii S., Yoshida W., & Yoshimoto J. (2002). Control of exploitation-exploration meta-parameter in reinforcement learning. *Neural Netw, 15,* 665-87.
130. Usher M., Cohen J. D., Servan-Schreiber D., Rajkowski J., & Aston-Jones G. (1999). The role of locus coeruleus in the regulation of cognitive performance. *Science, 283,* 549-54.
131. Voigt C. A., Kauffman S., & Wang Z. G. (2000). Rational evolutionary design: the theory of in vitro protein evolution. *Adv Protein Chem, 55,* 79-160.
132. Freeman W. J. (1994). Characterization of state transitions in spatially distributed, chaotic, nonlinear, dynamical systems in cerebral cortex. *Integr Physiol Behav Sci, 29,* 294-306.
133. Tsuda I. (2001). Toward an interpretation of dynamic neural activity in terms of chaotic dynamical systems. *Behav Brain Sci, 24,* 793-810.
134. Jirsa V. K., Friedrich R., Haken H., & Kelso J. A. (1994). A theoretical model of phase transitions in the human brain. *Biol Cybern, 71,* 27-35.
135. Breakspear M. & Stam C. J. (2005). Dynamics of a neural system with a multiscale architecture. *Philos Trans R Soc Lond B Biol Sci, 360,* 1051-74.
136. Bressler S. L & Tognoli E. (2006). Operational principles of neurocognitive networks. *Int J Psychophysiol, 60,* 139-48.
137. Werner G. (2007). Brain dynamics across levels of organization. *J Physiol Paris, 101,* 273-9.

138. Pasquale V., Massobrio P., Bologna L. L., Chiappalone M., & Martinoia S. (2008). Self-organization and neuronal avalanches in networks of dissociated cortical neurons. *Neuroscience, 153*, 1354-69.
139. Kitzbichler M. G., Smith M. L., Christensen S. R., & Bullmore E. (2009). Broadband criticality of human brain network synchronization. *PLoS Comput Biol, 5*, e1000314.
140. Ordaq G. W. & Fields R. B. (1977). A biochemical mechanism for bacterial chemotaxis. *Journal of Theoretical Biology, 68*, 491-500.
141. Berg H. C. (2004). *E. coli in Motion*. Series: *Biological and Medical Physics, Biomedical Engineering XI*. New York: Aip Press.
142. Fiorillo C. D., Tobler P. N., & Schultz W. (2003). Discrete coding of reward probability and uncertainty by dopamine neurons. *Science, 299*, 1898-902.
143. Niv Y., Duff M. O., & Dayan P. (2005). Dopamine, uncertainty and TD learning. *Behav Brain Funct, 1*, 6.
144. Fletcher P. C. & Frith C. D. (2009). Perceiving is believing: a Bayesian approach to explaining the positive symptoms of schizophrenia. *Nat Rev Neurosci, 10*, 48-58.
145. Phillips W. A. & Silverstein S. M. (2003). Convergence of biological and psychological perspectives on cognitive coordination in schizophrenia. *Behav Brain Sci, 26*, 65-82.
146. Friston K. & Kiebel S. (2009). Cortical circuits for perceptual inference. *Neural Netw, 22*, 1093-104.

Section 3

Social Embodiment

Expanding Perspectives: The Interactive Development of Perspective-Taking in Early Childhood

Sanneke de Haan*, Hanne De Jaegher°, Thomas Fuchs*
and Andreas Mayer*

* University of Heidelberg, Department of Phenomenological
Psychopathology and Psychotherapy, Germany
{sanneke.de-haan, thomas.fuchs, andreas.mayer}@med.uni-heidelberg.de
° University of the Basque Country, Department of Logic
and Philosophy of Science, Spain
h.de.jaegher@gmail.com

Introduction

We propose an account of the child's development of perspective-taking as a process of de-centring and expanding perspectives, in which the child gradually learns how its own and the other's perspectives differ and are interrelated. This growing complexity in perspective-taking develops through interactions with the environment in general and with the main caregivers in particular. We take 'perspective' to mean the subjective access to the world, centred in the lived body and mediated by it. The novelty of our approach lies in the proposal that interaction is the 'mechanism of change'.

In a way we offer an alternative account of the development of the capacities that Theory of Mind theory (ToM) aims to explain. ToM-theorists explain the possibility of second-person understanding out of the ability to implicitly or explicitly theorize on a social interaction from a third-person perspective (Bogdan, 1997; Hutto, 2004). Crudely put, the picture of social capacities that arises from ToM-theories resembles a game of battleship: a board game where two people try to localize each other's hidden submarines. They do so by 'dropping bombs' on a coordinate system, at first randomly but gradually, depending on the 'hits,' more precisely. Likewise, we could say that on a ToM-story, one has to guess beneath the surface to infer the hidden mental states of the 'opponent'.

Gallagher and others (Gallagher, 2001, 2008; Hutto, 2004) have extensively criticized this model of social cognition for being neither embodied nor interactive. Gallagher argues that the kinds of situations and capacities that ToM investigates concern only a small segment of our social lives. The explanation and prediction of another person's behaviour in terms of their hidden mental states is something that we might occasionally engage in, but it is not the pervasive form of our social interactions. Rather than regarding primary and secondary intersubjectivity as pre-cursors to the real thing, Gallagher points out that these embodied interactions are primary and pervasive, both developmentally and pragmatically. That is, these ways of understanding develop first and remain central throughout our lives.

In accordance with this viewpoint — that second-person embodied interactions are the pre-requisite for acquiring both a first- and third-person perspective — we propose that perspectives expand from pre-reflective to reflective through interactions.

Describing the child's developmental process as one of de-centring and perspective-taking is a well-established approach. Introduced by Piaget (1928), and taken up by, for instance, Hobson (2002), we in turn want to highlight the embodied and interactive dimension of these processes in the social realm. Our proposal is in line with the enactivist account of social understanding as participatory sense-making (De Jaegher & Di Paolo, 2007; De Jaegher, 2009a,b; Fuchs & De Jaegher, 2009). Here, we elaborate on the developmental side of this account.

In this paper, we have a twofold aim: firstly, we describe the child's social development in terms of expanding perspective-taking (sections I and III), and secondly, we criticize the narrow identification of social capacities with false belief understanding as is commonly done in the ToM tradition (section II).

I. Expanding familiarity with perspectives through interactions

We describe the development of some typical examples of what is generally considered social cognition[1]. We do so in terms of a continuity that ranges from the personal perspective with which each human being comes into the world to the multi-layered, multi-aspect richness of human social interactions. We propose that this development consists in the growing complexity and differentiation of recognising and understanding one's own and others' perspectives. This expansion of perspectives does not happen in separated, clear-cut stages, but simultaneously and through mutual influence. Discovering one's own perspective and that of others are processes that reciprocally constrain and enable each other.

Perspective expansion can be conceived both in terms of the interactions that children engage in as well as in terms of their growing awareness. Interactions become increasingly complex and can offer more and more possibilities for action and further interaction. Awareness begins focused and becomes more and more excentric and thereby enlarges its domain.

---

[1] We prefer not to use the term "social cognition" because it already entails a cognitive bias and connotes a modular approach to the development of social understanding.

More in particular, we discuss a few kinds of interactions that play a role in the development of perspective-taking: the games of peek-a-boo and hide-and-seek (A), joint attention and pointing (B), and triangulation (C). Then we discuss the changing awareness of perspectives that characterises and accompanies these kinds of interactions: awareness of the other, awareness of the relation, and imagining the other's perspective as such (D). Like we said, we do not consider these interactions nor the accompanying changes in awareness as clear-cut phases; they can rather be seen as elements in the child's development, that take place in different periods and with varying intensities. In other words, we highlight some important components of what we consider to be the continuous theme in the child's social development: the expansion of perspective-taking.

A. Peek-a-boo and hide-and-seek

As soon as infants are born, they engage in social interactions; they imitate (Meltzoff & Moore, 1983), they regulate interactions through vocalizing and through (averting) their gazes (Stifter & Moyer, 1990), and participate in 'protoconversations' with their caregivers (Bateson, 1971; Trevarthen, 1977). This comes down to what Trevarthen has termed 'primary intersubjectivity', where infants and caregivers are "mutually regulating one another's interests and feelings in intricate, rhythmic patterns," showing the infant's "active and immediately responsive" sensitivity to his surroundings (Trevarthen & Aitken, 2001).

Within dyadic interactions infants already familiarize themselves with perspectives. Interactions are playgrounds for developing and practicing perspective-taking. This can be most clearly illustrated in games like peek-a-boo and hide-and-seek.

Peek-a-boo and, later on, hide-and-seek are very popular games that can be repeated over and over again, without diminishing the joy and excitement of the infant. These games are interesting for our purpose because they reveal a very early and increasing awareness of the difference between one's own and the other's perspective. Both show a similar structure of staying in contact while interrupting visual communication, indicating that perspectives are not just visual but may involve all the other senses as well: touch, taste, smell, and hearing. To play peek-a-boo, all that is needed is that there is some obstruction between the eyes of the infant and of the other person, whereas in hide-and-seek not only the gaze is interrupted, but also physical proximity and sometimes verbal communication. In peek-a-boo, both the infant and the other can regulate the reunion of the gazes by removing the obstruction, or by moving their heads. In games of hide-and-seek there is a clear division of roles in which it is usually the child that hides and the adult that seeks, but the reverse is also possible.

We argue that both games assume the awareness of the other person's perspective. In the case of hide-and-seek, this is obvious since the ability to hide presupposes the ability to put yourself in the other's position. For instance, the child hides behind the couch because it knows that it is out of daddy's view there when he enters the living room.

Peek-a-boo rests on an even more basic capacity. Infants 'know' early on when someone is looking at them (Reddy, 2003) and are sensitive to the contingency of the interaction. In Murray & Trevarthen's famous double video experiment, infants first communicate with their mothers through a live television link (Murray & Trevarthen, 1986). When they are then shown a recording of the mother's earlier behaviour, they become upset, suggesting that the infants are aware that the interaction with the mother is now not live. More generally, the infants' reactions show their sensitivity to the timing and contingency of the interaction[2].

The excitement of peek-a-boo is that the infant knows that the other person is looking at him without being able to see her gaze directed at him. It is a kind of magic — the other's gaze is gone, but not really — the gaze goes on behind the cloth so to say. Without any visual confirmation the infant senses that the other is not only still present, but also remains directed at him.

Some variations may cause extra excitement: popping up from an unexpected angle, popping up with a silly face, or wearing a hat, etc. But these variations cannot be stretched endlessly: when a different person pops up, the infant is not amused (Parrott & Gleitman, 1989). And of course, in that case, it is not really a game of peek-a-boo anymore: the infant supposes to still be in contact with a specific other while in fact he is not.

To stay in contact is crucial for hide-and-seek too: through the act of seeking, the attention is still directed at the child. Hiding only remains hiding as long as the other person is indeed seeking. If not, there is no real interaction and thus no game going on. The father should be really 'searching': he cannot just do the dishes while the child is hiding and then go straight to the child's favourite hiding place to 'find' it. The thrill for the child is not only whether dad will find him, but also to trust that dad will search for him. Are we really still in contact? To trust in this contact even though one is not only out of direct sight, but even hidden, is the scary element, with the worst-case scenario of being forgotten. To affirm that the contact is still sustained, the seeker will often wonder aloud: I wonder where Amelie could be...?

---

[2] Whether this sensitivity can be relayed to an internal 'contingency detection module' as Gergeley and Watson (1999) propose, or is rather constituted in the interaction process itself is a matter of debate (De Jaegher et al., 2010; De Jaegher, 2010).

Moreover, both games require an attuned timing of the interaction: the time to reappearance or finding should not be too short (for building up the suspense) and not too long either (the child might worry if it is still in contact). This varies not only from child to child, but also depends on age: hide-and-seek is already more of a challenge than peek-a-boo.

From peek-a-boo to hide-and-seek we can already witness an increase in the possibilities for interaction: Interaction can take place without direct visual contact, and even without physical proximity, relying on both the child and the other continually being directed at each other.

How do these forms of interaction enable perspective-taking and growing awareness? In peek-a-boo and hide-and-seek, infants experience and sustain a partially interrupted contact for some time, and thereby sense the other's awareness of themselves outside of immediate contact. Thus, they develop an awareness of the other's perspective as detached from the immediate contact. This is an early form of taking an excentric position in the sense of de-centring from the primal perspectival point, and thus gradually loosening the tie with the here and now.

Peek-a-boo and hide-and-seek are good illustrations of this sensitivity to perspectives, which is also present in other kinds of interactions. Reddy has pointed out that, from the age of two months already, infants "react to attention to self with a variety of emotional reactions" (Reddy, 2003, p. 397). She argues that this is already a form of joint attention, in which the 'object' attended to is the infant himself.

B. Joint attention & pointing

Joint attention is taken as a hallmark of the infant's acknowledgement of the fact that the other person has a perspective of her own. Infants are generally taken to start being able to do this between 9-12 months of age, but whether it is only then that infants start to realise that others have their own perspective is a matter of contention (Reddy, 2003; Racine & Carpendale, 2007). This debate is a good starting point for our purposes. As Racine & Carpendale (2007) point out, divergent approaches to joint attention are possible: it can be conceived minimally as involving little more than simply looking "where someone else is looking" (Butterworth, 1998, p. 171, cited by Racine & Carpendale, 2007), and, at the other extreme, it can be thought to involve the participants' *knowing* that they are sharing attention (Tomasello, 1995). It is the second, more cognitively demanding conception that is at the basis of the idea that joint attention develops at around 12 months.

Here we will, rather than concur with either side of the debate and thereby continue to think in dichotomies, again attempt to capture the continuum. Rather than trying to establish which is 'the true underlying competence', which Racine & Carpenter rightly advise against (Racine &

Carpendale, 2007, p. 8), we will, like they suggest is necessary, attempt to get to grips with the idea that infants pass through different forms of understanding (see also Chapman 1987, cited in Racine & Carpendale, 2007). In order to do this we will, like before, take a phenomenological route.

Simply looking where someone else is looking is too minimal a requirement for joint attention, because there is not necessarily awareness of the jointness. Only when both participants are *aware* that they are looking at this thing can we speak of true joint attention. At the basis of this shift between what could in principle be a merely coincidentally converging attention to being aware of sharing this object of attention lie the interactional activities of emotion and feeling sharing. In experiencing and establishing this, the interaction of gazes, or eye contact, is crucial. For, as Stawarska indicates, referring to Gomez (Stawarska, 2006, p. 19), "in eye contact you not only observe the eyes of the other person but are also checking her attention, while the other person who attends to your eyes is checking your attention as well. In other words, the other is attending to your attention while you are attending to hers".

The joint activity of *pointing* can illuminate how infants develop new possibilities for acting and interacting. They expand their perspectival capacities through and in their ongoing experience of recurring activities that they engage in with others. Pointing develops into a form of joint attention when both infant and caregiver are aware of their shared attention to an object.

Originally, pointing is only a simple, but incomplete grasping movement directed towards a desired object. The child's failed reaching may provoke a helping reaction from the caregiver. Thus, it is exactly by the occurrence of a 'mismatch' that the meaning of the action changes. In the 'thwarting' of a goal, a gap opens up for potential new meaning. The individual reaching movement can then turn into a 'gesture for others'. The meaning of reaching changes, and develops into a new possibility for interacting with the (social) world: pointing. Gradually the child learns to use this new meaning-in-movement, which is also shown by his looking back towards the mother to make sure that she has seen the object as well. As we can see, the intention of pointing does not reside within the child's mind, but emerges as an outcome of their ongoing social interactions. This example shows that intentions may be formed not only individually but arise through participatory sense-making. Meaning and intentions are emergent products of socially embedded interaction, and in many situations they can be viewed as distributed phenomena rather than as individual, private mental acts or properties (De Jaegher, 2009a,b).

A behaviouristic refutation of our interpretation would be Perner's argument that infant pointing follows an associative schema established between his own actions and his mothers' reactions (Perner, 1991). The infant could have learned by conditioning how to successfully control his mother's gaze. We agree with Reddy & Morris (2004) that this kind of argument establishes a dualistic opposition of an exclusively behavioural exterior and an unobservable interior mind, where the mentalistic abilities develop on a separate track, unconnected to a meaningful interaction. This is indeed an undisprovable position, since "any pointing, however complex, and even if performed by adults, could always be seen to have prior associations with people's reactions and reinforcements" (Reddy & Morris, 2004, p. 657).

The only way to solve this problem is to take behaviour as intentional from the very beginning, in line with what phenomenologists and enactivists have argued in detail (Merleau-Ponty, 1945/2002; Scheler, 1954/1923; Thompson, 2007). Reddy & Morris argue that we are in a better position to grant the inherent meaningfulness of behaviour if we as researchers adopt an engaged, second-person approach rather than work as detached third-person observers. Only by engaging with the infant are we able to appreciate the fact that there really is interaction going on, even with very young infants.

Even though this approach cannot be 'proved' either, it is both phenomenologically more justified (experience as explanandum is taken seriously) and more parsimonious. A behaviouristic or mind-reading account has to construct a potentially endless number of 'epicycles' in order to account for, in the first place, the 'labelling problem': How to know which external events to apply the results of the internal mentalisation to? How to connect these results with certain observable behaviours? In order to solve this problem, the cognitivist account needs to postulate extra modules, such as an 'eye-direction-detector' for understanding gazes, or even an 'intentionality detector' (Baron-Cohen, 1995). In sum, if actions were not meaningful in themselves and perceived as embodied, animate and agentive, social understanding would either require an inordinately complicated mechanism, or the capacity would be much more fragile than it is in real life. The approach we put forward here is parsimonious in that meaning is created in the lived experience of connection and disconnection, which is inextricably bound up with the dynamic physicality of interaction (Fuchs & De Jaegher, 2009).

C. Triadic interactions

To date, primary intersubjectivity has mostly been investigated in dyadic interactions. However, already in the first year of life the child also engages in interactions including a third person who is often the father. This expands the possible scope of awareness of perspectives: When a third person witnesses a dyadic interaction, the infant becomes aware of a view on this interaction itself. This triangulation of interaction has recently been investigated, above all, by the Lausanne group of Fivaz-Depeursinge (Fivaz-Depeursinge & Corboz-Warnery, 1999).

Just as in the games of peek-a-boo or hide-and-seek, the third person is present and absent at the same time. The child becomes aware of his interaction with the mother being witnessed by the father who may at first not take part in it. This already opens the enclosed cycle of dyadic interaction where the intensity of the mutual exchange mostly overrides the awareness of the difference of the perspectives. Now there is an additional view from outside, a view on the relation itself — a perspective that is not occupied by mutuality, so to speak. Breaking up the dyadic cycle, the third person's perspective may also be called an excentric view (Plessner, 1975).

Moreover, in triadic interactions the perspectival role often changes: At one time, the child and the caregiver playing with each other are observed by the third person, at another time, the child himself will become the observer of his parents interacting with each other. This variable dynamics of triangulation is a decisive presupposition for acquiring an understanding of perspectives as such: Being the other, the witness or observer is not bound to a certain person, but is possible for each of us, or for everybody. The child begins to understand what one can see or do from a certain point of view. In Mead's terms, he realizes the 'generalized other' (Mead, 1962). This is the foundation for acquiring self-consciousness in the full sense: to reflect on oneself presupposes an excentric position, or to look at oneself from the point of view of the other.

The psychosocial development of the child is thus crucially dependent on acquiring the capacity to change between the dyadic and the triadic mode of interaction. Including the third person into one's awareness means to integrate the external or social space into the present interaction, thus gaining distance and additional degrees of freedom in one's relationships. The child is no more 'at the mercy' of the person he interacts with, because there is, in principle, always still another point of view. Thus, he increasingly acquires a sense of objectivity, neutrality and equality. Triadic intersubjectivity is necessary in order to become a person in the full sense: to recognize oneself as one among others who are intentional agents like oneself.

On the other hand, realizing the interaction of the other and the third (or mother and father) is also the fundamental experience of exclusion, and thus of emotions such as jealousy and envy. The resulting oedipal constellation has been famously emphasized by psychoanalysis as the crucial basis of child development: The father is a threat to the primary dyad, but at the same time the representative of the generalized other, of the rules of society or 'the law' (Ruskin, 1971, Bürgin, 1998). Coping with the affective challenge of triangulation, for example through identification, internalization or by other means, is thus an essential part of acquiring the capacity of perspective-taking.

D. Awareness

In the above descriptions of the more and more complex forms of interactions that infants engage in, we saw that these changes in interactions involve changes on the level of the infants' awareness as well. We now summarize the impact of these interactions in terms of the infants' growing scope of awareness. First of all, infants have an *awareness of themselves and others*. This awareness is both expressed and practiced in different forms of dyadic interactions — such as the games of peek-a-boo and hide-and-seek that we analyzed. We can already speak here of a *mutual awareness*, since both infant and caregiver attune, and coordinate their interactions through looking, moving, touching, and vocalizing and thus are obviously aware of each other.

When the interactions start to involve objects as well, infants become familiar with *joint awareness*. In dyadic interactions, the infant experiences that his actions can have certain effects, for instance that his mother comes when he cries, that she answers his smiles, etc. In cases of joint attention, the sphere of influence of the infant is considerably expanded, since he can now not only try to modulate the other's attention to him, but to objects as well. In a sense, he can stretch the scope of his own perspective to include the perspective of the other. It is likely that this will further increase his awareness of what the other person is capable of, thus making the other's perspective and experience of the world more tangible.

Triadic interactions happen from the very start of the infant's life. They foster yet another level of awareness, for when a third person witnesses the dyadic interaction that the infant is engaged in, he becomes aware of the possibility of a perspective on this interaction. Thus, although the infant was already engaged in such mutual interactions, and was aware of both himself and of the persons he was interacting with, he can now become *aware of the relation itself*. This transition from simply engaging to awareness of one's engagement means an increase in reflectivity (De Haan, 2010). The child senses the other's view and this opens up the possibility to experience an outside perspective on the interaction.

Even more advanced is the ability to imagine the other's perspective as such — that is, outside of a direct interaction. Both in the games of peek-a-boo and hide-and-seek and in triadic interactions, the infant gets familiar with the presence of an absent perspective, so to speak. In peek-a-boo and hide-and-seek we saw that there is an interruption of the immediate contact between the infant and the other person. The other person is still there, but her perspective is not directly visible at that moment[3]. In a similar way, in triadic interactions, there is the presence of a perspective that is not an immediate part of the interaction, for instance when the infant and his mother are observed by his father. The infant does not have a direct contact with his observing father; their contact is in a sense suspended. This is not to say that there is a complete lack of engagement, it is rather an indirect form of engagement. In these ways the infant gets to know absence, and can practice his imagination of another's perspective as such.

This ability to speculate about others who are not present is usually taken to be the ultimate proof of the child's awareness of the other's perspective. As such it is the common target of theories on social cognition, as measured by false belief tasks. In the next section, we will criticize the importance that is attached to these tasks and to what they measure. The focus on this last step in the development of the child's sensitivity to his own and others' perspectives may easily lead to overlooking the importance of the interaction process. Although the development of social understanding expands to this very abstract ability, we argue that it is through social interaction that we practice and acquire the skills that we eventually learn to use outside of direct interaction as well.

We can describe this expansion of the awareness of perspectives as a growing capacity to distance oneself from the here and now. The first forms of interactions are all 'here and now contact'. It is not hard to see their embodied nature since much contact involves touch and gestures. However, already in the here and now contact an element of transcendence is involved. A dimension of transcendence is already present in the infant's engagement with his own body. In discovering his body and its possibilities, he experiences his body both from within and as a 'thing'. This learning is of both 'what can *I* do' and 'what can *it* do'. Phenomenologists refer to these aspects as the 'lived body' (*Leib*) and the 'living body' (*Körper*) respectively (Husserl, 1952; Merleau-Ponty, 1945/2002; Fuchs, 2008; Legrand, 2006)

Another way of transcending the present is through the experience of expectations. Husserl (1985) describes time-consciousness as a process in which the present moment inherently contains a reference to both the moment that has just passed ('retention') and the moment to come ('protention'). He famously refers to hearing a melody to argue for the continuity of experience rather than a string of single experiences. These implicit expectations expand with experience, reaching into the further future and past. Stern (1985) describes the formation of what he calls 'generalized episodes' such as a "breast-milk" episode' (p.95): interactional patterns that the infant gets familiar with. Similar situations elicit

---

[3] In the psycho'-analytic literature, this trust that what is not directly visible still goes on existing, is called 'object constancy'. See for instance: Mahler, Pine & Bergmann (1975).

related expectations. Although one could describe the formation of expectations as a matter of the child building 'associative schemas' à la Perner (1991), we propose that these generalized episodes are interactional patterns — which are best understood as embedded and embodied forms of memory, rather than heapings of representational contents. As noted before, only by acknowledging that the infant perceives behaviour that is already inherently meaningful, can we avoid the so-called 'labeling problem' (in this case how, starting from a variety of actions from the mother, the infant can expect to be fed).

A further step comes with the development of fantasy and *imagination*. Although these may seem highly 'internal' activities, it is likely that they too are practiced in interactions, such as playing and reading stories. Pretend play marks an important transition in this respect. *Pretend play* is an excellent example of participatory sense-making, because the new meaning attached to an object requires the endorsement of both participants. Together they make it true that the banana is a telephone (Leslie, 1987). Finally, *language* acquisition, itself interactionally realised, is crucial both as a means to and application of the ability to reach beyond the immediately given.

The acquisition of language is often hailed as a decisive step in the child's growing reflective capacities. Although obviously of great importance, Stern (2009) points out that linguistic experience is not the only form of reflective experience available[4]. Besides, language use too has a bodily dimension and is interpersonally structured. He furthermore argues that the transition to language should not be seen as a breach in development: we witness here the same process of trial and error that characterizes all learning. Instead, Stern emphasizes the *continuity* between different forms of expression and experience. On his view, this continuity comes from what he calls 'dynamical forms of vitality' that characterize the 'form' or the 'how' of the experience or expression. For instance: "Anger can appear on the scene explosively, or build progressively, or arrive sneakily, or coldly, and so on. So could happiness and its smile." (p.314). He explicitly links these forms of vitality with the body: "it is these dynamic qualities that give the impression of 'an inhabited body' — an 'inhabited thought process', that is in action and alive, now. Without this, we would not experience a vital human being behind the words being said" (p. 326-7).

---

[4] Stern (2009) makes a distinction between pre-reflective, non-verbal reflective, and verbal reflective experiences. He argues that affect attunement and delayed imitation are examples of non-verbal reflective experiences, because in those cases infants register and compare (at least) two previous events. "This is tantamount to a reflexive experience." (p. 321) Although we agree with Stern that reflection is not exclusively verbal (De Haan 2010), we prefer to reserve the term "reflective" for those processes that are in some way self-referential — unlike his own examples.

Another advantage of speaking of forms of vitality is their obvious link with the affective dimension. Emotions, like the excitement and gratification in peek-a-boo and hide-and-seek, play a big role in the interaction process. Infants engage their whole body in the excitement, joy and apprehension of these games. We would however be a little bit more cautious when it comes to separating form from content: we would rather describe dynamical forms of vitality as expressions of emotional involvement. 'Expression' is not so much the form in which a neutral content gets shaped, but the expression is the involvement itself (Merleau-Ponty, 1945/2002).

II. The false belief about the false belief task

We have argued that it is an important step in children's development to imagine another's perspective outside of a direct interaction, but that this ability is itself learnt in interactions such as peek-a-boo, hide-and-seek, and triadic interactions specifically. For the last decades, the *false belief task* was considered to measure the 'most developed' form of this ability and was thought to be a definite test of mental state reasoning (Wellman et al., 2001) at least by the majority of researchers. In the original version, Wimmer & Perner (1983) describe the task as follows:

> A story character, Maxi, puts chocolate into a cupboard x. In his absence his mother displaces the chocolate from x into cupboard y. Subjects have to indicate the box where Maxi will look for the chocolate when he returns. Only when they are able to represent Maxi's wrong belief ('Chocolate is in x') apart from what they themselves know to be the case ('Chocolate is in y') will they be able to point correctly to box x. This procedure tests whether subjects have an explicit and definite representation of the other's wrong belief.[5] (p. 106)

The false belief test has been treated as the hallmark of a full-fledged and so-called representational ToM (Perner, 1991). But the clear-cut nature of the false belief task, distinguishing only between children who either pass or fail the task, is exactly what thwarts any attempt to give a gradual, continuous account of children's developing awareness of an other's perspective. It lies in the nature of experimental tasks to establish a dichotomy between those who pass and those who fail. In fact, it is the establishing of such a dichotomy that makes experimental tasks like the false belief task possible. The clear distinction between two groups must be explained and is consequently more easily related to ideas of a

---

[5] The false belief task is sometimes referred to as the 'Sally-Anne test' after a popular version of the task (Baron-Cohen et al., 1985). Here, the child watches two dolls, Sally and Anne. Sally has a basket and Anne has a box. Sally has a marble, which she puts in her basket. Sally leaves, and Anne takes the marble and puts it in her own box. Sally returns, and the child is asked where Sally will look for her marble.

conceptual change or the ripening of inner modules. Any attempt to give a continuous developmental account seems to stop at the clear-cut dichotomy of the false belief task. For this reason, we will take a closer look at this task.

In spite of its popularity, the history of the false belief task's application and success (success mainly in reproducing the finding that most of the 3-year-olds fail and most of the 5-year-olds succeed) is only slightly longer than the history of its critique. Bloom & German (2000) correctly stated that there is more to a ToM than understanding false belief and that passing the false belief task requires other abilities like inhibitory control, for instance. Although there have been many more critical voices, the false belief task is still considered to be a measure of social capacities. Here, we want to reconsider what the false belief task actually is about and what it says about the awareness of other persons in children who fail or pass the task. Interestingly, it is hard to find a satisfying answer to this question. The false belief test, again, is said to be a definite proof of children's ToM. But here the next question arises: What is a ToM? Premack & Woodruff (1978) defined it as follows:

> An individual has a theory of mind if he imputes mental states to himself and others. A system of inferences of this kind is properly viewed as a theory because such states are not directly observable, and the system can be used to make predictions about the behaviour of others. As to the mental states the chimpanzees may infer, consider those inferred by our own species, for example, purpose or intention, as well as knowledge, belief, thinking, doubt, guessing, pretending, liking, and so forth. (p. 515)

This is probably the most explicit expression of the fact that ToM is about inference, something that is easily forgotten when one takes for granted that ToM tasks are assessing social abilities or awareness of others.[6]

At this point, we want to draw an apparently obvious distinction. One has to distinguish between genuinely social skills and skills from other domains that can be used in social situations, for example logical inference or abstract mathematical thinking. If I think that Peter thinks that I am an idiot because I took his car last week without asking for permission and Peter thinks that I am probably angry with him because he thinks that I think that he knew that I needed the car urgently and he didn't offer it to me, we have a problem if we do not talk with each other

---

[6] ToM comes in two main flavours: Theory Theory and Simulation Theory, and some hybrid combinations of those two. Theory Theory argues that we rely on a folk psychological theory in order to predict and explain others. This theory is thought to be innate or acquired. Simulation Theory, on the other hand, assumes that we do not need a theory, because we can use our own experiences as a model: we can imaginatively put ourselves in the position of the other and work out what we would do in this case. The ability to simulate is also regarded by some as innate, and by others as an acquired ability. For a comprehensive overview, see the introduction of Dokic, & Proust (2002).

anymore and this problem could be labelled a social problem. However, the problem would certainly vanish into thin air if we just talked to each other and really interacted socially. In a way, the problem arises because we do *not* use our social skill to interact. Instead, we engage in something that resembles solving a difficult math problem. But exactly this kind of thinking has always been understood as the core of ToM because it is said to prove that we know about the fact that other people have their own thoughts, beliefs, etc. There is, in fact, more and more theoretical as well as empirical support to reconsider the false belief task as rather measuring reasoning abilities (Bowler et al., 2005; Riggs & Peterson, 2000; Riggs et al., 1998). Once again: if Peter thinks that I think he has a red King and I think that Peter thinks that I have a black Seven, this kind of thinking is relevant in a social situation like for example poker. But it would be a mistake to take this kind of thinking as the basis of our intersubjective grasp of the other. The same kind of thinking is involved in other domains, for example when experimental psychologists design experiments. Although the ability to think about others' beliefs or thoughts can be important in social encounters, it would be a mistake to think that this kind of thinking is the cradle of our awareness of other human beings *as having* thoughts and emotions, etc.

We have suggested that it is important to distinguish between genuinely social skills and skills that can be used and applied in social situations. One could ask at this point what is actually meant by a genuinely social skill or by a genuinely social measure, respectively. We do not want to present a perfect definition here, but the label 'social' would at least presuppose a situation where at least two persons are interacting with each other — rather than thinking about each other outside of a direct interaction. Interestingly, all false belief tasks – the explicit as well as the implicit, the verbal as well as the non-verbal ones – are about *absence*. The skills they measure are skills that become important if I am not able to really interact with the other person because she is not present or because she is present, but not interacting in a transparent manner or not interacting with me. This raises, once again, the question whether false belief understanding should really be considered as a genuinely social ability.

To put this argument forward, let us take a look at two examples that put the false belief task as the hallmark of our social-cognitive skills into question. In Nicaragua, deaf adult Nicaraguan home signers are reported to fail false belief tasks (Pyers, 2006). If the false belief really was the hallmark of a full-fledged ToM, these adults wouldn't have achieved it. Pyers (2006) reports that "although first-cohort signers struggle to accurately predict human behaviour when a false belief is involved, they lead otherwise normal lives, living with extended families, raising children, holding down jobs, and even navigating the Managuan bus system"

(p. 223). She consequently raises the question how important the understanding of false belief actually is to the human experience. Although those Nicaraguan adults often fail the false belief task, they are far from being autistic members of their society.

On the subject, let's jump from Nicaragua to the non-geographical, inner landscape of autism. Children with autism are severely impaired in ToM tasks and many of them fail the false belief task (Baron-Cohen et al., 1985). There are, however, high-functioning adults with Asperger who pass the explicit false belief task with ease despite having problems in social communication in their real lives as well as in more implicit measures (Senju et al., 2009).

Bringing together the findings from deaf Nicaraguans and adults with Asperger, we can say that there are people without a full understanding of false belief who lead a perfectly normal social life and people who pass the false belief task but live in isolation because of severe difficulties in engaging socially. How, then, can such great importance be attached to the false belief task? How can it be considered to measure something of great importance for social interaction?

Recent findings cast even more doubt on its importance. Different studies demonstrated an early understanding of false belief with eye measurement (Clements & Perner, 1994; Onishi & Baillargeon, 2005; Southgate et al., 2007) as well as with more behavioural measures (Buttelmann, 2009; Southgate et al., in press). As the age of onset of false belief understanding is dropping with every study, it is no longer reasonable to speak of a major developmental step or 'conceptual change'. What is measured seems to be 'there' from very early on. The representational interpretation of false belief understanding (Perner, 1991) is far from intuitive, as it is very difficult to imagine such young children reasoning with embedded propositions or from a detached observational stance.

Despite this critique, the understanding of a false belief remains an interesting case that deserves explanation. Herschbach points out that whereas representatives of more embodied approaches to cognition and social interaction (Gallagher, 2005; Reddy, 2008) have no difficulties in explaining early social competencies of children in non-mentalistic, non-representational terms, "the phenomenological critics say little about false beliefs" (Herschbach, 2008, p. 41). The phenomenological critics of ToM propose that we perceive emotions and intentions of others in their expressive behaviour and do not have to infer them. Herschbach agrees on that, but "the cases they use to make this point and present their alternative conception of social understanding do not obviously cover the case of false belief" (p. 41). According to Herschbach, although we can adjust our behaviour depending on what we unreflectively know about other people's beliefs, it remains unsatisfying to call this a purely embodied practice that does not involve mental state attribution or mindreading at all.

Obviously, a lot depends on how one defines 'mental states' and 'mindreading'. We do not want to deny the contribution of reasoning or drawing inferences about others' intentions per se, but we think that it is important to connect these abilities with the primary embodied interactions from which they arise. The problem with talk of 'mental states' and 'mindreading' is that they are used in opposition to (bodily) behaviour, assuming a dichotomy between the outward behaviour and the hidden inner mental states. The critique of phenomenologists is precisely directed against such a view (Zahavi & Gallagher, 2008). Behaviour and intention cannot be taken apart like that, for we encounter the other's meaningful actions, not mere behavioural responses.

False belief tasks measure the child's ability to take into account the limitations of someone's perspective, usually as a result of being absent. Precisely this could be explained in our account, because the development of perspective-taking entails also a growing sensitivity to the limitations of perspectives. For instance, in hide-and-seek, children practice with the inherent limits of the viewpoint of their seekers. The ability to assume the perspective of the other on themselves increases as they learn that merely covering their eyes is not enough not to be seen. They find better and better hiding places, but within the boundaries of the current game (e.g. hiding outside when the game is taking place inside overshoots the participation in this particular game). Also in joint attention, the infant knows whether or not the caregiver is paying attention to the same object, thus showing that he understands that her attention might be somewhere else too. Again, we would like to stress that it is through these interactions that children learn these capacities.

To illustrate the differences in explanation, let us look at Southgate et al.'s study (2007). They show that two-year old children already have correct expectations about another person's expectations — even if they are 'false'. The child apparently knows that when the experimenter looks away, she cannot see what goes on behind her back (i.e. that the ball is put in the other box). For the experimenter, it makes perfect sense to look for the ball in the box where she last saw it, and apparently, the same goes for the child.

It may seem difficult to explain the children's correct anticipation without any reference to a concept of belief or mental states. One way to do it would be to assume that children behave according to behavioural rules like "A person will look for a thing where he or she has seen it at last" — a quick and ready explanation that is hard or even impossible to refute. However, it is intentionally meagre in a way that, in our opinion, does not do justice to the infant's abilities.

Another possible non-conceptual explanation, but one that does justice to the intentionality of behaviour, could be that the continuous process of expanding perspectives as described here gives rise to an understanding of false beliefs. On the basis of our description of the development of perspective-taking, it seems safe to assume that children at that age have enough experience with perspectives and perspective-taking to correctly anticipate the experimenter's actions. On our account, no dichotomy in the child's ability arises; it is part of his increasingly sophisticated grasp of perspectives.

False belief understanding presupposes that the child can take the perspective of other persons, including the implications of their having been absent. Although we have offered an alternative explanation, much still needs to be worked out. The false belief task shows that, in order to strengthen an integrative account, we need to further develop not only the phenomenology of interaction but also the phenomenology of absence.

III. Mechanisms of change

In their review 'Social cognition in the first year', Striano & Reid (2006) conclude that "identifying the mechanisms of change should be among the major tasks for developmental scientists" (p. 471). What could these 'mechanisms of change' be?

The mechanisms of change should describe and explain how infants move from one stage in their development to the next. One option would be to postulate innate modules that 'ripen' in some way (Baron-Cohen, 1995; Carruther, 1996; Cosmides & Tooby, 2004). The difficulty lies in how to conceive of this ripening. If, on the one hand, we would take this as a completely automatic and internal process, then it would become impossible to explain the ample research that has shown that without the right circumstances certain abilities will not develop, or only in a distorted way (Schore, 2003). On the other hand, if we add the condition that these modules need 'favourable circumstances' to develop then the mechanisms of change are no longer (only) the innate modules, but rather the circumstances that lead them to develop or not. Even an appeal to innateness could not rule out the influence of the environment, since 'innate' simply refers to a developmental process that takes place in the womb, which is itself an environment.

The longstanding nature-nurture debate is heading, unsurprisingly, towards a synthesis of the two. If we acknowledge the influence of the environment, one of the central questions is how to define the 'favourable circumstances' that the infants need to proceed in their development. Now, 'favourable circumstances' sounds as if certain background conditions just need to be fulfilled, as if these were merely the stage on which the action (e.g. the mechanisms of change) can then take place. Such a static and passive description is treacherous, however, because it causes us to overlook that these conditions may in fact be processes — including the process of interaction between infant and caregiver.

This is in line with the commonsensical view that an infant needs, first and foremost, somebody who cares for him — not only in the sense of meeting his basic physical needs, but also as emotional involvement in the infant's well-being in general. There is more to favourable circumstance than merely being kept alive. It is important to note that there is no one-answer-fits-all to this question: proper care is about attending to the needs and joys of this specific infant. Therefore, in order to find out what the infant needs, the caregiver has to communicate with him. The better this communication is attuned, the more likely it is that the child's needs are met. Thus, no matter how we specify the favourable circumstances exactly, the need for communicating with the infant will inevitably be part of the process of tailoring the care to this infant. Thus, interaction is indispensable.

We suggest that it is this interaction process that stands at the basis of a healthy development in general, and of the development of the sensitivity to others' perspectives in particular. The interaction process is an important part of the mechanisms of change.

Conclusion

We will end by summing up the advantages of an embodied and embedded account of social development compared to the cognitivist model. Firstly, the account that we have presented here allows to conceive of social development on a continuum, rather than as a matter of separate stages and abilities that stack on top of each other much like building blocks. We have tried to avoid using dichotomous terminology such as implicit versus explicit or pre-reflective versus reflective, in order to bring out the developmental process spanning both ends, instead of opposing them as separable categories.

Secondly, we have conceived of the mechanism of change in this social development as the interaction process itself. The advantage of this is that it elucidates the connection between experience and the developmental mechanism. This development is a form of learning by doing, where the capacities that are needed for specific interactions develop in these interactions. Even the mechanism is learned. Traditional accounts often presuppose that capacities should already be acquired before one can put them to practice. In our view, capacities are themselves practiced. They are not ready-made but adjust dynamically to the developmental path.

Thirdly, following this view, we can say that social skills are themselves interactional (Di Paolo et al., forthcoming; McGann & De Jaegher, 2009). This means that what the child is able to do depends not only on the child, but also on whom he is interacting with and on the environment in which the interaction takes place.

Fourthly, on this approach, it becomes unnecessary to postulate conceptual knowledge at the basis of social capacities. The mechanisms we propose are not so cognitively demanding. Moreover, no invisible entities are needed for the explanation of social interaction. With its focus on the visible and experiential, this approach has the advantage that it lends itself very well to experimental investigation, where it becomes possible to rely only on what is there in the interaction instead of assuming hidden modules. In other words, to consider what is at stake in social understanding as accessible in the interaction process makes explanations more parsimonious and direct.

We can also conclude that a lot more work still needs to be done. On a theoretical level, the challenge will be to elaborate on the phenomenology of absence. Is it possible to do justice to the phenomenon of false beliefs without buying in to the whole representationalist ToM framework? On an empirical level, the challenge is to design experiments that start from a more interactive approach – and investigate how their outcomes compare to the traditional experiments on the development of social skills.

References

Bateson M. C. (1971). The interpersonal context of infant vocalization. *Quarterly Progress Report of the Research Laboratory of Electronics, 100,* 170-6.

Baron-Cohen S. (1995). *Mindblindness: An Essay on Autism and Theory of Mind.* Cambridge: MIT Press.

Baron-Cohen S., Leslie A. M., & Frith U. (1985). Does the autistic child have a "theory of mind"? *Cognition, 21,* 37-46.

Bloom P. & German T. P. (2000). Two reasons to abandon the false belief task as a test of theory of mind. *Cognition, 77,* 25-31.

Bogdan R. (1997). *Interpreting Minds: The Evolution of a Practice.* Cambridge: MIT Press.

Bowler D. M., Briskman J., Gurvidi N., & Fornells-Ambrojo M. (2005). Understanding the mind or predicting signal-dependent action? Performance of children with and without autism on analogues of the false-belief task. *Journal of Cognition and Development, 6,* 259-83.

Bürgin D. (1998). *Triangulierung. Der Übergang zur Elternschaft.* Stuttgart: Schattauer.

Buttelmann D., Carpenter M., & Tomasello M. (2009). Eighteen-month-old infants show false belief understanding in an active helping paradigm. *Cognition, 112,* 337-42.

Butterworth G. (1998). What is special about pointing in babies? In F. Simion & G. Butterworth (eds.), *The Development of Sensory, Motor, and Cognitive Capacities in Early Infancy: From Perception to Cognition* (pp. 171-91). Hove: Psychology Press.

Carruthers P. (1996). Simulation and self-knowledge: a defence of theory-theory. Theories of Theories of Mind. In P. Carruthers & P. K. Smith (eds.), *Theories of Theories of Mind* (p. 22-38). Cambridge: Cambridge University Press.

Chapman M. (1987). Inner processes and outward criteria: Wittgenstein's importance for psychology. In M. Chapman & R. A. Dixon (eds.), *Meaning and the growth of understanding: Wittgenstein's significance for developmental psychology* (pp. 103-27). Berlin: Springer.

Clements W. A. & Perner J. (1994). Implicit understanding of belief. *Cognitive Development, 9*, 377-95.

Cosmides L. & Tooby J. (2004). Social exchange: the evolutionary design of a neurocognitive system. In M. S. Gazzaniga (ed.), *The Cognitive Neurosciences* (p. 1208-95). Cambridge: MIT Press.

De Jaegher H. & Di Paolo E. (2007). Participatory Sense-Making: An enactive approach to social cognition. *Phenomenology and the Cognitive Sciences, 6*, 485-507.

De Jaegher H. (2009a). Social understanding through direct perception? Yes, by interacting. *Consciousness and Cognition, 18*, 535-42.

De Jaegher H. (2009b). What made me want the cheese? A reply to Shaun Gallagher and Dan Hutto. *Consciousness and Cognition, 18*, 549-50.

De Jaegher H., Di Paolo E. A., & Gallagher S. (2010). Does social interaction constitute social cognition? *Trends in Cognitive Sciences, 14*, 441-7.

De Jaegher H. (2010). Enaction versus representation: an opinion piece. In T. Fuchs, H. Sattel & P. Henningsen (eds.), *The Embodied Self: Dimensions, Coherence and Disorders* (pp. 218-24). Stuttgart: Schattauer.

Di Paolo E., Rohde M., & De Jaegher H. (forthcoming). Horizons for the enactive mind: Values, social interaction, and play. In J. Stewart, O. Gapenne, & E. Di Paolo (eds.), *Enaction: Towards a New Paradigm for Cognitive Science*. Cambridge: MIT Press.

Dokic J. & Proust J. (2002). *Simulation and Knowledge of Action.* Amsterdam/ Philadelphia: John Benjamins.

Fivaz-Depeursinge E. & Corboz-Warnery A. (1999). *The primary triangle: A developmental systems view of mothers, fathers, and infants.* New York: Basic Books.

Fuchs T. (2008). *Das Gehirn – Ein Beziehungsorgan.* Stuttgart: Kohlhammer.

Fuchs T. & De Jaegher H. (2009). Enactive Intersubjectivity: Participatory sense-making and mutual incorporation. *Phenomenology and the Cognitive Sciences, 8*, 465-86.

Gallagher S. (2001). The practice of mind: theory, simulation or primary interaction? *Journal of Consciousness Studies, 8*, 83-108.

Gallagher S. (2005). *How the body shapes the mind.* Oxford: Clarendon Press.

Gallagher S. (2008). Inference or interaction: Social cognition without precursors. *Philosophical Explorations, 11*, 163-74.

Gergely G. & Watson J. S. (1999). Early socio-emotional development: Contingency perception and the social-biofeedback model. In P. Rochat (ed.), *Early Social Cognition: Understanding others in the first months of life* (p. 101-37). Hillsdale: Erlbaum.

De Haan S. (2010). The minimal self is a social self. In T. Fuchs, H. Sattel, & P. Henningsen (eds.), *The embodied self. Dimensions, coherence and disorders* (pp. 12-8). Stuttgart: Schattauer.

Herschbach M. (2008). False-belief understanding and the phenomenological critics of folk psychology. *Journal of Consciousness Studies, 15*, 33-56.

Hobson R. P. (2002). *The cradle of thought. Exploring the origins of thinking.* London: Mcmillan.

Husserl E. (1952). *Ideen zu einer reinen Phänomenologie und phänomenologische Philosophie. Zweites Buch: Phänomenologische Untersuchungen zur Konstitution.* Den Haag: Martinus Nijhoff.

Husserl E. (1985). *Texte zur Phänomenologie des inneren Zeitbewusstseins (1893 - 1917).* Hamburg: Meiner.

Hutto D. D. (2004). The limits of spectatorial folk psychology. *Mind and Language, 19*, 548-73.

Kleeman J. A. (1973). The Peek-A-Boo game: Its evolution and associated behavior, especially bye-bye and shame expression during the second year. *Journal of the American Academy of Child Psychiatry, 12*, 1-23.

Legrand D. (2006). The bodily self: The sensorimotor roots of pre-reflective self-consciousness. *Phenomenology and the Cognitive Sciences, 5*, 89-118.

Leslie A. M. (1987). Pretense and representation: The origins of "Theory of Mind". *Psychological Review, 94*, 412-26.

Mahler M., Pine F., & Bergmann A. (1975). *The psychological birth of the human infant: symbiosis and individuation.* New York: Basic Books.

McGann M., & De Jaegher H. (2009). Self-Other Contingencies: Enacting Social Perception. *Phenomenology and the Cognitive Sciences, 8*, 417-37.

Mead G. H. (1962). *Mind, Self and Society.* Chicago: The University of Chicago Press.

Meltzoff A. N. & Moore M. K. (1983). Newborn infants imitate adult facial gestures. *Child Development, 54*, 702-9.

Merleau-Ponty M. (1945/2002). *Phenomenology of Perception.* London: Routledge.

Mitchell P. & Riggs K. J. (eds.) (2000). *Children's reasoning and the mind.* Hove: Psychology Press.

Murray L. & Trevarthen C. (1986). The infant's role in mother-infant communication. *Journal of Child Language, 13*, 15-29.

Onishi K. H. & Baillargeon R. (2005). Do 15-month-old infants understand false beliefs? *Science, 308*, 255-8.

Parrott W. G. & Gleitman H. (1989). Infants' Expectations in Play: The Joy of Peek-a-boo. *Cognition & Emotion, 3*, 291-311.

Perner J. (1991). *Understanding the representational mind.* Cambridge: MIT Press.

Piaget J. (1928). *The Child's Conception of the World.* London: Routledge and Kegan Paul.

Plessner H. (1975). *Die Stufen des Organischen und der Mensch.* Berlin: De Gruyter.

Premack D. & Woodruff G. (1978). Does the chimpanzee have a theory of mind? *Behavioral and Brain Sciences, 1*, 515-26.

Pyers J. E. (2006). Constructing the social mind: Language and false-belief understanding. In N. J. Enfield & S. C. Levinson (eds.), *Roots of human sociality* (p. 207-28). New York: Berg.

Racine T. P. & Carpendale J. I. M. (2007). The role of shared practice in joint attention. *British Journal of Developmental Psychology, 25*, 3-25.

Reddy V. (2003). On being the object of attention: implications for self-other consciousness. *Trends in Cognitive Sciences, 7*, 397-402.

Reddy V. & Morris P. (2004). Participants Don't Need Theories: Knowing Minds in Engagement. *Theory Psychology, 14*, 647-65.

Reddy V. (2008). *How infants know minds.* Cambridge: Harvard University Press.

Riggs K. J, Peterson D. M., Robinson E. J., & Mitchell P. (1998). Are errors in false belief tasks symptomatic of a broader difficulty with counterfactuality? *Cognitive Development, 13*, 73-91.

Riggs K. J. & Peterson D. M. (2000). Counterfactual thinking in pre-school children: Mental state and causal inferences. In P. Mitchell & K. J. Riggs (eds.), *Children's reasoning and the mind* (pp. 87-99). Hove: Psychology Press.

Ruskin M. (1971). Structural and unconscious implications of the dyad and the triad: An essay in theoretical integration. Durkheim, Simmel, Freud. *The Sociological Review, 19*, 179-201.

Scheler M. (1954/1923). *The Nature of Sympathy.* London: Routledge.

Schore A. N. (2003). *Affect Dysregulation and Disorders of the Self.* New York: W.W. Norton.

Senju A., Southgate V., White S., & Frith U. (2009). Mindblind eyes: An absence of spontaneous theory of mind in Asperger syndrome. *Science, 14*, 883-885.

Southgate V., Senju A., & Csibra G. (2007). Action anticipation through attribution of false belief by 2-year-olds. *Psychological Science, 18,* 587-592.

Southgate V., Chevallier C., & Csibra G. (in press). Seventeen-month-olds appeal to false beliefs to interpret others' referential communication. *Developmental Science.*

Stern D. N. (1985). *The Interpersonal World of the Infant: A View from Psychoanalysis and Developmental Psychology.* New York: Basic Books.

Stern D. (2009). Pre-Reflexive Experience and its Passage to Reflexive Experience: A Developmental View. *Journal of Consciousness Studies, 16,* 307-31.

Stifter C. A. & Moyer D. (1990). The regulation of positive affect: Gaze aversion activity during mother-infant interaction. *Infant Behavior & Development, 14,* 111-23.

Striano T. & Reid V. M. (2006). Social cognition in the first year. *Trends in Cognitive Sciences, 10,* 471-6.

Thompson E. (2007). *Mind in Life: Biology, Phenomenology, and the Sciences of Mind.* Harvard: Harvard University Press.

Tomasello M. (1995). Joint attention as social cognition. In C. Moore & P. Dunham (eds.), *Joint Attention: Its Origins and Role in Development* (pp. 103-31). Hillsdale: Erlbaum.

Trevarthen C. (1977). Descriptive analyses of infant communicative behaviour. In H. R. Schaffer (ed.), *Studies in Mother-Infant Interaction* (p. 227-70). London: Academic Press.

Trevarthen C. & Aitken K. J. (2001). Infant intersubjectivity: research, theory, and clinical applications. *Journal of Child Psychology and Psychiatry, 42,* 3-48.

Wellman H. M., Cross D., & Watson J. (2001). Meta-analysis of theory-of-mind development: The truth about false belief. *Child Development, 72,* 655-84.

Wimmer H. & Perner J. (1983). Beliefs about beliefs: Representation and constraining function of wrong beliefs in young children's understanding of deception. *Cognition, 13,* 103-28.

Zahavi D. & Gallagher S. (2008). The (in)visibility of others: a reply to Herschbach. *Philosophical Explorations, 11,* 237-44.

Basic Body Rhythms:
From Individual to Interpersonal Movement Feedback

Sabine C. Koch

University of Heidelberg, Institute of Psychology, Germany
sabine.koch@urz.uni-heidelberg.de

Abstract. This chapter provides an overview of embodiment approaches departing from static body feedback and moving toward dynamic body feedback. It outlines the influence of kinesthetic movement feedback in individuals and tactile movement feedback in interaction, using movement qualities and movement rhythms as independent variables. Research on the causal influence of afferent feedback from the body on affect, attitudes and cognition is extended into the dynamic realm and systematized into the separate influence of movement shape and movement quality. Movement quality — with movement rhythms as its most basic aspect — is an important component of an embodiment framework. Rather than with the 'what', it deals with the 'how' of movement. The empirical studies described here outline the implications of movement qualities on both the individual and interpersonal level.

Embodiment research in psychology is thriving. Building on the phenomenological philosophy of Merleau-Ponty (1962), embodiment approaches have shifted the focus from the former computational model of human experiencing and behavior to the more organismic view (Semin & Smith, 2008; Smith & Semin, 2004), stressing that the body plays a central role in thinking, feeling, perceiving and acting (Barsalou, 1999; Niedenthal et al., 2005).

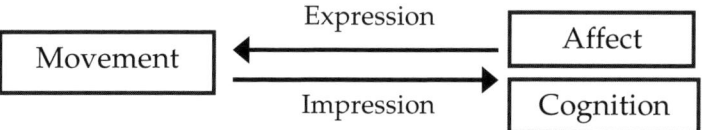

Fig. 1: Bidirectionality assumption between the motor system and the cognitive-affective system; afferent body feedback (impression) plays a causal role in the perception of emotion, the formation of attitudes and behavior regulation (cf. Wallbott, 1982; Zajonc & Markus, 1984)

One important premise of embodiment research is the bidirectionality assumption (Izard, 1977; Laird, 1984; Neumann & Strack, 2000; see Fig. 1). This assumption puts forth that not only do we express our thoughts and feelings in motor behavior (expression function; cf. Darwin, 1872), but motor behavior also causally influences affect and cognition via body feedback (Adelman & Zajonc, 1987; Zajonc & Markus, 1984). This body feedback on the kinesthetic level is not only functional for survival, but also causally relevant for experiencing empathy (Lipps, 1903) or appreciating beauty (aesthetic experience; e.g., Leder et al., 2004) by providing resonance in the living body (Merleau-Ponty, 1962).

1. Body feedback effects

Body feedback experiments have shown that our bodily behavior can change our perceptions, emotions, cognitions or reaction times in certain tasks (for a systematic overview, see Hatfield et al., 1994). Strack et al. (1988), for example, had their participants hold a pen either between their teeth or between their lips and found that participants holding the pen between their teeth judged a cartoon as funnier than participants who held the pen between their lips. The authors see the reason for this effect in the fact that the facial muscles needed for smiling are inhibited in the lip condition. Riskind (1984) showed that participants who sat in a slumped position (spine bowed with head hanging down) versus an upright position (spine upright with head held high) recalled more negative life events when asked to generate memories. The mechanism that is assumed to be responsible for these effects is proprioceptive combined with exteroceptive body feedback (Neumann & Strack, 2000). All these experiments assume that afferent feedback from the body plays a causal role in the experience of emotions and the formation of attitudes, as well as in cognition and behavior regulation (Adelman & Zajonc, 1987; Zajonc & Markus, 1984).

Psychological research has succeeded in integrating formerly singular approaches on body feedback and body-related effects into an overarching embodiment approach by the extension of the cognitive model of knowledge representation (Niedenthal et al., 2005). However, embodiment researchers have not yet fully recognized the basic meaning of movement (dynamic, qualitative aspects) within this new paradigm.

2. From static to dynamic

We are moving beings. However, embodiment research has usually focused on static body feedback (Laird, 1984; LaFrance, 1985; Riskind, 1984; Rossberg-Gempton & Poole, 1992). One of the present challenges of embodiment research is to integrate dynamic body feedback as an independent variable and to extend the definition of embodiment to the dynamic realm. This is what our research set out to do.

Cacioppo and colleagues, with their arm flexion and arm extension experiments (1993), have brought a dynamic component to body feedback research by employing force either toward the body or away from the body (see also Neumann & Strack, 2000; Raab & Green, 2005; Wentura et al., 2000). They had their participants either press on a table from below (a held approach movement) or press on a table from above (a held avoidance movement) while they showed valence-free Chinese ideographs to them. Participants with the held approach movement later rated these stimuli as significantly more positive than participants in the held avoidance condition. The authors explained this in an evolutionary fashion by pointing out the ontogenetic and phylogenetic functional value of bringing good things (such as good food and benevolent people) toward the body and pushing bad things (such as bad food and maleficent people) away from the body, emphasizing the lifelong practice of these actions.

Wells & Petty (1980), as well as Förster & Strack (1996), in their 'head shaking experiments' had earlier been working with dynamic movement. They demonstrated the motor-congruency effect that participants — presumably testing earphones — categorized positive words faster while nodding and categorized negative words faster when shaking their heads. However, the researchers did not take into account the influence of movement qualities within their manipulation. Scholarly work has very rarely included movement quality as an independent variable. As exceptions, we can name the research of Aronoff and colleagues (1992), Maass & Suitner (2010), and Wallbott (1985). Hatfield et al. (1992; 1994) investigated vocal qualities related to emotions.

We wanted to go further with the research on dynamic movement feedback. For reasons of external validity, working with actual movements was indicated instead of working with static postures in experimental settings. In everyday life, it is rather artificial to hold a certain posture for more than a minute. We are in motion most of the time. Employing movement makes the designs more realistic, but also more complex. Theories of body philosophy (Merleau-Ponty, 1962; Sheets-Johnstone, 1999; 2009) and movement analysis (Laban, 1960; Kestenberg, 1995) suggest that, next to movement shape (e.g., approach vs. avoidance), *movement quality* must be taken into account as another factor of influence in such designs. Movement qualities such as quick, slow, strong, light, smooth, sharp, etc. develop throughout life and can occur in a more automatic or a more deliberate way. We decided to start with the most basic movement qualities that have been described in clinical and developmental movement analysis: movement rhythms (Kestenberg, 1995; Loman, 1998). Movement rhythms are periodic alternations of muscle tension and relaxation. They play a role in dynamic body feedback on an individual level as well as on an interaction level, for example, in human communication. Here, we investigated their role in *kinesthetic* and *haptic* body feedback.

3. A theory of movement rhythms

Theories of movement analysis suggest that movement qualities and movement shape are factors of equal influence in the perception and production of a movement. Movement shapes fall into open and closed shapes, directional movement, movement toward or away from the body, and growing and shrinking movements (e.g., to move upward or downward, to widen, to narrow, to enclose or to spread (Kestenberg, 1995; Laban, 1960). Movement qualities generally fall into smooth and sharp movement rhythms, indulgent and fighting movement qualities, or relaxed and tense movement as Judith Kestenberg conceptualized in the Kestenberg Movement Profile (KMP; Kestenberg, 1995).

In her theory, as a sub-category of indulgent and fighting movement qualities, Kestenberg distinguished 10 basic movement rhythms[1] that correspond to the physiological and psychological needs of a person (Kestenberg, 1995; Kestenberg Amighi et al., 1999; Kestenberg & Sossin, 1979). These rhythms refer to the constant changes of tension and relaxation in our bodies (tension-flow). They fall into two basic categories: indulgent rhythms (libidinal; with smooth reversals/transitions) and fighting rhythms (aggressive; with sharp reversals/transitions). An overview of the rhythms as distinguished in Kestenberg's theory is graphically provided in section 7.2. Grounded in psychodynamic developmental theory, the rhythms — as the most basic movement qualities — are assumed to originate in the psychosexual zones: mouth, anus, bladder, internal and external genitals. Each indulgent rhythm, serving playful exploration of a new movement quality, is followed by a fighting rhythm, serving separation from this quality (cf. Erickson, 1950). Rhythms can be observed from the fetal stage forward, throughout the life span, and serve the function of expressing needs and affect. They further provide primary body feedback to oneself and in communication, all without conscious awareness. Indulgent rhythms indicate the 'giving in' to a situation or yielding to an experience, and are characterized by smooth transitions in tension-flow; fighting rhythms indicate the direct focusing on a goal, serving separation and dissociation, and are characterized by sharp tension-flow transitions. Rhythms can be presented on a graph by a time line by use of kinesthetic empathy; i.e., transforming the tension-flow in the observed person into the observer's body, arm, and finally her handwriting (i.e., the pen as an extension of one's own body), resulting in graphs with either smooth or sharp transitions. The interrater reliability of the Kestenberg rhythms has been demonstrated in several studies with Cronbach's alphas > .80 (Koch et al., 2002; Koch, 2006; Sossin, 1987).

---

[1] The 10 rhythms corresponding to 10 developmental movement stages are: sucking, biting, twisting, straining/releasing, running/drifting, starting/stopping, swaying, surging/birthing, jumping, and spurting /ramming.

The investigation of smooth versus sharp rhythms is not a brand new phenomenon in psychological research. Poffenberger & Barrows showed in 1924 that participants related smooth and sharp forms — such as the ones received from rhythm writing — to states such as sad, joyful, calm, irritated, angry, playful or weak with a high degree of agreement ('dead' was related to the straight line; see Fig. 2).

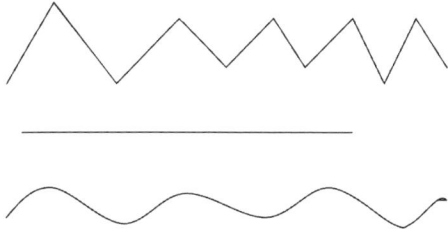

Fig. 2: Sharp, straight and round forms of Poffenberger and Barrows (1924; cf. Johnson, 2008) resemble smooth and sharp rhythms in Kestenberg rhythm writing (Kestenberg & Sossin, 1979; cf. Fig. 6).

These forms can be intermedially transformed into dance, music and other art modalities. The resulting forms are based on a kinesthetic resonance that causes corresponding inner qualities (Merleau-Ponty, 1962). We can find the distinction between smooth and sharp also in the classical Gestalt experiments of Köhler (1929). Köhler asked his participants to assign the names of *bouba* and *kiki* to two geometric forms — one round curved ink blot and one sharp-edged star. Ninety-five to 98% of the participants assigned *kiki* to the sharp-edged form and *bouba* to the round curved one. The effect was replicated in many studies — also interculturally — including one study with two-and-a-half year olds (Maurer et al., 2006). In addition, Bar & Neta (2006) found that attitudes toward everyday objects were more positive when they were presented with soft edges instead of sharp edges. Köhler (1929) described a similar effect for smooth and sharp forms and their relation to musical sounds.

Ramachandran & Hubbard (2001) put forth that the *kiki/bouba*-effect has implications for the evolutionary development of language because it suggests that the naming of objects is not totally arbitrary (even with the function of voice quality not yet taken into account). Due to its intermodality, the effect has been of interest in research on synesthesia also. Synesthesia is the experience of a particular sensual input in more than one sensory modality, such as the hearing of colors or the tasting of words. It offers one approach for investigating consciousness and its processes. By creating additional sensual experiences in atypical channels, the synesthetic experience can contribute to the investigation of qualia (e.g., Gray et al., 2002; Gray et al., 1997).

In clinical movement analysis, the basic distinction of fighting and indulgent movement qualities (Laban & Lawrence, 1947/1974) and smooth versus sharp rhythms (Kestenberg, 1995) is assumed to correspond to different psychological needs as meaning correlates (Kestenberg, 1995). The round, smooth transitions can be observed in playful exploration and indulgent situations, where one yields to the pleasure of the movement. An example would be jumping for the joy of jumping, or twisting for the joy of twisting. The sharp rhythms can be observed in situations in which fighting, controlling or vigilant behavior is functional. They serve the voluntary following through with a goal, against the bodily tendency to relax. We used Kestenberg's theory (1995) to operationalize movement qualities.

In our empirical studies, our general aim was to investigate the meaning of the movement qualities, in particular, whether indulgent rhythms versus fighting rhythms were basic dimensions of movement with differential implications for cognition and affect. In a second step, we combined movement qualities with the better-investigated factor of movement shapes (here: approach and avoidance motor behavior) to explore their single contribution to differential affect and attitudes. And in a third step, we investigated interpersonal implications of movement rhythms on person perception, particularly the affect and the judgment of personality characteristics.

4. Establishing movement quality as a source of influence on affect

In order to test movement quality as a source of influence, we first conducted a number of experiments on the influence of smooth versus sharp rhythms on affect and cognition. In our first study (Günther, 2006), 30 participants were instructed to spring (using a jumping rhythm as in elastically hopping) versus kick (using a spurting/ramming rhythm as in kicking an imaginary ball), while performing a word categorization task with a wireless mouse. We were able to show that the jumping rhythm (smooth, indulgent) versus the spurting/ramming rhythm (sharp, fighting) caused congruent affect in participants ($p < .05$): Smooth rhythms caused more positive affect (i.e., more relaxed, joyful, indulgent, peaceful, playful feelings as measured by the KMP-affect questionnaire; Koch & Müller, 2007), whereas sharp rhythms caused more negative affect (i.e., more tense, intruding, fighting, aggressive, retaining feelings). We chose these particular movement rhythms for the first study because they were particularly easy to observe and embody due to their large size. Because of their high intensity, they were particularly clear and easy to distinguish from one another. No effect was found on the cognitive measure.

In a second study ($n = 60$), we replicated this effect with two different movement rhythms (a swaying vs. a biting/starting-stopping rhythm) to make sure that the results were not specific to the movement rhythms used in Study 1. The variables, design, cover story, procedure and hypotheses of Study 2 were parallel to those of Study 1. Participants sat on a table and either swung their legs when performing a categorization task (smooth rhythm) or pulled both feet up and down while performing the task (sharp rhythm). As in Study 1, the results indicated an effect of the affective measure ($p < .01$), and no effect of smooth versus sharp rhythms on the cognitive measure (recognition of faces; neither online — in a direct categorization — nor offline from memory). When participants performed indulgent movements, they felt more relaxed, joyful, etc.; when they performed fighting movements, they felt more tense, more aggressive, etc.

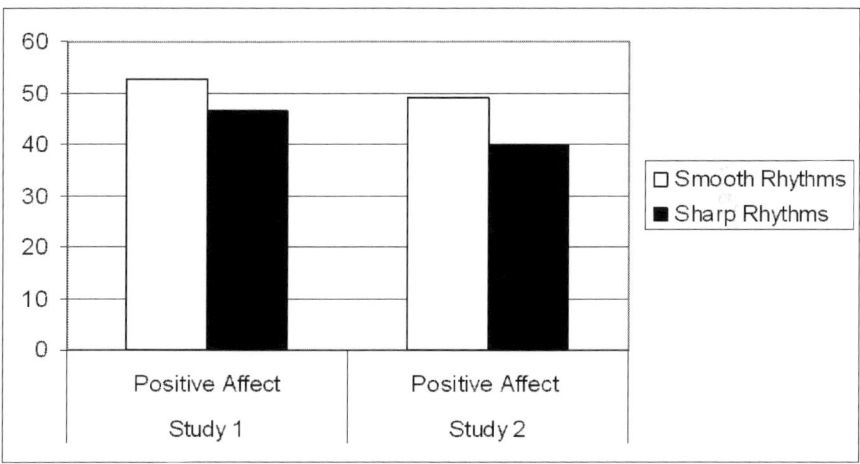

Fig. 3: Effects of movement rhythms on affect; the y-axis yields the approximated sum scores on the brief KMP-affect questionnaire (Koch & Müller, 2007).

Study 2 thus replicated the results of Study 1, suggesting that indulgent versus fighting rhythms and movement qualities are the underlying basic dimensions to which the effect can be traced back. Single movement rhythms are thus subcategories for the specification of affect.

In sum, these studies indicated that the basic movement dimensions (indulgent vs. fighting rhythms) are linked to the affect system. Cognition — as operationalized here — remained unaffected. Generally, we were encouraged to carry our studies further.

5. The joint influence of movement qualities and movement shape on affect and attitudes

In the next two studies, in addition to the affect measure, an evaluation measure was introduced: participants were presented valence-free Chinese ideographs in a learning phase while performing an approach or avoidance movement combined with an indulgent versus fighting rhythm

(4 conditions), and then had to evaluate the ideographs in a judgment phase (cf. Cacioppo et al., 1993). These studies stem from the research tradition of the influence of approach and avoidance motor behavior on attitudes. In the experiment by Cacioppo and colleagues (1993), participants performed either an approach movement (i.e., an arm flexion where they pressed their palms against the downside of a table), thereby mobilizing force upward and toward the body, or an avoidance movement (i.e., an arm extension where they pressed their palms against the surface of a table), thereby mobilizing force downward and away from the body. While performing the movement, participants watched a series of 24 initially valence-free Chinese ideographs. When they later evaluated the ideographs on a scale ranging from -2 to +2 (very negative to very positive), participants in the approach condition evaluated the ideographs more positively than participants in the avoidance condition. Cacioppo and his colleagues (1993) interpreted this finding as a direct effect of motor behavior on attitude. Their evolutionary explanation is that during ontogenesis, we learn to take in good things and push away bad things (e.g., food, other persons, etc.). This life-long learning process causes a *conditioned evaluative preparedness* of our cognitive-affective system. This system in turn enables us to differentiate "on a preconscious level between toxic and nourishing stimuli and provide the appropriate response" (Eberhard-Kaechele, 2007).

In the third study ($n = 40$), we wanted to replicate the findings of Cacioppo and colleagues (1993), and to introduce movement qualities (smooth vs. sharp rhythms) as a second independent variable. This allowed us to see whether movement quality (indulgent vs. fighting rhythms) or movement shape had the greater influence on attitudes and affect and whether moderations of one by the other occurred (Fig. 4).

We used a more dynamic manipulation than Cacioppo and colleagues (1993). Since we were interested in the effects of movement proper rather than the mere expense of force or muscle activation, we introduced four movement conditions. Participants were instructed to move their arms rhythmically either toward the body or away from the body (palm direction oriented accordingly) in either smooth rhythms or sharp rhythms (video examples were provided, and we asked them to imitate the movement until they had understood it). We hypothesized two main effects: one for movement shape (approach vs. avoidance), and one for movement quality (smooth vs. sharp rhythms): The smooth rhythms (indulgent quality) — just as approach movement — was hypothesized to cause more positive attitudes and affect. Dependent variables were the offline-evaluation of 12 of the Chinese ideographs from the original experiment (cognitive measure), an open affect question and the 12 affect items from Studies 1 and 2 (affective measure).

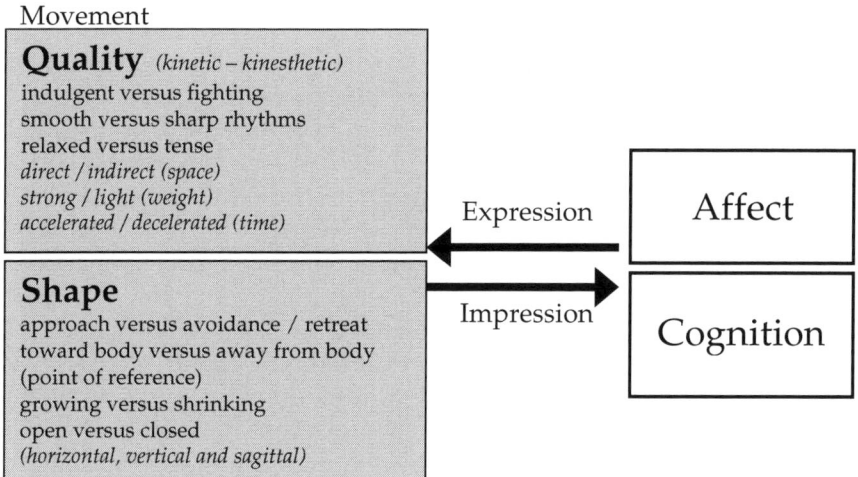

Fig. 4: Extended bidirectionality model: Cognition and affect play central roles in movement behavior and both movement shape and movement quality play causal roles in the perception of emotions, the formation of attitudes and behavior regulation (impression side). Self-referential movement must be distinguished from object-referential movement, and can be easily altered under instructions of perspective change (Markman & Brendl, 2005; Seibt et al., 2008).

Results indicated that the movement condition had a systematic influence on attitudes and affect. Movement shape (approach vs. avoidance) had no influence on attitudes, but influenced affect in a systematic way ($p < .05$): after approach movements, participants felt significantly more relaxed, peaceful, etc., independent of the rhythm employed; after the avoidance movement, they felt significantly more tense, aggressive, etc. Movement rhythms had no influence on the affective measure, but influenced attitudes in a systematic way: Participants judged the initially valence-free ideographs significantly more positively in the indulgent condition than in the fighting condition ($p < .05$). The interaction of movement rhythms and shapes was marginally significant for the cognitive measure ($p < .01$). The influence of shape on affect was predicted by KMP-theory (Kestenberg, 1995) just the way it occurred in the experiment, yet the influence of rhythms on attitudes was new. The marginal interaction of movement rhythms and shape may suggest that rhythm is a moderator for shape or vice versa. Overall, the effect size was small and the sample too small to generalize from. Therefore, Study 4 replicated Study 3 with a larger sample ($n = 66$).

On the basis of the findings from Study 3, we hypothesized a main effect for both movement shape (approach vs. avoidance) and movement quality (indulgent vs. fighting rhythms) on affect and attitudes. Just as in Studies 1 and 2, participants received the information that the study was investigating the effects of physical arousal on the perception of different stimuli and that they were in the low-arousal condition. The focus of attention was thus distracted from the movement qualities. Independent and dependent variables were exactly the same as in Study 3.

Results suggested a main effect of movement shape on affect and attitudes: approach movements caused significantly more positive affect than avoidance movements ($p < .01$) and a significantly more positive attitude toward the initially valence-free Chinese ideographs ($p < .05$). Further, there was a significant interaction of movement shape and movement rhythm, suggesting that (a) fighting (but not indulgent) rhythms make a difference in the influence on affect: avoidance movement with fighting rhythms caused significantly more positive affect than approach movements with fighting rhythms (clashing movement quality and shape caused more aversive reactions); and that (b) indulgent qualities make the difference in the influence on attitudes: ideographs that had been learned with approach movements and indulgent rhythms were later evaluated significantly more positively than the ones learned with avoidance movements and indulgent rhythms.

This effect of movement shape under smooth rhythms may be interpreted as due to the indulgent attitude that smooth rhythms produce. Sharp rhythms create a fighting and defensive attitude, thus possibly preventing the approach and avoidance information from unfolding its effect, making the system not permeable enough to let the information pass. It can consequently be hypothesized that sharp rhythms overwrite approach and avoidance effects, whereas smooth rhythms bring them to their full effect by raising the permeability ('Durchlässigkeit'; Lewin, 1935) of the organismic system. Furthermore, for both dependent variables (i.e., affect and attitudes), incongruence of movement quality and shape caused more negative reactions.

In sum, experiments 3 and 4 provide further evidence that the basic dimensions of the shape-system are related to affect and attitudes. There are hints to interaction processes between rhythms and shapes that need further exploration.

6. The influence of palm direction

Finally, we conducted two studies in which we reversed the *palm direction*, resulting in incongruent shapes of arm movement and hand position (Koch, 2009). Movements were all performed in smooth rhythms (for better permeability; Lewin, 1935).

Results suggest that palm direction alone does not exert an influence on affect or attitudes (only marginally for state affect measured with the PANAS; Watson et al., 1988). However, as expected, we found an effect of congruency of palm direction (toward body vs. away from body) and movement direction (approach vs. avoidance), with congruent shapes causing more positive affect ($p < .05$; see Fig. 5). The congruency of two movement shapes thus had a positive influence on the affect of participants.

Body feedback operates directly on the kinesthetic and haptic channels and indirectly on the visual channel via mirroring and mapping processes (employing kinesthetic empathy). For the kinesthetic channel, it provides feedback to the individual in the manner just reviewed. For the haptic channel, it directly transmits information from one person to another, as in an embrace or a handshake. In the next study, we investigated the communication of movement rhythms via handshakes.

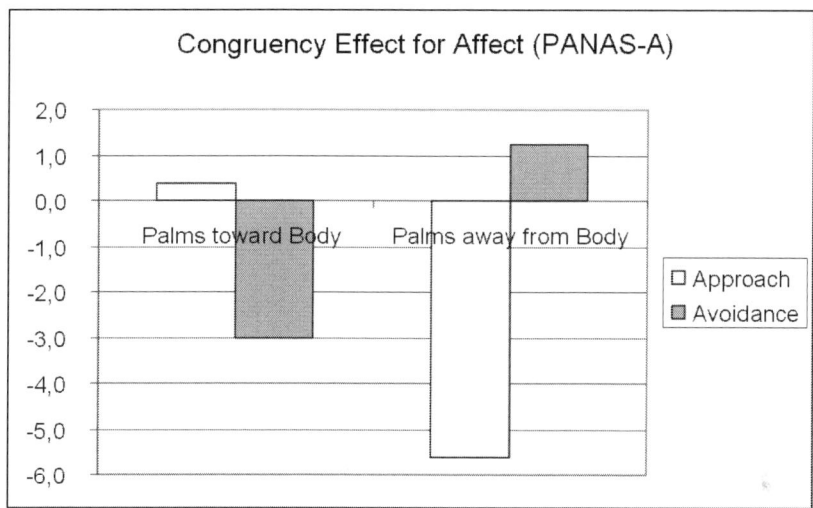

Fig. 5: Congruency Effect (n = 69): If palm direction and movement direction of the arms were incongruent, more negative affect resulted; y-axis: positive digits indicate amount of positive affect, negative digits indicate amount of negative affect.

7. The interpersonal dimension: The influence of tactile feedback

In all studies described here, effects of movement were observed on the affective or the evaluative measures, but not on the cognitive ones. All studies so far included the proprioceptive-kinesthetic feedback on only one's own affect and attitudes (individual level). To go one step further, we included the interactive processes and consequences of dynamic motor feedback. In this interactive study, we focused on the *haptic channel of communication* and investigated the communicative implications of movement rhythms.

Touch is a domain rarely investigated in the social sciences (for an exception, see Schubert et al., 2008). Ashley Montagu (1971) formulated how essential and central touch is for the development of a human being.

He stated that "the personal identity has only insofar substance and structure, as it has its fundament in the reality of our bodily experiences" (Montagu, 1971). The sense of touch can already be observed in eight week old fetuses retreating after a touch of the lips. At this point in time, the fetus is only 2½ centimeters tall and has neither eyes nor ears. In agreement with Montagu (1971) on the role of tactile communication, Fuchs (2000) wrote that

> the reciprocity of the relation is in no other sense modality as pronounced as in the sphere of touch. Visual, auditory and the other 'distance senses' use mediating means such as light and air. The skin is both the separating and the connecting interface, both a sense organ (impression) and an active communication organ (expression). (Fuchs, 2000; p. 114; author's translation)

An example of how we use rhythms in haptic communication is provided by Kestenberg Amighi et al. (1999). When we say goodbye to a dear friend, we often embrace him/her starting with an indulgent smooth rhythm that can be observed as a gentle back rub. When the embrace is getting too long for one of us, the person starts to use a sharp fighting rhythm, indicating the wish to separate from the friend. Most friends intuitively understand this message and terminate the embrace, i.e., they gently separate. Very few individuals will not understand this completely nonverbal tactile message. Inspired by this example, we planned to investigate the influence of movement rhythms on interpersonal communication. However, since we did not want to strain our participants' privacy, we decided not to use an experimental setup with an embrace. We used the less intimate form of a handshake instead.

7.1 Communicative meaning of body rhythms in handshakes

Former studies on communication via handshakes (e.g., Bailenson et al., 2007; Chaplin et al., 2000) had found relations between motor properties and personality measures. Chaplin et al. (2000) had four trained confederates shake the hands of 112 participants who judged the handshake. For the judges, a strong handshake was associated (more strongly) with *extraversion*, emotional expressiveness, and — for women only — with *openness to experience*, and less strongly with shyness and *neuroticism*. On this basis, reliable behavior predictions were possible in this experiment. Bailenson et al. (2007) found in a virtual touch environment/human-machine interaction, that seven emotions could be recognized better than chance via handshakes, but worse than in face-to-face interactions.

In our study, we investigated for the first time the relation between movement rhythms and personality characteristics and the relation between movement rhythms and affect as transmitted through handshakes. We proceeded from the proprioceptive level (individual) to the exteroceptive level (interpersonal) of analysis of dynamic movement feedback. We assumed that movement rhythms would have specific effects on the judgment of affect in self and other (handshaking confederate), and further tested the influence of movement rhythms on the judgment of personality characteristics, as hypothesized in the big five personality factors (Costa & McCrae, 1992).

We hypothesized that individuals distinguish the affective and personality features of their interaction partners on the basis of smooth versus sharp movement rhythms. In particular, we assumed that participants would judge smooth rhythms as transmitting positive affect and sharp rhythms as transmitting more negative affect; and that smooth rhythms would be positively related to perceived openness to experience, conscientiousness and agreeableness, whereas sharp rhythms would be related to perceived neuroticism of the partner.

7.2 Method: Providing handshakes and measuring reactions

Fifty-nine participants (37 women, 22 men; age: $M = 24.2$, $SD = 7.4$; *range*: 18 – 59) received a handshake from a female confederate three times during the experiment, for 25 sec each time. Confederates used either three different smooth (condition 1) or sharp rhythms (condition 2). In a one-factorial between-groups design, 30 participants were randomly assigned to the 'smooth rhythm' condition — receiving one out of three smooth-rhythm handshakes; 29 to the 'sharp rhythm' condition — receiving one out of three sharp-rhythm handshakes (see overview in Fig. 6).

KMP-rhythms overview

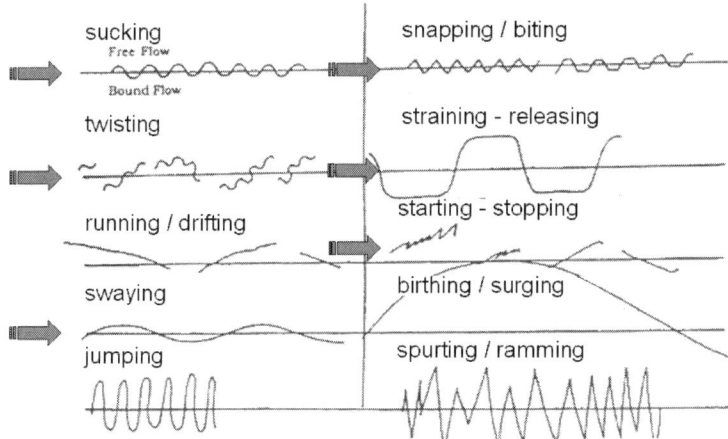

Fig. 6: Movement rhythms employed in the handshake study indicated by blue arrows: three indulgent rhythms (sucking, twisting and swaying) versus three fighting rhythms (biting, straining-releasing and starting-stopping); between-groups design (n = 59).

After the intervention, participants evaluated their own affect, the perceived closeness to the hand-shaker, the affect and personality of the hand-shaker as transmitted by the handshake, as well as their own personality. For personality ratings, we employed the personality questionnaire 24AM (with 24 items; Herzberg & Brähler, in prep.), measuring the big five personality dimensions (extraversion, openness to experience, agreeableness, conscientiousness and neuroticism). For affect ratings, we employed the KMP-affect questionnaire (short version, 13 Items; Koch & Müller, 2007). The experienced closeness to the hand-shaker was measured with the item *"How close did you feel to the person shaking your hand?"* on a rating scale from 1 (not at all) to 6 (very much). In the end, participants provided demographic data and received some sweets for participation. The experiment lasted 30 min. Participants were randomly assigned to the conditions. The sequence of the handshakes was balanced (three sequences).

7.3 Results: Body rhythms transport information on affect and personality

A MANOVA showed that in the smooth condition, the handshaking confederate was judged as transmitting higher positive affect than in the sharp condition ($p=.000; \eta^2=.28$). In the smooth condition, the confederate was perceived as significantly more agreeable ($p=.000; \eta^2=.25$), open ($p=.000; \eta^2=.22$), and extraverted ($p=.004; \eta^2=.14$; Fig. 7). The experienced closeness to the confederate was higher in the smooth condition ($p<.05$).

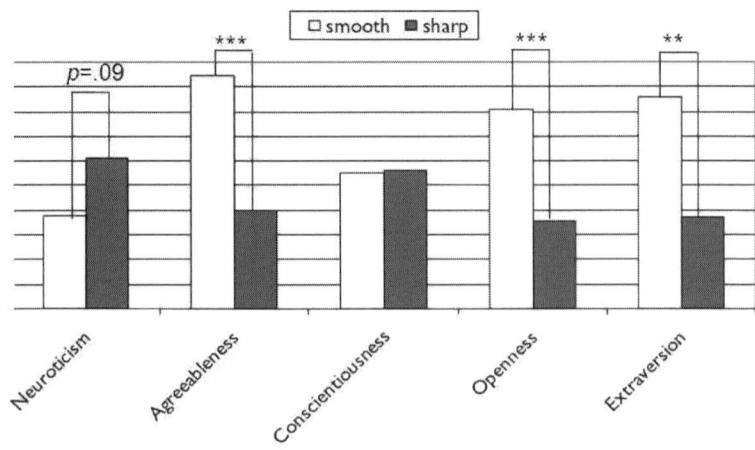

Fig. 7: Personality ratings by handshakes in smooth versus sharp rhythm; neuroticism, $p < .09$; personality measured with 24AM (Herzberg & Brähler, in prep.) on a scale from 1 = strong disagreement to 7 = strong agreement; high values = high disposition; $n = 59$).

7.4 Discussion: Embodied intercorporality

Smooth versus sharp movement rhythms in handshakes transmitted affect and personality characteristics identified by all participants in a similar manner. The hypotheses of the study were confirmed. More specifically, smooth rhythms conveyed agreeableness, extraversion, openness to experience and positive affect. They further transmitted a higher experienced closeness to the confederate. There was a tendency for sharp rhythms ($p < .09$) to convey more neuroticism and negative affect. Participants high on neuroticism showed the most biased rating of the confederate. Participants' affect was not influenced significantly.

Limitations of the study concern the external validity of handshakes provided in this manner: They were longer and different from handshakes in realistic settings. However, our aim was not to test handshakes per se, but rather to examine the difference caused by tactile contact in smooth versus sharp rhythms. Next to sharp and smooth reversals, future research should look more closely at intensity and amplitude of rhythms as carriers of meaning. Furthermore, there was a stimulus sampling problem with just one experimenter providing the handshake (Wells & Windschitl, 1999). Thus, future studies in this line of research should vary experimenters to achieve intersubjective reliability of these findings. Future studies should also include a control group without movement, but with bodily contact (just holding the participants' hand for the same amount of time as the conditions carried out here). By including a control group, the specific effects of the rhythms can be better experimentally separated from the mere effects of touch.

In sum, in the smooth rhythm condition, the handshaking confederate was evaluated as more agreeable, extraverted and open to experience. She further was attributed more positive affect than in the sharp rhythm condition. In the sharp rhythm condition, she was attributed more negative affect and marginally more neuroticism than in the smooth rhythm condition. This demonstration of the effects of haptic movement qualities on person perception (personality characteristics and affect) has important implications for research in personality and social psychology, opening a new field of investigation of intra- and interpersonal differences in the application of certain movement qualities and their implications. In communication research, the meaning of early parent-child interaction is of focal importance (Loman, 1998; Loman & Foley, 1996). Movement analysis offers possibilities for systematically investigating the influence of movement qualities and movement shapes on the communication with and the attitude toward interaction partners in family and work relations. 'Holding patterns' in romantic relationships and between mothers and infants (attunement and clashing) are two exemplary domains of interest that can be investigated with this paradigm.

8. The bigger picture:

8.1 Taking interaction into account

Extending the bidirectionality model to incorporate interactions between individuals is the next step (see Fig. 8). For the understanding of others, mirroring and mapping on the body level is necessary. Movement via kinesthetic resonance is the carrier of all sensorimotor experience and thus the primary modality of this 'bridging' between persons (Merleau-Ponty, 1962; Sheets-Johnstone, 1999, 2009).

Other attempts to re-integrate the interaction aspect within embodiment research have been put forth by Semin & Cacioppo (2008), as well as De Jaegher & Di Paolo (2007). Semin & Cacioppo (2008) concluded that "The converging research evidence we have selectively reviewed suggests that the architecture of the human perceptual and neural system is specifically designed for the recognition of movements of conspecifics in a privileged way." While much of the evidence they reviewed was a compilation of already existing knowledge, the much needed 'new' proposal is to go back to the social/interpersonal level instead of using the individual as the unit of analysis. De Jaegher & Di Paolo (2007) went one step further by employing an enactive approach that allowed them to drop, for example, the assumption of mental representations.

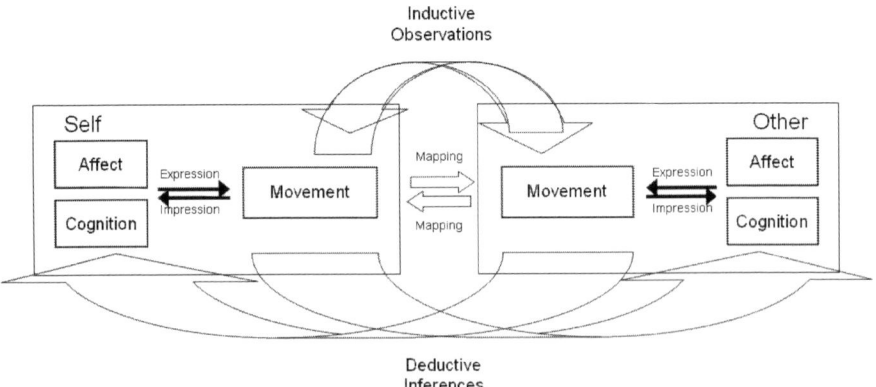

Fig. 8: Interactional Bidirectionality Model (Koch, 2010): Movement is seen in its primary function with kinesthetic resonance as the basis of all other sensual perceptions and expressions including verbal production. Mapping can lead either to mirroring or to inhibition. The model applies to human conspecifics and implies the unity of perception and action (v. Weitzsäcker, 1940).

8.2 Communicative and clinical implications

There are multiple reciprocities between movement and meaning, some of which have been addressed in our studies. In the future, it would be interesting to include the level of symbolization in studies in order to better understand, for example, the clinical and communicative implications of movement.

In psychotherapy, the symbolic function of movement (as a nonverbal metaphor) is particularly relevant (see also Ramseyer, this volume). In cases in which verbal methods of psychotherapy are not possible or useful, nonverbal methods gain importance in order to gain access to the patients' inner world and for the patients to gain access to their own emotions and problems. In body psychotherapy, arts therapies, mindfulness meditation and similar 'embodied' approaches, entirely nonverbal therapy processes are possible (even though verbalization is an important part of these therapies). The nonverbal part of the healing process is as of now not well researched and needs specification of theoretical grounding and methodological differentiation. Nonverbal processes are difficult to access scientifically; however, they are particularly interesting because it is often in movement that the un-speakable or the not-yet-to-be-verbalized becomes denser, expresses itself in nonverbal symbols and metaphors and searches to break through to the verbal.

The clinical or communicative situation is a well-suited field for investigating and documenting the translational processes from the nonverbal-fleeting to the verbal-manifest. The body and the interpersonal space are the sites of these translations, their resonance the precondition of the experiencing of the qualia (Merleau-Ponty, 1962) on the individual level, and empathy (Lipps, 1903) on the interpersonal or intercorporeal level. The expressive level has functional as well as symbolic-representative aspects. Both play an important role in communication. Although in everyday life the functional aspects of movement and language predominate, in cultural forms such as dance and improvisation, the symbolic-representational aspect plays a more important role. A secure space for expressive, symbolic movement is indispensable, for example, for psychiatric and psychosomatic patient groups — that have suffered trauma or depression — in order to return to their own vitality and bodily resonance. For many of them, therapy provided via nonverbal media such as movement, music or art often seems to be particularly effective, as has been, for instance, demonstrated with a single dance intervention for depressed patients (Koch et al., 2007). In some diseases such as schizophrenia, dementia and autism, this symbolic-representative function or the capacity for rhythm and resonance is impaired and needs to be implicitly addressed in therapy; for others, this function has a more explicit healing function, such as for trauma patients. With regard to therapy, it is particularly useful to investigate the communicative use of movement qualities and rhythms and to train students in employing the already existing knowledge and methods in their work with their clinical groups.

9. Conclusions

The research compiled in this chapter shows that movement qualities and movement rhythms exert an important influence on individual affect and attitudes as well as on person perception. The dynamic component of movement needs to be taken into consideration in studies that operate with any form of movement as an independent variable. An extended definition of embodiment can be: *"Embodiment* denominates a field of research, in which the reciprocal influence of the *body* as a living, animate organism, as well as its *movements* (in quality and shape), and *cognition, affect* and *behavior* are investigated with respect to their expressive and impressive functions on the individual, the interactional and the extended level (i.e., including person-person and person-environment interactions)." The studies presented here provide a method for the experimental investigation of basic movement dimensions and their meaning. From here, scholars can take on the call to drive these attempts further and build a firm knowledge base on the most important building blocks of the basic dimensions of movement.

References

Adelman P. K. & Zajonc R. B. (1987). Facial efference and the experience of emotion. *Annual Review of Psychology, 40,* 249-80.

Aronoff J., Woike B. A., & Hyman L. M. (1992). Which are the stimuli in facial displays of anger and happiness? Configurational bases of emotion recognition. *Journal of Personality and Social Psychology, 62,* 1050-66.

Bailenson J. N., Yee N., Brave S., Merget D., & Koslow D. (2007). Virtual interpersonal touch: Expressing and recognizing emotions through haptic devices. *Human-Computer Interaction, 22,* 325-53.

Bar M. & Neta M. (2006). Humans prefer curved visual objects. *Psychological Science, 17,* 645-48.

Barsalou L. W. (1999). Perceptual symbol systems. *Behavioral and Brain Sciences, 22,* 577-660.

Cacioppo J. T., Priester J. R., & Berntson G. (1993). Rudimentary determinants of attitudes II: Arm flexion and extension have differential effects on attitudes. *Journal of Personality and Social Psychology, 65,* 5-17.

Chaplin W. F., Phillips J. B., Brown J. D., Clanton N. R., & Stein J. L. (2000). Handshaking, gender, personality and first impressions. *Journal of Personality and Social Psychology, 79,* 110-7.

Costa P. T. & McCrae R. R. (1992). *Revised NEO Personality Inventory (NEO-PI-R) and NEO Five-Factor Inventory (NEO-FFI) manual.* Odessa: Psychological Assessment Resources.

Darwin C. (1872/1965). *The expression of emotions in men and animals.* Chicago: University of Chicago Press.
De Jaegher H. & Di Paolo E. M. (2007). Participatory sense making. An enactive approach to social cognition. *Phenomenology and the Cognitive Sciences , 6,* 485-507.
Eberhard-Kaechele M. (2007). The regulation of interpersonal relationships by means of shape flow: A psychoeducational intervention for traumatized individuals. In S. Koch & S. Bender (eds.), *Movement Analysis. The Legacy of Laban, Bartenieff, Lamb and Kestenberg.* Berlin: Logos.
Erickson E. (1950). *Childhood and society.* New York: Norton.
Förster J. & Strack F. (1996). Influence of overt head movements on memory for valenced words: A case of conceptual-motor compatibility. *Journal of Personality and Social Psychology, 71,* 421-30.
Fuchs T. (2000). *Leib Raum Person.* Stuttgart: Klett-Cotta.
Gray J. A., Chopping S., Nunn J., Parslow D., Gregory L., Williams S., Brammer M. J., & Baron-Cohen S. (2002). Implications of synesthesia for functionalism: Theory and experiments. Journal *of Consciousness Studies, 9,* 5-31.
Gray J. A., Williams S. C. R., Nunn J., & Baron-Cohen S. (1997). Possible implications of synesthesia for the hard question of consciousness. In S. Baron-Cohen, & J. E. Harrison (eds.), *Synesthesia: Classic and contemporary readings* (pp. 173-81). London: Blackwell.
Günther N. (2006). *Rhythmus geht unter die Haut – Auswirkungen runder und eckiger Bewegungsrhythmen auf Affekt, Kognition und Verhalten.* Unpublished Diploma Thesis: University of Heidelberg.
Hatfield E. Cacioppo J. T., & Rapson R. L. (1992). Primitive emotional contagion. In M. S. Clark (ed.), *Review of Personality and Social Psychology: Vol. 14, Emotions and social behavior* (pp. 151-77). Newbury Park: Sage.
Hatfield E., Cacioppo J. T., & Rapson R. L. (1994). *Emotional contagion.* Paris: Cambridge University Press.
Herzberg P. Y. & Brähler E. (in prep.). *The 24 AM: Assessing the Big-Five Personality Domains via a 24 Item Short Form.*
Izard C. E. (1977). *Human emotions.* New York: Plenum Press.
Johnson M. (2008). *The meaning of the body.* Chicago: University of Chicago Press.
Kestenberg J. S. (1995). *Sexuality, body movement and rhythms of development.* Northvale: *Jason Aronson.* (Originally published in 1975 under the title Children and Parents).
Kestenberg J. S. & Sossin K. M. (1979). *The role of movement patterns in development, Vol. 2.* New York: Dance Notation Bureau Press.
Kestenberg Amighi J., Loman S., Lewis P., & Sossin K. M. (1999). *The Meaning of Movement: Development and clinical perspectives of the Kestenberg Movement Profile.* New York: Routledge.
Koch S. C. (2006). Gender at work: Differences in use of rhythms, efforts, and preefforts. In S. C. Koch & I. Bräuninger (eds.), *Advances in dance/movement therapy. Theoretical perspectives and empirical findings* (pp. 116-27). Berlin: Logos.
Koch S. C. (2009). *Embodiment: Der Einfluss von Eigenbewegung auf Affekt, Einstellung und Kognition.* Habilitationsschrift University of Heidelberg.
Koch S. C., Cruz R., & Goodill S. (2002). The Kestenberg Movement Profile (KMP): Reliability of Novice Raters. *American Journal of Dance Therapy, 23,* 71-88.
Koch S. C., Morlinghaus K., & Fuchs T. (2007). The joy dance. Effects of a single dance intervention on patients with depression. *The Arts in Psychotherapy, 34,* 340-49.
Koch S. C. & Müller S. M. (2007). The KMP-questionnaire and the brief KMP-based affect scale. In S. C. Koch & S. Bender (eds.), *Movement analysis – Bewegungsanalyse. The legacy of Laban, Bartenieff, Lamb and Kestenberg* (pp. 195-202). Berlin: Logos.

Köhler W. (1929). *Gestalt psychology*. New York: Liveright.
Laban R. v. (1960). *The mastery of movement*. London: MacDonald & Evans.
Laban R. v. & Lawrence F. C. (1974). *Effort: Economy in body movement*. Boston: Plays. (Originally published in 1947)
LaFrance M. (1985). Postural mirroring and intergroup relations. *Personality and Social Psychology Bulletin, 11*, 207-17.
Laird J. D. (1984). The real role of facial response in the experience of emotion: a response to Tourangeau and Ellsworth, and others. *Journal of Personality and Social Psychology, 47*, 909-17.
Leder H., Belke B., Oeberst A., & Augustin D. (2004). A model of aesthetic appreciation and aesthetic judgments. *British Journal of Psychology, 95*, 489-508.
Lewin K. (1935). A dynamic theory of personality. New York: McGraw-Hill.
Lipps T. (1903). *Leitfaden der Psychologie* (pp. 187-201). Leipzig: Wilhelm Engelmann.
Loman S. (1998). Employing a developmental model of movement patterns in Dance/movement therapy with young children and their families. *American Journal of Dance Therapy, 20*, 101-15.
Loman S. & Foley F. (1996). Models for understanding the nonverbal process in relationships. *The Arts in Psychotherapy, 23*, 341-50.
Maass A. & Suitner C. (2010). Personal Communication 03/02/2010.
Markman A. B. & Brendl C. M. (2005). Constraining theories of embodied cognition. *Psychological Science, 16*, 6-10.
Maurer D., Pathman T., & Mondloch C. J. (2006). The shape of boubas: Sound-shape correspondences in toddlers and adults. *Developmental Science, 9*, 316-22.
Merleau-Ponty M. (1962). *Phenomenology of perception*. London: Routledge.
Montagu A. (1971). *Touching: The human significance of the skin*. New York: Columbia University Press.
Neumann R. & Strack F. (2000a). Approach and avoidance: The influence of proprioceptive and exteroceptive cues on encoding of affective information. *Journal of Personality and Social Psychology, 79*, 39-48.
Niedenthal P., Barsalou L. W., Winkielmann P., Krauth-Gruber S., & Ric F. (2005). Embodiment in Attitudes, Social Perception, and Emotion. *Personality and Social Psychology Review, 9*, 184-211.
Poffenberger A. T. & Barrows B. E. (1924). The Feeling Value of Lines. *Journal of Applied Psychology, 8*, 187-205.
Raab M. & Green N. (2005). Motion as input: A functional explanation of movement effects on cognitive processes. *Perceptual and Motor Skills, 100*, 333-48.
Ramachandran V. S. & Hubbard E. M. (2001), Synesthesia: A window into perception, thought and language, *Journal of Consciousness Studies, 8*, 3-34. http://psy.ucsd.edu/~edhubbard/papers/JCS.pdf Retrieved 03/09/09.
Riskind J. H. (1984). They stoop to conquer: Guiding and self-regulatory functions of physical posture after success and failure. *Journal of Personality and Social Psychology, 47*, 479-93.
Rossberg-Gempton I. & Poole G. D. (1992). The relationship between body movement and affect: From historical and current perspectives. *The Arts in Psychotherapy, 19*, 39-46.
Schubert T. W., Waldzus S., & Seibt B. (2008). The embodiment of power and communalism in space and bodily contact. In G. R. Semin & E. R. Smith (eds.), *Embodied grounding: Social, cognitive, affective, and neuroscientific approaches* (pp. 160-83). New York: Cambridge University Press.
Seibt B., Neumann R., Nussinson R., & Strack F. (2008). Movement direction or change in distance? Self- and object-related approach–avoidance motions. *Journal of Experimental Social Psychology, 44*, 713-20.

Semin G. R. & Smith E. R. (2008). *Embodied grounding.* Cambridge: Cambridge University Press.
Sheets-Johnstone M. (1999). *The primacy of movement.* Philadelphia: John Benjamin.
Sheets-Johnstone M. (2009). *The corporeal turn. An interdisciplinary reader.* London: Imprint Academic.
Sossin K. M. (1987). *Reliability of the Kestenberg Movement Profile. Movement Studies: Observer Agreement, Vol. 2* (pp. 23-8). New York: Laban/Bartenieff Institute of Movement Studies.
Smith E. R. & Semin G. R. (2004). Socially situated cognition. Cognition in its social context. In M. P. Zanna (ed.), *Advances in Experimental Social Psychology, Vol. 36* (pp. 53-117). Amsterdam: Elsevier.
Strack F., Martin L., & Stepper S. (1988). Inhibiting and facilitating conditions of the human smile: A non-obtrusive test of the facial feedback hypothesis. *Journal of Personality and Social Psychology, 54,* 768-77.
Wallbott H. G. (1982). *Bewegungsstil und Bewegungsqualität: Untersuchungen zum Ausdruck und Eindruck gestischen Verhaltens.* Weinheim: Beltz.
Watson D., Clark L. A., & Tellegen A. (1988). Development and validation of brief measures of positive and negative affect: The PANAS Scale. *Journal of Personality and Social Psychology, 54,* 1063-70.
Wells G. L. & Petty R. E. (1980). The effects of head movement on persuasion: Compatibility and incompatibility of responses. *Basic & Applied Social Psychology,1,* 219-30.
Wells G. L. & Windschitl P. D. (1999). Stimulus sampling and social psychological experimentation. *Personality and Social Psychology Bulletin, 25,* 1115-25.
Wentura D., Rothermund K., & Bak P. (2000). Automatic vigilance: The attention-grabbing power of approach- and avoidance-related social information. *Journal of Personality and Social Psychology, 78,* 1024-37.
Zajonc R. B. & Markus H. (1984). Affect and cognition: The hard interface. In C. Izard, J. Kagan, & R. B. Zajonc (eds.), *Emotions, cognition and behavior* (pp. 73-102). Cambridge: Cambridge University Press.

Dance: the Human Body as a Dynamic Motion System

Karl Grammer*, Elisabeth Oberzaucher*, Iris Holzleitner*
and Silke Atmaca**
* Department of Anthropology, Faculty of Life Sciences, University of Vienna,
Althanstrasse 14, A-1090 Vienna, Austria
{karl.grammer, elisabeth.oberzaucher, iris.holzleitner}@univie.ac.at
** Max Planck Institute for Human Cognitive and Brain Sciences, P.O. box
500355, 04303 Leipzig, Germany
atmaca@cbs.mpg.de

DANCING: A MATE SELECTION RITUAL

Thinking about dancing, several stereotypical pictures probably arise in your mind: a discotheque full of twitching people; a ballet ensemble, performing Swan Lake; a couple dancing an erotic tango; perhaps even a tribal dance around a fire, celebrating some special occasion. We find dance in all cultures around the world and in various styles. "In dance, man (...) cultivates his movements (...) into their most artistic skillfulness, affecting movements into an aesthetically most delightful ritual." (Eibl-Eibesfeld, 1989, p. 697). Various ethnographic records, as well as dance reviews in popular media, emphasize the aesthetic and artistic facets and the cultural importance of dance, judging individual dancers, dance companies, and choreographers, and telling us much about styles and quality of dancing. But as literature research shows us, we do not know much about the deep roots of this beautiful and ubiquitous form of human expression. This is why we want to focus on the evolutionary meaning of this motion behavior: Why do we dance?

Studies on the function of dance have shown that dance may serve various functions. It is clear that it occurs in the context of mate selection in almost all cultures. Usually dancing in the context of mate-selection is highly culturally elaborated with its basis being rhythmic body motion.

Our hypothesis is that one of the prominent functions of dance is that it serves as sexual indicator used in mate choice. The evolutionary argumentation is simple: If a behavior causes high costs for an individual, it must also have a positive effect on its reproductive or survival success. "Moving has energetic costs, so animals are expected to move only when the fitness benefits of movement exceed these costs." (Blythe et al., 1999). Considering that "music production and dancing would have had particularly high costs for our ancestors" (Miller, 1999, p. 334), dancing skills are also thought to have fitness benefits for the individual, probably formed by sexual selection. Since "mate seeking animals often evolve extremely complex courtship behaviors with special features designed to display their health, strength, size, status, intelligence, or creativity" (Blythe et al., 1999), dance might also be a courtship behavior, indicating one or more aspects of the overall fitness value of the dancing person. This line of reasoning fits with the closely related and much better explored topic 'evolution of music'. Many authors consider music to be an adaptation. Miller, for example, states: "Human music shows all the classic features of a complex biological adaptation." (Miller, 1999, p. 329). In terms of courtship behavior "we may assume that musical tones and rhythm were used by our half-human ancestors, during the season of courtship." (Darwin 1871, p. 880)

In 1998, Miller & Todd posited a two-stage lens model for assessing mate quality by integrating perceived sexual cues (Miller & Todd, 1998). According to this lens model, there are several sexual cues (e.g. waist-hip-ratio) that indicate different actual traits (e.g. fertility). Following this idea, music and dance could also be sexual cues for reproductive success, for instance fertility, health, or neuro-physiological efficiency.

A SHORT HISTORY OF DANCE RESEARCH

Grammer et al. (2003) stated that motion alone can provide a lot of information about a person. For instance, on the basis of motion perception alone, people can identify two of the major aspects of mate-choice which are identified up to now: Youth and gender. This is already well-known in scientific fields dealing with human gait. Hausdorff et al. (2001) showed that stride-to-stride fluctuation in gait patterns changes characteristically with maturation in children and older adults. From point-light display experiments[1], we know that subjects are very good in identifying the sex of walkers without seeing direct bodily cues of sex (e.g., Kozlowski & Cutting, 1977). But that is not all: There are also hints that diseases are reflected in gait patterns (Hausdorff et al., 2001). Additionally, Grammer et al. (1997) report differences in female movement quality during their menstruation cycle: Females were asked to turn around 360° in front of a video camera. They showed slower and more complex movements when they had high estrogen levels and were in the presence of a male experimenter. These findings support the idea that motion conveys a lot of information about a person and that movement quality is an indicator for the fertility of that person.

Additional hints of the importance of movement during courtship come from research of nonverbal courtship behavior. People in zero acquaintance scenarios tend to establish a personality profile (the 'big

---

[1] A point light display is a reduced visual representation of a moving human or animal body, produced in the dark, with the actor wearing lights on the independently moving body segments (typically on the joints).

five': extroversion, neuroticism, conscientiousness, agreeableness and openness) of a stranger in less than ten minutes (e.g. Borkenau & Liebler, 1992). Considering the very short time necessary for such assessments, this information is very likely to be extracted from behavior such as motion quality rather than from verbal exchange. Intelligence can be accurately accessed within a few minutes as well (e.g., Murphy et al., 2003). Furthermore, Walk & Homan (1984) and Dittrich et al. (1996) report that emotions expressed by educated mimes or dancers and taped as point-light displays are identified with remarkable accuracy. Grammer and others conducted several experiments in which two strangers of the opposite sex met for the first time and had a conversation (e.g., Grammer, 1990; Grammer et al., 1998; Grammer et al., 1999). These strangers show, for example, synchronization of nonverbal behavior with highly complex time structures (Grammer et al., 1998). Furthermore, female movement quality (number of movements, duration, size, speed, and complexity) covaries with female interest in her interlocutor (Grammer et al., 1999), whereas in both sexes a lack of interest is communicated through closed postures (Grammer, 1990). Thus, movement quality seems to indicate not only the mate value, but the interest of a potential partner as well, which could denote the probability of successful mating with this person.

FACIAL AND BODILY ATTRACTIVENESS

Evolutionary principles indicate that the more time or energy an individual invests in a bodily feature, the more reliable the feature is as an indicator for this person's genetic quality (e.g., Skamel, 2003). Since we are a species that has developed very complex language systems, we have generated a simple term for the complex judgment: "I very much enjoy perceiving a feature that indicates a high genetic quality." We call it 'beautiful' or 'attractive'. In other words: Instead of saying that "beautiful bodily features indicate high gene quality", we prefer to say that "high gene quality is manifested in certain bodily features, which we call beautiful".

Thornhill & Grammer (1999) suggested that the attractiveness of female faces and bodies is a reliable indicator of good health, fertility, and immunocompetence. Many female body features develop under the influence of estrogen. Estrogen is not only essential for the functioning of the female reproductive physiology (e.g., Dixson, 1998), but has negative effects on the immune system as well, for example, the promotion of certain hereditary diseases (Service, 1998). Therefore, females who carry bodily indicators of a high estrogen level show that they i) are able to reproduce, and ii) have such a powerful immune system that they can afford having such high estrogen levels. Thus, the simultaneous occurrence of two features, say a particular waist-hip-ratio signaling high estrogen levels, and even skin texture signaling immunological estrogen resistance, should be perceived as extremely attractive. Averageness and symmetry, in contrast, indicate a good immune system per se, because no diseases or parasites were able to disturb the physiological development (Grammer & Thornhill, 1994). The same relation exists for male body features and testosterone. Experiments have shown that female preference for testosterone-related facial characteristics is most apparent during their follicular phase of menstrual cycle, when conception is most likely.

Manning et al. (1998) found that the mean male second digit (index finger) to fourth digit (ring finger) ratio (2D:4D) is lower than the mean female ratio. Men tend to have longer ring fingers than index fingers, while in women the index finger is on average as long or even longer than the ring finger (Manning, 2002). Furthermore, Manning et al. (1998) found that in adult subjects lower digit ratios correlate with higher testosterone levels (for both men and women). This relation can also be found in sperm counts, number of offspring, and marital status (Manning et al., 1998, 2000; Manning, 2002). These findings are reflected in the perception of hand attractiveness: Manning & Crone (manuscript) have found that in men long ring fingers were positively associated with perceptions of attractiveness and sexiness.

How can finger digit ratio give us information about fertility? To answer this question, we have to go back to the 'ontogenetical descent of man', to about the seventh week of pregnancy. At this time, the genetically controlled sex differentiation begins by hormone-induced shaping of the sex specific gonad cells (testes in male and ovaries in female embryos) that immediately start to produce sex hormones. In male fetuses, there is a testosterone production peak in week 13 (Migeon & Wisniewski, 1998). Relative digit length, which appears to be fixed by week 14 (Garn et al., 1975), is influenced by the testosterone level via a number of tissues making up the fourth digit that are sensitive to testosterone (Manning, 2002). Manning et al. (1998) also found an insignificant but positive relation between prenatal estrogen level and the growth of the second digit. Therefore, the fetal digit length seems to reflect prenatal levels of sex hormones. The relationship between 2D:4D ratio and fetal hormone levels is of course difficult to measure directly. However, digit length seems to be "an indicator of steroid hormone levels at an important period for brain organization, sexual orientation, and the formation of the heart and major blood vessels and of the breasts." (Manning, 2002, p. xiv)

Sex-specific digit ratios affect not only the number of offspring and the likelihood to get married, but seem as well to be an indicator for musical and athletic ability. Sluming & Manning (2000) found out that there is a negative relationship between high musical ability (measured by the status of 54 men in a British symphony orchestra) and the musician's 2D:4D ratio. The same holds for athletic abilities. Manning & Taylor found in 2001 that professional football players had lower 2D:4D ratios than men of a control group. Football players in the reserve team had higher 2D:4D ratios than players in the first team, and players that had played in the national team had lower 2D:4D ratios than those who had not. Thus, musical ability and sportiness seem to be fertility indicators.

HORMONES AND MOTION

As we have seen above, 2D:4D ratio is negatively correlated to both prenatal and adult testosterone levels (e.g., Manning et al., 2001). Sex hormones control maturation of reproductive cells in both sexes. In males, testosterone is not only essential for spermatogenesis, but it is also known that high levels of testosterone suppress immunocompetence (e.g., Folstad & Karter, 1992). That is to say, only males with high immunocompetence can afford a high testosterone level. Females look for parasite-resistant males to increase their offspring's likelihood of surviving and to increase the probability of male parental care in species where males are involved in breeding. Thus, species-specific hormone markers that indicate high testosterone levels show high immunocompetence as well.

Two examples from the animal world demonstrate what further influence testosterone can have: Parker et al. (2002) showed that testosterone levels in male junglefowls were positively correlated to dominance rank. Individuals that transferred to smaller flocks showed reduced comb growth (a testosterone marker) and decreased testosterone levels. Olsson et al. (2000) treated male sand lizards with testosterone. These lizards showed greater mobility than control males, which resulted in higher mating success.

MOTION: ATTRACTIVENESS AND PERSONALITY

Further data for the connection between movement quality and courtship behavior come from attractiveness ratings of dancing subjects. Grammer et al. (2003) videotaped 71 persons in a dance club performing free dancing movements and transformed these short movies into dynamic quantized displays, which save the information about movement expressiveness, but do not allow identification of any body details. These quantized displays were rated for attractiveness and eroticism. It revealed that the mean rating for each stimulus person was correlated with its movement qualities (speed, emphasis, expressiveness, and complexity) (Grammer et al., 2003). It led the researchers to the conclusion that "movement quality is related to sex and attractiveness, and movement can be used as a stand-alone indicator for attractiveness" (Grammer et al. 2003, p. 316).

Indeed there are two studies which show a direct relation of body build and hormones to the attractiveness of dance. Brown et al. (2005) found in a Jamaican sample — using motion captured dances on neutral stick figures as stimuli — that bodily symmetry, one of the indicators of physical attractiveness, predicted perceived attractiveness of dance motions. The second study by Fink et al. (2007) shows that male saliva testosterone levels also predicted the attractiveness of male dancing motions. Both studies are thus able to link attractiveness and body motion via two crucial factors which link mate-quality and body motion.

But there are other factors than mere attractiveness ratings which could be conveyed by dancing. Bechinie & Grammer (2003) were able to use motion energy[2] data in training time delayed neural networks (TDNN, Waibel et al., 1989) to recognize personality traits (Big-Five, Costa, 1985) from male and female dancing motions. Koppensteiner & Grammer (2010) showed that personality can be decoded reliably from body and head motions of politicians which were transferred on stick figures. In this research also motion parameters were identified which lead to the decoding of the big five personality traits.

Personality also might function as a mate selection criterion because personality predicts the lines of action a person can take (Buss & Craik, 1983). Moreover on a proximate level, personality controls levels of cognitive functioning and is aimed at attaining or avoiding affective states central to a person. On an ultimate level, personality would allow predictability for self and others. It could serve as a social resource marker which facilitates ecological and social niche finding which matches a continuous distribution of viable strategies. McDonald (1999) thus concludes that personality is an evolved motivational system which has an affective core and its variance is maintained by frequency dependent selection. Studies of twins reared apart have also shown that the core of personality traits might be highly heritable (Pervin, 2003).

The high agreement among observers regarding the personality of a target has been demonstrated in several studies. Albright et al. (1988) assume that any impact of the stimulus target can be attributed to the physical features of the target. But they are not able to indicate which physical stimuli carry which information. Among researchers it is completely unclear how such a consensus might be reached and what information is used to assess the targets.

Previously, these finding have been explained by a social constructivist hypothesis which rests upon the assumption that there is no true association between appearance and personality, rather the consensus might reflect a commonly accepted covariation between certain facial features. This would reflect culturally acquired stereotypes about these links (cf. McArthur, 1982).

We will argue here that personality predicts the bandwidth of affect and affect then becomes visible in the quality of motion. This would make

---

[2] For a definition of motion energy see section on methodological issues (below).

the communication of personality possible in real time and allow a spectator to assess action tendencies in a potential mate via the 'shared manifold' (Gallese, 2001). Indeed our brain seems to be able to simulate motion in real time with the help of the so-called F-5 neurons which can be found in the prefrontal cortex. This could provide the pathway for the perception of dance by simulation in the brain.

BODY MOTION AND DYNAMIC SYSTEMS

Although we find some links between potential mate quality and dance — the signal which humans use for its assessment is less than clear. Here we propose that there has to be a relationship between cognition, the general construction of the body and the resulting body motion. This relation also might be called embodiment (Wachsmuth et al., 2008)

The actual intelligence of motion becomes visible through its expression by the body construction (Pfeiffer, 2007). In this view the body itself is a dynamical system with a limited number of degrees of freedom — in a simplified way this can be regarded as a number of joint pendulums which are controlled by the physical construction. In a simplified model (using head, arms, trunk, and legs) we would get a 12-dimensional dynamic system.

Thus, an organism's actual behavior is not only the outcome of internal control (brain) but also morphology, materials, and interaction with the environment. In this view the neurological structures exploit physical constraints in order to achieve robust movement and induce statistical regularities through sensor-motor activity. As a result motion ability is not only a result of motor control strategies, but the physical construction characteristics of the body, like length of levers, tendons, muscles and their weight, which determine the ability to move.

If this is the case we can suggest that prenatal sex hormone levels will determine the relative growth of brain regions in the two sexes (Goldstein et al., 2001). Relative differences caused by hormone exposure could be responsible for gender identification and moreover for different personalities. DeYoung et al. (2010) indeed were able to show in an fMRI study that the 'big five' personality dimensions are associated with the relative size of brain structures.

Following this line of thought — at the same time sex hormones create the blue print for later body development and affect differential growth of brain regions — it is at hand to expect a relation between personality, body build and body motion (Fig. 1). In terms of evolutionary biology (Oberzaucher & Grammer, 2008) body motion would consequently be an unfalsifiable signal and thus paramount to mate selection.

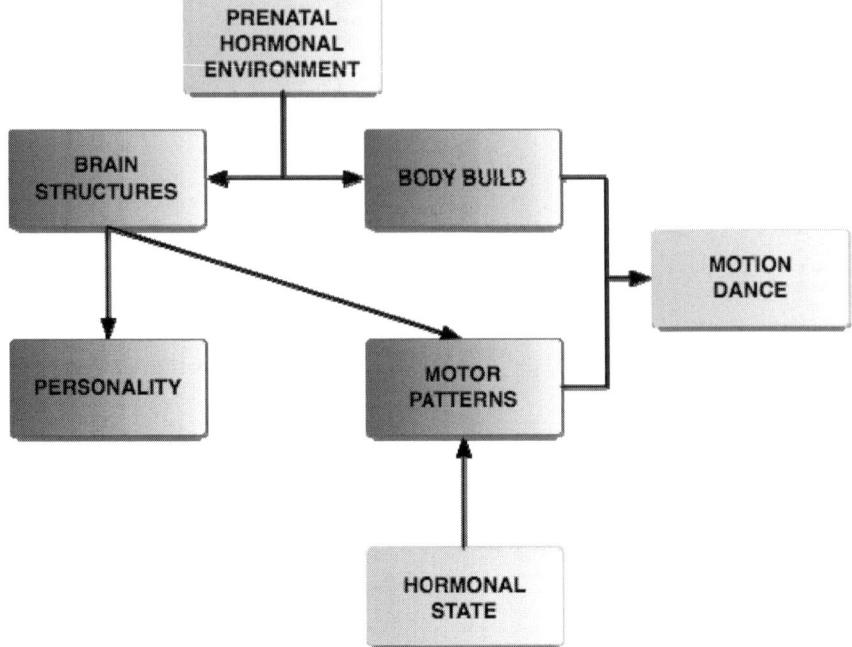

Fig. 1: Hormonal influences on differential growth and functioning of body regions. The prenatal hormonal environment affects the growth of brain structures and body proportions. Brain structures and body proportions affect motion quality, which is also affected by current hormonal state.

One problem for mate selection is that the cues which are used for assessing mate quality have to be honest and non-falsifiable. Body construction is the basis for motion and the influence of sex-hormones is difficult to falsify. Thus individuals should rely on the signals they see in movement, for example in dancing.

Early sex hormone levels are expressed in 2D:4D ratios — this measure would reflect the basic quality of brain build, body build and dancing. In addition we find relations between 2D:4D and the expression of personality (Fink et al. 2004). Thus the logical conclusion would be that these features are interrelated.

We will test our concept on data of a preliminary study we conducted on dancing, 2D:4D and personality. The methodological approach consists of the assessment of personality, 2D:4D ratios as a cue for prenatal hormonal environment, anthropological measurements which are associated with attractiveness to the opposite sex, and finally the analysis of the dynamic features of dance. These relations should be sex specific and allow us to identify the signal which people use for the assessment of the attractiveness of dance.

METHODOLOGICAL ISSUES AND ANALYSIS PROCEDURE
DATASET

The dataset consisted of 50 male (mean age 21) and 50 female students (mean age 20) who were recruited at the University of Vienna. They were instructed to dance for 30 seconds without music in presences of spectators of the same and opposite sex. This dance was videotaped (Fig. 2). In addition the subjects filled out a general demographic questionnaire and the German version of the NEO-FFI short version (Costa & McCrae, 1989).

After the dancing we measured finger length and took several anthropometric measures like body height, weight, breast, waist and hip circumference. Body fat was measured with a body fat analyzer (Tanita TBF-105). Finger length for the determination of the 2D:4D ratio was measured with a caliper from the distal crest to the finger tip (Fig. 3). Finger length is the sum of all four fingers measured (2D-5D). In addition we measured body symmetry by comparing the elbow, wrist, knee and ankle circumference of the left and right body side. All anthropometric measures were taken twice and averaged.

Fig. 2: Setup for videotaping dance motions.

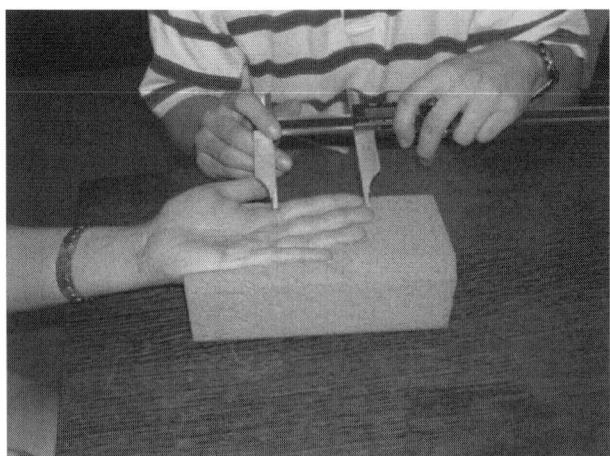

Fig. 3: Measuring of digit length

MOTION ANALYSIS

The videotaped dances were analyzed with Motion Energy Detection (MED, Bechinie & Grammer, 2003). MED basically is the first derivate of the video stream which actually produces one value for the amount of motion for each video frame. This method can be used to estimate the change of motion on a frame to frame basis (Fig. 4).

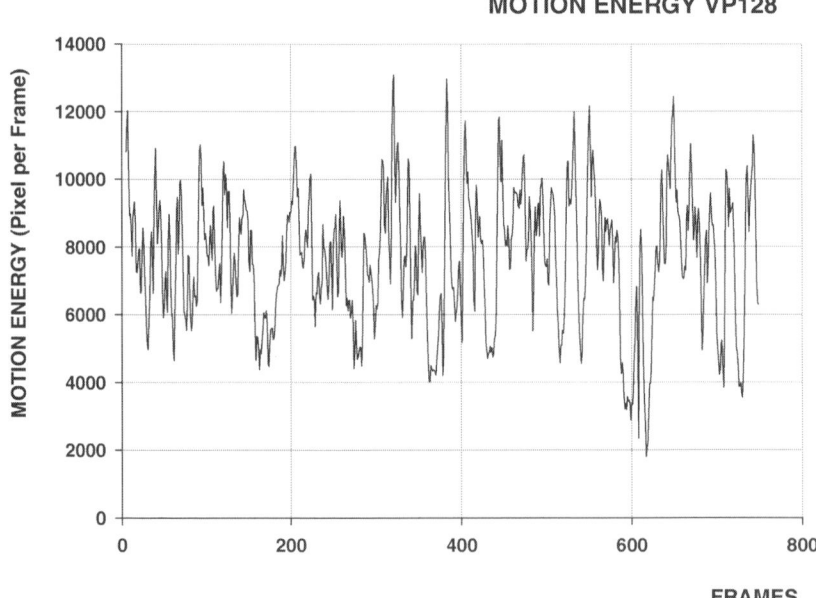

Fig. 4: The motion energy is based on the first derivate of a movie. It corresponds to the number of pixels that have changed their grey value.

RECURRENCE QUANTIFICATION ANALYSIS (RQA)

For the analysis of the dynamic properties of the motion energy curves we applied recurrence quantification analysis. Recurrence plots refer to the fact that deterministic dynamical systems diverge and converge in their patterns over time. Recurrence plots (RP) were introduced by Eckman et al. (1987). In such a plot all values of the time line are plotted against each other value. In a random series no patterns occur, but in more deterministic series patterns will form. A recurrence plot reveals distant correlations in a time series. RPs make it instantly apparent whether a system has periodic elements or is completely chaotic.

The measures introduced for the RQA were developed heuristically between 1992 and 2002 (Zbilut & Webber, 1992; Webber & Zbilut, 1994; Marwan et al., 2002). They are actually measures of complexity. The main advantage of the recurrence quantification analysis is that it can provide useful information even for short and non-stationary data, where other methods fail. RQA can be applied to almost every kind of data. It is widely used in physiology, but was also successfully applied on problems from engineering, chemistry and earth sciences (see Marvan et al, 2002). Here we will describe only the nature of the measures (for a mathematical outline see Marvan et al., 2002).

The dynamic features which can be assessed from an RP are:

Recurrence. Recurrence is the density of the recurrence points in an RP. This is the probability that a specific state will recur. In terms of dancing it will indicate that the same motion energy will occur again with a high probability — this would mean that the dancing motions are fluent and stereotypical.

Determinism. This measure is related to the predictability of the dynamic system — in terms of dancing it could be interpreted that no erratic or additional single elements are added.

Laminarity. Laminarity is related to the amount of linear phases in the system or its intermittency. In dynamical systems intermittency is the alternation of phases of apparently periodic and chaotic dynamics. In terms of dancing this would mean the fraction of time the dance is uncoordinated and turbulent.

Trapping Time. This measure indicates how long a system stays in a certain state — in dancing this would be how long a person holds a steady rhythm, for instance.

Divergence is the maximal diagonal line length, and as such a measure of the determinism of the system.

Entropy. This reflects the complexity of the deterministic structure in the system — and it is a measure of uncertainty — in terms of dancing with unpredictable motions.

Trend. This measure provides information about the stationarity of the system.

The recurrence analysis was done in the program Visual Recurrence Analysis by A. Koronov[3]. In Fig. 5 we show a recurrence plot of the dance data from Fig. 4. It shows that the moving body indeed is a dynamical system, which in dancing movements undergoes different recurrence states.

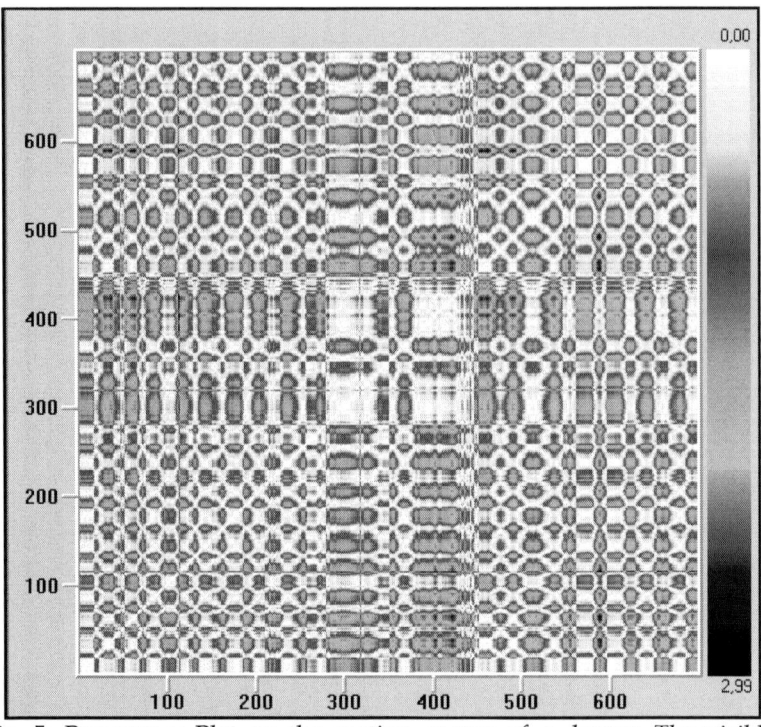

Fig. 5: Recurrence Plot on the motion energy of a dancer. The visible pattern shows the high degree of determinism in the dancing movements.

DYNAMICS OF DANCE

Prenatal hormonal environment

The 2D:4D relation is significantly different between the sexes in the predicted direction. The difference for both hands in males is -4.3 mm and for females it is -1.3 mm (ANOVA, $F = 7.3$, $p = 0.008$). The results do not change when corrected for body height (ANOVA, $F = 6.2$, $p = 0.015$). Independent of body height, male 2D:4D is lower than female 2D:4D. This indicates a pronounced sex difference in early hormonal environment.

---

[3] http://nonlinear.110mb.com/vra/

Body Measurements

For the body measurements we found the expected sex differences. Males are significantly taller and heavier than females and have more muscle mass and less fat than females. Their body mass index and their waist to hip ratio is higher than in females, whereas there are no differences in shoulder to hip ratio and body symmetry.

The question is how early hormonal development relates to body build. Weight (n = 45, r = -.32, p = 0.03), hip circumference (n = 45, r = -.42, p = 0.004), body fat (n = 26, r = -.48, p = 0.01) and finger length (n = 45, r = -.30, p = 0.04) correlate negatively with 2D:4D — this implies that the absence of prenatal testosterone correlates with a more feminine body build in males — for females no relations emerge.

Table 1: Sex differences in body build

	male		female	
	Mean	SD	Mean	SD
Height	180.09$_a$	5.44	166.46$_b$	5.75
Breast	93.0$_a$	8.6	87.8$_b$	6.2
Waist	82.8$_a$	7.9	71.3$_b$	6.9
Hip	94.6$_a$	7.1	89.4$_b$	7.5
Finger length	307.90$_a$	17.72	279.88$_b$	16.55
Weight	74.4$_a$	11.3	58.5$_b$	7.6
Percentage body fat	11.97$_a$	6.84	17.19$_b$	7.10
Muscle mass	63.09$_a$	6.06	42.68$_b$	3.12
Body Mass Index	.23$_a$	0.03	.21$_b$	0.03
Waist to Hip Ratio	.88$_a$	0.06	.80$_b$	0.05
Shoulder to Hip Ratio	.99$_a$	0.08	.99$_a$	0.07
Body Symmetry	.821$_a$	0.072	.822$_a$	0.092

Note: Values in the same row and subtable not sharing the same subscript are significantly different at p < 0.05 in the two-sided test of equality for column means.

Personality

Personality traits were analyzed with the standard procedure of the NEO-FFI (which measures the 'big five'). Sex differences were found as follows: Females show higher scores on neuroticism (n = 50, mean = 2.0, SD = 0.7) than males (n = 50, mean = 1.6, SD = 0.5, ANOVA F = 12.4, p = 0.001) and females score higher (n = 50, mean = 2.7, SD = 0.5) than males (n = 50, mean = 2.4, SD = 0.4) in agreeableness (ANOVA F = 4.3, p = 0.039).

Prenatal hormonal environment (2D:4D) correlates only with extraversion in males (n = 44, r = -.33, p = 0.02). Extraversion further shows a correlation with body fat (n = 25, r = .41 p = 0.04), waist to hip ratio (n = 45, r = .36 p = 0.02), and shoulder to hip ratio (n = 45, r = .33, p = 0.02). Openness correlates with finger length (n = 45, r = .34, p = 0.02). Conscientiousness correlates with shoulder to hip ratio (n = 45, r = 0.30, p = 0.04). In females no significant correlations between body build and personality traits were found.

Motion dynamics

As males and females differ considerably in body build, we should be able to show that the dynamic features from the RQA differ — if the argument holds true that body build indeed affects motion quality. Indeed recurrence rate (males 15.4, SD = 33, females 27.8, SD = 24, t-test, p = .04), determinism (males 31.9, SD = 24, females 45.1, SD = 28, t-test, p = .01), and laminarity (males 18.2, SD = 27, females 31.6, SD = 37, t-test, p = .05) are significantly higher in males than in females. The female dance is less chaotic and shows more fluent motions with continuous repetitions.

In order to reduce the data we applied a Principal Component Analysis to the motion quality variables. The resulting three factors explained 78.5% of the variance. 1) The rhythmic dancer shows high recurrences of specific states and high intermittency along with high levels of determinism and predictability of the occurrence of elements. The motion system stays in the same state for a long time and the deterministic structure is highly complex. 2) The smooth and slow dancer's style is a low dimensional dynamic system with high divergence of the trajectories. And finally 3) the wild dancer shows high determinism, low recurrence and low stationarity with high trends in motion changes (turns body around). Prevalence of dancing styles is not significantly different between the sexes.

Motion, body measurements and personality

The final part of the analysis will now deal with motion, personality and prenatal hormonal environment. Agreeable males use the slow dancer style (n = 45, r = .37, p = 0.02) and conscientious males use the rhythmic dancer style (n = 45, r = .31, p = 0.04). Agreeable females in contrast avoid the slow dancer style (n = 45, r = -.28, p = 0.05) and conscientious females also avoid the rhythmic dancing style (n = 45, r = -.32, p = 0.03) but prefer the wild dancer style (n = 45, r = .28, p = 0.05). This is also reflected in correlations of prenatal hormonal environment and dancing style. In males there is a positive correlation between 2D:4D and rhythmic dancing (n = 45, r = .35, p = 0.02) while no such relationships are found in females.

When we take a look at the body measurements themselves we find that rhythmic male dancers (n = 45) are symmetric (r = .38, p = 0.01), show a high waist to hip ratio (r = .35, p = 0.02), a high shoulder to hip ratio (r = .41, p = 0.006), and have shorter fingers (r = -.32, p = 0.04). The last two relations hold also true for female finger length (r = -.30, p = 0.05) and shoulder to hip ratio (r = .33, p = 0.03). Females who dance with the wild style usually have small breasts (r = -.30, p = 0.04).

RÉSUMÉ: THE BODY AS A DYNAMIC SYSTEM

We believe that dance is one of the last unexplored mysteries of human behavior. After carefully reviewing past research, we think we have identified useful methods for revealing evolutionary explanations for this mysterious motion pattern. Correlations of movement quality with selected cues that are known to indicate reproductive success (2D:4D ratio, personality and body features) only partially support our hypothesis that dance quality is used as one of many cues for mate choice. In this first exploratory study our hypothesis was that prenatal environment influences both personality and body build and then finds its expression in dancing could not be fully supported.

Kretschmer (1921, 1961) and later Sheldon (1940) tried to find correlational relationships between body build and personality or temperament. Both assumed a causal relationship — but later it became clear that the results were artifacts originated in methodological shortcomings. The more serious problem was that this type of research in all its naïveté discredited psychological analysis of human gestalt. But newer work by Borkenau & Liebler (1995) suggests a link between appearance and personality. A second problem is that the assumed somatotypes as such are not supported by empirical data when analyzed with modern statistical methods. This is why we concentrated on sex differences. Our model is completely different in that we assume a common variable, which is only partially genetic, i.e. sex hormone levels during early ontogeny.

Our basic idea was that both personality and body build are determined by prenatal sex hormones and — when dancing is embodied — personality could find its embodied expression. A complete model for this hypothesis could not be established in the course of this project. But we find a row of interesting isolated results, which still prevail after correction for the amount of statistical tests. Therefore the reason why TDNNs can be trained to assess personality from dancing movements remains still unveiled. One basic problem of this study is the small number of subjects — we will try to increase this in future studies.

The interactions between 2D:4D and personality is weak — as has been shown in other research. One reason for that could be that the NEO-FFI questionnaire does not cover the dimensions of personality which are affected by prenatal concentrations of sex hormones. Only male extraversion can be related to 2D:4D.

In contrast, 2D:4D is correlated to a high number of bodily features — in males, but not in females. It seems that prenatal testosterone is not responsible for variations in bodily features in the female sex. The lack of relations between 2D:4D and other measures in women could be due to the basic female mechanism. Whereas the construction of a male organism requires the presence of sex hormones, female organisms develop in the absence of sex hormones (Panksepp, 1998). Consequently, positive relations between 2D:4D and other variables are more likely to occur in males, where higher sex hormone concentrations are present. Nevertheless we find profound sex-differences in body build and in the dynamic features of dancing. Females dance recurrently and apparently with smoother motions, whereas heavier males dance not so smooth — it seems that heavier bodies cannot be exploited as well for dancing moves.

Another question is whether traits, which are responsible for bodily attractiveness, covary with dancing style. In males apparently shoulder to hip ratio might depend on sex hormones as expressed in 2D:4D, moreover high shoulder to hip ratio correlates with the loading on rhythmic dancing style in both sexes. Finger length shows the same pattern in both sexes: The longer the fingers, the higher the degree of rhythmic dancing. The mechanism of action suggests that sex steroids exert both an indirect and a direct effect on longitudinal bone growth. Sex steroids influence growth hormone secretion in humans (Frantz & Raben, 1965; Illig & Prader, 1970), which is responsible for bone length growth. If this is the case, we have to take the length of long bones and the resulting proportional differences between subjects and the sexes into account. On the level of the assumption that the human body is a combination of pendulums (at least when dancing) this relation between bone lengths and motion patterns would make perfect sense in terms of physics.

Interestingly enough female breast size, probably because of the inertia moment produced by their weight seems to prohibit the wild dancing. Moreover dancers using the rhythmic stile show a higher body symmetry which is clearly a trait in mate selection.

As we can show the human body can be described as a dynamic system in its motion. The dynamic system is partially sex specific — with respect to body build, and relates, at least in males, to early hormonal environment. In the next step of our research we will try to determine how motion attractiveness fits into the whole picture.

The problem with this study is that the number of subjects apparently is too small so we could not control for spectator effects, which can play a considerable role in the emergence of the typical dance styles. Another problem is that Motion Energy Detection and/or RQA do not pick up the signal completely. And a last, but serious problem could be that the NEO-FFI items are not the personality traits which play a role in mate choice. Besides sex-differences in personality we also find correlations between body build and personality within males and females. This gives rise to the question which variable causes both, within and between sex effects.

A final problem is an analytical problem — some of the bodily traits do not behave in a linear way, like i.e. waist to hip ratio, where an average female waist to hip ratio is attractive rather than a minimum or a maximum. This might be the case for many body measurements and should receive attention in our future research.

In this research area it seems too early to accede to Knight Dunlap's statement from 1928:

> At the present time many so called character analysts, consultants, and experts are presenting both plausibly and earnestly methods of judging character based on physical criteria, such as head measurements. Respectably psychology almost without exception repudiates such methods and its foundations on physiological and neurological grounds. The futility of character judgments by any form of phrenology is refuted theoretically to the queen's taste in a conclusive onslaught. (Cleeton & Knight, 1928, p.255).

They conclude that the physical measurements which underlie character analysis agree neither with themselves nor with other measures of character. These authors at this point in time (1928) set an end to a hype in society where everybody believed that personal character is encoded in bodily and facial appearance. Physiognomy and phrenology were based on the assumption that different traits and abilities of an individual were manifested in the shape and form of the skull and the face. And indeed no scientific evidence was found to support the ideas of physiognomy (Alley, 1988) and the proposed links between character and appearance are mystical (Brandt, 1980).

However, in recent research a new paradigm has arisen, which creates surprising results: The zero acquaintance paradigm is a condition were one person observes another, but the two have never engaged in social interaction before. Surprisingly it seems that people's first impressions of a stranger are remarkably similar regarding some traits. Borkenau & Liebler (1993) showed short 90 second video clips of participants to strangers who assessed the stimulus persons on Big Five Personality Scales (Costa & McCrae, 1985). They also obtained ratings by the target's cohabiting partners. There were significant acquaintance-partner-stranger correlations for extraversion and openness dimensions. Berry (1990) found significant acquaintance-stranger correlations based on static facial photographs for impressions of warmth, honesty and social power.

These results have been replicated over and over under various conditions. Norman & Goldberg (1966) report statistically significant self-stranger correlations for the big five (openness, conscientiousness, neuroticism, extraversion, and openness) when strangers meet for 20 minutes in a waiting room. This finding was replicated by Watson (1989). Borkenau & Liebler (1993) manipulated the amount of information presented to strangers (video and sound) and found high self-strangers correlations for extraversion and conscientiousness. Correlations were highest in the video and sound condition. We are currently pursuing this line of research in social interactions and dancing.

Whereas we are still cautious with the conclusions about the relation between hormones, body build and personality, we think that this line of research is worth further effort. The picture is far from being complete, but each study casts a little more light on the complex developmental and functional processes involved in the creation of such signals.

References

Albright L., Kenny D. A., & Malloy T. E. (1988). Consensus in Personality judgments at zero acquaintance. *Journal of Personality and Social Psychology, 55,* 387-95.

Bechinie M. & Grammer K. (2003). Charisma Cam: a Prototype of an Intelligent Digital Sensory Organ for Virtual Humans. Intelligent Virtual Agents. In T. Rist et al. (eds.), *Intelligent Virtual Agents* (pp. 212-6). Berlin: Springer.

Blythe P. W., Todd P. M., & Miller G. F. (1999). How Motion Reveals Intention. In G. Gigerenzer, P. M. Todd, & the ABC Research Group. *Simple heuristics that make us smart* (pp. 257-85). New York: Oxford University Press.

Borkenau P. & Liebler A. (1992). Trait inferences – sources of validity at zero acquaintance. *Journal of Personality and Social Psychology, 62,* 645-57.

Borkenau P. & Liebler A. (1995). Observable attributes as manifestations and cues of personality and intelligence. *Journal of Personality, 63,* 1-25.

Buss D. M. & Craik K. H. (1983). The act frequency approach to personality. *Psychological Review, 90,* 105-26

Costa P. T. Jr. & McCrae R. R. (1985). *The NEO Personality Inventory manual.* Odessa: Psychological Assessment Resources.

Darwin C. (1871). *The Descent of Man, and Selection in Relation to Sex.* London: Murray.

DeYoung C. G., Hirsh J. B., Shane M. S., Papademetris X., Rajeevan, N., & Gray J. R. (2010). Testing Predictions from Personality Neuroscience: Brain structure and the Big Five. *Psychological Science, 21,* 820–8.

Dittrich W. H., Troscianko T., Lea S. E. G., & Morgan D. (1996). Perception of emotion from dynamic point-light displays represented in dance. *Perception, 25,* 727-38.

Dixon A. F. (1998). *Primate sexuality. Comparative studies of the prosiminans, monkeys, apes, and human beings.* Oxford: Oxford University Press.

Eckmann J. P., Kamphorst S. O., & Ruelle D. (1987). Recurrence Plots of Dynamical Systems. *Europhysics Letters, 5,* 973–7.

Eibl-Eibesfeldt I. (1989). *Human Ethology.* New York: Aldine de Gruyter.

Fink B., Manning J. T., & Neave N. (2004). Second to fourth digit ratio and the 'big five' personality factors. *Personality and Individual Differences, 37,* 495–503.

Fink B., Seydel H., Manning J. T., & Kappeler P. M. (2007). A preliminary investigation of associations between digit ratio and women's perception of men's dance. *Personality and Individual Differences, 4,* 381-90.

Folstad I. & Karter A. J. (1992). Parasites, Bright Males, and the Immunocompetence Handicap. *American Naturalist, 139,* 603-22.

Frantz A. G. & Rabkin M. T. (1965). Effects of estrogens and sex difference on secretion of human growth hormone. *J. Clin. Endocrinol. Metab., 25,* 1470-80.

Gallese V. (2001). The "Shared Manifold" Hypothesis: from mirror neurons to empathy. *Journal of Consciousness Studies, 8,* N° 5-7, 33-50.

Garn S. M., Burdi A. R., Babler W. J., & Stinson S. (1975). Early prenatal attainment of adult metacarpal-phalengeal rankings and proportions. *American Journal of Physical Anthropology, 43,* 327-32.
Goldstein J. M., Seidman L. J., Horton N. J., Makris N., Kennedy D. N., Caviness V. S. Jr., Faraone S. V., & Tsuang M. T. (2001). Normal sexual dimorphism of the adult human brain assessed by in vivo magnetic resonance imaging. *Cereb Cortex, 11,* 490-7.
Grammer K. (1990). Strangers meet: Laughter and nonverbal signs of interest in opposite-sex encounters. *Journal of Non-Verbal Communication, 14,* 209-35.
Grammer K., Fieder M., & Filova V. (1997). The communication paradox and possible solutions. In A. Schmitt, K. Atzwanger, K. Grammer, & K. Schäfer (eds.), *New aspects of human ethology* (pp. 91-120). New York: Plenum Press.
Grammer K., Honda M., Juette A., & Schmitt A. (1999). Fuzziness of Nonverbal Courtship Communication. Unblurred By Motion Energy Detection. *Journal of Personality and Social Psychology, 77,* 509-24.
Grammer K., Keki V., Striebel B., Atzmüller M., & Fink B. (2003). Bodies in Motion: A Window to the Soul. In E. Voland & K. Grammer (eds.), *Evolutionary Aesthetics* (pp. 295-323). Berlin, Heidelberg, New York: Springer-Verlag.
Grammer K., Kruck K. B., & Magnusson M. S. (1998). The courtship dance: patterns of non-verbal synchronisation in opposite sex-encounters. *Journal of Non-Verbal Behavior, 22,* 3-29.
Grammer K. & Thornhill R. (1994). Human (Homo sapiens) facial attractiveness and sexual selection: the role of symmetry and averageness. *Journal of Comparative Psychology, 108,* 233-42.
Hausdorff J. M., Ashkenazy Y., Peng Ch. K., Ivanov P. Ch., Stanley H. E., & Goldberger A. L. (2001). When human walking becomes random walking: fractal analysis and modeling of gait rhythm fluctuations. *Physica A, 302,* 138-47.
Illig R. & Prader A. (1970). Effects of testosterone on growth hormone secretion in patients with anorchia and delayed puberty. *J Clin Enocrinol Metab, 30,* 615-8.
Koppensteiner M. & Grammer K. (2010). Motion patterns in political speech and their influence on personality ratings. *Journal for Research in Personality 44,* 374-9.
Kozlowski L. & Cutting J. E. (1977). Recognizing the sex of a walker from a dynamic point-light display. *Perception & Psychophysics, 21,* 575-80.
Manning J. T. (2002). *Digit Ratio: A Pointer to Fertility, Behavior, and Health.* New Brunswick: Rutgers University Press.
Manning J. T., Barley L., Walton J., Lewis-Jones D. I., Trivers R. L., Singh D., Thornhill R., Rohde P., Bereczkei T., Henzi P., Soler M., & Szwed A. (2000). The 2nd:4th digit ratio, sexual dimorphism, population differences, and reproductive success: evidence for sexually antagonistic genes? *Evolution and Human Behavior, 21,* 163-83.
Manning J. T. & Crone (manuscript). Cited in J. T. Manning (2002). *Digit Ratio: A Pointer to Fertility, Behavior, and Health.* New Brunswick: Rutgers University Press.
Manning J. T., Henzi P., & Bundred P.E. (2001). The ratio of 2nd to 4th digit length: a proxy for testosterone, and susceptibility to HIV and AIDS? *Medical Hypotheses, 57,* 761-3.
Manning J. T., Scutt D., Wilson J., & Lewis-Jones D. I. (1998). The ratio of the 2nd to 4th digit length: A predictor of sperm numbers and levels of testosterone, LH and oestrogen. *Human Reproduction, 13,* 3000-4.
MacDonald K. B. (1999). What about Sex Differences? An Adaptationist Perspective on 'the Lines of Causal Influence' of Personality Systems. Commentary on 'Neurobiology of the Structure of Personality: Dopamine Facilitation of Incentive Motivation & Extraversion' by R. A. Depue & P. F. Collins. *Behavioral and Brain Sciences, 22,* 530–1.
McArthur L. Z. (1982). Judging a book by its cover: A cognitive analysis of the relationship between physical appearance and stereotyping. In A. Hastorf & A. Isen (eds.), *Cognitive social psychology* (pp. 149-211). New York: Elsevier.

Marwan N., Romano M. C., Thiel M., & Kurths J. (2007). Recurrence Plots for the Analysis of Complex Systems. *Physics Reports, 438,* 237.

Marwan N., Wessel N., Meyerfeldt U., Schirdewan A., & Kurths J. (2002). Recurrence Plot Based Measures of Complexity and its Application to Heart Rate Variability Data. *Physical Review, E 66,* 026702.

Marwan N. & Kurths J. (2002). Nonlinear analysis of bivariate data with cross recurrence plots. *Physics Letters A, 302,* 299-307.

Migeon C. J. & Wisniewski A. B. (1998). Review – Sexual differentiation: From genes to gender. *Hormone Research, 50,* 245-51.

Miller G. F. (1999). Evolution of Human Music through Sexual Selection. In N. L. Wallin, B. Merker, & S. Brown (eds.), *The Origin of Music.* Cambridge, London: MIT Press.

Miller G. F. & Todd P. M. (1998). Mate choice turns cognitive. *Trends in Cognitive Sciences, 2,* 190-8.

Murphy N. A., Hall J. A., & Colvin C. R. (2003). Accurate Intelligence Assessments in Social Interactions: Mediator and Gender Effects. *Journal of Personality, 71,* 465.

Oberzaucher E. & Grammer K. (2008). Everything is movement: on the nature of embodied communication. In I. Wachsmuth, M. Lenzen, & G. Knoblich (eds.), *Embodied communication* (pp. 151-77). Oxford: Oxford University Press.

Olsson M., Wapstra E., Madsen T., & Silverin B. (2000). Testosterone, ticks and travels: a test of the immunocompetence-handicap hypothesis in free-ranging male sand lizards. *Proceedings of the Royal Society of London Series B-Biological Sciences, 267,* 2339-43.

Panksepp J. (1998). Affective Neuroscience: The Foundations of Human and Animal Emotions (Series in Affective Science). New York: Oxford University Press,.

Parker T. H., Knapp R., & Rosenfield J. A. (2002). Social mediation of sexually selected ornamentation and steroid hormone levels in male junglefowl. *Animal Behavior, 64,* 291-8.

Pervin L. A. (2003). *The science of personality.* New York: Oxford University Press.

Pfeifer R. & Bongard J. (2007). *How the Body Shapes the Way We Think: A New View of Intelligence.* Cambridge: The MIT Press.

Service R. (1998). New role of estrogen in cancer. *Science, 279,* 1631-2.

Skamel U. (2003). Beauty and Sex Appeal: Sexual Selection of Aesthetic Preferences. In E. Voland & K. Grammer (eds.), *Evolutionary Aesthetics* (pp. 173-200). Berlin, Heidelberg, New York: Springer-Verlag.

Sluming V. A. & Manning J. T. (2000). Second to fourth digit ratio in elite musicians: Evidence for musical ability as an honest signal of male fitness. *Evolution and Human Behavior, 21,* 1-9.

Thornhill R. & Grammer K. (1999). The body and face of woman: one ornament that signals quality? *Evolution and Human Behavior, 20,* 105-20.

Wachsmuth I., Lenzen M., & Knoblich G. (2008) *Embodied communication.* Oxford: Oxford University Press.

Waibel A. H., Hanazawa T., Hinton G. E., Shikano K., & Lang K. J. (1989). Phoneme Recognition Using Time-Delay Neural Networks. *IEEE Transactions on Acoustic, Speech, and Signal Processing, 37,* 328-39.

Walk R. D. & Homan C. P. (1984). Emotion and dance in dynamic light displays. *Bulletin of the Psychonomic Society, 22,* 437-40.

Watson D. (1989). Strangers' ratings of the five robust personality factors: Evidence of a surprising convergence with self-report. *Journal of Personality and Social Psychology, 57,* 120-8.

Webber C. L. Jr. & Zbilut J. P. (1994). Dynamical assessment of physiological systems and states using recurrence plot strategies. *Journal of Applied Physiology 76,* 965-73.

Zbilut J. P. & Webber C. L. Jr. (1992). Embeddings and delays as derived from quantification of recurrence plots. *Physics Letters A, 171,* 199-203.

Nonverbal synchrony in psychotherapy: embodiment at the level of the dyad

Fabian Ramseyer

University Hospital of Psychiatry, University of Bern, Switzerland,
Stanford University, Department of Psychology,
450 Serra Mall, Stanford, CA 94305
fabian.ramseyer@spk.unibe.ch

"There are no chaste minds. Minds copulate wherever they meet."
"When people are free to do as they please, they usually imitate each other"
Eric Hoffer (1902 – 1983) American Author and Philosopher

Introduction

Like Eric Hoffer, who does not believe in chaste minds, Watzlawick et al. (1967) have pointed out that 'non-behaving' individuals do not exist: behaviour has no opposite, so non-behaviour is not defined. This chapter concerns nonverbal behaviour in dyadic interaction, where non-behaviour is especially difficult to imagine. However, traditional research on nonverbal behaviour has primarily focused on the behaviour of single individuals in a dyadic interaction, as though each of two interacting individuals might be examined independently. In psychotherapy research, for example, behaviour has been assessed either at the level of the patient or the therapist, largely ignoring the system level of the dyad (see overview in Hall et al., 1995). In contrast, this paper uses a different strategy that focuses on the dyad as the unit. Instead of concentrating on specific nonverbal acts, the dynamic quality of behaviour will provide information about the psychological state of the dyad. Later, we shall specifically suggest that the quality of the therapeutic relationship is embodied in the amount of coordinated movement between patient and therapist, which we call 'nonverbal synchrony'. Nonverbal synchrony may be considered a Gestalt which humans are capable of perceiving on a flexible time basis (Bernieri et al., 1988), and which does not reside in any particular behaviour (Davis, 1982; Grammer et al., 1998). For the study reported here, we have adopted a theoretically neutral concept of movement coordination. We were interested in the manifestation of coordinated dynamics, not in specific gestures, postures, or other isolated acts. This 'dynamical systems view' (Haken et al., 1985; Newtson, 1994; Schmidt & Richardson, 2008; Vallacher & Nowak, 2009) is an appropriate framework for defining nonverbal synchrony. Before doing so for the case of psychotherapy, we present a brief overview of nonverbal synchrony in dyadic interaction more generally and its relationship to the concept of embodiment.

Nonverbal synchrony in social interaction

During social interaction, people frequently adapt to each other without awareness of doing so (Bernieri & Rosenthal, 1991; Burgoon et al., 1995; Davis, 1982; Hatfield et al., 1994). Such mutual influence takes place in a variety of behavioural domains, in cognition, in emotion, and on a physiological level. Synchrony has been conceptualised from a neural perspective (*mirror neurons*; Gallese et al., 1996; Iacoboni, 2009), from a representational perspective (*neuronal coherence*; Dumas et al., 2010; Rodriguez et al., 1999), and from a perspective of self-organised behavioural dynamics (*synergetics*; Haken et al., 1985; Oullier et al., 2008). Condon & Ogston (1966) were the first authors to empirically analyse the phenomenon during verbal interaction. They used the term 'interactional synchrony' to refer to the coordination of body movements between interaction partners. In this chapter, our usage of the general term 'synchrony' includes the coordination of body movement (Bernieri & Rosenthal, 1991), the imitation of specific actions or mannerisms (Chartrand & Bargh, 1999), congruence in posture (Scheflen, 1964), mimicry of facial displays (Sonnby-Borgström et al., 2003), convergence of voice quality (Neumann & Strack, 2000), synchrony in physiology (Marci et al., 2007) and contagion of emotional states (Hatfield et al., 1994). These concepts all share the common notion that participants of social exchange have an effect upon each other during their interactive behaviour. According to Cappella (1981)

> ... mutual influence in expressive behaviors is a pervasive feature of social interaction, found across a variety of behaviors. This pervasiveness extends not only across behaviors but across developmental time. ... One must be awed by the flexible yet patterned responses that social actors make to one another. (p. 123)

Movement behaviour and embodiment

Merleau-Ponty (2002) noted in the mid-20th century that sensation, perception and cognition are inseparably connected to the physical body. "It is through my body that I understand other people, just as it is through my body that I perceive 'things'." (Merleau-Ponty, 2002, p. 216). This observation is receiving strong neuroscientific support, e.g. in the domain of the perception of emotion (de Gelder, 2009).

We view embodiment and embodied cognition as the larger framework in the investigation of synchrony and similar phenomena (Semin & Cacioppo, 2008). Cognitive functions as well as interpersonal attributions are not sufficiently understood as computation or information processing and, therefore, the computer metaphor of the mind has been found to be ill-advised. Modern psychology has proceeded towards acknowledging the intrinsic embedding of the mind in its body and in its environment, which amounts to Lewin's concept of *Lebensraum* (Lewin, 1936; cf., Haken & Tschacher, this volume). Contemporary systems theory (Haken, 1988) with its emphasis on self-organisation provides the formal foundation of a dynamical system approach to the mind (Tschacher & Dauwalder, 2003), which may shed a new light on attributes of cognition as well as attributes of interpersonal functioning. When considered from an evolutionary viewpoint, a person needs to be able to transform the raw perception of a partner's acts, into an interpretation of the partner's mood and intentions. Most of these processes are very fast and occur outside conscious awareness (Tamietto & de Gelder, 2010).

Research in the domain of nonverbal behaviour has traditionally focused on facial behaviour, while whole-body actions have received less scientific attention (de Gelder, 2009). This bias is currently changing, possibly due to the relevance of motor action for the mirror neuron system. This shift towards a better inclusion of motoric movement is justified, as exemplified by a study which showed that the accuracy of detecting facial emotion from movies (i.e. with visible movements of the face) is significantly higher compared to still photographs (Brick et al., 2009). That is, the whole body (not just the face) can hence be viewed as an important 'signalling device' in emotional processing (de Gelder, 2006). Body movement during social interaction thus serves as an indicator of the type of interpersonal exchange that is taking place. Such information can be assessed at the level of the individual (Blake & Shiffrar, 2007; Grammer et al., 1997, 2003; Kupper et al., 2010) as well as at the level of the dyad: "The most parsimonious reason may be that rapport is primarily a physically manifested construct; it is a construct that is visible at the surface and readily apparent. ... In other words, rapport simply may be visible." (Grahe & Bernieri, 1999, p. 265).

Based on the relevance of synchrony for dyads and on the importance of body movement, we hypothesised that nonverbal synchrony would be meaningfully associated with various measures of therapeutic success.

Synchronisation and the quality of a relationship

In their definition of rapport, Tickle-Degnen & Rosenthal (1990) explicitly addressed three nonverbal components that shape rapport: attentiveness, positivity-negativity, and coordination. Here, we focus on coordination, because this feature resides solely in the dyad and it is very closely related to the concept of synchrony as described above.

In humans, synchrony occurs very early in life (Meltzoff & Moore,

1977) and it plays a crucial role for a child's successful development (Feldman, 2007; Harrist & Waugh, 2002). Early examples of synchrony have been documented in the domain of body movement (O'Toole & Dubin, 1968), voice and language (Cappella, 1981), emotions (Feldman et al., 1999), and in relationship with the development of attachment (Isabella et al., 1989). Stronger or more synchrony was associated with favourable development and more successful social adaptation later in life (Barber et al., 2001). For adults, the so called chameleon effect (Chartrand & Bargh, 1999) has instigated a renewed interest in synchronised processes during social interaction. Most of the available studies generally acknowledge a beneficial effect of synchrony for both imitator and imitatee (see overview in Chartrand & van Baaren, 2009). In the domain of purely dynamic or rhythmic synchronisation of movement, there are several recent studies that have revealed that synchronised motor activity increases both cooperation (Wiltermuth & Heath, 2009) and liking (Hove & Risen, 2009), and is associated with higher ratings of rapport. Even rather basic body movements, such as walking, are more synchronised in dyads with positive relationships (Miles et al., 2010). The degree of movement synchronisation also has an impact for an observer's rating of how much two persons form an entity and how well they seem to get along together (Lakens, 2010). Taken together, there is ample evidence that synchrony during emotionally positive valenced interactions is associated with positive aspects of relationship quality.

Evolution theory (Lakin et al., 2003) is an appropriate background for these principles, because advantages to survival are evident both phylogenetically (e.g. a synchronised flight response in threatening situations: Preston & de Waal, 2002), as well as ontogenetically, (e.g. positive developmental outcomes: Harrist & Waugh, 2002). The perception-action model (Preston & de Waal, 2002) and the shared circuits model (Hurley, 2008) emphasise the importance of the biological foundation of behavioural correspondence. The social advantages are, among others, improved perception and encoding of actions (internal simulation) as well as improved inferences about the other person (understanding and empathy), providing important cues about intentions of others, and their relation to one's own social group (Carr et al., 2003).

Nonverbal Synchrony in Psychotherapy

In the study reported here (Ramseyer & Tschacher, 2010a), we used the term 'nonverbal synchrony' in accordance with Condon & Ogston (1966), who first described the phenomenon of movement coordination between interacting persons as interactional synchrony. Our conceptualisation of nonverbal synchrony has three unique features: a) it is a *dynamic* quality (Bernieri & Rosenthal, 1991), i.e., movement characteristics are assessed, irrespective of the specific postures or gestures displayed; b) it is measured *objectively* and *automatically* by a video-computer interface; c) it includes *simultaneous* movement (Condon & Ogston's definition) as well as *time-lagged* coordinated movement in a window of ± 5 seconds.

Synchrony quantification with motion energy analysis, MEA

Digitised sequences of therapy interactions were analysed with video-analysis software for motion-energy detection (Rokeby, 2006). Motion energy was defined as differences in grey-scale pixels between consecutive video-frames (Grammer et al., 1997; Grammer et al., 1999). Detection of frame-by-frame change allowed an objective quantification of movement present in pre-defined regions of interest (one region per subject, covering the upper body from the chair's seating-base upwards), as shown in Fig. 1A. Time-series of raw pixel-change were filtered and corrected prior to further analyses (for details, see Grammer et al., 1999; Ramseyer, 2008). As nonverbal synchrony was conceived as a dynamic quality, it reflected an objective quantification of the dynamic movement characteristics displayed by patient and therapist.

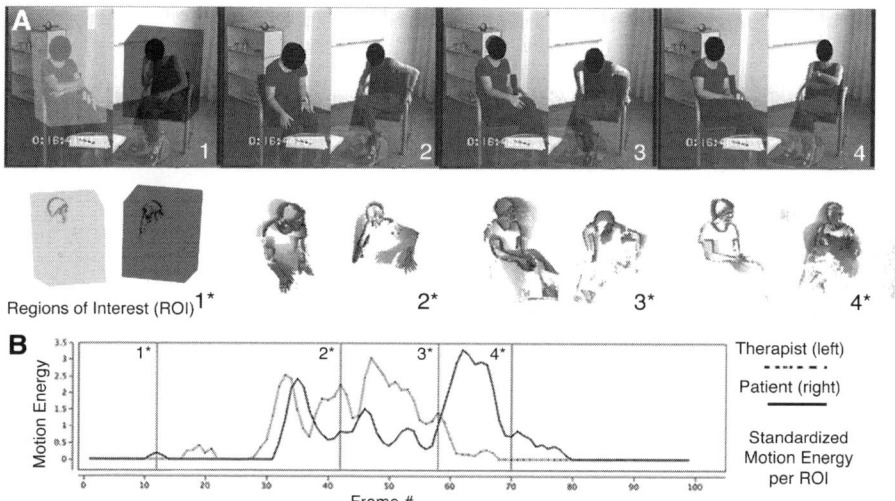

Fig. 1: Motion energy analysis (MEA).

Quantification of synchrony

Time-series of motion energy (Fig. 1B) were cross-correlated (Boker et al., 2002; Derrick & Thomas, 2004) in window segments of one minute duration, thus taking into consideration the non-stationarity of movement behaviors. Movements were cross-correlated with time-lags up to 5 seconds, in order to allow for both exact synchronisation (lag of 0) and delayed synchronisation (lags of various steps up to 5 seconds). Absolute values of cross-correlation were aggregated over the entire interval of 15 minutes. Apart from this global measure, we were interested in whether the direction of imitation goes from patient to therapist, vice-versa or both ways: who is acting as the *Zeitgeber* for whom? Using the time-lagged cross-correlations, we could identify when the therapist was imitating the patient (*pacing*), or guiding the patient (*leading*, Bandler & Grinder, 1979). These two distinctions are represented on either the left or right side of each of the cross-correlation displays in Fig. 2A. Cross-correlations with negative lags (-5 seconds up to 0 seconds) were said to reflect *pacing*, while positive lags (greater than 0 seconds up to +5 seconds) were said to reflect *leading*.

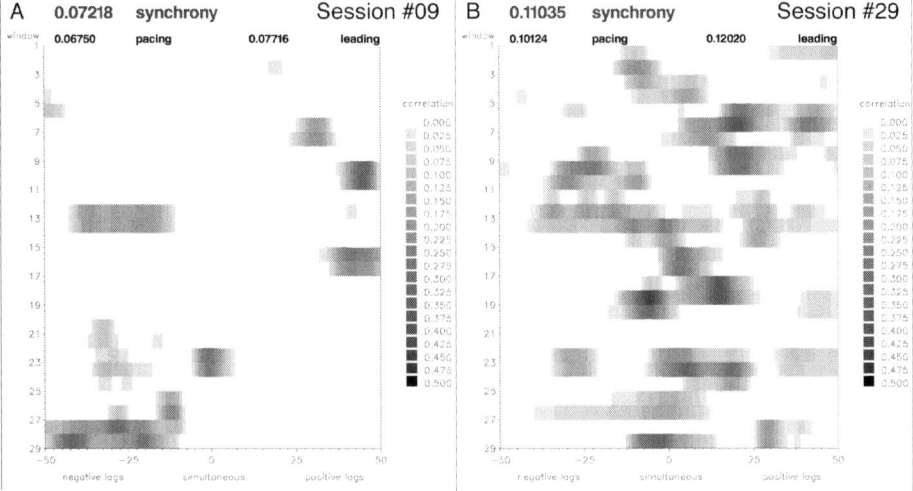

Fig. 2: Cross-correlation graphs. Panel A: session with low synchrony and low relationship quality. Panel B: session with high synchrony and high relationship quality.

Control for spurious correlations

Surrogate datasets ($N = 100$) were produced by segment-wise shuffling of the original data, preventing cross-correlations of movement segments that actually occurred at the same time. Surrogate synchrony in shuffled datasets was calculated identically to the synchrony of the original data. For the comparison of nonverbal synchrony versus surrogate synchrony, the mean value of 100 shuffled surrogate data was computed (Ramseyer & Tschacher, 2010).

Nonverbal synchrony in a randomised sample of psychotherapy sessions

Sample

Out of more than 5000 available sessions that were administered at the ambulatory psychotherapy research centre of the University of Bern (Grawe, 2004), a randomised sample was drawn (Ramseyer & Tschacher, in press). The sample included only patient-therapist dyads of the same sex. Sessions were taken from the individually calculated first third of therapy (T1) or last third of therapy (T3). Based on these conditions, 70 patients with 104 sessions were included (37 women). Patients belonged to diagnostic groups of anxiety disorders (35%), affective disorder (28%) and a mixed group with other disorders (37%). The limitation on same-sex dyads was based on previous research showing that mixed-gender dyads were less prone to exhibit nonverbal synchrony (Grammer et al., 1998).

Assessment Scales

Post-session questionnaires (BPSR-P/BPSR-T; Flückiger et al., 2010) were administered after each therapy session, as was routinely done in all archived sessions as part of ongoing research activity. These self-report measures comprised 22 (patient, PAT) and 27 (therapist, TH) items covering five global factors determined by previous factor analysis (Tschacher et al., 2007). Two factors captured the patient's view of the therapy process (quality of therapeutic bond PAT; and patient's self-efficacy), and three factors reflected the therapist's perspective (quality of therapeutic bond TH; therapist's mastery interventions; and therapist's insight interventions).

Outcome of therapy was measured at termination of therapy with a battery of standard questionnaires addressing the following domains: interpersonal behaviour, attachment style, psychopathology, coping style, attainment of individual treatment goals, and experienced changes in behaviour and cognition. All self-report assessments were combined into one global outcome measure by averaging the z-standardized scores of individual scale results.

Results

The comparison of synchrony with surrogate synchrony revealed significant differences ($p < .001$) of a medium effect size (Cohen's $d = 0.5 - 0.6$). Nonverbal synchrony was positively correlated with the patient's rating of the therapeutic bond ($r = .33$ in both T1 and T3). The compound effect-size of therapy outcome (mean effect size of outcome assessments at termination of therapy) correlated with nonverbal synchrony. Associations of psychopathology, self-efficacy and changes in experiencing and behaviour were in the range of medium effect sizes ($r = .2$ to $.4$) and pointed all in the same direction: synchrony was positively associated with outcome. Worthy of note are the correlations in the domain of interpersonal behaviour: nonverbal synchrony correlated with less interpersonal problems ($r = -.25$ to $-.35$), and with a secure attachment style ($r = .30$ to $.39$).

Concerning the question of who imitates whom, no significant differences in the amount of synchrony were found. Nonverbal synchrony is characterised by imitative behaviour of both patient and therapist. However, associations with therapy outcome revealed an interesting characteristic pattern: at the beginning of therapy (T1), therapist's *pacing* correlated more strongly with measures of success (patient's self-efficacy), while at the end of therapy (T3), therapist's *leading* correlated more strongly with relationship quality (quality of therapeutic bond PAT). The following points can be summarised:

- nonverbal synchrony was significantly higher in comparison to surrogate synchrony (synchrony that would be expected by chance)
- nonverbal synchrony was positively associated with process measures of psychotherapy (questionnaires administered after each therapy session)
- the overall outcome of therapies was positively associated with nonverbal synchrony
- variables of interpersonal behaviour (relationship quality, interpersonal problems, attachment style) were meaningfully associated with nonverbal synchrony: patients with impairments in these domains showed less synchrony
- a characteristic pattern of pacing and leading was found: during the initial phase of therapy, therapist's imitation (pacing) was more strongly associated with positive characteristics (which could be interpreted as a kind of relationship establishment via imitation), while in the final phase of therapy, therapist's leading was more strongly associated with positive outcome (which could be interpreted that the therapist served as a role model).

Apart from the dyadic synchrony measure, the individual movement patterns also revealed interesting differences between patient's and therapist's movement behaviour. Characteristic patterns for female and male patients and for different diagnostic groups were found. However, due to small group sizes (SEX X DIAGNOSIS), results should be interpreted with caution. The following list summarises the most interesting findings and may serve as a starting point for further investigations in a larger population.

- generally, patients showed greater movement than therapists (25.6%

vs. 20.9%; $d = 0.67$)

- patients showed an increase in the total amount of movement from T1 to T3 (24.1% vs. 26.8%; $d = 0.34$), but therapists did not (21.5% vs. 20.4%; $d = -0.19$)
- an interaction effect occurred between the variables SEX and DIAGNOSIS for patients' movement in the initial phase of therapy ($R^2 = 0.24$; $p < .05$), but not in the final phase of therapy ($R^2 = 0.02$); (see Fig. 3)
- therapist's movement behaviour did not show this interaction effect for SEX and DIAGNOSIS found in patients' diagnoses.

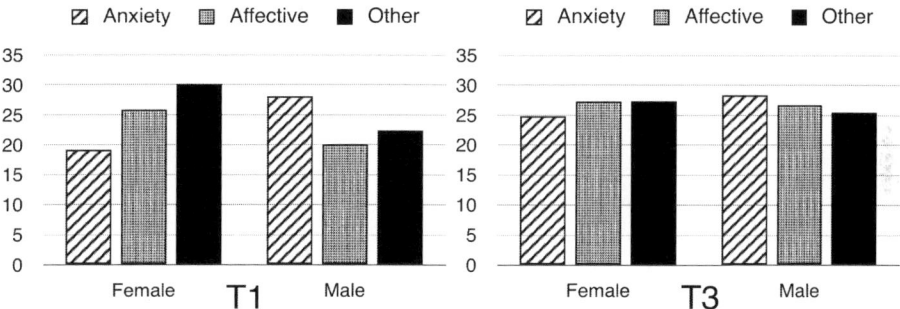

Fig. 3: Relative amount of movement in patients with different diagnosis.

Discussion

Over the past decade, empirical findings have documented the favourable effects of imitation in social interactions (Chartrand & van Baaren, 2009). In line with this research, the study summarised here has shown that nonverbal synchrony a) manifests itself significantly more often than would be expected by chance, b) is associated with the quality of the relationship and other process measures of psychotherapy, and c) dyads with high levels of synchrony show better outcomes at termination of therapy. The associations found here have a medium effect size and imply that the quality of the relationship between patient and therapist is indeed embodied by the coordination of their bodies' movement. Due to the correlational design, the study is not able to answer the question whether there is a causal connection between nonverbal synchrony and relationship quality. An experimental variation of nonverbal synchrony would be needed to determine the causal pathway between these two factors. It has to be noted that in this study, neither patients nor therapists had any conscious knowledge of nonverbal synchrony. The results reported here thus solely concern the *nonconscious* (normally occurring) manifestation of nonverbal synchrony. The study does not provide information to tell whether consciously altering movement behavior in the direction of more synchrony would have beneficial effects or not. Based on experimental evidence from social psychology (Chartrand & Bargh, 1999; Chartrand & van Baaren, 2009), one may speculate that such a deliberate creation of high synchrony might work in the psychotherapeutic setting too. It may well be that an optimal amount of synchronised behaviour between patient and therapist exists. Boker (2004) has called the two poles of too little and too much synchrony 'bored teenager effect' and 'mime effect'. This suggests that both extremes would have a detrimental effect on relationship quality (see Fig. 4). An empirical investigation with computer-generated characters (avatars) corroborates this interpretation: Avatars that mimic the head movements of an interaction partner are evaluated more favourably than avatars that do not display such imitative head movements (the head movements of the non-imitating avatar were those of the previous participant, i.e. a surrogate synchrony condition). Beneficial effects of imitation were present when the avatar mimicked the participant with a delay of 4 seconds. This imitation was noticed by very few participants (5%). However, if the avatar mimicked participant's head movement with a shorter delay of 1 second, more participants became aware of the imitation, which resulted in less favourable evaluations (Bailenson et al., 2004; Bailenson et al., 2008). A similar result was found in the domain of prosodic mimicry: when a computer always imitated the prosody of hummed sounds (100% of the time), positive effects were less evident in comparison to an 80% imitation rate (Suzuki et al., 2003). It thus seems that there is an upper limit of 'acceptable imitation'. These results are consistent with the observation that infants who do not yet recognise themselves in a mirror (before the age of 20 months) usually show both joy as well as embarrassment when they see themselves reflected in the mirror and thus perceive a 100% perfect copy of their own actions (Amsterdam, 1972). The same infants do not show negative reactions when they are copied by caregivers, i.e. when they perceive 'imperfect' copies of themselves, but copies that allow them to experience reciprocation (Rochat & Passos-Ferreira, 2009). It should be noted, however, that in the study reported here and in social interaction in general, not all movement is synchronous. During any session of psychotherapy, intermittent phases of unsynchronized movement were also present. Boker & Rotondo (2002) call this phenomenon 'symmetry breaking' and 'symmetry building' (Rotondo & Boker, 2002).

A hypothetical functional relationship between nonverbal synchrony and relationship quality is depicted in Fig. 4. Too little synchrony as well as too much synchrony both have a negative impact on the quality of the relationship (solid line). The optimal — and naturally occurring — amount of synchrony lies somewhere in between, and is thought to represent the normal amount of synchrony that is displayed when people are not consciously monitoring their nonverbal synchrony. It can be hypothesised (dashed line) that deliberately — and thus consciously — increasing the amount of synchrony, would result in an even more favourable relationship quality (peak of the dashed line), as long as it goes unnoticed (sudden drop of the dashed line). Experimental studies are needed to evaluate this hypothesis.

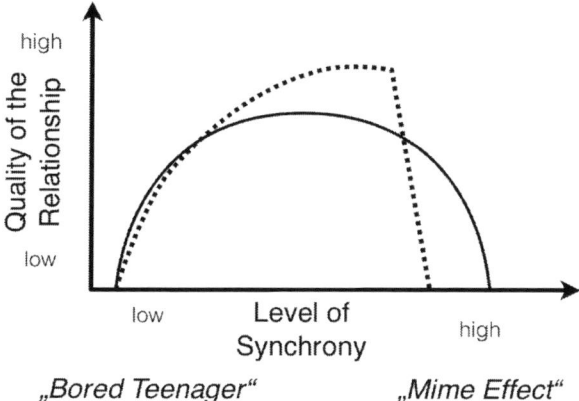

„Bored Teenager"   „Mime Effect"

Fig. 4: Hypothesized association between nonverbal synchrony and relationship quality

When we consider the movement behavior of individuals, the results for the global movement parameters (relative amount of movement) indicate that patients show a distinctive pattern of movement in comparison to therapists. Their diagnosis-specific movement behaviour shows a trend for convergence from T1 to T3, which may be interpreted as a successful normalisation of patient's movement. In T3, movement patterns are no longer significantly different between diagnostic groups, i.e. patients could no longer be distinguished based on their movement patterns. This effect does not occur in the therapist's movement: their relative amount of movement does not change from T1 to T3, nor is it significantly different with patients of different diagnostic groups. This finding of psychopathology-specific movement patterns is consistent with another study that used MEA and which found associations between the relative amount of movement and psychopathology in schizophrenic patients during social role play situations (Kupper et al., 2010).

Taken together, it can be noted that the movement quantification (MEA) described here, along with the statistical approach for synchrony, allow for an objective quantification of embodied phenomena in social interaction. Such an approach enables insight into processes that are normally not consciously controlled by individuals. MEA is a theory-free method that lends itself to numerous areas of psychological inquiry.

Using this kind of objective quantification of nonverbal behaviour may help in further advancing research on phenomena of embodiment in psychology.

References

Amsterdam B. (1972). Mirror self-image reactions before age two. *Developmental Psychobiology, 5,* 297-305.

Bailenson J. N., Beall A. C., Loomis J., Blascovich J., & Turk M. (2004). Transformed social interaction: Decoupling representation from behavior and form in collaborative virtual environments. *Presence: Teleoperators & Virtual Environments, 13,* 428-41.

Bailenson J. N., Yee N., Patel K., & Beall A. C. (2008). Detecting digital chameleons. *Computers in human behavior, 24,* 66-87.

Bandler R. & Grinder J. (1979). *Frogs into princes.* Moab: Real People Press.

Barber J., Bolitho F., & Bertrand L. (2001). Parent-Child synchrony and adolescent adjustment. *Child and Adolescent Social Work Journal, 18,* 51-64.

Bernieri F. J. & Rosenthal R. (1991). Interpersonal coordination: Behavior matching and interactional synchrony. In R. S. Feldman & B. Rime (eds.), *Fundamentals of nonverbal behavior. Studies in emotion & social interaction.* New York: Cambridge University Press.

Bernieri F. J., Reznick S., & Rosenthal R. (1988). Synchrony, pseudosynchrony, and dissynchrony: Measuring the entrainment process in mother-infant interactions. *Journal of Personality and Social Psychology, 54,* 243-53.

Blake R. & Shiffrar M. (2007). Perception of human motion. *Annual Review of Psychology, 58,* 47-73.

Boker S. M. (2004, September). Context dependence of interpersonal coordination in social interaction. *Learning and multimodal communication.* [Conference] Chicago, Il.

Boker S. M. & Rotondo J. L. (2002). Symmetry building and symmetry breaking in synchronized movement. In M. Stamenov & V. Gallese (eds.), *Mirror Neurons and the Evolution of Brain and Language.* Amsterdam: John Benjamins Publishing Company.

Boker S. M., Xu M., Rotondo J. L., & King K. (2002). Windowed cross-correlation and peak picking for the analysis of variability in the association between behavioral time series. *Psychological Methods, 7,* 338-55.

Brick T. R., Hunter M. D., & Cohn J. F. (2009). Get the FACS fast: Automated FACS face analysis benefits from the addition of velocity. *3rd international conference on affective computing and intelligent interaction,* 1-7.

Burgoon J. K., Stern L. A., & Dillman L. (1995). *Interpersonal adaptation: Dyadic interaction patterns.* Cambridge: Cambridge University Press.

Cappella J. N. (1981). Mutual influence in expressive behavior: Adult-Adult and infant-adult dyadic interaction. *Psychological Bulletin, 89,* 101-32.

Carr L., Iacoboni M., Dubeau M. C., Mazziotta J. C., & Lenzi G. L. (2003). Neural mechanisms of empathy in humans: A relay from neural systems for imitation to limbic areas. *Proceedings of the National Academy of Sciences, 100,* 5497-502.

Chartrand T. L. & Bargh J. A. (1999). The chameleon effect: The perception-behavior link and social interaction. *Journal of Personality and Social Psychology, 76,* 893-910.

Chartrand T. L. & van Baaren R. (2009). Human mimicry. *Advances in Experimental Social Psychology, 41,* 219-74.

Condon W. S. & Ogston W. D. (1966). Sound film analysis of normal and pathological behavior patterns. *Journal of Nervous and Mental Diseases, 143,* 338-457.

Davis M. (ed.) (1982). *Interaction Rhythms. Periodicity in communicative behavior.* New York: Human Sciences Press.

Derrick T. R. & Thomas J. M. (2004). Time series analysis: The cross-correlation function. In N. Stergiou (ed.), *Innovative analyses of human movement*. Champaign: Human Kinetics.

Dumas G., Nadel J., Soussignan R., Martinerie J., & Garnero L. (2010). Inter-Brain synchronization during social interaction. *PLoS ONE, 5*.

Feldman R. (2007). Parent-Infant synchrony and the construction of shared timing; physiological precursors, developmental outcomes, and risk conditions. *Journal of Child Psychology and Psychiatry, 48*, 329-54.

Feldman R., Greenbaum C. W., & Yirmiya N. (1999). Mother-Infant affect synchrony as an antecedent of the emergence of self-control. *Developmental Psychology, 35*, 223-31.

Flückiger C., Regli D., Zwahlen D., Hostettler S., & Caspar F. (2010). Der Berner Patienten- und Therapeutenstundenbogen 2000. *Zeitschrift für Klinische Psychologie und Psychotherapie, 39*, 71-9.

Gallese V., Fadiga L., Fogassi L., & Rizzolatti G. (1996). Action recognition in the premotor cortex. *Brain, 119*, 593-609.

de Gelder B. (2006). Towards the neurobiology of emotional body language. *Nature Reviews Neuroscience, 7*, 242-9.

de Gelder B. (2009). Why bodies? Twelve reasons for including bodily expressions in affective neuroscience. *Philosophical Transactions of the Royal Society of London. Series B, Biological Sciences, 364*, 3475-84.

Grahe J. E. & Bernieri F. J. (1999). The importance of nonverbal cues in judging rapport. *Journal of Nonverbal Behavior, 23*, 253-69.

Grammer K., Filova V., & Fieder M. (1997). The communication paradox and possible solutions. In A., Schmitt, K., Atzwanger, K., Grammer & K., Schaefer (eds.), *New aspects of human ethology*. New York: Plenum Press.

Grammer K., Honda R., Schmitt A., & Jütte A. (1999). Fuzziness of nonverbal courtship communication unblurred by motion energy detection. *Journal of Personality and Social Psychology, 77*, 487-508.

Grammer K., Keki V., Striebel B., Atzmüller M., & Fink B. (2003). Bodies in motion: A window to the soul. In E. Voland & K. Grammer (eds.), *Evolutionary aesthetics*. Heidelberg: Springer.

Grammer K., Kruck K. B., & Magnusson M. S. (1998). The courtship dance: Patterns of nonverbal synchronization in opposite-sex encounters. *Journal of Nonverbal Behavior, 22*, 3-29.

Grawe K. (2004). *Psychological therapy*. Seattle: Hogrefe.

Haken H. (1988). *Information and self-organization (A macroscopic approach to complex systems)*. Berlin: Springer.

Haken H., Kelso J. A. S., & Bunz H. (1985). A theoretical model of phase transitions in human hand movements. *Biological Cybernetics, 51*, 347-56.

Hall J. A., Harrigan J. A., & Rosenthal R. (1995). Nonverbal behavior in clinician-patient interaction . *Applied and Preventive Psychology, 4*, 21-37.

Harrist A. W. & Waugh R. M. (2002). Dyadic synchrony: Its structure and function in children's development. *Developmental Review, 22*, 555-92.

Hatfield E., Cacioppo J. T., & Rapson R. L. (1994). *Emotional contagion*. Cambridge: Cambridge University Press.

Hove M. J. & Risen J. L. (2009). It's all in the timing: Interpersonal synchrony increases affiliation. *Social Cognition, 27*, 949-60.

Hurley S. (2008). The shared circuits model (SCM): How control, mirroring, and simulation can enable imitation, deliberation, and mindreading. *Behavioral and Brain Sciences, 31*, 1-22.

Iacoboni M. (2009). Imitation, empathy, and mirror neurons. *Annual Review of Psychology, 60*, 653-70.

Isabella R. A., Belsky J., & von Eye A. (1989). Origins of infant-mother attachment: An examination of interactional synchrony during the infant's first year. *Developmental Psychology, 25,* 12-21.

Kupper Z., Ramseyer F., Hoffmann H., Kalbermatten S., & Tschacher W. (2010). Video-based quantification of body movement during social interaction indicates the severity of negative symptoms in patients with schizophrenia. *Schizophrenia Research, 121,* 90-100.

Lakens D. (2010). Movement synchrony and perceived entitativity. *Journal of Experimental Social Psychology, 46,* 701-8.

Lakin J. L., Jefferis V. E., Cheng C. M., & Chartrand T. L. (2003). The chameleon effect as social glue: Evidence for the evolutionary significance of nonconscious mimicry. *Journal of Nonverbal Behavior, 27,* 145-62.

Lewin K. (1936). *Principles of topological psychology.* New York: McGraw-Hill.

Marci C. D., Ham J., Moran E., & Orr S. P. (2007). Physiologic correlates of perceived therapist empathy and social-emotional process during psychotherapy. *Journal of Nervous & Mental Disease, 195,* 103-11.

Meltzoff A. N. & Moore M. K. (1977). Imitation of facial and manual gestures by human neonates. *Science, 198,* 75-8.

Merleau-Ponty M. (2002). *Phenomenology of perception.* London, United Kingdom: Routledge.

Miles L. K., Griffiths J. L., Richardson M. J., & Macrae C. N. (2010). Too late to coordinate: Contextual influences on behavioral synchrony. *European Journal of Social Psychology, 40,* 52-60.

Neumann R. & Strack F. (2000). "Mood contagion": The automatic transfer of mood between persons. *Journal of Personality and Social Psychology, 79,* 211-23.

Newtson D. (1994). The perception and coupling of behavior waves. In R. R. Vallacher & A. Nowak (eds.), *Dynamical Systems in Social Psychology.* San Diego: Academic Press.

O'Toole R. & Dubin R. (1968). Baby feeding and body sway: An experiment in George Herbert Mead's "taking the role of the other". *Journal of Personality and Social Psychology, 10,* 59-65.

Oullier O., de Guzman G. C., Jantzen K. J., Lagarde J., & Kelso J. A. S. (2008). Social coordination dynamics: Measuring human bonding. *Social Neuroscience, 3,* 178-92.

Preston S. D. & de Waal F. B. M. (2002). Empathy: Its ultimate and proximate bases. *Behavioral and Brain Sciences, 25,* 1-72.

Ramseyer, F. (2008). *Synchronisation nonverbaler Interaktion in der Psychotherapie.* [Nonverbal synchrony in psychotherapy]. Dissertation, University of Bern, Switzerland.

Ramseyer F. & Tschacher W. (in press). Nonverbal synchrony in psychotherapy: Coordinated body-movement reflects relationship quality and outcome. *Journal of Consulting & Clinical Psychology.*

Ramseyer F. & Tschacher W. (2010). Nonverbal synchrony or random coincidence? How to tell the difference. In A. Esposito, N. Campbell, C. Vogel, A. Hussain, & A. Nijholt (eds.), *Development of multimodal interfaces: active listening and synchrony.* Berlin: Springer.

Rochat P. & Passos-Ferreira C. (2009). From imitation to reciprocation and mutual recognition. In J. A. Pineda (ed.), *Mirror neuron systems.* New York: Humana Press.

Rodriguez E., George N., Lachaux J. P., Martinerie J., Renault B., & Varela F. J. (1999). Perception's shadow: Long-Distance synchronization of human brain activity. *Nature, 397,* 430-3.

Rokeby D. (2006). *SoftVNS 2.17* [Computer Software]. Toronto, Canada.

Rotondo J. L. & Boker S. M. (2002). Behavioral synchronization in human conversational interaction. In M. I. Stamenov & V. Gallese (eds.), *Mirror Neurons and the evolution of brain and language*. Amsterdam: John Benjamins Publishing Company.

Scheflen A. E. (1964). The significance of posture in communication systems. *Psychiatry*, 27, 316-31.

Schmidt R. C. & Richardson M. J. (2008). Dynamics of interpersonal coordination. In A. Fuchs & V. Jirsa (eds.), *Coordination: Neural, Behavioural and Social Dynamics*. Heidelberg: Springer.

Semin G. R. & Cacioppo J. T. (2008). Grounding social cognition: Synchronization, coordination, and co-regulation. In G. R. Semin & E. R. Smith (eds.), *Embodied Grounding: Social, Cognitive, Affective, and Neuroscientific Approaches*. New York: Cambridge University Press.

Sonnby-Borgström M., Jönsson P., & Svensson O. (2003). Emotional empathy as related to mimicry reactions at different levels of information processing. *Journal of Nonverbal Behavior*, 27, 3-23.

Suzuki N., Takeuchi Y., Ishii K., & Okada M. (2003). Effects of echoic mimicry using hummed sounds on human-computer interaction. *Speech Communication*, 40, 559-73.

Tamietto M. & de Gelder B. (2010). Neural bases of the non-conscious perception of emotional signals. *Nature Reviews Neuroscience*, 11, 697-709.

Tickle-Degnen L. & Rosenthal R. (1990). The nature of rapport and its nonverbal correlates. *Psychological Inquiry*, 1, 285-93.

Tschacher W. & Dauwalder J.-P. (eds.) (2003). *The dynamical systems approach to cognition: concepts and empirical paradigms based on self-organization, embodiment, and coordination dynamics*. Singapore: World Scientific.

Tschacher W., Ramseyer F., & Grawe K. (2007). Der Ordnungseffekt im Psychotherapieprozess: Replikation einer systemtheoretischen Vorhersage und Zusammenhang mit dem Therapieerfolg. *Zeitschrift für Klinische Psychologie und Psychotherapie*, 36, 18-25.

Vallacher R. R. & Nowak A. (2009). The dynamics of human experience: Fundamentals of dynamical social psychology. In S. J. Guastello, M. Koopmans, & D. Pincus (eds.), *Chaos and Complexity in Psychology: The Theory of Nonlinear Dynamical Systems*. New York: Cambridge University Press.

Watzlawick P., Beavin Bavelas J. H., & Jackson D. D. (1967). *Pragmatics of human communication: A study of interactional patterns, pathologies, and paradoxes*. New York: Norton.

Wiltermuth S. S. & Heath C. (2009). Synchrony and cooperation. *Psychological Science*, 20, 1-5.

The Role of Embodied Communication in Therapeutic Change: A Multiple Code Perspective

Wilma Bucci

Adelphi University, New York
wbucci@adelphi.edu

The basic goal of psychotherapy, shared across widely different approaches, is change in emotion schemas that have been dissociated or distorted — change in how people experience themselves in relation to others, what they expect, how they feel and the strategies for living that they have devised. In these psychological terms, the changes in symptoms and behaviors that are sought in treatment occur as a function of reorganization of these internal processes. The various schools of psychotherapy utilize different theoretical frameworks, and different definitions of these internal processes, and propose different types of interventions designed to achieve therapeutic change, but the psychological common core remains.

The commonalities among therapeutic approaches are supported by similarities in treatment effects as demonstrated statistically by many researchers (Luborsky et al., 2002; Wampold, 2010; Westen et al., 2004). In a review of meta-analytic studies of psychotherapy forms, Beutler (2009) reported that systematic and direct comparisons of cognitive, cognitive behavioral, psychodynamic and other treatments revealed essentially equivalent effects among all treatments, with some meta-analyses showing greater effects for one or another of the treatment forms, and some showing null effects. The implication of these findings is that to understand the processes of therapeutic change it is necessary to move from the comparative study of different treatment forms that has dominated the psychotherapy research field to a study of processes that contribute to therapeutic change in all approaches. As Beutler (2009) emphasizes, only when a mix of common factors such as the role of patient, therapist and the relationship was added to the comparative analyses were significant treatment effects revealed.

The researchers cited above have emphasized a statistical approach to identifying common factors in therapeutic change. In my work I have attempted to approach the question of common factors from a different perspective, identifying basic psychological processes associated with change in emotion schemas; then examining the degree to which these apply in various types of psychotherapy, and their relation to treatment effects. The basic psychological processes are defined in the context of the theory of multiple coding and the referential process, derived from current work in cognitive psychology, affective neuroscience, and related fields. Recent research in the areas of enactive perception and embodied communication has provided new perspectives on aspects of this theory. Multiple code theory also provides certain concepts, particularly the concept of subsymbolic processes in multiple modalities, that potentially contribute to the understanding of how embodied communication operates. In this paper I will briefly outline the basic concepts of the multiple code theory, which have been presented in detail elsewhere, and will then introduce an elaboration of this theoretical model incorporating processes of embodied communication, and show its application in the therapeutic setting.

Multiple Code Theory and the Referential Process

The theory of multiple coding and the referential process provides a general framework for understanding the nature of the problems that bring patients to treatment, and the process of change in psychotherapy. The theory is based on the premise of the human organism as a multi-state, multi-format information processor — including emotional information — with substantial but limited integration of systems (Bucci 1997, 2002, 2007a,b). The multiple systems include two basic formats: the *symbolic* and what I call the *subsymbolic* (or nonsymbolic) codes. Both systems may operate within and outside of awareness; both incorporate verbal and nonverbal components. Both subsymbolic and symbolic processes operate in their own formats throughout normal, rational, adult life, and are also connected to a limited degree. The multiple modalities are connected by the *referential process;* components of the multiple modalities are organized into relatively enduring interconnected systems that I term *emotion schemas*. I'll briefly explain each of these concepts of the multiple code theory here.

Symbolic Codes

Symbols (in the technical, semiotic sense used here) are discrete representations with properties of reference and generativity (see also discussion on intentionality in this volume: Friston, 2010; Haken & Tschacher, 2010); that is, they are representations that refer to other entities and that may be combined to generate an infinite array of new forms; symbols may be images in all sensory modalities, or words. Language is deeply generative: starting from a limited set of the smallest meaning bearing elements in each language, the morphemes, speakers (and writers) form words, then phrases, then sentences — all the way up to the limitless and infinitely varied arrays of written texts and spoken discourse that humans produce. Images may be generative as well; for example, the police artist combines eyes, nose, hair, chin and other discrete elements following a witness's description, to generate an image of a perpetrator's face. We are all familiar with verbal thought and images. Most people carry an implicit assumption of symbolic thought as verbal, but also understand the operaion of nonverbal images as symbols — in a narrow sense, as symbolic entities such as the flag of a nation, the Christian cross, or the Star of David; in a broader sense as the prototypic representations of objects that we can bring to mind or draw (an orange, a cat, a chair).

The Subsymbolic System

The subsymbolic system is less clearly recognized but ubiquitous and dominant in our daily lives. Like symbols, *subsymbolic processes* are systematic, organized forms of thought, with their own formats and their own operating systems that continue to develop throughout life, and that may occur within as well as outside of awareness. Technically, subsymbolic processing is characterized as formally analogic, i.e., processed as variation on continuous dimensions. The special nature of subsymbolic processing, distinguishing it from symbolic forms, is the continuous flow; the felt similarities and relationships are known through patterning and analogy rather than generated from discrete elements. Subsymbolic processes operate in sensory, motoric and somatic systems, as sounds, smells, feelings of many different sorts. They contribute to verbal processing as well, in forms such as prosody, speech rhythm patterns and modulation of intensity and pitch.

Subsymbolic processing is involved constantly in the activities of daily life, from recognizing a familiar voice to entering a lane of traffic, and accounts as well for complex skills in sports and for creative work in sciences and the arts. People in all types of creative fields — painters, sculptors, musicians, dancers, actors, geometers, physicists, and many others — operate in highly complex, systematic, and differentiated ways in the subsymbolic mode. The police drawing of a face based on combining elements as described by a witness will not be experienced as capturing the sense of the individual; the difference will be obvious when the generated image is eventually compared with a picture of the actual person. What is missing is the subsymbolic patterning that we recognize without being able to articulate the elements. A talented artist viewing the subject could represent the emotional nuances with a few strokes of the pen, although he probably could not explicate what he does; he is drawing on some different kind of perceptual response pattern within himself. Many writers have struggled, with limited success, to articulate the elements of the Mona Lisa's expression; but we all respond to it immediately within the subsymbolic zone.

For all of us, subsymbolic processing underlies knowing one's own bodily states and responding to the facial and bodily expressions of others, without being able to measure them in discrete units or categorize them in symbolic form. We know this processing as intuition, the wisdom of the body, and in other related ways. Like all people, therapist and patient communicate continuously in the subsymbolic mode. While this communication may occur without direct attention and without intention, this is not unconscious processing or unconscious communication, as it has been commonly discussed. The skilled athlete or dancer — or therapist — is aware of and attuned to such processing, although it is occurring in a zone that cannot be articulated in verbal form. Such processing may be experienced as outside of the self, outside of the zone over which one has direct control. Athletes and creative artists talk about being 'in the flow'; they do not know how they achieve this state; they prize it when they are there.

Subsymbolic processing is modeled in cognitive science by connectionist or parallel distributed processing systems with the features of dynamical systems (McClelland, Rumelhart & The PDP Research Group, 1989; Bucci, 1997). There is support in neurological observations for the operation of this format. Panksepp (1999) refers to global state processes of the brain, which are embodied and fundamentally analog — not able to be simulated by digital algorithms. As he says, the models that can handle the full complexity of emotions in the brain will require dynamical systems approaches that account for such analogic processes.

The Referential Process

The referential process is the integrating mechanism of the multiple code system. The multiple modes — subsymbolic and symbolic; verbal and nonverbal — are connected by the referential process, but only partially and to varying degrees. Some degree of dissociation is inherent in the human multiformat system; the global, analogic subsymbolic representations can be connected only partially and indirectly to the discrete, abstract symbols of the verbal code. Imagery, metaphor and narrative are central means of such connection (Bucci, 1997, 2002). The sensory and somatic processes of the subsymbolic mode are able to be connected to discrete sensory images that express and evoke these processes, and that eventually can be connected to words, often in the form of episodes and memories of one's life, fantasies and dreams. The referential process operates in intrapsychic organization and in interpersonal communication throughout life, and is central to the formation of the emotion schemas. The referential process is also the basic process underlying therapeutic change, as I will discuss below.

Emotion schemas

Emotion schemas as defined within multiple code theory are types of memory schemas that incorporate all components of the human information processing system, including subsymbolic information in all sensory, bodily and motoric systems, as well as all forms of imagery; later words are added to varying degrees. They are the fundamental organizers of emotional life in humans and probably in other species, formed through repeated interactions with other people from the beginning of life. The structure of the emotion schema is represented in language through memories, fantasies, dreams, the narratives and metaphors of our lives.

Schematic representations of this nature are similar to Bowlby's (1969) concept of *working models*, or Stern's (1985) concept of *representations of interactions that have been generalized (RIGs)*. They are similar as well to the psychoanalytic concepts of *object representation*, defined as representations of interaction between self and other in various emotional contexts, and the *transference*, understood as occurring in all interactions of life, not in therapy only. The therapeutic approaches that are dominant today, including general cognitive behavioral treatments, and specific forms of schema therapy and exposure treatments, as well as psychodynamic treatments, all incorporate versions of the concept of the schema and view changes in these schemas as therapeutic goals (Bucci, 2010).

Like all memory schemas, the emotion schemas are not registered as stable storehouses of knowledge, but as networks of processes that determine how we perceive and respond to the world and are themselves changed by each new activation (Bartlett, 1932). They differ from other memory schemas in the dominance of the subsymbolic sensory, somatic and motoric processes that make up the *affective core* of the schema, the basis on which the organization of the schema is initially built. The objects and settings of time and place constitute the specific contexts and contents of the emotion schemas, which continue to be elaborated throughout life.

Damasio's (1994, 1999) notion of *dispositional representations* provides a neurological basis for the construct of the emotion schema, and supports and extends this concept. Dispositional representations exist as potential patterns of neuronal activity distributed throughout the nervous system, connecting sensory and association cortices with limbic structures and structures subserving motoric and visceral response.

Embodied Communication and the Emotion Schemas

Recent research in the areas of mirror systems (Rizzolatti et al., 1996; Rizzolatti et al., 2001), and related work on enactive perception (Kinsbourne & Jordan, 2009), and embodied communication (Jordan, 2009) have provided new insight and new evidence concerning the emotion schemas as they develop in healthy and in maladaptive functioning. The operation of mirroring systems, initially discovered by Rizzolatti and his colleagues in macaque monkeys has now been demonstrated in humans as well in many complex forms. The subset of cells in the brain that constitutes the mirror neuron system fires when an individual carries out an action (hits a tennis ball, kisses a lover), sees others perform the actions, hears sounds associated with the actions, or says or reads or hears words associated with them (Iacoboni, 2009). These cells are characterized as *indifferent* to perception or action, firing in an equivalent manner in both contexts. They represent, in an individual's brain, the movements that the brain sees in another individual and produce signals toward sensorimotor structures so that the corresponding movements may be 'previewed' in simulation mode, or actually executed, at least in trace form, by the viewer.

According to Kinsbourne & Jordan (2009), the common coding of perception and action, which they refer to as *enactive perception,* enables individuals to continuously *entrain* to one another's actions and meanings. Entrainment involves a process of reciprocating interactions in which:

> … movements, postures, gestures, gazes, or languages generated by each can elicit expected similar or congruent movements, postures, gestures, gazes or languages from the other. These, in turn, can recursively elicit reciprocating movements, postures, gestures, gazes, and languages from the former. (Kinsbourne & Jordan, 2009, p. 104)

The recursive entrainment described by Kinsbourne and Jordan is present in some forms from the beginning of life, but also determined by learning and experience and affected by context. Imitation is the core of this early entrainment, and the most well demonstrated in neurological and behavioral research. Meltzoff & Moore (1994) and others have described the infant's imitation of gestures and facial expressions, such as protrusion of the tongue, observed from the first few hours of life. There is also considerable behavioral evidence for other types of entrained sequences, such as sequences with rhythmic synchrony across different motor patterns — for example, the child moving or blinking in time to the mother's speech rhythms (Stern, 1985). For the infant, these entrained processes are uninhibited, playing out repeatedly in their actions, and activating corresponding motor plans in the caregivers, who may then choose the degree to which they continue the entrainment. As the pre-frontal cortex develops, the child gains capacity to inhibit the realization of the action, but the common encoding of perception and action tendencies remains.

Anticipatory Perception and Networks of Consequences

There is now evidence that the mirroring systems are embedded in neural networks that incorporate regularities between motor planning and its consequences; thus perceiving the action of another will activate not only the neurons associated with the action but also representations of the consequences of the action were it to be carried out. Thus the process of enactive perception can enable people to plan responses to actions of others that are pending but have not yet occurred — in some cases to ward off or forestall such actions; in other instances to facilitate or cope with them.

Here the possibilities for human interaction become highly complex and variable. The patterns of consequences are to a large extent learned in the individual contexts of life, so that those patterns activated in the neural networks of the observer are different from those of the actor. In general, the operation of the mirror system depends on the individual's expertise with a given action. Dancers and football players show more mirroring actions when watching the movement forms they have learned; the mirror neurons of dancers will be more active when watching the dance at which they are expert than some other form. Ballet and capoeira dancers revealed more pre-motor activation in the mirror neuron area in response to the dance form in which they were experts; non-expert dancers showed less activation than experts for both forms, and their level of activation did not vary with dance types (Jordan, 2009). The mirror neurons of a non-tennis playing observer will fire to some extent when watching a game; the equivalent neurons of a tennis player will fire more strongly; particularly when watching someone like Roger Federer (Iacoboni, 2009). Here we can see the gap between an action plan as represented in mirror neurons and action involving the motor circuitry. While the perceptual/ motor neurons of the Federer fan may be firing wildly, a realization in action is unfortunately not likely to occur.

Application to Emotional Interaction

Much of the recent experimental and neurological research on embodied communication and enactive perception has focused on cognitive and motoric functions. The possibilities for emotional interaction are even more varied and complex. The nonverbal indicators associated with emotion, such as facial expression, gesture, body movements and postures, as well as the paralinguistic features such as speech rhythms and intonation patterns, have the features of common coding of perception and action — built in to some extent in evolution; also learned in the infinite variations of each individual's interpersonal history.

The operation of embodied emotional communication has been recognized in different terms by many researchers, writers and clinicians, from Darwin, Reik and James to Ekman and Gazzaniga, as well as clinicians representing a wide range of approaches, as I have discussed elsewhere (Bucci, 2001). Darwin (1872) showed the presence, across as well as within species, of characteristic patterns of facial expression and gesture associated with specific emotion states. Reik, writing over 60 years ago (Reik, 1948/1964), used insights from this work to explicate the communication that occurs in psychotherapy:

> What tells dog A., who has just met dog B., and prepares for a fight or a sexual interlude while B. circles round him, the secret intentions of his mate or adversary? (Reik, 1948/1964, p. 456).

As Reik notes, dog A responds to olfactory signals and other aspects of B's appearance and action; A also experiences internal reactions, such as muscle tension, changes in body temperature or heartbeat, hair standing on end, or alternatively, sexual arousal. A then knows B's experience in the terms of his or her own, and acts accordingly. Similarly, according to Reik, a broad range of cues are transmitted by the patient and received by the therapist, usually unintentionally and without awareness, that carry information concerning the patient's inner state. These include sensory information in all sensory modalities, and general impressions based on features of bearing, gesture and movement, as well as paralinguistic indicators accompanying speech.

Emotional mirroring has been demonstrated to affect both the central and autonomic nervous systems, in several experimental studies. Thus for example, observing another person looking disgusted has been shown to generate neural activation in the observer's anterior insula, the brain area that is known to underly disgust (Wicker et al., 2003). There is also evidence that people can distinguish their own emotional responses from those of others. Thus, whereas certain brain structures are activated during observation of another person's distress, this activation does not extend to areas of the brain that underly the sensory properties of pain.

The Perception/Response Anticipation Sequence

Here I will outline a model extending the processes of enactive perception and embodied communication as investigated in current research, to the processes of emotional information, as this occurs in the development of emotion schemas from the beginning of life; and in the reconstruction of dissociated and distorted schemas in the psychotherapy process. The model identifies a recursive sequence of perception/action mirroring, knowing the other's feelings, and anticipation of action, involving complex connections within individuals and interactions between them. This approach is based on an integration of concepts drawn from research on affective neuroscience, embodied communication and cognitive science; and is supported by behavioral and neurological observations in these fields. In outline form, the sequence includes:

a) **Perception/action mirroring.** This is the basic imitation function, dependent on activation of the mirror neuron system. The mother smiles at the child, the child's perception of the smile is encoded directly with the action plan. In the young infant the action itself will automatically play out; the child smiles. As the child develops, the immediate action may play out or be inhibited or redirected.

b) **Activation of motoric and emotion circuitry.** With the arousal of the motoric and emotional circuitry associated with the mirrored action, the child feels within herself how the other feels. The mother smiles, the child feels the emotional circuitry of pleasure within herself; the mother scowls, the child experiences a feeling of anger in herself. In the repeated experiences of life, these feelings become associated with the people with whom the child interacts, and with particular events.

c) **Anticipating the action of the other.** Through activation of the plan for action in herself, associated with the other, the child 'knows' not only what the other feels but what the other is likely to do — a loving action, an attacking one. For humans, there are some instinctive components in this anticipation, but learned components, specific to the familial context, are increasingly dominant as the child develops.

d) **Preparing a response.** The person who knows in her body what the other will do can 'plan' her response — to approach, attack, defend or withdraw — before the action of the other is completed. The playing out of this 'plan' in action will be regulated and directed in varying ways with physiological and cognitive development and learning.

e) **Anticipating the consequences of alternative responses.** There are sets of consequences, largely learned in the context of one's interpersonal experience, for each of these potential actions — what is likely to happen if I attack or cry or scream or run away or turn to another person for help. The actions that are most effective in reducing painful consequences or increasing pleasurable ones will be incorporated in the patterns of response that the child develops.

Development of the schema. The repetition of these sequences from the beginning of life determines the individual response patterns that make up the emotion schemas, the enduring representation of one's self in relation to one's interpersonal world. In adaptive development the sequences remain to some extent fluid and flexible throughout life; the nature of the consequences that are anticipated for a given action will change as the context of interaction changes and with development of the individual's powers. In less functional settings, the schemas become rigid and new learning is blocked, as will be discussed.

Parallel and recursive processes. It is necessary to recognize that parallel sequential processes are going on within the other (or the several) participants in any interpersonal interaction, but the emotional contexts and sets of learned consequences are different for each individual, dependent on the experiences of their lives. Each person reads, perceives, knows the other differently, depending on the patterns of entrainment they bring with them. This occurs in the patient-therapist interaction; this occurs in all the encounters of life.

Dependence on the subsymbolic mode. Every phase in this sequence of perceiving, responding, knowing the other's feelings, anticipating the other's responses, preparing to respond, and weighing the consequences of an action in its recursive interpersonal form is occurring in the subsymbolic mode — not able to be connected to language; operating far more quickly than could be articulated and directed in the symbolic mode. Subsymbolic processing may be conscious or unconscious, may be experienced as outside of the domain over which one has intentional control, but it is systematic nonetheless. It is possible to learn to focus attention on this level of processing and to direct it, by indirect means, to some extent; the rituals that athletes or performers rely on are indirect attempts at control of this processing zone.

Reik's example of emotional interaction can be paraphrased in terms of this model: What tells human A who has just met human B the secret intentions of his potential friend or adversary. Thus at a party, A may show various signs of interest in B before actually speaking to her, through means such as eye contact or facial expression. B perceives A's interest and anticipates his action, in the context of the emotional circuitry it activates in her. Her anticipation may be accurate or not, depending on the emotional history she brings with her. B's response of encouragement, avoidance or various forms of each will be experienced by A in his own emotional context, and the entrainment continues or breaks off.

Development of Maladaptive Schemas

This model, incorporating the operation of subsymbolic processing in relation to embodied communication, may be applied to the development of the dissociated and distorted emotion schemas that bring patients to treatment, and to the reconstruction of the maladaptive schemas in psychotherapy. The entrained sequences of perception, anticipatory planning and expectation of consequences that are formed at certain stages of life are likely not to fit at other times. The perception and planning mechanisms — how we see the world, how we respond, how we expect the other to respond — need to evolve as the individual grows and attains new powers, and need to be flexible in response to the changing contexts of life.

In some cases, however, this evolution does not occur, or occurs only partially, leaving the individual with fixed and rigid perceptions and patterns of response that were appropriate in earlier times and contexts, but that are maladaptive for the individual in his current life. These rigid mechanisms, with their multiple imagined and real consequences, are what bring patients to treatment.

In childhood, in the family constellation, expression of rage by the caretaker is perceived and experienced by the child within herself, accompanied initially by its own inherent action plan — perhaps to attack, to express rage in some other way, or to run away, or become numb. With development the child learns patterns of response that enable her to inhibit or manage her initial response, and to evaluate the consequences of alternate responses so as to ward off the attack or protect herself in some way. The child also needs to retain the attachment to the caretaker, the other on whom she depends for emotional and physical survival; thus seeks to avoid not only the attack but also recognition of it. The strategies that the child develops become entrained in the perception of the other's emotional expressions, determining in a basic and immediate way how these expressions are perceived and experienced. The various forms of acute or chronic abuse by the caretaker — rejection, abandonment, seduction, humiliation — will lead to development of particular entrained patterns of interaction.

In the future, in different situations, perception itself is likely to be distorted; the individual's attention is likely to be drawn to components of the other's expression that represented danger for him as a child, prematurely activating a particular anticipatory plan, and reducing the possibilities of flexible response. The individual may also hesitate to expose himself to situations associated with painful affect in the past, thus limiting the new information that might serve to change the schema. In the example of the party above, B may be unsure as to how to interpret A's signal and tentatively shows a neutral, mildly positive response. A perceives this as discouraging; he feels shame at exposing his interest and being rejected, and avoids contact with B. The entrainment is then likely to be self-perpetuating and recursive; A's response is likely to bring about the very consequences that are feared. B had also been interested in A but now becomes wary of him and wishes to avoid further contact with him. This interaction may play out without either participant intending or even being explicitly aware of it.

Reconstruction of Dissociated Schemas: The Referential Process

Therapeutic change, defined as change in the dissociated and distorted emotion schemas, involves taking in new knowledge about events in the world that may be experienced as threatening, although they are no longer dangers in the context of one's current situation and current powers; but the particular nature of dissociated schemas is that they are set up precisely to avoid such knowledge. The presenting problems that bring patients to treatment — the addictions, the isolation, the self-destructive behaviors, the somatic symptoms — reflect the strategies of management of the painful affect that the person devised in earlier times, the best they could do in situations that were experienced as dangerous or even catastrophic. The strategies are not working now and are themselves problems, but the dangers are still registered in the schema and must be dealt with. The therapist needs to enable a change in the problematic strategies while recognizing them as the achievements of the individual's early years and as incorporated in his/her sense of self; and also must gradually address the nature of the experience that is misperceived as danger today.

The person will utilize in treatment the patterns of response that have been effective in avoiding or managing painful affect in the past. Activation of painful affect, even in trace form, has the potential to reinforce avoidance rather than to provide new emotional information that can be taken in to change the schema. This is a core problem for treatments focused on extinction (LeDoux, 2002), and a major explanation for the high drop-out rates experienced in these therapies (Schottenbauer et al., 2008). This has also been recognized as a crucial therapeutic dilemma by psychoanalysts at least since Strachey (1934), writing about the vicious circle of treatment; and is a central rationale for schema therapy for borderline personality disorder, as well as for the relational approach in psychodynamic psychotherapy.

The management of this process is the core of therapeutic skill in all treatments. The dreaded schema, at least in trace form, must be activated in the session and in the relationship in order for change to come about; but activated in such a way that the tangle of avoidance and protection can be penetrated to some extent, so that the schema can potentially be reconstructed rather than the dissociation being reinforced.

The process of change in emotion schemas occurs in treatment through the operation of the referential process, which involves activation and exploration potentially leading to change. This has three major components, characterized as *Arousal, Narrative/Symbolizing* and *Reorganizing;* these operate in interactive and recursive ways in both therapist and patient.

Arousal Phase: Traces of the problematic dissociated emotion schema are activated within the relationship, in the interaction of the two participants and in different ways in the subjective experience of each. The affective core is communicated primarily on bodily and motoric levels; this is what I have termed emotional communication (Bucci, 2001, 2009). There is likely to be a fairly continuous flow of language during this phase, but the language that the patient speaks — at least the semantic level of the language — is largely dissociated from the affective core that has been aroused. The language that the analyst speaks needs to be connected to the patient's affective core; this must be through the analyst experiencing the patient in him/her self, as will be explained and illustrated in detail.

Narrative/Symbolizing Phase: The person talks about an episode of life, or tells a dream or fantasy whose connection to the problematic schema may not be recognized. The symbolizing of the emotion schema may also occur in the interactions of the treatment relationship. The images, narratives and interpersonal enactments have the potential to bring elements of the problematic emotion schema into explicit and shareable symbolic form. The power of this phase is to open new connections to the meaning of the painful affects; the risk is to touch on dreaded dissociated elements of the affective core before the patient has developed the capacity to contain the affect.

Reorganizing Phase: Once the material is shared, and the affect is activated but sufficiently contained, there is opportunity for a phase of reorganizing and reflection in which the source and meaning of the events that make up the schema may be further explored in the current context, new connections may be discovered, and new schemas constructed.

The phases do not necessarily occur in clear and orderly progression throughout a session; for example, the movement between arousal and symbolizing is likely to be recursive as the patient opens up small corners of the dreaded schemas, and pulls back to absorb — or deflect — the effects, but the three components operate in any effective session, in any treatment form. We are developing measures to identify and characterize these phases in our psychoanalytic process research (Bucci & Maskit, 2007).

In previous work on the referential process, and in our empirical research, I have focused primarily on the function of the Narrative/ Symbolizing phase in exploring emotion schemas and in providing representations of the emotion schemas that can be shared. In connecting emotional experience effectively to language, it is not sufficient to say 'I felt angry — or sad — or ashamed'. What is most useful in connecting to emotional experience and evoking corresponding experience in the other is to tell an episode or provide a fantasy incorporating such a feeling, in concrete and specific detail. There is considerable evidence for the power of such narratives, and reflection on them, in bringing about change in emotion schemas (Bucci, 1995, 2007a,b).

In this paper I focus on the interactions that are associated with embodied communication; these are dominant in the Arousal phase but active throughout the treatment as well. This bodily communication provides the emotional context for associated exploration in narrative and also in the enactments of the schema in the therapeutic relationship. The patient 'knows' the other and herself in relation to the other in her own subsymbolic system; the therapist also 'knows' the patient through the complementary entrainment. The therapist's response, in his own emotion circuitry, to the playing out of the patient's plan is the best available source of knowledge and entry into further shared knowledge of the patient's dissociated and distorted schema. This 'knowing' is unlikely to be explicit for the therapist, at least at first; he will need to go through a version of the referential process to recognize the nature of his experience. In this process, the therapist will have associations and memories and will also reflect on these — including examination of the way in which the experience of his own life contributes to his perception of the patient's experience.

The converse of this, which needs to be recognized in all treatment approaches, including the various forms of cognitive and behavioral and exposure treatments, as well as experiential and client centered approaches, is that the therapist's *real* emotional experience of the patient, including experience of which she/he may not be aware, will necessarily be received by the patient and responded to within his/her embodied emotional system. All therapists need to recognize that this is occurring in making their decisions as to how to work.

A Clinical Illustration: William Cornell's Case of Ann

William Cornell, who identifies with fields of Transactional Analysis as well as body work and psychoanalysis, describes an encounter with a patient whom he calls Ann, with whom he had been working for several years in weekly psychotherapy. He describes her as deeply anxious, hypersensitive to approval or disapproval, and often withdrawn:

> She was also sweetly naïve and maintained a subtly ironic sense of humor about the struggles in her lonely life. I knew that she was profoundly lonely, but I never quite understood how she kept herself so socially isolated.

One evening, he happens to see Ann as she enters a movie theatre where he is seated:

> In the theater, I barely recognized this woman hunched down into her overcoat, arms held tightly at her sides, unkempt hair over her face, moving like a street person with the thorazine shuffle. She walked up and down the aisle several times before choosing a seat far from others. I could not tell if she had seen me. (Cornell, 2008, p. 41)

As he watched Ann, Cornell saw someone very different from the woman he saw in his office, and began to have a sense of the mechanisms that kept her so alone.

In the next session, Ann indirectly acknowledged having seen him in the theatre — asking what he thought of the movie. After responding to that, he told her that he had seen her in the theater but couldn't tell if she had seen him. She said that it looked like he was with a friend so she didn't want to intrude. "I was alone, as usual" — , she said. With considerable care, Cornell then tells her that if he hadn't known her, he would have found her way of coming into the theater rather frightening, that her whole demeanor seemed to emanate "Leave me the fuck alone." Even knowing her, he said, he didn't feel he could approach her to say hello; all he could feel was the signal to stay away. He asked her if that was what she was feeling and if that was what she wanted to communicate:

> Ann was startled: "NO! Is that really what I look like? What I'm feeling is that everybody else is at the movies with a friend, a partner, a boyfriend, a family, and I'm alone, always alone, and people are staring at me. I hate it. I try to find a seat where I won't bother anybody, and where I don't have to see the couples. I hate it so much that most of the time I can't even get out the door to go to the movie. But I didn't know I looked so weird."(Cornell, 2008, pp.41-42)

He could see her anxiety and shame overwhelm her; he says that it felt important to tell her what he experienced, he was worried that it might shame her, but he thinks there is a lot they can learn from this. He then suggests that "they bring the body that was in the theater" into his office.

> I suggested that she put her coat back on, hunch into it, and shuffle into the office. I felt sick to my stomach as I watched. I wanted to move to her, to tell her to pull the hair out of her face, to look at me, to do or say something kind to her. I asked her to notice any feelings that came up in her and to allow her body to move in any way it needed. Gradually, she became still and then slumped to her knees, curling over, pulling her coat over her head. She looked to me now like she was awaiting a beating. I thought of her stories of beatings by her father, the teasing and taunting by her brothers, the delusional ravings of her mother. But I did not feel compassionate. I felt irritated.

He is moving from his complex subsymbolic bodily responses of revulsion and caring to begin to process the enactment in his symbolic system, through connecting to stories of her childhood and her family. His perception of Ann may also be arousing in him the feelings and associated responses she elicited in her family at that time.

> She just knelt there, curled over and inert. I wanted to kick her. I got bored. I started thinking ahead to my evening after work. My bladder began to ache. I wanted the session over. I felt I'd made a mistake in talking to her about the theater, in intervening this way.

He does not act on the response plan that is aroused; he recognizes it explicitly and manages it through various processes of avoidance, defense and reflection.

> Still, she did not move. I forced myself to look at her inert form. She looked like a supplicant. I began thinking of my Catholic upbringing (Ann was also raised Catholic) — forced to genuflect, to kneel, to pray for forgiveness, awaiting the sound of the nuns' clickers informing us we could stand up and move on. Submission. Defeat. Hatred. An object of derision and disgust.

Again, he is involved in a referential process, entering the symbolic mode, now making associations to his own life, naming the feelings as experienced in himself. The process begins to take a different form.

> Do I speak to Ann? Do I wait? I waited in silence.

> Ann began to stir. She placed her hands on the floor and pushed herself upright, brushing the hair out of her face. "This is a relief," she said. "This is what I feel all the time, but I've been afraid if you knew it you would give up on me. Did I scare you this time, too? I feel like a freak when I'm outside. But I'm glad we did this. I'm glad I could show you this. This is how my body feels all the time. (Cornell, 2008, p. 43)

The interaction of Ann and her therapist illustrates the recursive and interactive sequence of perception/action mirroring, emotional experiencing and anticipation that has been offered here, and how this may play out and be used in the therapeutic context. Ann's perception of the interpersonal world has grown to incorporate the experience of people as staring at her, shaming her, ridiculing her, abusing her. She has learned to respond to that before it happens. Her anticipatory response is self-fulfilling; Cornell feels sick to his stomach, he is bored, he wants to kick her, to get away from her, he suffers physically. He has learned through his body the set of feelings that perception of Ann's demeanor excites in the people around her. These lead him as well to explicit imagery and associations to her life, and to his own life, including the Catholic upbringing that he and Ann share, and the associated feelings.

The occurrence of his negative reactions in a sense seems to raise questions concerning the claim I made earlier — that the therapist's feelings will necessarily be communicated to the patient. He does not kick her as he has the urge to do, but he does feel boredom, anger, and the wish to escape. There are a number of additional distinctions that need to be made, which Cornell does not explicate. This interaction occurred in the context of several years of work together, several years of countless interactions in which he has seen and reacted to multiple aspects of her — her sweet naivete, her sense of humor; countless times in which he has perceived her differently, reacted differently from the reactions of her family in her early years. He is distressed in many ways, some of which he explicitly recognizes, some of which he may not. He wants to get away but does not, he endures his distress, manages it somehow, explores it, stays with her.

She recognizes that she has evoked distress in him, she 'scared him' again, as she did in the theatre; perhaps she intended to do so, perhaps it is one of her strategies of attack or warding off attack. She also sees that he has allowed her to show this depth of feeling that she has seen as unspeakable and he has stayed with her. The treatment doesn't end with the bodily communication, but moves on to exploration of experiences of the present and past.

As Cornell also emphasizes, this is both an exploration *within* each of them and a communication between them. The therapist explores within his own body, the patient within hers — to find the hidden bodily expectations of the past that have shaped her current confrontations with the world. The therapist must reflect as well on the contributions of his own life experience to his response to the patient. What is happening in him is in response to Ann's communication, but also determined by who he is.

Conclusions and Implications

Clinicians, at least from Freud onward, have struggled with the question of how one can know in some valid way what is in another person's mind. Freud addressed the question in terms of the unconscious mind and was not particularly troubled by the problem. He saw this communication as immediate and direct, similar to the mechanism of the telephone:

> Just as the receiver converts back into sound waves the electric oscillations in the telephone lines which were set up by sound waves, so the doctor's unconscious is able, from the derivatives of the unconscious which are communicated to him, to reconstruct the unconscious, which has determined the patient's free associations. (Freud, 1912, p. 115)

Reik attempted to place these processes in a scientific context, in his prescient work on emotional communication, and also drew on concepts of *introjection, projection,* and *reprojection* to account for more complex aspects of the analyst's understanding of the patient's experience. In the intervening years, some psychoanalytic explanations of these processes have grown increasing abstruse. As I have argued:

> The emphasis on projective identification and related concepts has deepened the epistemological mystique surrounding the question of how the analyst can 'know' the patient's experience and further widened the gap between psychoanalysis and scientific psychology. (Bucci, 2001, p. 41)

The findings concerning mirror neurons and their embedding in recursive interactive sequences take us an important step towards addressing these clinical issues and potentially placing them in a scientific context. As Iacoboni (2009) has argued, "this work will force us to rethink radically the deepest aspects of our social relations and our very selves" (p. 8). According to Ramachandran (2000) the discovery of mirror neurons is potentially of equivalent importance in neuroscience to the discovery of DNA in biology.

Some Caveats

It should be emphasized that the research on these processes in humans is just beginning, and the applications to the psychotherapy process that I have proposed here are complex and speculative. While a set of neurons that fire indifferently for perception and actions have been identified neurologically, these are of course only a subset of the neurological equipment of the human brain. Beyond this, systematic models on a psychological level that are compatible with these neurological observations need to be further developed.

The model of complex behavior chains outlined here clearly differs from standard conditioning paradigms. Rather than basing the process on connections of objects (S), e.g. food, to a response (R), e.g. salivate, or on complex networks of S-S connections, the new approach relies on a different basic set of processing units, a core of perceptions that themselves incorporate actions and affect. We should also note, however, that learning must occur in this perception/response core, as indicated experimentally by the role of expertise in the firing of the mirror neurons, and the nature of the learning remains to be explored.

It is also clear that the way of knowing the experience of others, as usually understood in traditional theories of mind, by making inference from observation of others to their inner experience, needs to be revised. The multiple code theory, with its component of subsymbolic processing, was developed in large part in recognition that human knowledge and information processing are not adequately modeled as symbol manipulating systems. This is a broader formulation that goes beyond the emphasis on action of the embodied communication theories but is compatible with it, and may provide some elaboration of the underlying psychological model.

It is also important to recognize that while the therapist 'knows' the other immediately through his/her own bodily experience, this knowledge may be valid or invalid. Therapists need constantly to examine the contribution of their own life experience to their knowledge of the other. The new findings should not lead psychodynamic therapists to say they have found a scientific basis for the elusive — and seductive — concept of projective identification; but a more nuanced understanding of factors in themselves as well as the patient that contribute to what they perceive.

Embodied Communication and Therapeutic Practice

Therapists today, in all treatment approaches, including empirically supported and manualized treatment need to be aware of what is going on emotionally and bodily in the patient, in themselves and between the two of them. As Robert Leahy, a leading cognitive therapist has written:

> ... many novices in cognitive-behavioral therapy (CBT) rely heavily on 'empirically supported treatments', manualized approaches, agenda-setting, or targeted behaviors and cognitions, but fail to recognize appropriately the role of the therapeutic relationship ... Empirically supported treatments 'work' ... but only if the patient enters therapy, maintains a therapeutic relationship ... Many patients drop out prematurely. If the patient is not in

treatment, then no help is found. (Leahy, 2009, p. 187)

The core of psychotherapy is the dyadic interchange. The patient must first and foremost be 'in treatment' in order for the treatment to work, as Leahy says, and this requires that a relationship be developed and sustained. Experienced clinicians have remained aware of this basic premise of psychotherapy through all the requirements of manualized treatments; psychotherapy researchers are increasingly aware of this as well, as shown in the work of Beutler and others cited above. Psychotherapy approaches differ as to the degree to which the operation and exploration of the relationship are central to the processes of therapeutic change, or simply a means of keeping a patient 'in treatment' so that other processes may be employed; but the basic premise of psychotherapy as a dyadic interchange remains. The new work on subsymbolic, bodily communication that has been outlined here opens pathways for scientific understanding of processes that on some level, all clinicians — and all humans — know do occur.

References

Bartlett F. C. (1932). *Remembering: A study in social psychology.* Cambridge: Cambridge University Press.

Beutler L. E. (2009). Making science matter in clinical practice: Redefining psychotherapy. *Clinical Psychology: Science and Practice, 16,* 301-17.

Bowlby J. (1969). *Attachment and Loss: Vol. 1: Attachment.* New York: Basic Books.

Bucci W. (1995). The power of the narrative; A multiple code account. In J. Pennebaker (ed.), *Emotion, Disclosure and Health* (pp. 93-122). Washington: American Psychological Association Books.

Bucci W. (1997). *Psychoanalysis and Cognitive Science: A multiple code theory.* New York: Guilford Press.

Bucci W. (2001). Pathways of emotional communication. *Psychoanalytic Inquiry, 20,* 40-70.

Bucci W. (2002). The Referential Process, Consciousness, and the Sense of Self. *Psychoanalytic Inquiry, 22,* 766-93

Bucci W. (2007a). Dissociation from the perspective of multiple code theory: Part I; Psychological roots and implications for psychoanalytic treatment. *Contemporary Psychoanalysis, 43,* 165-84

Bucci W. (2007b). Dissociation from the perspective of multiple code theory: Part II; The spectrum of dissociative processes in the psychoanalytic relationship. *Contemporary Psychoanalysis, 43,* 305-26

Bucci W. (2010). *Components of the referential process as common factors in therapeutic change.* Paper presented at Society for Psychotherapy Research, Asilomar, CA.

Bucci W. & Maskit B. (2007). Beneath the surface of the therapeutic interaction; The psychoanalytic method in modern dress. *Journal of the American Psychoanalytic Association, 55,* 1355-97.

Cornell W. F. (2008). Self in Action: The Bodily Basis of Self-Organization In F. S. Anderson (ed.), *Bodies in Treatment; The Unspoken Dimension* (pp. 29-49). Hillsdale: The Analytic Press, Inc.

Damasio A. R. (1994). *Descartes' Error: Emotion, Reason and the Human Brain.* New York: Avon Books.

Damasio A. R. (1999). *The Feeling of What Happens*. New York: Harcourt Brace.
Darwin C. (1872). *The Expression of the Emotions in Man and Animals*. New York: Philosophical Library.
Freud S. (1912). Recommendations to Physicians Practising Psycho-Analysis. *Standard Edition*, 12, (pp. 109-20). London: Hogarth Press.
Iacoboni M. (2009). *Mirroring People: The Science of Empathy and How We Connect to Others*. New York: Farrar, Straus and Giroux.
Kinsbourne M. & Jordan J. S. (2009). Embodied anticipation: A neurodevelopmental interpretation. *Discourse Processes, 46*, 103-26.
Jordan J. S. (2009). Forward-looking aspects of perception-action coupling as a basis for embodied communication. *Discourse Processes, 46*, 127-44.
Leahy R. L. (2009). Resistance: An emotional schema therapy (EST) approach. In S. E. Gregoris (ed.), *Cognitive Behavior Therapy: A Guide for the Practising Clinician, Vol. 2*. (pp. 187-204). New York: Routledge/Taylor & Francis Group.
LeDoux J. E. (2002). *The synaptic self*. New York: Viking.
Luborsky L., Rosenthal R., Diguer L., Andrusyna T. P., Berman J. S., Levitt J. T., Seligman D. A., & Kraus E. D. (2002). The dodo bird verdict is alive and well — mostly. *Clinical Psychology: Science and Practice, 9*, 2-12.
McClelland J. L., Rumelhart D. E., & Hinton G. E. (1989). The appeal of parallel distributed processing. In D. E. Rumelhart, J. L. McClelland, & the PDP Research Group (eds.), *Parallel Distributed Processing: Explorations in the Microstructure of Cognition* (Volume 1: Foundations), (pp. 3-44). Cambridge: MIT Press.
Meltzoff A. N., & Moore M. K. (1994). Imitation, memory and the representation of persons. *Infant Behavior and Development, 17*, 83-99.
Panksepp J. (1999). Emotions as Viewed by Psychoanalysis and Neuroscience. *Journal of Neuropsychoanalysis, 1*, 15-38
Ramachandran V. S. (2000). *Mirror neurons and imitation learning as the driving force behind 'the Great Leap Forward' in human evolution*. Edge 69 (cited in Iacoboni, 2009, p. 281)
Reik T. (1948/1964). *Listening with the Third Ear: The Inner Experience of a Psychoanalyst*. New York: Pyramid Books.
Rizzolatti G., Fadiga L., Gallese V., & Fogassi L. (1996). Premotor cortex and the recognition of motor actions. *Cognitive Brain Research, 3*, 131-41.
Rizzolatti G., Fogassi L., & Gallese V. (2001). Neurophysiological mechanisms underlying the understanding and imitation of action. *Nature Reviews Neuroscience, 2*, 661-70.
Schottenbauer M. A., Glass C. R., Arnkoff D. B., Tendick V., & Gray S. H. (2008). Nonresponse and Dropout Rates in Outcome Studies on PTSD: Review and Methodological Considerations. *Psychiatry, 71*, 134-68
Stern D. N. (1985). *The Interpersonal World of the Infant*. New York: Basic Books.
Strachey J. (1934/1963). The nature of the therapeutic action of psycho-analysis. In L. Paul (ed.), *Psychoanalytic Clinical Interpretation*. New York: Free Press.
Wampold B. E. (2010). The research evidence for common factors models: A historically situated perspective. In B. L. Duncan, S. D. Miller, B. E. Wampold, & M. A. Hubble, (eds.), *The heart and soul of change: Delivering what works in therapy* (2nd ed.), (pp. 49-81). Washington: American Psychological Association.
Westen D., Novotny C. M., & Thompson-Brenner H. (2004). The empirical status of empirically supported psychotherapies: Assumptions, findings and reporting in controlled clinical trials. *Psychological Bulletin, 130*, 631-63.
Wicker B., Keysers C., Plailly J., Royet J. P., Gallese V., & Rizzolatti G. (2003). Both of us disgusted in my insula: The common neural basis of seeing and feeling disgust. *Neuron, 40*, 655-64.

Section 4

Embodiment & Ecological Psychology

Affordances, Effectivities, and Extension of the Body

Naoya Hirose

Department of Psychology, Kyoto Notre Dame University,
1 Minami-Nonogamicho, Shimogamo, Sakyoku,
Kyoto 606-0847 Japan
nhirose@notredame.ac.jp

Introduction

This chapter attempts to describe some aspects of embodiment from the perspective of ecological psychology. Ecological psychology aims to study perception-action coupling in animal-environment systems. When considering the relationship between animals and the environment, traditional psychology would ask how animals perceive the surrounding environment and behave in it. Ecological psychology, in contrast, asks first if there is information in the environment that enables animals to regulate their behavior. In other words, ecological psychology puts emphasis on the environment, rather than on animals. The environmental property that animals use to regulate their behavior is called affordance. The concept of affordance is central to ecological psychology and also useful in understanding embodiment in animal-environment systems. In this chapter, we will discuss affordance and its complementary concept, effectivity, in reference to embodiment.

Before turning to the discussion of affordance and effectivity, it will be useful to clarify the relation between the body and the perception-action systems. The term 'body' has various meanings, so that the body can be described from different viewpoints. In particular, the biological and psychological views of the body seem to be important for our present purposes. What we mean by the biological and psychological here is in agreement with Gibson's classifications: "Biology begins with the division between the nonliving and the living. But psychology begins with the division between the inanimate and the animate" (Gibson, 1986, p. 7). From the biological view, the body is delineated as living, separated from nonliving objects in the surroundings of the animal. It is compatible with the common meaning that body refers to the physical structure of an organism. From this view, the boundary of the body is fixed at the surface of the skin. For example, clothes are not part of the wearer's body and a shell is not part of the body of a hermit crab; they belong to the surroundings of the animals.

On the other hand, from the psychological view, the body can be described as animate, namely, moving spontaneously. What makes an organism animate is its capability to regulate its behavior with its surroundings (Reed, 1996). In order to regulate its behaviors, the organism needs to perceive information in the environment. Thus, the body should have the means to interact with the environment: perceiving its information and acting upon it. Gibson (1986) maintained that animals perceive in order to move and also move in order to perceive. He also asserted that "Moving from place to place is supposed to be 'physical' whereas perceiving is supposed to be 'mental', but this dichotomy is misleading" (Gibson, 1986, p. 223). Action is commonly assumed to be related to the body, but perception is also related to the body. Since perception and action are closely coupled, the body can be described as a perception-action system. According to this view, the boundary of the body should be the point where the animal perceive and act on its surroundings; it may not always be at the surface of the skin. From this psychological view, clothes are part of the wearer's body and a shell is part of the body of a hermit crab. In this chapter, we describe the body from the psychological view, that is, the view of the body as a perception-action system. With this view in mind, we will explore aspects of embodiment in the animal-environment systems.

In the following sections, we examine the definitions of affordance and describe the linkage between affordances and the body. Then we discuss the concept of effectivity and show some examples of extension of effectivities. Next, we consider whether extensions of effectivities modify perception of the body. Finally, we discuss the extension and boundary of the body from the perspective of animal-tool-environment systems.

What are affordances?

The term *affordance* was invented as the noun form of the verb *afford* by Gibson (1986). Inventing such a word, Gibson tried to express what could not be expressed by the existing concepts. The concept of affordance is essential in ecological psychology (Chemero, 2003, 2009; Heft, 1989, 2003; Sanders, 1997, 1999; Stoffregen, 2000a, 2003; Turvey, 1992). The concept, however, has not been fully articulated, thus ecological psychologists have discussed what affordances are (e.g., Jones, 2003; Stoffregen, 2000b). Roughly speaking, there are two different definitions of affordance among them (Chemero, 2003).

One definition is that affordances are properties of the environment referring to an animal (Heft, 1989, 2001; Michaels, 2000; Reed, 1996; Shaw et al., 1982; Turvey, 1992). This view stems from Gibson's most acknowledged definition of affordance: "The *affordances* of the environment are what it *offers* the animal, what it *provides* or *furnishes*, either for good or ill" (Gibson, 1986, p. 127). Several authors generally share the view that affordances are properties of the environment; however, they disagree about what kind of properties affordances should be.

According to Reed, affordances refer to the resources encountered by an animal in the environment (Reed, 1996). An animal makes use of available resources (i.e., affordances) to regulate its behaviors in the environment. Reed proposed that affordances create selection pressure on behavior of an animal and thus its behavior is regulated with respect to the affordances of the environment. Accordingly, this view of affordance as a resource is closely linked to evolution by natural selection.

On the other hand, in his development of the notion of affordance, Turvey (1992) argued that affordances are dispositional properties of the environment. Disposition is a property of a thing that is potential or latent. A disposition ought to be paired with a particular condition that actualizes it. If affordances are dispositional properties, then they must be complemented by animals' properties that actualize the dispositions. For example, the affordance of the object being graspable is not defined without a complementing animal property of capability to grasp the object. This complemented property is called effectivity. Accordingly, whereas affordances are properties of the environment, effectivities are properties of the animals. The notion of effectivity is particularly significant for extension of the body that we will discuss later on.

The other definition of affordance is that affordances are relational properties of the animal and the environment. Some ecological psychologists do not share the view that affordances are properties of the environment, and maintain that affordances are emergent properties of the animal-environment system (Stoffregen, 2003) or relations between the abilities of animals and features of the environment (Chemero, 2003, 2009). This view is well matched to Gibson's frequent quotation about affordances:

> An affordance is neither an objective property nor a subjective property; or it is both if you like. An affordance cuts across the dichotomy of subjective-objective and helps us to understand its inadequacy. It is equally a fact of the environment and a fact of behavior. It is both physical and psychical, yet neither. An affordance points both ways, to the environment and to the observer. (Gibson, 1986, p. 129)

This passage seems to suggest that affordances should be properties of the animal-environment systems. In order to avoid the subject-object dichotomy, Gibson emphasized the relation between the animal and the environment. This may obscure the definition of affordance. In an earlier draft of the theory of affordances, Gibson offers more specific definition of affordance: "Subject to revision, I suggest that *the affordance of anything is a specific combination of the properties of its substance and its surfaces taken with reference to an animal*" (Gibson, 1977, p. 67). Jones (2003) pointed out that Gibson changed the wording of his final book to be rather unclear. Ambiguity in Gibson's (1986) book may lead to two irreconcilable definitions of affordance.

We suggest that confusion between the two definitions of affordance, affordance as environmental property and affordance as relation, might be brought about by different standpoints that researchers have taken. The theory of affordances discussed so far seems to include two distinct viewpoints (see also Şahin et al., 2007, for a similar view). One is the viewpoint of an observer; the other is that of an animal. To dispel the confusion about definition, we will now examine these two viewpoints more closely.

Let us first examine affordances from the viewpoint of an observer. An observer can perceive relations between the animal and the environment. Studies suggest that laypersons can accurately perceive other persons' affordances (Mark, 2007; Ramenzoni et al., 2008a, 2008b; Stoffregen et al., 1999). Meanwhile, the observer's viewpoint is typical of the researchers who want to elucidate the animal-environment systems. Researchers can focus attention on different aspects of the animal-environment systems (Fig. 1A). Following their interest, they can focus on the environment or on the animal, or on the relation between them. Some can focus on the environment in the animal-environment system (Fig. 1A, a). This is the view of affordances as properties of the environment that is postulated by many ecological psychologists, such as Reed (1996) and Turvey (1992). Additionally, some may direct attention toward the animal (Fig. 1A, c). This case is referred to as effectivity, not as affordance.

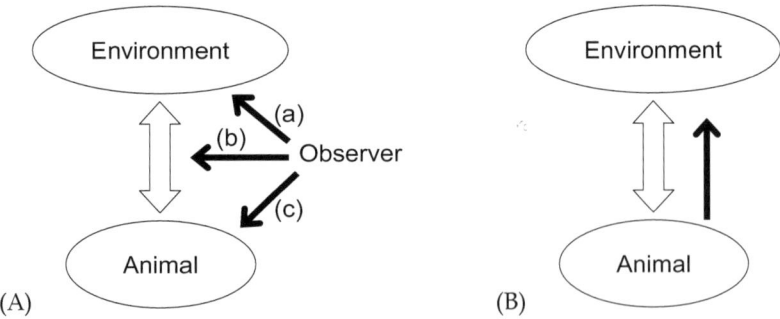

Fig. 1: Different viewpoints of animal-environment system: from an observer (A) and from an animal (B).

Other psychologists have focused on the relation between the animal and the environment (Figure 1A, b). This is the view of affordances as relations that Chemero (2003, 2009) and Stoffregen (2003) advocate. If ecological psychology is concerned with the animal-environmental fits, it is natural that ecological psychologists spotlight the animal-environment relations. Hence, they insist that affordances, the fundamental concept of ecological psychology, should be relational properties of the animal and the environment.

The main point is that the two conflicting definitions of affordance are derived from two different focuses of the researchers. The question we ask here is which definition of affordance is more consistent with what Gibson (1986) wished to articulate. In order to answer the question, we ought to consider affordances from the viewpoint of an animal. This is because it is an animal that perceives and utilizes affordances.

Let us turn now to the viewpoint of an animal (Fig. 1B). When perceiving and realizing affordances, an animal should attend to the properties of the environment, rather than those of the animal itself. The animal does not need to care about its capabilities because they are relatively constant. For the animal, its capabilities are the frame of reference and, accordingly, not usually attended to. Meanwhile, the animal needs to give attention to the environmental properties because they are changeable and diversified. From the viewpoint of an animal, affordances must be perceived as properties of the environment. Therefore, the definition of affordance as environmental property is more qualified than that of affordance as relation from the animal's viewpoint.

Furthermore, the definition of affordance as relation is less eligible, considering the original meaning of affordance. Recall that the word *affordance* is the noun form of the verb *afford*. This implies that the environment affords animals. In this statement, the environment and animals do not have the equivalent status; it is unequivocal that the focus is on the environment. There is an asymmetry between the environment and animals in the ecological approach.

The view of affordance as relation makes light of this asymmetry. The term *affordance* does mean that the environment affords animals; it does not mean that animals utilize the environment. Gibson remarked, "The organism depends on its environment for its life, but the environment does not depend on the organism for its existence" (Gibson, 1986, p. 129). Reed (1996) also pointed out that there is always an asymmetry between an environment and its inhabitants. Consequently, we should emphasize the environmental property when defining affordance. Even if we assume affordance as relation, the emphasis should be on the environmental side.

We propose that affordances are properties of the environment, but we also suggest that they are related to the animal that perceives and utilizes them; affordances are related to the perception-action system, that is, the body of the animal. Whereas traditional psychology has assumed that perception is measured independently from the properties of the observer, this postulation does not apply to perception of affordances. Gibson (1986) insisted that an affordance cannot be measured as we measure in physics and that it must be measured relative to the animal. For example, an affordance for sitting is different between adults and children because of their different leg lengths. Studies on perception of affordances have shown that an observer perceives properties of the environment in relation to the observer's body.

Warren's (1984) study on affordances for stair climbing is the first attempt to show that perception of affordances is related to the body. To analyze affordances in relation to the body, Warren employed the principle of intrinsic metrics. In intrinsic metrics, the variable of the animal-environment system is expressed by dimensionless ratios, called π numbers:

$$\pi = E/A, \quad (1)$$

where E is an environmental property and A is an animal one. In the case of stair climbing, the π number is formulated by the ratio of riser height to climber's leg length. Because the π number is scaled by the leg length, it is expected to be a constant regardless of the size of the climber. To test this hypothesis, both shorter and taller participants were asked to judge each stair as climbable or unclimbable. As expected, the taller participants judged higher riser as climbable than did the shorter. Nevertheless, when the perceptual judgments were normalized as a function of π number, the difference between two groups disappeared. As a result, perception of affordances for stair climbing was independent of the climber's height and scaled by the climber's leg length.

Warren's study demonstrated that the action boundary of stair climbing can be scaled by the actor's body dimension (i.e., leg length). Scaling affordances by body dimension were also applied to research on stepping (Mark, 1987; Pufall & Dunbar, 1992), walking through apertures (Warren & Whang, 1987), sitting (Mark, 1987; Mark & Vogele, 1987), and reaching (Carello et al., 1989). Later studies, however, have demonstrated that affordances should not be scaled by one geometrical body dimension as Warren hypothesized. Rather, affordances should be scaled dynamically by action or multi dimensions (Cesari et al., 2003; Cesari & Newell, 1999, 2000; Choi & Mark, 2004; Konczak et al., 1992; Snapp-Childs & Bingham, 2009; Warren, 1995). For instance, Choi & Mark (2004) showed transitions between reaching styles were predicted by reach distance, object weight and participant's strength of isometric pull. Hence, Warren's study on stair climbing can be said to be an exceptional case where the affordance is scaled by just one geometrical dimension. Typically, affordances are measured by several geometrical and dynamical constraints of the body.

Effectivities and their extensions

As mentioned earlier, effectivity is the complementary concept of affordance. Effectivities are means for acting that an animal adopts to realize a specific affordance. They are properties of the animal that show the reciprocity between the animal and the environment (Shaw et al., 1982; Turvey, 1992; Turvey & Shaw, 1979). Turvey (1992) mentioned that a disposition and its complement are interchangeable. If the focus is on the environmental capability, the affordance is the disposition and the effectivity is the complement. On the contrary, if the focus is on the animal's ability, the effectivity is the disposition and the affordance is the complement. Thus, affordances and effectivities are complementary to each other.

Unfortunately, the status of effectivity in ecological psychology has not been well established. Michaels (2003) pointed out that there are two usages of effectivity among researchers. One the one hand, Shaw (2001) took a similar view to Turvey's (1992), asserting that the affordances and effectivities are dual components. On the other hand, Sanders (1997) argued that an affordance does not require its complement because the concept of affordance already connotes the animal's ability. Similarly, Stoffregen (2003) maintained that effectivities are not distinct complements of affordances but subordinate to affordances. As discussed above, there is an asymmetry between the environment and animals, and the ecological approach should highlight the environmental aspect. Thus, the concept of affordance is primary in the ecological approach; effectivity has only a secondary significance. Despite this, we propose that effectivity is a valuable concept to describe animal-environment systems. Effectivity is especially useful when we examine extensions of the body.

Since effectivity is a property of the animal in the animal-environment system, it can be altered by changes in the animal's state. Tool use is a typical case where effectivities can be extended, enhanced or recovered. For instance, a rake extends reaching ability; a hammer enhances striking ability; a pair of glasses recovers visual ability. Attachments to the body can also change effectivities. For example, a wet suit restricts movability of the wearer. In many cases of attachment, changes in capability may arise as an incidental result of attaching to the body. Despite the discrepancy between tools and attachments, in this chapter, we will not discriminate attachments from tools as far as changes in effectivity are concerned.

Tools can extend perception-action capabilities of animals, especially of humans (Lockman, 2000, 2005; Shaw et al., 1995; Smitsman, 1997; Smitsman & Bongers, 2003). Tools extend and focus certain effectivities, and therefore enable humans to make use of certain affordances. From the ecological perspective, tools have a dual function (Gibson, 1986; Shaw et al., 1995). Before used, a tool is a detached object of the environment, separated from the user's body. Thus, the tool not in use is regarded as functional extension of the environment; it has its specific affordances and provides new opportunities for action. A tool in use, however, is not a mere object. The tool in use is considered as functional extension of the user; it plays a central role in extending the user's effectivities to realize affordances of the environment. Consequently, tool use involves the task to detect affordances, not of the tool itself, but of functional relations between the tool and the environment (Smitsman, 1997; Smitsman & Bongers, 2003; Smitsman & Cox, 2008). Whereas tool use entails extension of the environment, this chapter mainly concerns the functional extension of the user.

Extended haptic perception is a typical example of extending a perceptual system by tools (Burton, 1993). Extended haptic perception refers to the capacities of animals to perceive by artificial tools or by biological appendages such as vibrissae. An appendage is a natural prolongation from a part of an organism; it is organic whereas a tool is inorganic. Because such tools and appendages are neurally inert, a potential receptive surface is not necessarily nervous tissue of perceptual organs. In the ecological approach, perception is the process to pick up information in the environment, not the process of mental construction (Gibson, 1986; Reed, 1996). If an inorganic tool, such as a blind person's stick, supports information pick-up activities, the tool can be regarded as a component of the perceptual system. Thus, appendages and tools can constitute a potential receptive surface, provided they have a susceptibility to physical influence. Properties of the environment, especially affordances, can be perceived through nonneural extensions.

A hand-held object is a good example of extended haptic perception. Ecological psychologists have studied perception of hand-held objects in the area of dynamic touch (see, Carello & Turvey, 2004; Turvey, 1996). Dynamic touch is the kind of touch that occurs when one grasps an object firmly and wields it. Studies have shown that one can perceive various properties of a hand-held object by wielding and hefting the object. In addition, one can perceive not only properties of a hand-held object itself, but also properties of a distal object by probing with it. Research on haptic probing has demonstrated that one can distinguishably perceive the length of a rod used for probing and the distance to a surface to be probed (Carello et al., 1992; Chan & Turvey, 1991). One also can perceive haptically the length of a target rod by probing with a second probe rod (Peck et al., 1996). Therefore, haptic perception of objects can be extended beyond the hand.

Extended haptic perception is also evident in the studies on perception of affordances by probing. Burton (1992) investigated nonvisual perception of affordances for gap crossing. In the experiments, participants were asked to judge by probing or vision whether a gap could be stepped over. As was done in Warren's (1984) study, two groups of different heights participated. The results showed that the taller participants categorized larger gap as crossable than did the shorter, and that the difference between two groups disappeared when gap size was normalized by leg length. These results correspond to the principle of intrinsic metrics discussed earlier. Moreover, participants could make nonvisual judgments as reliably as visual judgments, and both judgments were less variable. Thus, haptic perception of gaps has some parallels with visual perception. This finding agrees with the ideas of the equivalence of different perceptual systems (Gibson, 1966; see also Wagman et al., 2009).

The equivalence of haptic probing and visual exploration was further investigated by Fitzpatrick and colleagues (1994). Fitzpatrick and colleagues examined perception of affordance for supporting upright stance. Participants were asked to either visually or haptically judge whether a slanted surface supports upright stance. In the experiments, participants stood about 1 m from an inclined board, and either looked at the surface or explored the surface with a probe. The perceived transitional point between supporting and not supporting did not differ for haptic and visual judgments. In addition, whereas the exploration time was longer in haptic judgments than that in visual judgments, the profiles of the response time were similar for both judgments: the exploration time increased around the transitional point. These results suggest that the pickup of information is independent of particular sensory organs. That is, different stimulus energies can carry the same information (Gibson, 1966, 1986).

Tool use can extend not only perceptual systems but also action systems (see Hirose, 2002). Bongers and colleagues (2003) examined effects of rod properties on approaching and displacing an object with a hand-held rod. Adult participants were asked to walk toward a table while holding a rod upward, select a place to stop, and then displace an object off the table with the tip of the rod. In order to determine how properties of the rod affect the reaching distance and the displacing posture, length, mass and mass distribution of the rod were manipulated. Analysis revealed that rod length was most important for determining the reaching distance. The distance was also prospectively adapted to the upcoming posture of displacing the object. Mass and mass distribution contributed slightly and reliably to determining the distance and the posture (but not applying to children, see Bongers et al., 2004). These findings show that both geometrics and kinetics of rods changed participants' reaching effectivities, allowing them to perceive the affordance for reaching with rods. Hence, participants could prospectively modify their reaching behaviors to changes in geometrics and dynamics of the body plus rod system.

Steenbergen and colleagues also showed that a tool changes dynamics of action systems (Steenbergen et al., 1997). They investigated the effect of perturbations of the tool-environment relation upon the action of tool use. They introduced perturbation by manipulating some features of the tool without nullifying its affordances. If young children can use a modified tool so as to preserve its original functional relation, this seems to be good evidence that they perceive an object in terms of its functional properties, that is, its affordances (Reed, 1997). Steenbergen and colleagues examined whether young children could perceive and maintain affordance of spoons in the face of perturbation by manipulating the geometrical relation of the bowl and the stem. They employed a normal spoon and five transformed spoons that were bent at the intersection of the bowl and the stem. Young children from 2 to 4 years were asked to use one of the spoons to carry rice from a full container to an empty one. To maintain the affordance for scooping, children must scoop substance with the concave side facing upward even at the cost of the arm and body posture. Therefore, children were expected to show various grip patterns to adapt their handlings to perturbations. The results showed that children tried to use spoons in the functional way, inserting them into rice with the concave side keeping upwards. To preserve this functional relation, children changed their grip type and position according to the type of spoon. This allowed children to carry rice successfully at most of the attempts. Hence, children adapted their tool use actions to the transformations of the tool, preserving the functional relation between the tool and the environment.

As described earlier, studies on scaling affordances demonstrate that perception of affordances is based on the body. Attachments to the body alter the user's body dimensions, thus changing the user's effectivities. In order to fit the environment, the user needs to adjust their perception of affordances to this change. How is this perceptual adjustment attained?

Consider putting on thick-soled shoes, for example. Mark and colleagues (Mark, 1987; Mark et al., 1990) investigated perception of affordance for sitting with altering observers' leg length by strapping 10-cm blocks on their feet. Because the blocks extend sitting abilities, the maximum seat height that a person with 10-cm blocks can actually sit on is 10 cm higher than that without blocks. The question then arises: can observers perceive their extended capability of sitting without practicing sitting? In their experiments, participants were allowed to walk around with blocks during the interval between trials, but were not allowed to practice sitting with blocks. At the beginning of the trials, participants with blocks tended to underestimate their actual sitting ability. As trials progressed, however, their perception became less underestimated, approaching their actual sitting heights. In other words, the gap between the perceived and actual height decreased over trials without practice of the relevant action. This result suggests that participants gradually retuned their perception of affordances to the changes in their effectivity. This retuning process was also found in studies of stir climbing (Mark, 1987) and bar crossing (Hirose & Nishio, 2001). It should be noted that retuning is not improvement of object perception. Mark (1987) reported that perception of the block height did not improve over trials; participants consistently overestimated its heights. This suggests that retuning pertains to changes in perception of body plus blocks, not of blocks only.

Carrying luggage is another example of changing effectivities by attachments to the body. Malek & Wagman (2008) investigated perception of affordances for standing on an inclined surface with wearing a weighted backpack. The weighted backpack alters the wearer's body dimension, thus changing the effectivity of maintaining upright posture. Participants' task was to judge whether they could stand on an inclined surface with wearing a weighted backpack. Results showed that perception of affordances for standing on the inclined surface depended on whether a weighted backpack shifted the center of mass toward or away from the inclined surface. Regia-Corte & Wagman (2008) also found that perception of this affordance depended on the degree to which a weighted backpack raised the center of mass. In a developmental study, Adolph & Avolio (2000) explored adaptation to altered body scales on infant walking by having them put on a weighted vest, suggesting that infants could retune their perceptual judgments to their altered action capabilities. Studies on affordances for walking through apertures while carrying an object also suggests that people are sensitive to changes in effectivities by attachments to the body (Higuchi et al., 2006; Wagman & Malek, 2007; Wagman & Taylor, 2005).

Perception of the body

Next we consider the sense of embodiment during tool use and attachment to the body. We have noted above that tool use and attachment to the body change effectivities and affordances. The question now arises as to whether this change leads to an extension of the sense of embodiment. The hypothesis that tools and attachments change our sense of embodiment seems to be accepted as commonplace. For instance, contact lens wearers rarely feel their lenses being worn, and furthermore, they are usually unconscious of their vision being amplified. Skillful drivers are often said to be able to feel a car body as if it were part of their own; for example, they can pass through a narrow passage without difficulty. Thus the hypothesis about extension of the sense of embodiment appears sufficiently promising. We will now examine whether empirical studies support this hypothesis.

As described above, tool use changes effectivities and perception of the affordance. The question that we ask here is whether tool use changes perception of the body. There has been no study addressing this topic in ecological psychology, but a number of studies in cognitive neuroscience and neuropsychology have been conducted on perception of the body in using a tool (e.g., Farne et al., 2005; Farne et al., 2007; Goldenberg & Spatt, 2009; Johnson-Frey, 2004; Ladavas & Serino, 2008; Maravita et al., 2001;

Maravita & Iriki, 2004).

Let us consider the seminal study of tool use by macaque monkeys (Iriki et al., 1996; Ishibashi et al., 2000). Japanese macaque monkeys can be trained to use a rake to retrieve distant food although they rarely use tools in their natural habitat. Iriki and colleagues analyzed the monkeys' bimodal neurons responding to both somatosensory and visual stimulation to the hand. Before tool use, the visual receptive fields were located near the hand corresponding to the somatosensory ones. After tool use, however, the visual receptive fields included not only the hand but also the entire tool. This expansion of the visual receptive fields was interpreted as evidence for the modification of body schema: when the monkeys intended to use a rake to retrieve distal food, the rake was incorporated into the monkey's schema of the hand. Although ecological psychologists might cast a doubt on existence of such body schemas, it is fair to say that intensive tool use changed the monkey's perception of the hand.

Another example of the extension of the hand by tool use can be seen in the study examining a patient with cross-modal visual-tactile extinction (Maravita et al., 2001). Cross-modal extinction refers to the case that some patients with right-hemisphere lesions fail to report a touch on the left hand when a visual stimulus is presented near the right hand (peripersonal space). However, such cross-modal extinction is reduced when a visual stimulus is presented far from the hand (extrapersonal space). If a hand-held object extends the hand, cross-modal extinction may not be reduced for a visual stimulus far from the hand but near the hand-held object (i.e., peripersonal space). Maravita and colleagues tested whether a patient could report a tactile stimulus on the left hand when a visual stimulus was presented far from the right hand. They found that the amount of cross-modal extinction was greater when the patient held a long stick (i.e., the visual stimulus was presented just above the far end of the stick) than when the stick was not present. Furthermore, the condition in which the stick was not gripped and laid on the table reduced cross-modal extinction as much as the no-sticks condition. The result that holding a stick increased cross-modal extinction suggests that the use of a stick could expand the spatial extension of the peripersonal space. In other words, the hand could be extended through tool use.

An attachment to the body also changes effectivities, thus altering perception of the affordance. Does the attachment also change perception of the body? The studies on this topic were provided by the works on perception of limb orientation (see Pagano & Turvey, 1998, for a review). Because the shape of limbs seems to be cylindrical, moving an arm can be considered to be wielding a cylindrical object. Thus, perception of limbs may be similar to perception of a hand-held object. Research on orientation of hand-held objects found that perceived orientation is specified by the eigenvectors of the object's inertia tensor, the invariant quantities corresponding to the symmetrical axes of rotation (Pagano & Turvey, 1992; Turvey et al., 1992). Consequently, it is likely that perceived orientation of the limb is also specified by the eigenvectors of the limb's inertia tensor.

Pagano & Turvey (1995) investigated how one perceives spatial orientation of an occluded arm. In normal situations, the arm's longitudinal axis is coincident with the arm's inertial eigenvectors. They hypothesized that, if this normal relation was broken, the perceived orientation of the arm would be dependent on the arm's inertial eigenvectors, just as was the case with object orientation. To test this hypothesis, the arm's eigenvectors were manipulated by attaching a splint to the arm. Participants were asked to point at visual targets with the occluded arm. When the arm's spatial axes were not consistent with its eigenvectors, the angles in which the arm was positioned were biased by the direction in which the eigenvectors of the limb plus splint were directed. In other words, participants pointed with the arm's inertial eigenvectors rather than the arm's longitudinal axis. In line with Pagano and Turvey's study, Pagano et al. (1996) found that participants matched their forearms with reference to the forearms' eigenvectors rather than the elbow angles. Garrett et al. (1998) also demonstrated that positioning a limb was based on the limb's inertial eigenvectors rather than on joint angles or gravitational torques. Therefore, these studies supported the hypothesis about the central role of inertial eigenvectors in limb proprioception.

In later studies, however, the inertial eigenvector hypothesis has been called into question (Craig & Bourdin, 2002; van de Langenberg et al., 2007, 2008). Van de Langenberg and colleagues tested, against the inertial eigenvector hypothesis, the alternative hypothesis that limb orientation depends on the center of mass vector. In the experiments, participants pointed at visible targets while the arm's inertial eigenvectors and center of mass were manipulated independently by attaching a weighted carbon fiber frame to the arm. Results show that pointing errors were affected not by the inertial eigenvectors but by the center of mass, suggesting that the center of mass plays a predominant role in the perception of limb orientation. The emphasis here is not on whether perception of limb orientation depends upon the inertial eigenvectors or upon the center of mass, but on whether this perception depends upon the limb alone or upon the limb plus object system. These studies clearly show that the perception of limb orientation is significantly affected by attachments to the limb. The phenomenon that attachments change perception of the body applies not only to the perception of limb orientation but also to that of the direction of gravity, the subjective vertical (Fourre et al., 2009). Thus, it is fair to say that attachments to the body extend the sense of embodiment.

Extension of the body

In this section, we would like to discuss whether tool use and attachment to the body extend the boundary of the user's body. Thus far, we have seen how tool use and attachment affect perception of affordance and of the body. Tools and attachments change the user's effectivities. This change leads to changes in affordances of the environment. In order to adapt to the environment, the user must retune their perception of affordances. Furthermore, the user should modify perception of his/her own body. Accordingly, what was discussed so far implies that tools and attachments extend the boundary of the body.

The claim that tools and attachments extend the body is not new. Phenomenologists have argued in favor of extension of the body by tool use. Merleau-Ponty (1962) argued that the blind person's stick extends the scope of touch and therefore extends the bodily space. Heidegger (1962) also claimed that the tool in use becomes 'ready-to-hand', in other words transparent to the user, implying that the user is immersed in the activity, not concerned about the tool itself.

Correspondingly, ecological psychologists have claimed that tools shift the boundary between the body and the environment. Gibson (1986) maintained that a tool in use is a sort of extension of the hand and that clothing being worn is a part of the wearer's body. As described earlier, extension of the body is exemplified in studies of extended haptic perception: extensive use of the rod as a probe makes the rod a transparent medium, becoming part of the user's arm (Peck et al., 1996); a hand-held object is treated as an extension of the body, forming a person-plus-object system (Wagman & Taylor, 2005). For most psychologists, as Burton (1993) argued, extended haptic perception seems to be 'eccentric perception'. Some philosophers argue that there are no interesting scientific laws of human-tool systems because behaviors of such systems depend on the diversity of tools (Adams & Aizawa, 2001). Research on hand-held tools, however, has shown that extended haptic perception depends on the physical laws (i.e., inertia tensor or center of mass), thus suggesting that there may be meaningful scientific laws in human tool use.

Hirose & Nishio (2001) insisted that extension of the body by attachments, a process of embodying, is crucial for the retuning of affordance perception. Participants in the retuning experiments are forbidden to practice the relevant actions such as sitting and stepping, but are allowed to walk around with blocks during the interval between trials. As trials proceed, the blocks may become part of the legs. This process of embodying enables participants to adapt themselves to the relevant action capabilities that are extended by wearing blocks. Consequently, participants retune their perception of affordance for the relevant actions. This explanation describes why retuning of affordance perception occurs without the exercise of relevant actions (see Cardinali et al., 2009, for a similar view).

In contrast to the view of tool as extension, some authors argue that a tool is a mediator or a medium between an animal and its environment (see Smitsman, 1997; Smitsman & Bongers, 2003, for criticism). The view of tool as a mediator, however, seems to complicate the relation between the animal and the environment (Shaw et al., 1995). In order to examine whether a tool is a mediator or extension, we should draw attention to animal-tool-environment systems (here we use *'tool'* instead of *'tool and attachment'* for the sake of brevity). As was done previously in animal-environment systems, we can distinguish two standpoints: that of an observer and that of an animal. Different viewpoints seem to offer the key to an understanding of the boundary of the body.

From the viewpoint of an observer, researchers can focus on any components or relations in the animal-tool-environment system (Fig. 2A). A boundary between the animal and the environment cannot be uniquely defined. According to their interest, some may draw a boundary between the animal and the tool; others may draw one between the tool and the environment. In association with this, there has been considerable debate as to whether cognition can be extended or not (e.g., Adams & Aizawa, 2001; Adams & Aizawa, 2008; Chemero, 2009; Clark, 2008; Clark & Chalmers, 1998; Rupert, 2004; Weiskopf, 2010). It is beyond the scope of this chapter to describe the extensive controversy, but we still suggest that such a boundary dispute may arise because scholars can arbitrarily define the boundary of cognition. To avoid arbitrary definition of the boundary, we should take the view from the standpoint of an animal.

From the viewpoint of an animal, two boundaries — one between the animal and the tool, and the other between the tool and the environment — cannot be focused at the same time. Accordingly, there are two possible states in an animal-tool-environment system (see Shaw et al., 1995, for a similar view). One is the state that an animal does not have a tool and seeks one in the environment (Fig. 2B). In this state, the tool belongs to the environment, not to the animal. For the animal, a tool is an object of interest to be perceived; thus it is extension of the affordance of the environment. We can say that the boundary of the body is set at the surface of the skin in this state. The other is the state that an animal is using a tool (Fig. 2C). In this situation, the tool belongs to the animal, not to the environment. For the animal, the environment is an object of interest. A tool seems to be transparent and incorporated; thus the tool is an extension of the effectivity of the animal. One can say that the boundary of the body is extended beyond the surface of the skin.

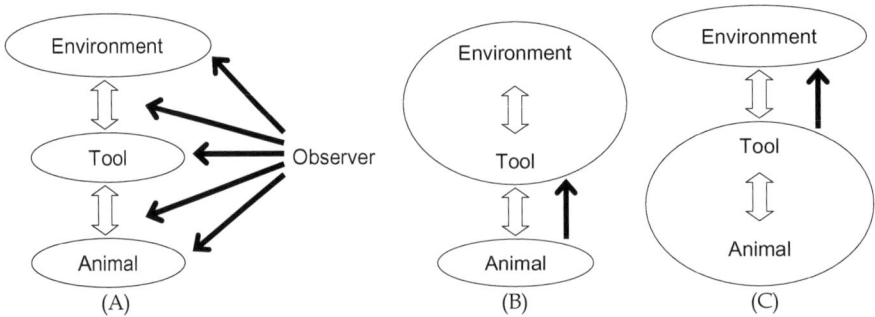

Fig. 2: Different viewpoints of animal-tool-environment system: from an observer (A), from an animal when a tool is not in use (B), and from an animal when a tool is in use (C).

Thus far, we have argued that the boundary of the body is changeable and can be extended by tools and attachments. If we admit that the boundary is not fixed, we may encounter the problem of ambiguity in the boundary. Burton (1993) argued that extended haptic perception obscures the distinction between the animal and the environment. For this reason, it seems difficult to demarcate the boundary of the animal and the environment. How can we define the extended boundary in empirical studies? There seems to be at least two methods by which we can demarcate the body boundary.

One is to scrutinize the user's perception of the body, as described earlier. If a user with an attachment perceives his/her body differently due to the influence of the attachment, it can be said that the user and the attachment form a unified system and that the body is extended by the attachment. Such a study depends on the user' subjective sense of embodiment, and thus cannot be applied to animals and infants that have no ability to give verbal reports. In contrast, cognitive neuroscientific and neuropsychological studies of body perception in tool use, as mentioned above, offer objective neurophysiological and behavioral measurements. Future research on perception of the body needs to include both subjective and objective measurements.

The other is to corroborate the equivalence of perception-action systems. If we observe that a perceptual system with a tool is functionally equivalent to one without a tool, we can confirm that the system is extended by the tool; thus the body is considered as being extended by the tool. Let us note that the equivalence of perceptual systems was shown in the studies of haptic probing (Burton, 1992; Fitzpatrick et al., 1994). These findings suggest that extended haptic systems correspond to other perceptual systems. In other words, a probe plus limb system can be regarded as a united perceptual system; that is, a probe must be embedded in the body. Another good example of the equivalence of action systems is provided by the work of Steenbergen and colleagues

(1997). They demonstrated that perturbation in the spoons affected the children's spoon-handling actions. In their experiments, the functional characteristics of the affordances were maintained despite perturbations in spoons. To keep the spoon's concave side upward, children altered their grip configurations; the prehensile system and the spoon worked together to realize the specific function of scooping. Thus, a child plus spoon formed a unified action system.

Additionally, a recent study examined a different aspect of action systems in tool use (Dotov et al., 2010). Dotov and colleagues demonstrated the transition between ready-to-hand and unready-to-hand modes in interactions with tools, originally proposed by Heidegger (1962). They examined this transition using a simple video game with a computer mouse. When smoothly playing the game, participants experienced the mouse as ready-to-hand. During the experiment, participants encountered the tool as unready-to-hand when the connection between mouse and pointer movements was perturbed. The recordings of trajectory of the hand-tool system showed that the system exhibited a correlated character of a smoothly coping, self-assembled system during proper functioning and that this character was reduced during perturbation. Most previous studies have not concerned malfunctioning of the system; hence the method used in Dotov's study appears quite promising.

Conclusion

We have considered embodiment from the perspective of ecological psychology, animal-environment systems. This perspective views animal as animate: they move around the environment, perceive it and act on it. What animals perceive in the environment is affordances. Animals utilize affordances to fit the environment. Affordances are properties of the environment, but also depend on effectivities, properties of the animal. Tools and attachments change effectivities of the animal, resulting in changes in affordances. From the perspective of ecological psychology, the boundary of the body is set at the interface with the environment that the animal perceives and acts on. Therefore, if a person with a stick perceives the object at the tip of the stick rather than the stick itself, then it can be safely said that the hand is extended to incorporate the stick. Whether the body can be extended or not depends on how the body is defined. From the view of the body as a perception-action system as discussed so far, the body can be extended beyond the surface of the skin.

References

Adams F. & Aizawa K. (2001). The bounds of cognition. *Philosophical Psychology*, 14, 43-64.
Adams F. & Aizawa K. (2008). *The bounds of cognition*. Malden: Blackwell Publishing.

Adolph K. E. & Avolio A. M. (2000). Walking infants adapt locomotion to changing body dimensions. *Journal of Experimental Psychology: Human Perception and Performance, 26*, 1148-66.

Bongers R. M., Smitsman A. W., & Michaels C. F. (2003). Geometrics and dynamics of a rod determine how it is used for reaching. *Journal of Motor Behavior, 35*, 4-22.

Bongers R. M., Smitsman A. W., & Michaels C. F. (2004). Geometric, but not kinetic, properties of tools affect the affordances perceived by toddlers. *Ecological Psychology, 16*, 129-58.

Burton G. (1992). Nonvisual judgment of the crossability of path gaps. *Journal of Experimental Psychology: Human Perception and Performance, 18*, 698-713.

Burton G. (1993). Non-neural extensions of haptic sensitivity. *Ecological Psychology, 5*, 105-24.

Cardinali L., Frassinetti F., Brozzoli C., Urquizar C., Roy A. C., & Farne A. (2009). Tool-use induces morphological updating of the body schema. *Current Biology, 19*, R478-9.

Carello C., Fitzpatrick P., & Turvey M. T. (1992). Haptic probing: Perceiving the length of a probe and the distance of a surface probed. *Perception & Psychophysics, 51*, 580-98.

Carello C., Grosofsky A., Reichel F. D., Solomon H. Y., & Turvey M. T. (1989). Visually perceiving what is reachable. *Ecological Psychology, 1*, 27-54.

Carello C. & Turvey M. T. (2004). Physics and psychology of the muscle sense. *Current Directions in Psychological Science, 13*, 25-8.

Cesari P., Formenti F., & Olivato P. (2003). A common perceptual parameter for stair climbing for children, young and old adults. *Human Movement Science, 22*, 111-24.

Cesari P. & Newell K. M. (1999). The scaling of human grip configurations. *Journal of Experimental Psychology: Human Perception and Performance, 25*, 927-35.

Cesari P. & Newell K. M. (2000). Body-scaled transitions in human grip configurations. *Journal of Experimental Psychology: Human Perception and Performance, 26*, 1657-68.

Chan T. C. & Turvey M. T. (1991). Perceiving the vertical distances of surfaces by means of a hand-held probe. *Journal of Experimental Psychology: Human Perception and Performance, 17*, 347-58.

Chemero A. (2003). An outline of a theory of affordances. *Ecological Psychology, 15*, 181-95.

Chemero A. (2009). *Radical embodied cognitive science*. Cambridge: MIT Press.

Choi H. J. & Mark L. S. (2004). Scaling affordances for human reach actions. *Human Movement Science, 23*, 785-806.

Clark A. (2008). *Supersizing the mind*. Oxford, UK: Oxford University Press.

Clark A. & Chalmers D. J. (1998). The extended mind. *Analysis, 58*, 7-19.

Craig C. M. & Bourdin C. (2002). Revisited: The inertia tensor as a proprioceptive invariant in humans. *Neuroscience Letters, 317*, 106-10.

Dotov D. G., Nie L., & Chemero A. (2010). A demonstration of the transition from ready-to-hand to unready-to-hand. *PLoS ONE, 5*, e9433.

Farne A., Bonifazi S., & Ladavas E. (2005). The role played by tool-use and tool-length on the plastic elongation of peri-hand space: A single case study. *Cognitive Neuropsychology, 22*, 408-18.

Farne A., Serino A., & Ladavas E. (2007). Dynamic size-change of peri-hand space following tool-use: Determinants and spatial characteristics revealed through crossmodal extinction. *Cortex, 43*, 436-43.

Fitzpatrick P., Carello C., Schmidt R. C., & Corey D. (1994). Haptic and visual perception of an affordance for upright posture. *Ecological Psychology, 6*, 265-87.

Fourre B., Isableu B., Bernardin D., Gueguen M., Giraudet G., Vuillerme N., et al. (2009). The role of body centre of mass on haptic subjective vertical. *Neuroscience Letters, 465,* 230-4.

Garrett S. R., Pagano C., Austin G., & Turvey M. T. (1998). Spatial and physical frames of reference in positioning a limb. *Perception & Psychophysics, 60,* 1206-15.

Gibson J. J. (1966). *The senses considered as perceptual systems.* Boston: Houghton Mifflin.

Gibson J. J. (1977). The theory of affordances. In R. E. Shaw & J. Bransford (eds.), *Perceiving, acting, and knowing* (pp. 67-82). Hillsdale: Lawrence Erlbaum Associates.

Gibson J. J. (1986). *The ecological approach to visual perception.* Hillsdale: Lawrence Erlbaum Associates.

Goldenberg G. & Spatt J. (2009). The neural basis of tool use. *Brain, 132,* 1645-55.

Heft H. (1989). Affordances and the body: An intentional analysis of Gibson's ecological approach to visual perception. *Journal for the Theory of Social Behaviour, 19,* 1-30.

Heft H. (2001). *Ecological psychology in context: James Gibson, Roger Barker, and the legacy of William James's radical empiricism.* Mahwah: Lawrence Erlbaum Associates.

Heft H. (2003). Affordances, dynamic experience, and the challenge of reification. *Ecological Psychology, 15,* 149-80.

Heidegger M. (1962). *Being and time.* J. MacQuarrie & E. Robinson (transl.). New York: Harper & Row.

Higuchi T., Cinelli M., Greig M., & Patla A. (2006). Locomotion through apertures when wider space for locomotion is necessary: Adaptation to artificially altered bodily states. *Experimental Brain Research, 175,* 50-9.

Hirose N. (2002). An ecological approach to embodiment and cognition. *Cognitive Systems Research, 3,* 289-99.

Hirose N. & Nishio A. (2001). The process of adaptation to perceiving new action capabilities. *Ecological Psychology, 13,* 49-69.

Iriki A., Tanaka M., & Iwamura Y. (1996). Coding of modified body schema during tool use by macaque postcentral neurones. *Neuroreport, 7,* 2325-30.

Ishibashi H., Hihara S., & Iriki A. (2000). Acquisition and development of monkey tool-use: Behavioral and kinematic analyses. *Canadian Journal of Physiology and Pharmacology, 78,* 958-66.

Johnson-Frey S. H. (2004). The neural bases of complex tool use in humans. *Trends in Cognitive Sciences, 8,* 71-8.

Jones K. S. (2003). What is an affordance? *Ecological Psychology, 15,* 107-14.

Konczak J., Meeuwsen H. J., & Cress M. E. (1992). Changing affordances in stair climbing: The perception of maximum climbability in young and older adults. *Journal of Experimental Psychology: Human Perception and Performance, 18,* 691-7.

Ladavas E. & Serino A. (2008). Action-dependent plasticity in peripersonal space representations. *Cognitive Neuropsychology, 25,* 1099-113.

Lockman J. J. (2000). A perception-action perspective on tool use development. *Child Development, 71,* 137-44.

Lockman J. J. (2005). Tool use from a perception- action perspective: Developmental and evolutionary considerations. In V. Roux & B. Bril (eds.), *Stone knapping : The necessary conditions for a uniquely hominid behaviour* (pp. 319-30). London: McDonald Institute for Archaeological Research.

Malek E. A. & Wagman J. B. (2008). Kinetic potential influences visual and remote haptic perception of affordances for standing on an inclined surface. *The Quarterly Journal of Experimental Psychology, 61,* 1813-26.

Maravita A., Husain M., Clarke K., & Driver J. (2001). Reaching with a tool extends visual-tactile interactions into far space: Evidence from cross-modal extinction. *Neuropsychologia, 39,* 580-5.

Maravita A. & Iriki A. (2004). Tools for the body (schema). *Trends in Cognitive Sciences, 8,* 79-86.

Mark L. S. (1987). Eyeheight-scaled information about affordances: A study of sitting and stair climbing. *Journal of Experimental Psychology: Human Perception and Performance, 13,* 361-70.

Mark L. S. (2007). Perceiving the actions of other people. *Ecological Psychology, 19,* 107-36.

Mark L. S., Balliett J. A., Craver K. D., Douglas S. D., & Fox T. (1990). What an actor must do in order to perceive the affordance for sitting. *Ecological Psychology, 2,* 325-66.

Mark L. S. & Vogele D. (1987). A biodynamic basis for perceived categories of action: A study of sitting and stair climbing. *Journal of Motor Behavior, 19,* 367-84.

Merleau-Ponty M. (1962). *Phenomenology of perception* (C. Smith, Trans.). New York: Routledge & Kegan Paul.

Michaels C. F. (2000). Information, perception, and action: What should ecological psychologists learn from Milner and Goodale (1995)? *Ecological Psychology, 12,* 241-58.

Michaels C. F. (2003). Affordances: Four points of debate. *Ecological Psychology, 15,* 135-48.

Pagano C. C., Garrett S. R., & Turvey M. T. (1996). Is limb proprioception a function of the limbs' inertial eigenvectors? *Ecological Psychology, 8,* 43-69.

Pagano C. C. & Turvey M. T. (1992). Eigenvectors of the inertia tensor and perceiving the orientation of a hand-held object by dynamic touch. *Perception & Psychophysics, 52,* 617-24.

Pagano C. C. & Turvey M. T. (1995). The inertia tensor as a basis for the perception of limb orientation. *Journal of Experimental Psychology: Human Perception and Performance, 21,* 1070-87.

Pagano C. C. & Turvey M. T. (1998). Eigenvectors of the inertia tensor and perceiving the orientations of limbs and objects. *Journal of Applied Biomechanics, 14,* 331-59.

Peck A. J., Jeffers R. G., Carello C., & Turvey M. T. (1996). Haptically perceiving the length of one rod by means of another. *Ecological Psychology, 8,* 237-58.

Pufall P. B. & Dunbar C. (1992). Perceiving whether or not the world affords stepping onto and over: A developmental study. *Ecological Psychology, 4,* 17-38.

Ramenzoni V. C., Riley M. A., Shockley K., & Davis T. (2008a). Carrying the height of the world on your ankles: Encumbering observers reduces estimates of how high an actor can jump. *The Quarterly Journal of Experimental Psychology, 61,* 1487-95.

Ramenzoni V. C., Riley M. A., Shockley K., & Davis T. (2008b). An information-based approach to action understanding. *Cognition, 106,* 1059-70.

Reed E. S. (1996). *Encountering the world: Toward an ecological psychology.* New York: Oxford University Press.

Reed E. S. (1997). Comments on Smitsman. In C. Dent-Read & P. Zukow-Goldring (eds.), *Evolving explanations of development: Ecological approaches to organism-environment systems* (pp. 331-33). Washington: American Psychological Association.

Regia-Corte T. & Wagman J. (2008). Perception of affordances for standing on an inclined surface depends on height of center of mass. *Experimental Brain Research, 191,* 25-35.

Rupert R. D. (2004). Challenges to the hypothesis of extended cognition. *Journal of Philosophy, 101,* 389-428.

Şahin E., Çakmak M., Doğar M. R., Uğur E., & Üçoluk G. (2007). To afford or not to afford: A new formalization of affordances toward affordance-based robot control. *Adaptive Behavior, 15,* 447-72.

Sanders J. T. (1997). An ontology of affordances. *Ecological Psychology, 9,* 97-112.

Sanders J. T. (1999). Affordances: An ecological approach to first philosophy. In G. Weiss & H. F. Haber (eds.), *Perspectives on embodiment: The intersections of nature and culture* (pp. 121-41). New York: Routledge.

Shaw R. E. (2001). Processes, acts, and experiences: Three stances on the problem of intentionality. *Ecological Psychology, 13*, 275-314.

Shaw R. E., Flascher O. M., & Kadar E. E. (1995). Dimensionless invariants for intentional systems: Measuring the fit of vehicular activities to environmental layout. In J. M. Flach, P. A. Hancock, J. Caird & K. Vicente (eds.), *Global perspectives on the ecology of human-machine systems* (pp. 293-357). Hillsdale: Lawrence Erlbaum Associates.

Shaw R. E., Turvey M. T., & Mace W. M. (1982). Ecological psychology. The consequence of a commitment to realism. In W. Weimer & D. Palermo (eds.), *Cognition and the symbolic processes Vol. 2* (pp. 159-226). Hillsdale: Lawrence Erlbaum Associates.

Smitsman A. W. (1997). The development of tool use: Changing boundaries between organism and environment. In C. Dent-Read & P. Zukow-Goldring (eds.), *Evolving explanations of development: Ecological approaches to organism-environment systems* (pp. 301-29). Washington: American Psychological Association.

Smitsman A. W. & Bongers R. M. (2003). Tool use and tool making: A developmental action perspective. In J. Valsiner & K. J. Connolly (eds.), *Handbook of developmental psychology* (pp. 172-93). London: Sage Publications.

Smitsman A. W. & Cox R. F. A. (2008). Perseveration in tool use: A window for understanding the dynamics of the action-selection process. *Infancy, 13*, 249-69.

Snapp-Childs W. & Bingham G. (2009). The affordance of barrier crossing in young children exhibits dynamic, not geometric, similarity. *Experimental Brain Research, 198*, 527-33.

Steenbergen B., van der Kamp J., Smitsman A. W., & Carson R. G. (1997). Spoon handling in two- to four-year-old children. *Ecological Psychology, 9*, 113-29.

Stoffregen T. A. (2000a). Affordances and events. *Ecological Psychology, 12*, 1-28.

Stoffregen T. A. (2000b). Affordances and events: Theory and research. *Ecological Psychology, 12*, 93-107.

Stoffregen T. A. (2003). Affordances as properties of the animal-environment system. *Ecological Psychology, 15*, 115-34.

Stoffregen T. A., Gorday K. M., Sheng Y. Y., & Flynn S. B. (1999). Perceiving affordances for another person's actions. *Journal of Experimental Psychology: Human Perception and Performance, 25*, 120-36.

Turvey M. T. (1992). Affordances and prospective control: An outline of the ontology. *Ecological Psychology, 4*, 173-87.

Turvey M. T. (1996). Dynamic touch. *American Psychologist, 51*, 1134-52.

Turvey M. T., Burton G., Pagano C. C., Solomon H. Y., & Runeson S. (1992). Role of the inertia tensor in perceiving object orientation by dynamic touch. *Journal of Experimental Psychology: Human Perception and Performance, 18*, 714-27.

Turvey M. T. & Shaw R. E. (1979). The primacy of perceiving: An ecological reformulation of perception for understanding memory. In L. G. Nilsson (ed.), *Perspectives on memory research* (pp. 145-66). Hillsdale: Erlbaum.

van de Langenberg R., Kingma I., & Beek P. J. (2007). Perception of limb orientation in the vertical plane depends on center of mass rather than inertial eigenvectors. *Experimental Brain Research, 180*, 595-607.

van de Langenberg R., Kingma I., & Beek P. J. (2008). The perception of limb orientation depends on the center of mass. *Journal of Experimental Psychology: Human Perception and Performance, 34*, 624-39.

Wagman J. B., Carello C., Schmidt R. C., & Turvey M. T. (2009). Is perceptual learning unimodal? *Ecological Psychology, 21*, 37-67.

Wagman J. B. & Malek E. A. (2007). Perception of whether an object can be carried through an aperture depends on anticipated speed. *Experimental Psychology, 54*, 54-61.

Wagman J. B. & Taylor K. R. (2005). Perceiving affordances for aperture crossing for the person-plus-object system. *Ecological Psychology, 17*, 105-30.

Warren W. H. (1984). Perceiving affordances: Visual guidance of stair climbing. *Journal of Experimental Psychology: Human Perception and Performance, 10*, 683-703.

Warren W. H. (1995). Constructing an econiche. In J. M. Flach, P. A. Hancock, J. Caird, & K. Vicente (eds.), *Global perspectives on the ecology of human-machine systems* (pp. 210-37). Hillsdale: Lawrence Erlbaum Associates.

Warren W. H. & Whang S. (1987). Visual guidance of walking through apertures: Body-scaled information for affordances. *Journal of Experimental Psychology: Human Perception and Performance, 13*, 371-83.

Weiskopf D. A. (2010). The Goldilocks problem and extended cognition. *Cognitive Systems Research, 11*, 313-23.

Embodiment and the Arts

Wolfgang Tschacher* and Martin Tröndle**

*University Hospital of Psychiatry, University of Bern, Switzerland
tschacher@spk.unibe.ch
**Department of Communication and Cultural Management, Zeppelin University, Friedrichshafen, Germany
mt@kunstpartner.com

Introduction

Why should we study embodiment in connection with the arts? At first sight, art has little in common with 'bodies': A work of art is associated with the pure beauty intrinsic to the artifact, and hence with the aesthetic involvement of the viewer; we may expect a viewer's thoughtful responses instigated by the artwork. Art is also involved with the cultural context and the historical tradition in which an artwork is situated. The literature on art theory and on aesthetics shows that art is a major topic in philosophy, not biological science. Seen from a still different angle, one may consider the sociological influences on art, the tidal waves of fashion and avantgarde; or the dynamics of art marketing, of hype and gossip. One may finally consider the politics of art, how nations and even governments are represented by certain artists or art movements; or how works of art can provide potent oppositional statements. It is therefore not at all obvious why art should have to do with the body.

When we approach art and aesthetics from a psychological perspective, however, there are several entry points by which the body permeates the aesthetic perception of art. The first is through cognition: aesthetics is perceived and appraised through the viewer's cognitive system. Cognition however is only understood appropriately as *embodied* cognition: this is the convergent result of different fields of research in psychology and cognitive science (Storch et al., 2010). Thus, probably no 'pure' cognitive processes exist. Even mathematics, since it has been invented and applied by real people, relies on metaphors and constructs that have their origins in embodied experience (Lakoff & Núñez, 2000). The same is true for aesthetic perception.

The second point is emotion: it is not feasible to disentangle aesthetic judgments from emotional and motivational responses. This is apparent in the analysis of self-reports of viewers in the art gallery. Factor analyses show that viewers in general combine aesthetic assessments ("this artwork is beautiful") with emotional evaluations ("this artwork is likable, joyful, interesting"). An important component of emotion is physiological response. Therefore, via its link with emotion, aesthetic perception is necessarily embedded in the physiology, i.e. the body, of the perceiver.

The third reason for art perception being embodied is that viewers of art are not passive receptors of artistic stimuli. Be it in the museum or in the theatre, the audience is using and moving their bodies continuously. Recipients may often be unaware of this, yet they respond with facial expression, body posture and gestures to the contents on display. Thus, through expressive movements the body is again a part of the sensori-motor loop of art reception. The underlying processes here are emotional contagion and synchronization (Ramseyer & Tschacher, 2011) with protagonists on the screen or stage and with the contents displayed in a picture.

Finally, art must be viewed in an architectural and curatorial context. Thus, we should also consider visitor behavior and locomotion that is displayed in the space of an exhibition. Curators of exhibitions, for instance, are very deliberate and careful in their decisions on where to hang which artwork, or on the design of the interior of gallery space. The art must be put in the context of other artworks and of the physical environment. Many curatorial decisions are reflected in the overt 'mass behavior' of visitors. Ecological psychology has focused on such 'standing patterns of behavior' (Barker, 1978) that are afforded by the environment. These patterns can be seen clearly when the locomotions of visitors through a constant museum environment are visualized.

We will now introduce a project in which several of these points of embodied art perception have been monitored and analyzed.

The project 'eMotion'

In a large empirical project, eMotion[1], which was funded by the Swiss National Foundation, a wireless tracking system was installed to monitor visitors in an art museum. We obtained permission by the Kunstmuseum St. Gallen (Switzerland) to convert the museum into a large laboratory for several months in the year 2009. The exhibition "11 : 1 (+3) = Eleven Collections for a Museum" was curated particularly for this study. It consisted of 76 pieces of modern and contemporary paintings, drawings and sculptures. The show started with works of Claude Monet, Max Liebermann and Edvard Munch (Space 2); continuing to Swiss art of the early 20th century by Ferdinand Hodler und Giovanni Giacometti (Space 3) and works from classical modernity by Max Ernst, Fernand Léger, Le Corbusier (Space 4). Spaces 5 and 6 will be described in a later section. Space 7 contained works by pop-artists such as Andy Warhol and Roy Lichtenstein, and Space 8 conceptual works by Imi Knoebel and On

---

[1] for information see the eMotion website: www.mapping-museum-experience.com

Kawara. Finally, the exhibition presented the intervention "A Label Level, 2009" by Nedko Solakov, specially created for this show. This work consisted of 32 small graffiti-like tags ('labels') written on the walls of the exhibition hall in more or less visible places.

At the exhibition entrance, visitors participating in the project (N=517) received an electronic glove that included measurement sensors and a sender, which transmitted data to wireless receivers in all Spaces. This equipment allowed the precise imaging of the path of each individual through the museum. From these position data we could infer movement speed and time spent in front of a picture or object (Fig. 1). In addition, two physiological parameters, heart rate and skin conductance level, with their respective variabilities, were monitored and transmitted on a second-by-second basis. Measurements were obtained continuously throughout each participant's visit of the exhibition. Duration of visits was optional, so that the viewers were completely unrestricted in their choice of artworks to be viewed.

Fig. 1: Participant with electronic glove in front of Günther Uecker "Antibild, Räumliche Struktur, Aggressive Reihung, 1974"

One may note here that the design of this project was especially adapted to investigate the embodiment of art perception. Whereas in typical psychological research on aesthetics, the art is usually presented as reproductions on a monitor in a psychology lab, the eMotion project set out to study art perception of real artworks in the real environment, giving participants maximal freedom of choice over the stimuli they attended. Art theorists have proposed that artworks possess a characteristic 'aura' (Benjamin, 1939/1980), i.e. they have effects that rest on the authenticity of the original. Therefore, research based on reproductions has dubious external validity: It may explore perceptual processes but miss the essentials of art perception.

The large corpus of position-imaging and physiological data was complemented by self-report assessments. We acquired demographic information together with art-related attitudes and knowledge in an entrance survey prior to the visit. At the termination of the visit, a structured interview was used to describe in detail the aesthetic-emotional judgments of participants with respect to the selected works they saw in the exhibition.

Mass locomotion behavior

Fig. 2 depicts the paths of 30 randomly chosen visitors at the entrance of the exhibition. Markers (in the original imaging procedure, orange and yellow clouds) are attached to the paths; they stand for physiological arousal (x, skin conductance; o, heart rate). Space 1, the museum's entrance hall, was equipped with two tables where visitors received the electronic gloves. The tables are visible as knots of paths (paths are represented by gray lines) from where visitors then walked across the hall, generally directly into Space 2, the first exhibition hall. When entering Space 2, Fig. 2 shows that visitors' physiology was apparently influenced by the exhibited artworks. Face validity indicates that locomotion patterns as well as the physiological shifts were related to the art on display. The physiological markers appeared to be not confounded by physical movement per se. Inside the exhibition hall, visitors' paths were complex, with a high concentration of markers in front of the artworks (the gloves were worn on right hands, leading to a slight translation of the markers and paths to the right). Interestingly, the attraction of the Corinth painting that was hung just outside the official entrance to the exhibition was minimal. This shows the environmental impact of curatorial staging on aesthetic perception; in the case of the Corinth painting we observe how the gallery environment, at least partially, 'makes' the aesthetic object. If not staged appropriately, a painting may almost disappear and not evolve its aura.

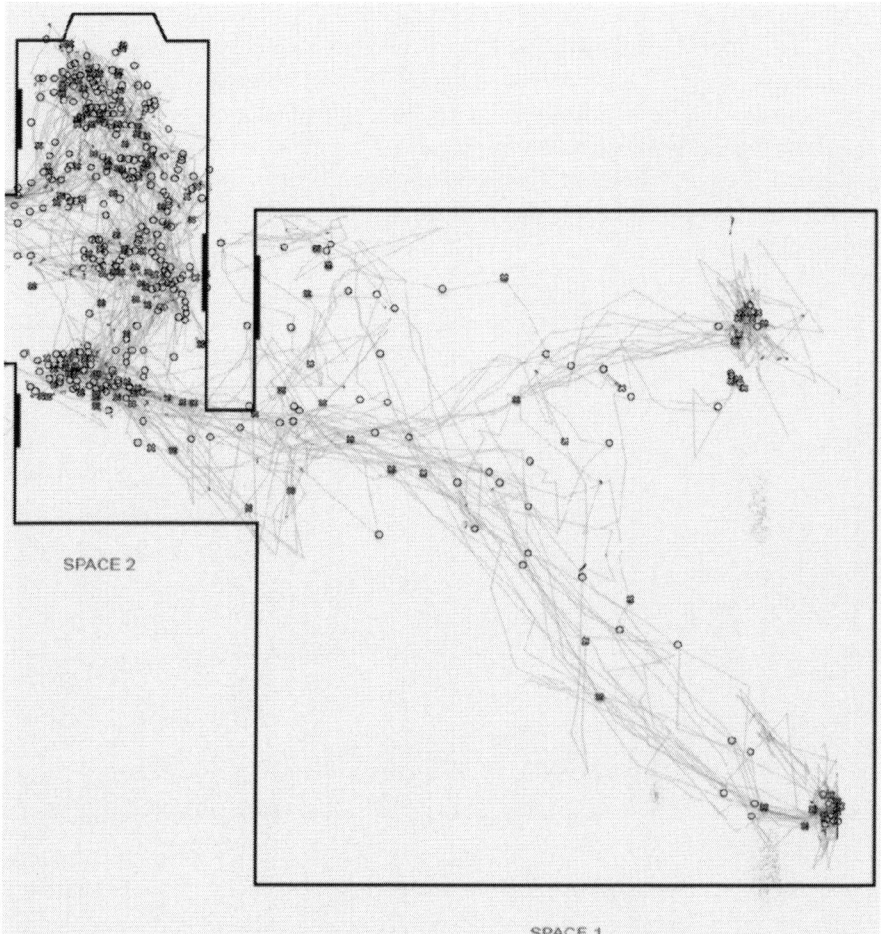

Fig. 2: Depiction of paths (gray lines) of 30 visitors in the entrance hall (Space 1) and first hall (Space 2) of the exhibition. Markers, attached to the paths, represent phasic shifts of skin conductance (x) and heart rate (o). Black solid lines depict walls, bars on the walls represent pictures. From right to left and bottom to top: works by Lovis Corinth, Claude Monet, Edvard Munch and Max Liebermann. Space 1 is approx. 10.5m x 11m

We may regard Fig. 2 as a visualization of Barker's (1978) standing patterns of behavior, a concept of ecological psychology. In the language of dynamical systems theory, the artworks appear to function as spatial attractors whose basins can be outlined using the visitors' trajectories in their vicinities. In analogy to dynamical systems, where trajectories approach the attractor, thereby compressing phase space, visitors' paths can be 'pulled into' the basins of these attractors, where the aura of the artwork is fully experienced. For each artwork, the museum director, the curator, and the principal investigator defined this space as the artwork's Region of Interest (RoI, see Fig. 3). In the eMotion project we measured the number of visits, the duration of visits, and the physiological states inside the RoIs. The ensuing dataset contains nomothetic information on longstanding hypotheses in the field of aesthetics. For instance, we modeled the association between physiological responses inside a RoI and the aesthetic assessments of the respective artwork (Tschacher et al., in preparation).

Fig. 3: Regions of Interest (RoI) of the artworks in two halls of the exhibition, Spaces 5 and 6 (approx. 8m x 14m). RoIs are shaded areas. Solid lines, walls; thin bars on walls, artworks; two squares with shaded areas, sculptures; two gray rectangles, benches; text posters, '⊥'; four small circles, columns.

Individual locomotion

In the following, we will proceed idiographically and discuss the paths of three individual visitors. We will compare their locomotion styles and physiological reactions in Space 5 and 6. The works displayed in Space 5 were by László Moholy-Nagy, Hans Arp, Paul Klee, Julius Bissier, Cy Twombly, Hans Hartung, Lucio Fontana and Yves Klein. In Space 6 visitors viewed conceptual art by Günther Uecker, Max Bill and others.

In Fig. 3, museum visitors enter from the right side. As in Fig. 2, the pictures on the walls are depicted as fat bars. The two sculptures of Space 5 are squares (the larger one is a work by Hans Arp, the small one a work by Yves Klein). The eleven small bars in a lighter shade represent the labels of the art intervention of Nedko Solakov, placed on the walls and three columns of the Spaces. Detailed text posters are represented by '⊥'s. Two seating benches are indicated by gray rectangles.

The visitor's path in Fig. 4 is visualized as a black/gray line, with markers at those locations where phasic physiological responses and fluctuations occurred. 'x' indicates shifts of skin conductance; 'o', shifts of heart rate. The path is displayed in a lighter shade of gray where the visitor moved faster.

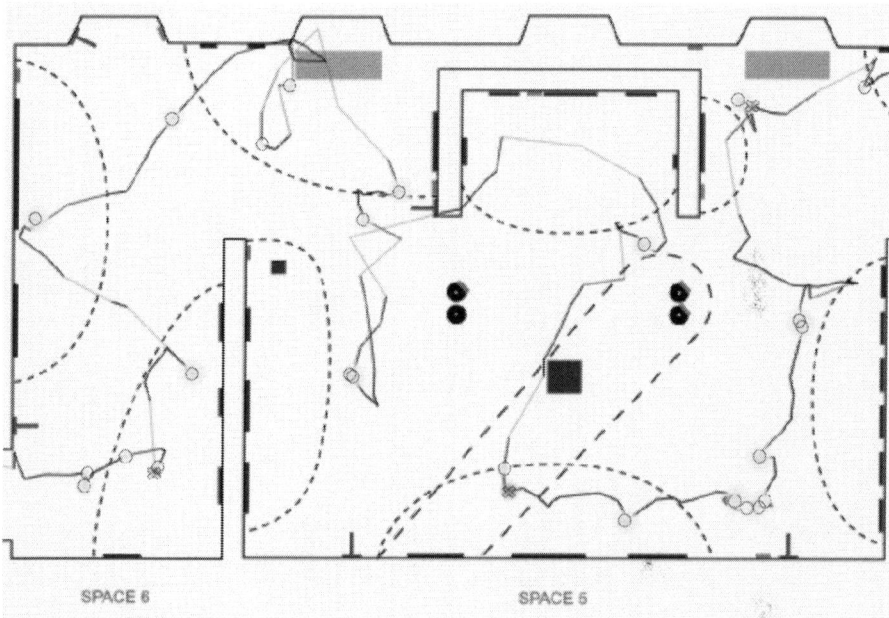

Fig. 4: Visitor SJ8 on her way through two halls of the museum. Symbols as in Fig. 3. Dotted lines indicate curatorial ensembles of connected artworks.

The path in Fig. 4 is from visitor SJ8, a woman of about 70 years. We see her entering Space 5 on the right side, passing slightly disinterestedly through these two exhibition halls (direction of locomotion is not visualized in the figures, but the raw data are in movie format). She does not view each single artwork, and keeps a rather large distance from the works. Very few shifts of skin conductance and some shifts of heart rate were measured. Significant shifts of heart rate can be found in front of two text posters (represented by '⊥'s) in Space 5. None of the works makes this visitor stop walking, and take a closer look, no marked physiological reactions are recorded. From this visitor's behavioral pattern one can infer that she is likely not engaged in viewing the artworks. Her art affinity index, a composite score derived from the entrance survey, combining a participant's knowledge of art, her motivation for visiting the museum and attitudes towards art, was very low.

The imaging in Fig. 5 comes from a female visitor (SJ24) in the age group of 18-29 years. According to the entrance survey she has little art affinity (on a scale of none, little, medium, high). Compared to visitor SJ8, she is moving slower, there are few sections of gray lines in her path. She again keeps large distances to most works and crosses Space 5 fast.

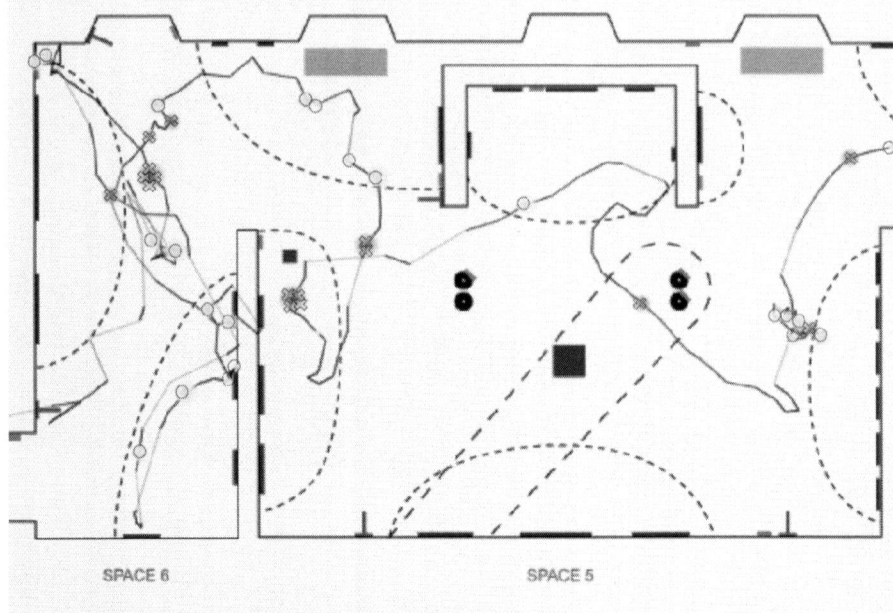

Fig. 5: Path and physiology of visitor SJ24

Several shifts of skin conductance ('x' markers) and of heart rate ('o') were recorded, significant skin conductance markers are displayed in the upper part of Space 6, inside the RoI of the work "Antibild" by Günther Uecker, which was shown in Fig. 1. In front of this work her trajectories become denser. One may notice that she also walks to the wall label in the corner next to this work. The reading of the label may cause shifts of heart rate. She then moves down Space 6 to view the other works hung there. Afterwards, SJ24 does not exit Space 6 to enter Space 7, but rather returns once more to explore the "Antibild". This work seems to exert a strong attractive pull on this visitor.

Interestingly, the other significant shift of skin conductance, a large 'x' marker, can be found in Space 5, probably referring to the work "Spaziale" by Lucio Fontana. Both the Uecker and Fontana works have a rather violent gesture: Fontana executed his work by cutting the canvas, Uecker by sticking long nails through the canvas, aggressively pointing at the visitors. To the other works, visitor SJ24 responds only sparsely and does not appear to be attracted or 'moved'.

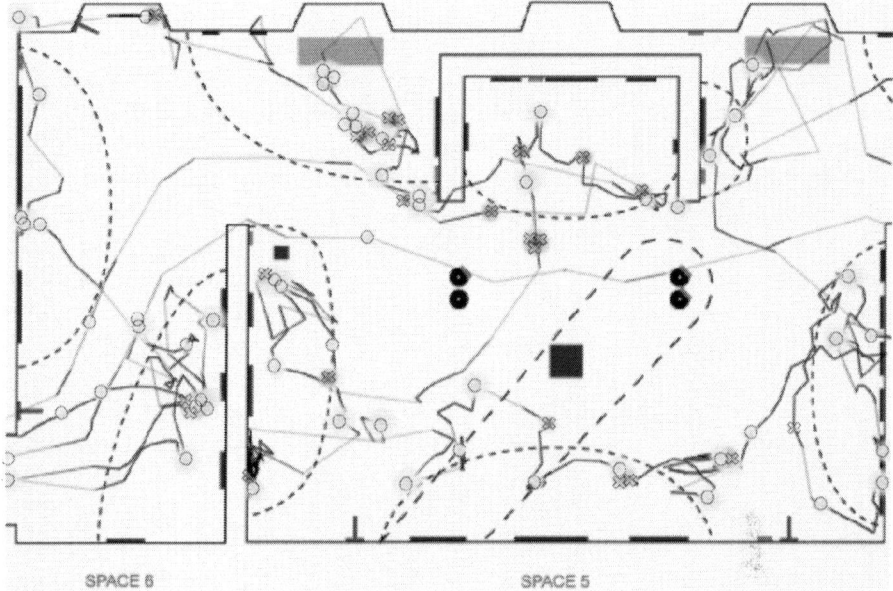

Fig. 6: Path and physiology of visitor SJ6.

Fig. 6 displays visitor SJ6, a 18-29 year old female, again with only little art affinity. This imaging dataset shows a high density of paths, which in some places are strongly accumulative (e.g. Space 5, bottom left corner). We recorded high frequencies of 'x' markers (shifts of skin conductance) as well as 'o' markers (shifts of heart rate). On several occasions, these markers overwrote and occluded the 'x' markers (visible in the original movies). Visitor SJ6 views the artworks thoroughly and in detail, moving from work to work. She reads carefully two of the five text posters (⊥), where several physiological markers occur. One may also notice that she traverses the exhibition halls two times quickly, prior to further exploration. This visitor perceives most of the tiny and often funny graffiti interventions by Nedko Solakov (represented by small gray rectangles on walls), responding physiologically (e.g., Space 6 top).

Discussion

The imaging data of the three individual paths in Spaces 5 and 6 show three different types of visitors. Idiographical analysis supported the validity of the recordings of both locomotion patterns and physiological responses and showed how they may relate to the artworks on display. The three examples do not allow generalizing. Statistical models of the complete sample of visitors included in the eMotion project, however, provide evidence that physiological responses are associated with aesthetic-emotional responses to the artworks (Tschacher et al., in preparation). For instance, heart rate variability recorded inside RoIs was significantly predictive of which aesthetic assessments of the respective artwork were made in the interviews after the visits. Aesthetic quality, as well as surprise/humor attributed to a work, were both linked to increased heart rate variability in the respective RoI. This corresponds well with the occurrence and location of the markers in the imaging dataset.

The findings of the project support the idea that art reception may be an example of embodied cognition. The imaging of the visitors SJ6, SJ8, and SJ24 (Fig.s 4-6) indicates clearly how artworks have an attracting and sometimes also repelling effect on the spatial behavior of visitors. Artworks are like attractors in museum psycho-geography. Locomotion inside the RoIs of the works may be seen as a specific type of the regulation of closeness and distance in social space. The perspective of embodiment in recent psychology (Barsalou et al., 2003; Ramseyer & Tschacher, 2011) implies that motor actions always modify experiences and judgments, in addition to being mere results *of* experiences and judgments. This is obviously true also in the field of aesthetics, but still very little research exists on the issue.

A further aspect of embodiment concerns the physiological reactions we measured in the context of viewing exhibited artworks. Aesthetics research in the era of neuroscience has produced several findings that identify the neurological bases (there are more than one!) of aesthetic experience (Ramachandran & Hirstein, 1999). Such research increasingly implements sophisticated measuring apparatuses such as functional magnetic resonance imaging (fMRI) and event-related EEG (Kawabata & Zeki, 2004; Jacobsen, 2010). To date, however, the constraints placed on such research are restrictive. Generally, the stimuli are presented in unnatural environments (in the case of the MRI scanner, participants have to rest supine and motionless) and underlie strict experimental variation (e.g. only simple geometrical forms, not genuine artworks, are presented), so that the experimental situation per se becomes artificial and disembodied. As reported, we have chosen a different way in the eMotion project by focusing on a less demanding neuronal signal while optimizing ecological and external validity.

The art world, in concord with traditional art theory, usually expresses severe concerns when it comes to quantitative research of artworks and their aesthetic attraction. Critics argue that one cannot cover the singularity of art reception by averaging out the idiographic experiences. They fear that statistical and experimental methods may damage the very object of investigation. We regard some of these concerns as quite justified: Psychological research has a long history of studying conditions that have been simplified beyond recognition; in numerous instances, complex processes in embodied social systems were investigated by severely reducing complexity, process, and embodiment. This poses a danger for aesthetics research, which relates to complex stimuli (i.e. artworks with their 'aura') that are being perceived by real embodied agents in their own time frames.

These well-justified concerns, however, must not rule out just any nomothetic research on art. Studying art is not in principle disastrous for art. To the contrary, there is a need for more empirical studies of art reception as an idiosyncratically human behavior, which is, judged by its social and psychological importance, rather under-researched. In the future, this research should better consider the external validity of its results and address real art in real environments.

Acknowledgements

This work was supported by the Swiss National Science Foundation (13DPD3-120799/1). We thank the Institute for Research in Design and Art, University of Applied Sciences of Northwestern Switzerland, for administrative support and Ubisense for providing the position-tracking technology. We would especially like to thank the eMotion-team: The media artist and technical director of eMotion Steven Greenwood; the sociologists Prof. Dr. Volker Kirchberg and Dr. Stéphanie Wintzerith; the art theorists Prof. Dr. Karen van den Berg and Prof. Sibylle Omlin; Sukandar Kartadinata and Christophe Vaillant for developing the electronic glove; Patricia Reed, Mauritius Seeger, Enrico Viola, Valentin Schmidt for information design and programming; Chandrasekhar Ramakrishnan for data sonification; Roman Rammelt and Behrang Alavi for database management and Nicolai Karl for managing the tracking technology. We warmly thank Roland Wäspe, director of the Kunstmuseum St.Gallen, who made it possible to turn the museum into a laboratory.

References

Barker R. G. (1978). *Habitats, environment, and human behavior.* San Francisco: Jossey-Bass.
Barsalou L. W., Niedenthal P. M., Barbey A. K. & Ruppert J. A. (2003). Social embodiment. *Psychology of Learning and Motivation, 43,* 43-92.
Benjamin W. (1939/1980). *Das Kunstwerk im Zeitalter seiner technischen Reproduzierbarkeit.* Frankfurt: Suhrkamp.
Jacobsen T. (2010). Beauty and the brain: Culture, history and individual differences in aesthetic appreciation. *J Anat, 216,* 184-91.
Kawabata H. & Zeki S. (2004). Neural correlates of beauty. *J Neurophysiol, 91,* 1699-705.
Lakoff G. & Núñez R. E. (2000). *Where mathematics comes from: How the embodied mind brings mathematics into being.* New York: Basic Books.
Ramachandran V. S. & Hirstein W. (1999). The science of art: A neurological theory of aesthetic experience. *Journal of Consciousness Studies, 6,* 15-51.
Ramseyer F. & Tschacher W. (2011). Nonverbal synchrony in psychotherapy: Relationship quality and outcome are reflected by coordinated body-movement. *Journal of Consulting and Clinical Psychology.*
Storch M., Cantieni B., Hüther G., & Tschacher W. (2010). *Embodiment. Die Wechselwirkung von Körper und Psyche verstehen und nutzen.* Bern: Verlag Hans Huber.
Tschacher W., Tröndle M., Greenwood S., Kirchberg V., Wintzerith S., & van den Berg K. (in preparation). Physiological correlates of aesthetic perception in a museum.

Name Index

A
Abbott L. F. 122
Abraham W. C. 122
Adams F. 244-245, 247
Adelman P. K. 151-152, 168
Adolph K. E. 241, 248
Aitken K. J. 131, 150
Aizawa K. 244-245, 247
Albright L. 178, 190
Amsterdam B. 202, 204
Anaxagor(as) 8
Angelucci A. 121
Anishchenko A. 122
Applebaum D. 119
Arendt H.-J. 11, 28
Aristotle 4, 7, 28
Aronoff J. 153, 168
Ashby W. R. 119
Atick J. J. 121
Atmaca S. ix, 173-192
Avolio A. M. 241, 248

B
Bailenson J. N. 162, 168, 202, 204
Baillargeon R. 143, 149
Bajcsy R. 46, 55
Baldi P. 120
Ballard D. H. 65, 69, 120-121
Bandler R. 198, 204
Banks E. C. 13-14, 28
Bar M. 155, 168
Barber J. 196, 204
Bargh J. A. 63, 69, 194, 196, 202, 204
Barker R. G. 80, 87, 249, 254, 257, 263
Barlow H. 100, 103, 121
Barnes J. 7, 28
Baron-Cohen S. 135, 140, 143, 145, 147, 169
Barrows B. E. 155, 170
Barsalou L. 51, 55, 151, 168, 170, 262-263
Bartlett F. C. 213, 227
Barto A. G. 123
Bateson M. C. 131, 147
Bauermeister M. 62, 69
Bays P. M. 50, 55, 123
Beal, M. J. 120
Bear M. F. 122
Bechara A. 62, 69
Bechinie M. 178, 182, 190
Beer R. 49, 55, 60-61, 69
Bell A. J. 121
Bellman R. 110, 123
Berg H. C. 25, 28, 125, 149, 263, 280

Bernard C. 119
Bernieri F. J. 193-195, 197, 204-205
Berridge K. C. 123
Beutler L. E. 209, 227
Bialek W. 121
Bienenstock E. L. 122
Bingham G. 236, 251
Blake R. 195, 204
Blickhan R. 36-37, 55
Bloom P. 141, 147
Blythe P. W. 173-174, 190
Bogdan R. 129, 147
Boker S. M. 197, 202, 204, 207
Bongard J. 32, 49, 57, 192
Bongers R. M. 237-239, 245, 248, 251
Borkenau P. 175, 187, 189-190
Borst C. 40, 55
Bourdin C. 243, 248
Bowlby J. 213, 227
Bowler D. M. 142, 147
Brähler E. 164, 169
Breakspear M. 124
Brendl C. M. 159, 170
Brentano F. 79, 85, 87
Bressler S. L. 124
Bressloff P. C. 121
Brick T. R. 195, 204
Brooks R. 54-55, 60, 69, 79-80, 87
Brown E. 40- 41, 55, 168, 177, 192
Bucci W. ix, 209-228
Buchli J. 35, 55
Burge T. 67, 69
Bürgin D. 136, 147
Burgoon J. K. 194, 204
Burton G. 238, 244, 246, 248, 251
Buss D. M. 178, 190
Buttelmann D. 143, 147
Butterworth G. 133, 147
Buytendijk F. J. J. 19, 23, 27-28

C
Cacioppo J. T. 63, 69, 152, 158, 166, 168-169, 195, 205, 207
Cairns H. 5, 29
Camerer C. F. 123
Cappella J. N. 194, 196, 204
Cardinali L. 245, 248
Carello C. 236, 238, 248, 250, 252
Carhart-Harris R. L. 119
Carr L. 196, 204
Carruthers P. 147
Cartmill M. 39, 55

Cesari P.   236, 248
Chalmers D. J.   245, 248
Chan T. C.   238, 248
Chaplin W. F.   162, 168
Chapman M.   57, 134, 148
Chartrand T. L.   194, 196, 201-202, 204, 206
Chawla D.   122
Chemero A.   60, 66-67, 69, 232-234, 245, 248
Chen S.   63, 69
Chiel H.   60-61, 69
Choi H. J.   236, 248
Christian P.   27, 28, 211
Churchland P. S.   46, 55, 61, 69
Clark A.   vii, x, 50-51, 55, 62, 64, 65-69, 82, 87, 169, 171, 245, 248
Clements W. A.   143, 148
Cohen J. D.   124
Cohen R. S.   13, 28
Coleman M.   35, 55
Collins S.   34-36, 55, 191
Condon W. S.   194, 196-197, 204
Corboz-Warnery A.   136, 148
Cornell W. F.   34-35, 41, 222-225, 227
Cosmelli D.   62, 69
Cosmides L.   145, 148
Costa P. T. Jr.   163, 168, 178, 181, 189-190
Cottingham J.   10, 28
Cox R. F. A.   238, 251
Craig C. M.   243, 248
Craik K. H.   178, 190
Crane T.   67, 69
Crauel H.   119
Crone   176, 191
Cruse H.   38, 55-56
Curcio A. C.   44, 56
Cutting J. E.   174, 191

D
Damasio A.   62, 69, 213, 227-228
Damian D.   42, 55-56
Darwin C.   81, 86, 98, 106, 107, 123, 151, 169, 174, 190, 215, 228
Dauwalder J.-P.   vii, x, 80-81, 86-88, 195, 207
Davis M.   69, 193-194, 204, 250
Daw N. D.   123
Dayan P.   120, 122-123, 125
De Gelder B.   194-195, 205, 207
De Haan S.   viii, 129-150
De Jaegher H.   viii, 67, 69, 129-150, 166, 169
De Palma A.   122
De Preester H.   56
De Vignemont F.   59-61, 67-68, 70
De Waal F. B. M.   196, 206
Derrick T. R.   197, 205

Descartes R.   9-10, 16, 18, 20, 22-23, 28, 69, 117, 119, 227
Desimone R.   122
Dewey J.   46, 56
DeYoung C. G.   179, 190
Di Paolo E.   69, 130, 146, 148, 166, 169
Dilthey W.   15, 28
Diogenes Laërtius   4, 28
Dittrich W. H.   175, 190
Dixon A. F.   148, 190
Dokic J.   141, 148
Dotov D. G.   247-248
Doya K.   57, 122-123
Dreyfus H. L.   79, 87
Dubin R.   196, 206
Dumas G.   194, 205
Dunbar C.   236, 250
Dur V.   38, 56
Durstewitz D.   122

E
Eberhard-Kaechele M.   158, 169
Eckmann J. P.   190
Edelman G. E.   50, 56, 123
Edelman S.   49, 56
Efron B.   120
Eibl-Eibesfeldt I.   173, 190
Erickson E.   154, 169
Evans D. J.   119

F
Farne A.   241, 248
Fearing R.   42, 56
Fechner G. Th.   11-13, 16, 23, 28-30
Feldman A. G.   27-28,
Feldman R.   196, 205
Felleman D. J.   120
Feynman R. P.   119
Field D. J.   121
Fields R. B.   119, 125
Fink B.   178, 180, 190-191, 205
Fiorillo C. D.   125
Fisette D.   24, 29
Fitzpatrick P.   239, 246, 248
Fivaz-Depeursinge E.   136, 148
Flandoli F.   119
Fletcher P. C.   125
Flückiger C.   199, 205
Foley F.   165, 170
Folstad I.   177, 190
Förster J.   153, 169
Fourre B.   243, 249
Franceschini N.   44, 56
Frantz A. G.   188, 190
Freeman W. J.   vii, x, 124

265

French R. 63, 6
Freud S. 21, 149, 225, 228
Fries P. 122
Friston K. viii, 76, 89-125, 210
Frith C. D. 125, 147, 149
Fuchs T. viii, 129-150, 162, 169, 207
Full R. J. 36, 56-57

G
Gallagher S. viii, 26, 29, 59-71, 129-130, 143-144, 148, 150
Gallese V. 51, 56, 179, 190, 194, 204-205, 207, 228
Garn S. M. 176, 191
Garrett S. R. 243, 249-250
Garrido M. I. 121
Gergely G. 148
German T. P. 141, 147
Ghahramani Z. 120, 122
Gibson J. 46, 56, 81, 85, 87, 231-233, 235, 237-239, 244, 249
Gilestro G. F. 122
Gleitman H. 132, 149
Glenberg A. M. 50, 56
Goldenberg G. 241, 249
Goldman A. 59-61, 67-68, 70
Goldstein J. M. 179, 191
Goldstein K. 23, 29
Gomez G. 38-39, 44, 57, 134
Grahe J. E. 195, 205
Grammer K. ix, 173-192, 193, 195, 197, 199, 205
Grawe K. 199, 205, 207
Gray C. M. 122
Gray J. A. 155, 169
Green N. 152, 170
Greeno J. G. 81, 87
Gregory R. L. 89, 119
Grinder J. 198, 204
Grist M. 119
Gros C. 124
Grossberg S. 121
Guillery R. W. 121
Günther N. 156, 169
Gurney K. 123

H
Haggard P. 50, 56
Haken H. vii-viii, x, 75-88, 119, 124, 193-195, 205, 210
Hall J. A. 192-193, 205
Haller R. 13, 29
Hamilton E. 5, 29
Harnad S. 48-49, 56
Harris C. S. 62, 70

Harrist A. W. 196, 205
Hatfield E. 152-153, 169, 194, 205
Hausdorff J. M. 174, 191
Heath C. 196, 207
Hebb D. O. 104-105, 122
Heeger D. J. 122
Heft H. 232, 249
Heidegger M. 79, 81, 87, 244, 247, 249
Heidelberger M. 11, 13, 23, 29
Heraclitus 4-5, 29
Hernandez Arieta A. 41, 56, 58
Herrmann J. M. 124
Herschbach M. 143, 148, 150
Herzberg P. Y. 164, 169
Hesslow G. 50, 56
Higuchi T. 50, 56, 241, 249
Hinton G. E. 119-120, 192, 228
Hirayama J. 123
Hirose N. ix, 231-252
Hobson R. P. 130, 148
Hoffmann H. 51, 56
Hoffmann M. viii, 31-58, 61, 79
Hollerbach J. 42, 56
Holzleitner I. ix, 173-192
Homan C. P. 175, 192
Hoshino K. 45, 56
Hove M. J. 147, 149, 196, 205
Huang G. 119
Hubbard E. M. 155, 170
Hubley P. 67, 71
Hurley S. 66, 70, 196, 205
Husserl E. 22, 24, 29, 138, 148
Hutto D. 67-68, 70, 129, 148

I
Iacoboni M. 194, 204-205, 214-215, 225, 228
Iida F. 38, 56-58
Ijspeert A. J 35, 55
Illig R. 188, 191
Iriki A. 242, 249-250
Isabella R. A. 196, 206
Ishibashi H. 242, 249
Ishii S. 123-124
Itti L. 120
Izard C. E. 151, 169

J
Jirsa V. K. 124, 207
Johnson M. vii, x, 63-64, 68, 70, 155, 169
Johnson-Frey S. H. 241, 249
Jones K. S. 232-233, 249
Jordan J. S. 213-215, 228
Jordan M. I. 123
Jordan S. 86, 87,
Jung T. 44, 56

K
Kahn C. H. 4-5, 29
Karter A. J. 177, 190
Kass R. E. 120
Kauffman S. 119, 124
Kawato M. 58, 120
Kelso J. A. S. 81, 87, 124, 205-206
Kersten D. 120-121
Kestenberg J. S. 153-156, 159, 162, 169, 171
Kiebel S. 120-121, 123, 125
Kinsbourne M. 213-214, 228
Kitzbichler M. G. 125
Kleeman J. A. 149
Knill D. C. 120
Knobloch F. 123
Knockaert K. 50, 56
Koch S. C. ix, 63, 151-171
Koditschek D. E. 36, 56
Köhler W. 81, 87, 155, 170
Konczak J. 236, 249
Koppensteiner M. 178, 191
Kozlowski L. 174, 191
Kubow T. M. 36, 57
Kuniyoshi Y. 49, 57-58
Kupper Z. 195, 203, 206
Kurths J. 192

L
Laban R. v. 153-155, 170
Ladavas E. 241, 248-249
LaFrance M. 152, 170
Laird J. D. 151-152, 170
Lakens D. 196, 206
Lakin J. L. 196, 206
Lakoff G. vii, x, 51, 56, 63-64, 68, 70, 253, 263
Lauer H. E. 10, 29
Laughlin S. B. 121
Leahy R. L. 226-228
LeDoux J. E. 220, 228
Lee T. S. 120
Legrand D. 26, 29, 138, 149
Leibniz 10
Leslie A. M. 139, 147, 149
Leutgeb S. 122
Lewen G. D. 121
Lewin K. 80-82, 84, 87, 160, 170, 195, 206
Lichtensteiger L. 45, 57
Liebler A. 175, 187, 189-190
Linden D. E. J. 66, 70
Linsker R. 103, 121
Lipps T. 152, 167, 170
Lockman J. J. 237, 249
Loman S. 153, 165, 169-170
Luborsky L. 209, 228

Lungarella M. 32, 43-44, 46-48, 56-58

M
Ma W. J. 120
Maass A. 153, 170
Maass W. 50, 57,
MacDonald K. B. 170, 191
Mach E. 13-14, 16, 23-24, 28-29
MacKay D. J. C. 120
MacKay D. M. 120
Mahler M. 138, 149
Malek E. A. 241, 249, 252
Manning J. T. 176-177, 190-192
Maravita A. 50, 57, 241-242, 249-250
Marci C. D. 194, 206
Mark L. S. 234, 236, 240, 248, 250
Markman A. B. 159, 170
Markram H. 31, 57
Markus H. 151-152, 171
Marr D. 43, 57
Martinez H. 44, 46, 48, 55-57
Marwan N. 183, 192
Marzke M. 39, 57
Marzke R. 39, 57
Maskit B. 221, 227
Maturana H. R. 124
Maunsell J. H. 122
Maurer D. 155, 170
Mayer, A. viii, 129-150
McArthur L. Z. 178, 191
McClelland J. L. 212, 228
McCrae R. R. 163, 168, 181, 189-190
McGeer T. 33, 35-36, 57
Mead G. H. 136, 149
Meltzoff A. N. 131, 149, 196, 206, 214, 228
Menary R. 68, 70
Merleau-Ponty M. 23-26, 29, 135, 138, 140, 149, 151-153, 155, 166-167, 170, 194, 206, 244, 250
Mesulam M. M. 120
Metta G. 44, 58
Miall R. 58, 123
Michaels C. F. 232, 237, 248, 250
Migeon C. J. 176, 192
Miller G. F. 173-174, 190, 192
Mitchell P. 149
Mittelstaedt H. 27, 29
Molina-Vilaplana J. 40, 57
Montagu A. 161-162, 170
Montague P. R. 123
Moore J. L. 81, 87
Moore M. K. 131, 149, 196, 206, 214, 228
Morris C. 120
Morris P. 135, 149
Moyer D. 131, 150

Müller S. M.   156-157, 164, 169
Mumford D.   120-121
Murphy N. A.   175, 192
Murray L.   132, 149
Murray S. O.   121

N
Nara S.   124
Nash J.   123
Neal R. M.   120
Neisser U.   vii, x, 120
Neta M.   155, 168
Neumann R.   151-152, 170, 194, 206
Newell K. M.   236, 248
Newtson D.   193, 206
Nicolis G.   119
Niedenthal P.   vii, x, 151-152, 170, 263
Nietzsche F.   28-29
Nishio A.   240, 244, 249
Niv Y.   125
Noë A.   65-66, 68, 70
Nolfi S.   49, 57
Nowak A.   193, 206-207
Núñez R.   vii, x, 63, 70, 253, 263

O
O'Regan K.   64, 66, 70
O'Toole R.   196, 206
Oberzaucher E.   ix, 173-192
Ogston W. D.   194, 196-197, 204
Oja E.   121
Olshausen B. A.   121
Olsson M.   177, 192
Onishi K. H.   143, 149
Optican L.   121
Ordaq G. W.   125
Oudeyer P.-Y.   48, 57
Oullier O.   194, 206

P
Pagano C. C.   242-243, 249-251
Panksepp J.   124, 188, 192, 212, 228
Pareti G.   122
Parker T. H.   177, 192
Parrott W. G.   132, 149
Pascal B.   28
Pasquale V.   125
Passos-Ferreira C.   202, 206
Paulin M. G.   120
Paulsen O.   122
Paus T.   121
Pavlov I.   23
Peck A. J.   238, 244, 250
Perner J.   134, 139-140, 143, 148-150
Pervin L. A.   178, 192

Petty R. E.   153, 171
Pezzulo G.   50-51, 57
Pfeifer R.   viii, 31-58, 61, 79, 86-87, 192
Phillips W. A.   125, 168
Piaget J.   130, 149
Plato   4-9, 29
Plessner H.   15-19, 23-26, 28-29, 136, 149
Poffenberger A. T.   155, 170
Poggio T.   48, 58
Poole G. D.   152, 170
Port R.   vii, x
Portmann A.   16
Pouget A.   120
Poulakakis I.   36, 58
Prader A.   188, 191
Premack D.   141, 149
Preston S. D.   196, 206
Price G. R.   123
Prigogine I.   119
Proust J.   141, 148
Pufall P. B.   236, 250
Pyers J. E.   142, 149
Pylyshyn Z.   31, 58
Pythagoras   4-5, 7-8, 11

R
Raab M.   152, 170
Rabinovich M.   124
Rabkin M. T.   190
Ramachandran V. S.   55, 69, 155, 170, 225, 228, 262-263
Ramenzoni V. C.   234, 250
Ramsey W.   67, 70
Ramseyer F.   ix, 83, 88, 167, 193-207, 254, 262-263
Rao R. P.   69, 121
Reddy V.   132-133, 135, 143, 149
Redgrave P.   123
Redlich A. N.   121
Reed E. S.   81, 87, 232-235, 238, 240, 250
Regia-Corte T.   241, 250
Reid V. M.   145, 150
Reik T.   215-216, 218, 225, 228
Rescorla R. A.   110, 123
Reynolds J. H.   122
Richardson M. J.   193, 206-207
Richeimer J.   27, 29
Richmond B. J.   121
Riesenhuber M.   48, 58
Riggs K. J.   142, 149
Ringrose J.   36, 58
Risen J. L.   196, 205
Riskind J. H.   152, 170
Rizzolatti G.   205, 213-214, 228
Rochat P.   148, 202, 206

Rock I. 62, 70
Rodriguez E. 194, 206
Rokeby D. 197, 206
Roll J-P. 62, 70
Roll R. 62, 70
Rosenthal R. 194-195, 197, 204-205, 207
Rossberg-Gempton I. 152, 170
Rotondo J. L. 202, 204, 207
Roweis S. 120, 122
Rowlands M. 64, 68, 70
Rupert R. D. 245, 250
Ruskin M. 136, 149

S
Şahin E. 234, 250
Sanders J. T. 232, 237, 250-251
Sandini G. 44, 58
Sanger T. 120
Saranli U. 36, 58
Scheflen A. E. 194, 207
Scheibert J. 42, 58
Scheier C. 32, 49-50, 58, 86-87
Scheler M. 15, 21, 135, 149
Schilder P. 20-25, 29
Schmicking D. 26, 29
Schmidt R. C. 193, 207, 248, 252
Schomaker L. 50, 58
Schore A. N. 145, 149
Schottenbauer M. A. 220, 228
Schroeder C. E. 122
Schubert T. W. 161, 170
Schultz W. 123, 125
Seamans J. K. 122
Seeger R. J. 13, 28
Seibt B. 159, 170
Sejnowski T. J. 55, 69, 120-123
Semin G. R. 151, 166, 171, 194, 207
Senju A. 143, 149-150
Serino A. 241, 248-249
Shapiro L. A. 61-63, 68, 70
Shaw R. E. 232, 236-237, 245, 249, 251
Sheets-Johnstone M. 153, 166, 171
Sherman S. M. 121
Shiffrar M. 195, 204
Shipp S. 120
Silverstein S. M. 125
Simoncelli E. P. 121
Singer W. 70, 122
Smith E. R. 151, 171
Smith J. M. 123
Smith L. 51, 58, 81, 87
Smitsman A. W. 237-238, 245, 248, 251
Snapp-Childs W. 236, 251
Socrates 5, 8
Sonnby-Borgström M. 194, 207

Sossin K. M. 154-155, 169, 171
Southgate V. 143-144, 149-150
Spatt J. 241, 249
Spinoza 10
Sporns O. 32, 43-44, 46-48, 57-58, 123
Spratling M. W. 122
Stadler F. 13, 29
Stadler M. vii, x, 81, 87
Stam C. J. 124
Steenbergen B. 239-240, 246, 251
Steffey D. 120
Stern D. 138-139, 150, 213-214, 228
Stifter C. A. 131, 150
Stoffregen T. A. 232-234, 237, 251
Strack F. 80, 87, 151-153, 169-171, 194, 206
Straus E. 23, 25, 29, 61, 70
Striano T. 145, 150
Stubenberg L. 14, 29
Suitner C. 153, 170
Sutton R. S. 123
Suzuki N. 202, 207

T
Tamietto M. 195, 207
Tani J. 113, 124
Thelen E. 51, 58, 81, 87
Thomas J. M. 197, 205
Thompson E. x, 62, 66-71, 135, 150
Thornhill R. 175-176, 191-192
Thornton C. 44, 58, 119
Tickle-Degnen L. 195, 207
Tipping M. E. 121
Todd P. M. 174, 190, 192
Todorov E. 123
Tognoli E. 124
Tomasello M. 133, 147, 150
Tooby J. 145, 148
Treisman A. 122
Treue S. 122
Trevarthen C. ix, 67, 71, 131-132, 149-150
Treves A. 122
Tröndle M. 253-263
Troxler I. P. V. 10-13, 23, 29-30
Tschacher W. vii-viii, x, 75-88, 124, 195-196, 198-199, 206-207, 210, 253-263
Tseng Y. W. 123
Tsuda I. 124
Turvey M. T. 232-234, 236-238, 242-243, 248-252
Tyukin I. 113, 124

U
Usher M. 124

269

V

Vallacher R. R.   193, 206-207
van Baaren R.   196, 201-202, 204
van Camp D.   119
van de Langenberg R.   243, 251
van den Berg J. H.   25, 28, 263
van Essen D. C.   120
van Gelder T. J.   vii, x
van Leeuwen C.   124
Varela F.   vii, x, 66-68, 70-71, 122, 124, 206
Verdaasdonk B.   35, 58
Versace M.   121
Verschure P. F.   123
Voigt C. A.   124
von der Malsburg C.   104, 122
von Holst E.   27, 29
von Uexküll J.   23-24, 30
von Weizsäcker C. F.   18, 27, 30
von Weizsäcker V.   18-20, 23-25, 27, 30
Vorovac B.   36, 58
Vukobratovic M.   36, 58

W

Wachsmuth I.   179, 192
Wackermann J.   viii, 3-30
Wagman J.   239, 241, 244, 249-250, 252
Wagner A. R.   110, 123
Waibel A. H.   178, 192
Walk R. D.   175, 192
Wallbott H. G.   151, 153, 171
Wampold B. E.   209, 228
Wapner S.   62, 70
Warren W. H.   236, 238, 252
Watkins C. J. C. H.   123
Watson D.   160, 171, 189, 192
Watson J. S.   132, 148,
Watzlawick P.   193, 207
Waugh R. M.   196, 205
Webb M.   32, 50, 58
Webber C. L. Jr.   183, 192
Weiskopf D. A.   245, 252
Wellman H. M.   140, 150
Wells G. L.   153, 165, 171
Wentura D.   152, 171
Werner G.   124
Werner H.   62, 70,
Westen D.   209, 228
Whang S.   236, 252
Wheeler M.   64, 68, 71
Wicker B.   216, 228
Widmer M.   10, 29
Wilson R. A.   65, 71
Wiltermuth S. S.   196, 207
Wimmer H.   140, 150
Windschitl P.   165, 171

Wisniewski A. B.   176, 192
Wolpert D. M.   50, 55-56, 58, 123
Womelsdorf T.   122
Woodruff G.   141, 149
Wunderlin A.   83, 87

Y

Yokoi H.   39, 56, 58
Yu A. J.   122, 124
Yu W.   41, 56, 58,

Z

Zahavi D.   144, 150
Zajac F. E.   61, 71
Zajonc R. B.   151-152, 168, 171
Zbilut J. P.   183, 192
Zeki S.   120, 262-263
Zemel R.   120
Zlatev J.   64, 71

Subject Index

A
action plan   215, 217, 219
accuracy   94, 97, 101, 104, 175, 195
actuality   7
adaptive behavior   108, 114-115
adaptive resonance theory   100
aesthetic experience   ix, 152, 262
aesthetics   ix, 11, 22, 253, 256, 258, 262
affect   136, 139-140, 151, 154, 156, 165,
   168, 178, 213, 219, 221, 226, 244
   − system   151, 157-158
affordance   ix, 66, 81, 84, 231 237, 239
   242, 244-245
agent   32, 38 41, 44, 48, 52, 54, 79, 80, 82,
   86, 89, 97, 107, 109, 112, 115 118,
   135-136, 263
analogic   211-212
anticipation   144, 214, 216, 219, 224
appendage   238
arousal   159, 160, 216-217, 221, 256
art   ix, 35-36, 155, 167, 173, 210 212,
   253-254, 256, 258, 263
artificial intelligence (AI)   viii, 31-55,
   79-80, 86, 270
Asperger   143
attachment
   − style   196, 199-200, 219
   − to the body   237, 240-247
attention   26, 62, 105-106, 116, 118,
   131-134, 137, 144, 212, 218-219
   −, joint   131 134, 137, 144
attractiveness   175-178, 180, 188-189, 260
attractor   viii, 83-84, 92, 102, 104, 107,
   110, 111, 113-114, 257
attunement   133, 137, 139, 146, 165, 212
autism   143, 167
autopoiesis   113-114, 116
awareness   130-138, 140-142, 154,
   194-195, 210-211, 216
   −, mutual   137

B
behavior regulation   151-152, 159
behavioristic   134-135
biased competition   106, 116
bidirectionality assumption   ix, 151, 159,
   166
bifurcation   113
big five   163-164, 178-179, 185, 189

biological
   − agent   viii, 89-95
   − embodiment   61-62, 68
   − system   38, 43-45, 54, 91-92, 95, 117
biology   vii-viii, 14-16, 19, 23-24, 27, 32,
   68, 76, 114, 117, 179, 225
body
   − build   177-190
   − dynamics   viii-ix, 35-38, 48, 53
   − feedback   ix, 151-168
   − image   20-22, 24, 26
   − -mind problem   vii, 3-28, 85
   − morphology   vii, 32-33, 38-47, 52-54
   − motion   173-190, 193-204
   − movement   151-168, 194 196, 215
   − proportions   174-189
   − psychotherapy   167
   − schema   20, 31, 33, 50, 62-63, 242
   − symmetry   181, 185, 188
   −, corporeal   10-12
   −, inhabited   139
   −, lived   138
   −, living   7, 17, 19, 138
   −, vital   10, 17
boundary   ix, 16-17, 20, 144, 236, 244 247
brain   viii, 21, 26, 31-33, 38, 40, 51, 54,
   59-62, 64-66, 68, 76, 80, 85, 89-118,
   176, 179-180, 212, 214, 216, 226

C
categorization   31-32, 48-51, 63, 113,
   156-157
causality   viii, 8, 18, 24, 77- 78, 90
   −, circular   viii, 77-78, 90
cell assemblies   104-106
chameleon effect   196
chaos   103, 183, 186
closed organization   17
cognition
   −, grounded   51
   −, higher level   32-33, 48, 65, 67-68
   −, social   59-61, 67-68, 80, 129-147
cognitive affective system   151, 158
cognitive science   viii, 26, 27, 31, 63,
   66-68, 79, 81, 119, 212, 216, 241, 253
cognitivism   9, 27, 28, 62, 64, 135, 146
complexity   9, 43-44, 47, 49, 81, 94, 97,
   101, 104, 129, 130, 175, 177, 183,
   212, 262

271

computation viii, 31, 45, 55, 66, 79-80, 113, 195
—, morphological viii, 32-33, 38, 45, 52, 54
computational 27, 31, 36, 43, 48, 50, 54, 59, 60, 62, 65, 79, 81, 86, 91, 110, 111, 116, 151
computationalism 55, 67
computer viii, 27, 32, 43, 48, 79, 195, 197, 202, 247
conditioning 135, 226
connectionism 64, 212
consciousness 16-17, 20-21, 24, 65-66, 94, 136, 138, 155
—, embodied 66
—, phenomenal 65
—, reflective 17
—, self- 20, 136
—, time- 138
constructivism 178
control 6, 8, 31 41, 47, 49, 52-54, 76-77, 83-86, 98, 105, 109 112, 115-116, 135, 141, 156, 165, 179, 203, 212, 218
— parameter 76-77, 83-86
coordination 27, 33, 38, 43, 46-49, 52-54, 76, 78, 85, 116, 183, 193-197, 201
correlation theory 104-105
cortex 179, 213-214
coupling viii, 46, 51, 66-67, 82, 86, 231
courtship behavior 174, 177
cross correlation 198
cross modal extinction 242
culture 16, 173

D
dance ix, 155, 167, 173-190, 215
Darwinism ix, 98, 106, 107
de centring 129, 130, 133
dementia 167
depersonalization 20
development (development studies) ix, 21, 48, 50, 67, 68, 89, 101, 118, 129-147, 153, 154, 161, 176, 179, 185, 190, 194, 196, 216-219, 241
—, social ix, 129-147
differential equation 82
digit ratio (2D:4D ratio) 176-177, 180-188
disembodied 48, 62, 86, 262
dissipative dynamics 111, 115
dissociation 154, 209, 212, 216, 218-222
dual aspect theory 11
dualism (psycho physical dualism) 9, 14, 16, 19, 22-23, 117
dyad (dyadic interaction) ix, 131, 135-137, 193-204, 227

dynamical system vii, 35, 75-86, 91, 114-116, 179-180, 183-188, 193- 195, 212, 257
dynamic walker 33, 34, 36, 44, 53, 54

E
ecological
 — niche 32, 34, 36, 52, 178,
 — psychology ix, 79 82, 84, 231-247, 254, 257
effectivity ix, 231-247
efficiency 25, 32-35, 53, 85, 100-101, 174
embedding vii-viii, 23, 32, 82, 116, 195, 225
embodied
 — categorization 48-50
 — consciousness 66
 — functionalism 64-66, 68
 — inference 89, 117
 — semantics 63-64, 68
embodiment
 —, biological 61-62, 68
 —, minimal viii, 59-61, 64, 68
 —, radical (enactive) 59, 66-68
 —, sense of 241, 243, 246
 —, simple 65
emergence viii, 21, 49, 82, 84, 106, 134, 188, 233
emotion
 — recognition 61
 — regulation 66
 — schema ix, 209-213, 216-221
emotional
 — involvement 140, 146
 — mirroring 216
empathy ix, 20, 152, 154, 161, 167, 196
enactive 59, 64-68, 166, 210, 213-216
 — perception 65-66, 210, 213-216
enactivism 130, 135, 166
enactment 223
entanglement 18-19, 24-25
entropy 44, 46-48, 90, 92, 94-96, 107, 116, 183
equilibrium viii, 75, 91, 111-113, 116-117
ergodicity 83, 96
eroticism 173, 177
estrogen 174-176
evolution 45, 49, 89-90, 105, 107, 114, 116 118, 153, 155, 158, 173-174, 179, 187, 195, 215, 233
expectation 20, 89, 96, 99, 102, 107, 112, 114, 117, 218
experiential 21, 65, 147, 222
exposure treatment 213, 222
extended mind 64, 68

extension
— of the body 31, 152, 154, 158, 231
233, 236-238, 241-245
— of cognition 65
—, spatial 9, 16-17, 23

F

facial expression vii, 67, 152, 194-195,
212, 214-215, 218, 254
false belief 130, 138, 140-145
— task 140-145
feedback ix, 36, 40-41, 46, 50, 52-53,
151-168
—, body ix, 151-168
—, movement 151-168
fertility 174 177
fluctuation 76-78, 83-84, 95-97, 102, 105,
107, 111, 174, 259
— Theorem 92
forward
— mapping 101
— model 31, 33, 50-51, 54
free energy viii, 76-77, 85, 89-119
— principle viii, 76, 89-119
functionalism 62, 64, 66-68

G

gait 37, 49, 53, 76, 174
Game Theory 110
Geist 10-12, 18
generalized other 136
generative model 94-98, 101-105,
107-110, 112, 115-117
generativity 210
Gestalt 20- 21, 23, 81, 155, 193
— psychology 20-21, 23, 81
Gestaltkreis viii, 18-20, 23, 25, 27
gesture vii, 63, 67, 134, 138, 193, 197,
214-216, 254, 260
gradient 20, 97, 102, 105, 113, 115
grasping 18, 31, 33, 39-43, 48-49, 51-53,
55, 134
grounded cognition 51
grounding problem 49

H

handshake 161-165
haptic 153, 161-162, 165, 238-239, 244,
246
— perception 238, 239, 244, 246
— probing 238, 239, 246
health 174-175
hide and seek ix, 131-133, 136-138, 140,
144

higher level cognition 32-33, 48, 65,
67-68
homeostasis 90, 92, 101
hormone ix, 176-177, 179-180, 187-188,
190

I

idealism 7-8, 11, 24
imitation 131, 139, 158, 193-194, 196,
198, 200-202, 214, 216
immunocompetence 175, 177
inference 64, 89, 93-94, 98-100, 103-107,
109, 115-116, 141, 226
— machine 89, 98
active inference 94, 107, 115
infomax principle 100-101, 103-104, 116
information viii, 27, 31-33, 38, 41-54,
61-65, 76, 79, 81, 91-94, 98, 100-104,
110, 117, 159 161, 164, 174 178, 183,
189, 193, 195, 201, 210, 213, 216,
219-220, 226, 231-232, 238-239
— structure 44-47, 52-53
— theory 33, 38, 41-47, 53, 91- 94, 98,
100
inhibition 166
intelligence 31-58, 79-80, 86, 174-175,
179
artificial intelligence (AI) 31 58, 79-80,
86
intentionality viii, 79, 84 86, 113,
135-136, 144, 210
interaction ix, 13, 18-19, 22, 25, 27, 31-33,
36, 38-41, 48-54, 62, 64, 67, 81-83,
89-91, 129-147, 151, 153, 161-162
166, 169, 179, 189-190, 193-194, 197,
201-203, 213-221, 224-225, 232, 247
—, dyadic ix, 131, 135-137, 193-194
—, triadic 135-145
internal simulation 51, 196
interpersonal 151, 156, 161-162, 165-167,
195, 199, 200, 212, 215, 217-218, 221,
224
intersubjectivity 67, 129, 131, 135-136,
142
intrinsic metrics 236, 238
introjection 225
intuition 4, 212
itinerancy 91-92, 110-116

K

kiki/bouba effect 155
kinesthetic ix, 151-155, 161, 166
Körper 10-12, 14, 17, 138
Kullback Leibler divergence 94, 96-97

273

L

labelling problem 135
language 11, 32, 63, 139, 155, 167, 175, 196, 210, 213, 218, 220-221, 257
learning ix, 48, 89, 91, 93, 98, 100, 102, 104-110, 113, 116, 118, 134-135, 138-140, 146, 158, 214-215, 217, 226
 —, machine 93, 100, 110
 —, reinforcement 102, 106-110, 116
 —, sensory 105
 —, value dependent 106
Lebensraum 80, 195
Leib 10-12, 14, 17, 21, 138
linear 83, 108, 183, 189
linearity 83
linguistics 31, 63
locomotion ix, 31-41, 44, 48-50, 55, 254, 256-261
Lyapunov function 111

M

mate selection (—choice) ix, 173, 175, 178-180, 187-188
materialism 11
mathematical formulation viii, 35, 76, 78, 80-84, 91-118, 183
mathematics 63, 141, 253
meaning 8, 21, 49, 63-64, 67, 79, 134-135, 139, 144, 152, 156, 162, 165, 167-168, 173, 210, 214, 221, 231
memory 14, 26, 50, 62, 65, 95, 97, 104, 139, 152, 157, 212-213, 222
mental
 — imagery 51, 63
 — rotation 63, 113
metaphor 25, 63, 80, 99, 113, 167, 195, 212
metastability 114
mind-body problem vii, 3-28, 85
mindfulness meditation 167
mind reading 135
mirror neuron system ix, 60-61, 166, 195, 214-216
mismatch 100, 108, 134
 — negativity (MMN) 108
model of the world 98, 116
monadology 10
monism 12
morphology vii-viii, 4, 32-33, 38-47, 52-54, 179
motion ix, 173-190, 193-204
 — energy ix, 178, 182-184, 197
 — energy analysis (MEA) ix, 197, 203
 — Energy Detection (MED) 182, 188
 — quality ix, 175, 180, 186

motor congruency effect 153
movement vii-ix, 33-55, 61, 67, 76, 92, 107-112, 134, 151-168, 173-190, 193-204, 214-216, 254-256
 — coordination 76, 193, 196
 — feedback 151-168
 — quality 151-168, 173-178, 180, 186-187
 — shape 151-154, 157-161, 165, 168
 —, approach 153, 158
 —, avoidance 153, 157-160
music 155, 167, 173-174, 176, 181

N

natural selection 106-107, 114, 116, 233
nature nurture debate 145
naturalism 8-9
neural vii, 9, 12, 17-19, 27, 31-32, 35-38, 45, 49, 54, 60-63, 64, 66-67, 98, 104, 106-109, 166, 178, 194, 214-216
 — Darwinism 106-109
 — network 38, 104, 178, 214-215
neurobiology vii, 80, 100, 104
neuronal 18, 60, 76, 92-93, 99-107, 112-113, 117, 194, 213, 262
neuroscience 31, 50, 68, 80, 91, 110, 117, 210, 216, 225, 241, 262
nonlinear 35, 66, 95, 97, 100, 102, 184
nonverbal ix, 139, 142, 162, 167, 174-175, 193-204, 210-212, 215
 — synchrony ix, 193-204

O

object constancy 138
ontogenesis 153, 158, 187, 196
optimal control theory viii, 98, 109-111, 115, 269
order parameter 77-78, 84-86

P

panpsychism 10, 12
parallel distributed processing 212
participatory sense making 67, 130, 134, 139
pattern formation 75-76, 81-82, 85
peek a boo ix, 131-133, 136-137, 140
pendulum 32, 35
perception
 — action system 82, 196, 216, 224, 231-232, 235, 237, 246-247,
 —, active 46-48
 —, enactive 65-66, 210, 213-216
 —, Gestalt 81
 —, haptic 238-239, 244, 246
 —, situated 26

274

—, visual   31, 33, 43-48, 55, 65-66, 101, 104, 112-113, 238-239, 242-243
perceptual adjustment   240
perceptual inference   89, 103, 106
periodic   35, 37, 42, 153, 183
permeability   160
personality   ix, 23, 156, 162-165, 174, 178-180, 185-190, 220
perspective taking   ix, 63, 65, 129-147, 159
—, second person   129-130, 135
—, third person   129-130, 135
phenomenalism   13, 24
phenomenology   viii, 16, 18, 20-27, 79, 134-135, 138, 143-145, 147, 151, 244
phenotype   89, 92, 107, 110, 118
phrenology   189
phylogenetic   153, 196
physicalist   8, 24
physics   viii, 24, 35, 75-77, 85, 91, 93, 188, 235
physiology   10, 18, 23, 92, 175, 183, 194, 254, 256, 260-261
plasticity   102-106, 108-109
point light display   174
positionality   15-18, 20, 24
posture   vii, 60, 62, 67, 80, 153, 175, 193-194, 197, 214-215, 239-241, 254
potentiality   7
prediction   50, 89, 94-105, 108-109, 111-113, 116-117, 129
prediction error   96-97, 99, 101, 104-105, 108, 112, 116-117
preparedness   158
pre reflective   130, 139, 146
probabilistic model   95, 98
projective identification   225-226
proprioceptive   62, 112, 152, 161-162
prosody   vii, 202, 211
psyche   4-7, 9, 19, 22-23
psychoanalysis   ix, 20-21, 136, 213, 221-222, 225
psychodynamic   154, 209, 213, 220, 226
psychophysics   11-13, 89
psychophysiology   5
psychosomatic   18, 23, 167
psychotherapy   ix, 83, 91, 167, 193-204, 209-227
—, body   167

Q
qualia   155, 167

R
rapport   195-196
ready to hand   244, 247
reafference   27
receptive field   100-101, 242
recognition density   93-97, 99, 101, 104, 109, 117-118
recurrence quantification analysis (RQA)   183-188
recursion   82, 106, 214, 216-221, 224-225
redundancy   100-101
reference   64, 85, 138, 210
referential process   ix, 210, 212, 219-223
reflective   17, 130, 139, 146
regularity   32, 104-105, 179, 214
repetition suppression   99, 105, 108
representation   viii, 31, 33, 48-51, 54-55, 60-61, 64-68, 82, 93-94, 96-97, 99-104, 109, 117-118, 140, 152, 166, 174, 210-213, 217
representationalism   61, 64-65, 67, 139,-140, 143, 147, 167, 194
reprojection   225
resonance   ix, 100, 152, 155, 166-167, 262
rhythm   ix, 131, 153-168, 173-174, 183, 186, 188, 196, 211, 214-215
robotics   viii, 31-55, 68, 79, 86, 113, 117

S
schema   ix, 10, 20-21, 31, 33, 50, 62-63, 134, 139, 209-213, 216-222, 242
— therapy   213, 220
—, associative   134, 139
—, body   20, 31, 33, 50, 62-63, 242
—, dissociated   219
—, emotion   ix, 209-213, 216-221
—, maladaptive   218
—, memory   213
schizophrenia   116, 167, 203
Seele   10-12
selective pressure   106-107
self -
— adaptation   39-40
— consciousness   20, 136
— organization   viii, 75-78, 81-86, 91-93, 111-114, 194-195
— reference   139
— regulation   41
— stabilization   35-37, 53
— structuring   45, 47
selfness (selfhood)   11, 15
sensori motor system   18-19, 25, 43, 46, 48, 53-54, 64, 66, 82, 86, 166, 214, 254

275

sex (gender) 174-177, 180, 184-189, 199, 201
— hormone ix, 179-180, 187-188
shared
— circuits model 196
— manifold 179
simulation
— Theory 141
—, cognitive 50-51, 61, 67, 179, 196, 214
—, artificial 31, 37, 44, 49-51, 102-103, 108, 111, 113, 212
slaving 77-78, 84
social
— ability (skill) ix, 141-142
— adaptation 196
— cognition 59-61, 67-68, 80, 129-147
— development ix, 129-147
— psychology ix, 80, 165, 202
— space 136, 262
— understanding ix, 130, 135, 138, 143, 147
soul 3-12, 22
space 3, 12, 17, 23-25, 62, 80-84, 103, 107, 109-115, 167, 242-244, 254, 257-258
—, extrapersonal 242
—, peripersonal 242
spatial orientation 243
stability 14, 32-34, 49, 83
subjectivity 17, 27
subsymbolic processing ix, 210-213, 218, 221, 223, 226-227
supervenience 64
surprise viii, 20, 33, 92-98, 100-101, 106-109, 111, 116, 262
—, Bayesian viii, 101
symbolic processing 27, 31, 49, 62, 79, 82, 167, 210-212, 220-223, 226
symmetry 100, 176, 178, 181, 185, 188, 202
synchronization 105-106, 196, 198
synchrony ix, 193-204, 214
—, interactional 194, 196
—, nonverbal ix, 193-203
synergetics viii, 75-76, 80-81, 84-86, 91, 113-114, 194
Synesthesia 155
system environment dynamics 49
systems theory 66, 76, 80, 82, 84, 114, 116, 195, 257

T
Theory
— of Mind Theory (ToM) ix, 129-130, 140-143, 147
— of multiple codings ix, 210-213, 226
— Theory 141
therapeutic
— bond (relationship) ix, 193, 199-200, 226
— change 209, 212, 227
therapy outcome ix, 195, 199, 200
thermodynamics 90, 93, 94
time
— delayed neural networks (TDNN) 178, 187, 272
— series 32, 83, 183, 197
tool use 237-247
trajectory 37, 46, 112, 115, 247
transference 213
transition 4, 54, 92, 137, 139, 247
transparent 142, 244, 245
triad 135-138, 140
triangulation 131, 135-136

V
vector autoregression 83
vitality 139-140, 167
vocal 153

W
waist to hip ratio 174-175, 185-186, 189
working model 113

Z
Zeitgeber 198

About the Authors

Dr. **Silke Atmaca** is a postdoc at the Max Planck Institute for Human and Cognitive Brain Sciences in Leipzig and works on social cognition.

Claudia Bergomi is currently writing her doctoral thesis in psychology at the University Hospital of Psychiatry (Bern) and studies mathematics at the University of Bern. Her current main interests are mindfulness-based approaches in psychotherapy, the psychometric assessment of mindfulness, and cognitive coordination in schizophrenia.

Wilma Bucci, Ph.D., is author of Psychoanalysis and Cognitive Science: A Multiple Code Theory, and many other publications in areas of language, emotion and psychotherapy research. She is Professor Emerita, Derner Institute, Adelphi University; Co-Chair, Research Education, American Psychoanalytic Association.

Hanne De Jaegher, Dr., is a philosopher and cognitive scientist, and investigates the role of the interaction process in social understanding, using the enactive concept of participatory sense-making. She is currently Marie Curie Fellow at the University of the Basque Country.

Karl Friston is a neuroscientist and authority on brain imaging. He invented statistical parametric mapping, voxel-based morphometry and dynamic causal modelling. These technical contributions were motivated by theoretical work on the disconnection hypothesis of schizophrenia, active inference and the free-energy principle. He is Principal Fellow and Scientific Director at the Wellcome Trust Centre for Neuroimaging and Professor at the Institute of Neurology, UCL, London

Thomas Fuchs, MD, PhD, is Karl Jaspers Professor of Philosophy and Psychiatry and Head of the Section Phenomenology at the Psychiatric Department of the University of Heidelberg. He is also coordinator of the interdisciplinary European Research Project "TESIS" on Embodied Intersubjectivity (2011-2015, www.tesis.rtn-eu). His main research areas are phenomenological psychopathology and theory of neuroscience.

Shaun Gallagher is Professor of Philosophy and Cognitive Sciences at the University of Central Florida. His research focuses on phenomenology, philosophy of mind, and the cognitive sciences. His recent books include How the Body Shapes the Mind (2005), Brainstorming (2008), and (with Dan Zahavi) The Phenomenological Mind (2008).

Karl Grammer is Professor at the Department of Anthropology at the University of Vienna. His research focuses on the evolution of human behavior, with emphasis on nonverbal communication and Darwinian aesthetics.

Sanneke de Haan, M.A., obtained a M.A. in Philosophy in Amsterdam and currently works as Marie Curie Fellow at the University of Heidelberg. She conducts interviews with young schizophrenic patients and writes her thesis on an integrative approach to psychiatry, arguing that a relational approach can connect the (neuro)biological, experiential and existential levels involved in psychiatry.

Hermann Haken is a mathematician and physicist. As founder of the transdisciplinary field of synergetics, he was chair of the Institute of Theoretical Physics and Synergetics at Stuttgart University. Honorary memberships of numerous international societies. Research fields are quantum optics, laser physics, bifurcation theory, and statistical physics.

Naoya Hirose is Associate Professor in the Department of Psychology at Kyoto, Notre Dame University. His research interests include perception of affordances, human tool use, and action errors in daily activities.

Matej Hoffmann is currently working towards the Ph.D. degree at the Artificial Intelligence Laboratory, University of Zurich, Switzerland. His research interests include legged locomotion, motor control, and embodied cognition in animals and robots.

Mag. **Iris Holzleitner** is doctoral student at the University of Vienna. She works on nonverbal behavior and physical attractiveness.

PD Dr. **Sabine C. Koch**, psychologist, dance/movement therapist, is a researcher and lecturer at the University of Heidelberg. She has specialized in Kestenberg Movement Profiling. Her present work is on embodiment and, in a National Research Project, on the "Language of Movement and Dance". Further research interests include personality and social psychology, psycholinguistics, nonverbal communication, gender, health psychology, phenomenology, and creative arts therapies.

Andreas Mayer, Dipl.-Psych., M.A., received a master degree in cultural geography, anthropology and psychology at the University of Heidelberg. He currently works there in the Psychiatric Department, Section 'Phenomenological Psychopathology'. His research focuses on the alleged phenomenon of an 'opacity of mind' in the Southern Pacific and combines experimental methods with phenomenological and anthropological reflections.

Elisabeth Oberzaucher is senior researcher at the Department of Anthropology at the University of Vienna. Her main research topics involve communication, social relationships and gender differences in behavior.

Rolf Pfeifer is Professor of Computer Science at the Department of Informatics, University of Zurich, Switzerland, and Director of the Artificial Intelligence Laboratory since 1987. His research interests are in the areas of embodiment, biorobotics, artificial evolution and morphogenesis, modular robotics, self-assembly, and educational technology. Recent book: How the body shapes the way we think - a new view of intelligence (with Josh Bongard).

Fabian Ramseyer is a researcher at the Department of Psychotherapy, University Hospital of Psychiatry, Bern. His focus is on nonverbal synchrony in dyadic interaction (psychotherapy sessions, healthy individuals). Currently he is a visiting scholar at Stanford University, CA, where he conducts an experimental investigation of nonverbal synchrony in a cooperative task.

Martin Tröndle, Dr. phil., is Professor for Art Management and Art Research at the Zeppelin University Friedrichshafen (Germany). He is also Senior Researcher at the Institute for Research in Design and Art, University of Applied Sciences of Northwestern Switzerland, and Head of the Swiss National Research project eMotion.

Wolfgang Tschacher is a psychologist and professor at the University of Bern, head of a research department at the University Hospital of Psychiatry. His interests are in empirical psychotherapy research and experimental psychopathology, with an emphasis on dynamical systems approaches, complexity science, and phenomena of cognitive self-organization.

Jiří Wackermann, DPhil (Charles University, Prague, 1985) is Head of the Department of Empirical and Analytical Psychophysics at the Institute for Frontier Areas of Psychology in Freiburg i.Br., Germany. Main research interests: perception of time and space, history and philosophy of science.